CODEGURU • COM
Visual C++
GOODIES

Nigel Quinnin, Subject Editor

que ®

201 W. 103rd Street
Indianapolis, Indiana 46290

CodeGuru.com Goodies

International Standard Book Number: 0789727773

Library of Congress Catalog Card Number: 2002110928

Printed in the United States of America

First Printing: January 2003

05   04   03   02   4   3   2   1

Trademarks

All terms mentioned in this book that are known to be trademarks or service marks have been appropriately capitalized. Que Publishing cannot attest to the accuracy of this information. Use of a term in this book should not be regarded as affecting the validity of any trademark or service mark.

Warning and Disclaimer

Every effort has been made to make this book as complete and as accurate as possible, but no warranty or fitness is implied. The information provided is on an "as is" basis. The author and the publisher shall have neither liability nor responsibility to any person or entity with respect to any loss or damages arising from the information contained in this book or from the use of the CD or programs accompanying it.

Associate Publisher
Paul Boger

Acquisitions Editor
Candace Hall

Development Editor
Kelly Talbot

Managing Editor
Charlotte Clapp

Project Editors
Carol Bowers
Sheila Schroeder

Indexer
Chris Barrick

Proofreader
Katie Robinson

Multimedia Developer
Dan Scherf

Interior Designer
Anne Jones

Cover Designer
Dan Armstrong

Page Layout
Stacey Richwine-DeRome

Contents at a Glance

Contents

II Visual Studio

III Windows Programming

IV Controls

About the Author

Nigel Quinnin, subject editor for the book, CodeGuru.com member, and frequent contributor, is the chief technology officer for Qubit Automation and the founder of Computerlink Technology, Inc., a top software research and development firm in San Diego, CA. Nigel has been working as a software development and test engineer for the past 18 years both in England and the United States.

Dedication

To Lisa

You fill my heart with joy. I love you.

Acknowledgments

This book would not contain the great articles and notes it does without the tireless help of everyone at the CodeGuru site. I would like to specifically thank Brad Jones, the Webmaster of CodeGuru, who has been a tremendous resource, as well as all of the many contributors to the site, without whom this book could not have been written.

I want to thank the authors of the articles selected for inclusion in this book. Their efforts are seldom acknowledged, but they should be seen and merited as having contributed the best articles on the site.

I also want to thank everyone at Que Publishing who did all of the hard work in making this book happen. I would especially like to thank Kelly Talbot, development editor, for all of his inspiration and guidance, and Candace Hall, acquisitions editor, for her enthusiasm and drive in pushing everything along.

The biggest thanks should go to you for buying this book and for being part of the development community at large. Without the generous and collaborative efforts of like-minded individuals, the programming community would not be as thriving or vibrant as it is today.

Finally, I want to thank Lisa Schmitt, who provided unlimited support and encouragement during the creation of this book and was always there as my sounding board and friend.

We Want to Hear from You!

As the reader of this book, *you* are our most important critic and commentator. We value your opinion and want to know what we're doing right, what we could do better, what areas you'd like to see us publish in, and any other words of wisdom you're willing to pass our way.

As an associate publisher for Que, I welcome your comments. You can email or write me directly to let me know what you did or didn't like about this book—as well as what we can do to make our books better.

Please note that I cannot help you with technical problems related to the *topic* of this book. We do have a User Services group, however, where I will forward specific technical questions related to the book.

When you write, please be sure to include this book's title and author as well as your name, email address, and phone number. I will carefully review your comments and share them with the author and editors who worked on the book.

Email: feedback@quepublishing.com

Mail: Paul Boger
                Associate Publisher
                Que Publishing
                201 West 103rd Street
                Indianapolis, IN 46290 USA

For more information about this book or another Que title, visit our Web site at www.quepublishing.com. Type the ISBN (excluding hyphens) or the title of a book in the Search field to find the page you're looking for.

Introduction

This book is aimed at the intermediate to advanced level programmer, and so I have assumed that readers have at least a working knowledge of Visual C++ 6.0 and an understanding of the Microsoft Foundation Classes (MFCs).

I did not set out with the intention of teaching any particular programming skills; instead, I wanted to peer into the darkest corners of the CodeGuru.com site to bring you a selection of its very best articles, comments, and other goodies.

From the vast amount of material available on the CodeGuru site began the seemingly overwhelming task of selecting which articles to use for this book. This was not easy, as the quality of the majority of the articles there is exceptional. Over 2,000 articles and almost a half million newsgroup threads were reviewed, and only the very best of these could be squeezed into the pages of this book.

The subject of the book, CodeGuru.com, is a vibrant and thriving site on the Internet and is an integral part of many programmers' lives. The site is a fountain of knowledge and the first stop for many of the hundreds of thousands of regular visitors, from novices to professional engineers.

For readers unfamiliar with the CodeGuru.com site, I would certainly recommend visiting the site, which is an invaluable resource for programmers everywhere, offering free content and discussions. The CodeGuru site is part of Developer.com and the EarthWeb Channel of Internet.com. The Internet.com family of Web sites is part of the INT Media Group.

Not only does the CodeGuru site provide a great programming resource for source code and answers to specific technical questions, it also offers a rich mixture of news, book reviews, and current affairs in the programming arena as well as in-depth interviews with key industry professionals.

The collaborative nature of the CodeGuru site is one of the main reasons that programmers are continually drawn to it, with its free code and free discussion forums that draw on the knowledge of countless gurus in an open and welcoming environment.

Not only should the articles within this book serve as great reference examples for anyone reading them, but the book itself should serve as a tribute to the endless amount of energy that the gurus from around the world have contributed to help others.

While reading, you should find the chapters organized and logical, allowing you to treat this as a purely technical reference to find a quick solution to a difficult problem or as a resource to be browsed to discover creative and innovative ideas to enhance your code.

The organizational structure of this book broadly reflects that of the CodeGuru site itself. The order of the topic matter is arranged in the same topic order as the site. The articles are immediately followed by relevant comments, just as they are on the site. I have tried to maintain some perspective throughout, tying the articles themselves to any relevant threads of discussion from the Visual C++ forum on the site. The excerpts from the forum are presented as sidebars. There are also additional references and notes along the way to help you.

Due to the subject nature of some of the articles, their textual content is rather brief. In these cases, the content is better demonstrated by the demos and the source code itself, which can be found on the accompanying CD-ROM. We have tried to present the material as faithfully as possible to the original articles on the site. There have, however, been occasions where we felt it was necessary to edit the material for context, presentation, or brevity, in addition to proofreading.

C++ and MFC

1

Getting Started

In this chapter

As was mentioned in the Introduction, every effort will be made to spare you from the basics wherever possible; however no good book is complete without a great tutorial to get everyone up to speed.

In this first chapter, you will find an excellent introduction and overview of MFC and the Visual Studio IDE by Brian Martin over the course of seven short but informative lessons, along with a discussion of multithreading by Gopal Mor.

- "Lesson 1: Behind the Scenes with Handles and Messages" introduces and explains the mechanism by which Windows applications talk to each other, and themselves at times.
- "Lesson 2: C++ Essentials" offers a recap of some C++ fundamentals.

- "Lesson 3: Visual C++ IDE and Workspaces" provides information about how to make the best of the Developer Studio.
- "Lesson 4: MFC Basics" is a feet-first introduction to the Microsoft Foundation Classes.
- "Lesson 5: Dialog-based Applications" describes different types of dialog boxes and how they can be used.
- "Lesson 6: SDI and MDI Applications" introduces the Document/View architecture, and the two flavors it comes in.
- "Lesson 7: Data Viewer" is a working project finally evolved from the preceding lessons in the form of a data-viewing application.
- "What Are Threads?" answers the frequently asked questions about the often misunderstood world of multithreaded applications.

Lesson 1: Behind the Scenes with Handles and Messages

This article was contributed by Brian Martin.

Though you think you want to dive right into the code, you really don't. Windows programming is overwhelming at first. Let's take a quick look at how Windows works. The backbone of all of your programming will be responding to and sending messages. What are messages? Messages are simply a 32-bit number designating some event. Example: You move the mouse, a message (defined as WM_MOUSEMOVE) is "posted" to the active window. You press a key, a message (WM_KEYDOWN) is "posted" to the active window. You resize the window, a message (WM_SIZE) is "posted" to the active window. Get the picture?

Now where do these messages go? They get queued up, and a window eventually takes them out of the queue and reacts to them. For instance, when a window gets the WM_MOVE message, it changes the coordinates of the window and redraws it on the screen.

Let's move on to handles. Windows is very much object oriented. You have several Window objects (like the desktop, the program you're reading this with, and so on). How does the programmer distinguish all of these things in an non-object-oriented language? He uses handles. Handles are a way to reference different Windows objects. You can have handles to windows, handles to files, handles to allocated memory, handles to images, and so on. You can think of them as pointers. You must create them somehow. And when you are done with them, you must destroy them. If you don't, you will end up with what is called a resource leak. This could bring your system to a grinding halt. So take care to always make sure they are destroyed at some time.

Now let's tie these two things together. Say you have a window. You will have a handle to it (called an HWND). Let's name your handle your_HWND. The operating system wants to tell you to redraw your window because it was just uncovered by some other window. Windows passes you a message like this:

```
PostMessage(your_HWND, WM_PAINT, 0,0);
```

This function posts a paint message to the window with the handle your_HWND. The last two parameters are used for extra information about the message. Don't worry about them for now.

Now your application will have a function with a big case statement in it to handle all of the messages. For example

```
void   HandleTheMessage(long Message)
{
 switch(Message)
 {
  case WM_PAINT:
   DrawWindow();
  break;
```

```
    case WM_KEYDOWN:
    break;

    //etc...
  }
}
```

OK, that is basically how Windows works under the hood. That should be enough to get you going when we start talking about MFC.

Lesson 2: C++ Essentials

This article was contributed by Brian Martin.

If you want to use Microsoft Visual C++, it helps a ton if you really know C++. Everything is about classes. If you are used to plain C, you won't really see the big deal with classes until you use them for a while. Let's review what you need to know about classes to get started with VC++.

A *class* is a structure for the most part. Let's work with an example instead of me just telling you rules. Let's make a class to represent a line. In the .h file you would define the class as follows:

```
class CLine
{
 int m_nX1;
 int m_nY1;
 int m_nX2;
 int m_nY2;

public:
 // constructors
 CLine();
 CLine(int x1, int y1, int x2, int y2);

 // destructor
 ~CLine();

 // set the line data
 void SetPoints(int x1, int y1, int x2, int y2);

 // draw the line
 void Draw();
}
```

A quick word about naming conventions. Class names usually start with C, and the member variables usually are prefixed by an m_. Then in the Microsoft way, you will have a letter to let you know what data type the name is and the name of the variable. Capitalize the first letter of all new words in the name. Don't use underscores and stuff like that. I recommend this Microsoft standard (called Hungarian notation) since it is widely accepted and very easy to read. If you see m_pPoint, you would assume this is a member variable of a class that points (it is a pointer) to a point. If you see fData, you would assume that it is a floating-point value.

Back to our class. The int variables are the end points of the line. Note that they are before the public part. This means that a programmer using this class will not be allowed to manipulate these guys directly. They are not for public use. The functions under the public statement are for public use. The first three are called constructors. These functions are called any time a new CLine class is created. Here are some examples when they are called:

```
// this calls CLine()
CLine MyLine;

// this is a pointer to a CLine class
CLine *pMyLine;

// this  calls CLine()
pMyLine = new CLine;

// this is a pointer to a CLine class
CLine *pMyLine;
// this calls CLine(int x1, int y1, int x2, int y2)
pMyLine = new CLine(0,0,10,10);

// this calls CLine(int x1, int y1, int x2, int y2)
CLine MyLine(0,0,10,10);
```

All of these construct a line. Some initialize it to its default settings and others copy coordinates. The new keyword is used to create new things in C++, like malloc in C. You need to call delete for everything you say new to, like free in C. This goes for classes as well as other data types. I could allocate an array of 100 integers with

```
// a pointer to some integers
int *pNumbers;

// make memory for 100 of them
pNumbers = new int[100];

// set the first element to 0
pNumbers[0]=0;

// set the last element to 99
pNumbers[99]=99;

// free the memory.
delete [] pNumbers;
```

Notice the [] after the delete. This is to tell the program to delete the entire array. If you say delete pNumbers; you will only free memory for the first element. You will then be "leaking" memory. Memory leaks are when you forget to delete memory. This may end up crashing your computer if you use all the computer's memory.

Sorry, let's get back to the constructors for CLine. The code for these constructor functions that automagically get called when a new line is created will look like

```
CLine::CLine()
{
 m_nX1=0;
 m_nX2=0;
 m_nY1=0;
 m_nY2=0;
}
CLine::CLine(int x1, int y1, int x2, int y2)
{
 m_nX1=x1;
 m_nX2=x2;
 m_nY1=y1;
 m_nY2=y2;
}
```

Notice that the function declaration is much like a regular C function except that we put the class name and two colons in front of the function name (CLine::). One difference with constructors is that they don't have a return value. This is the case for destructors also. A destructor is the function that automagically gets called when our CLine is deleted or goes out of scope. For instance

```
// this is a pointer to a CLine class
CLine *pMyLine;

// this  calls CLine()
pMyLine = new CLine;

// memory for the class is cleared up and ~CLine() is called
delete pMyLine;

{
 // this  calls CLine()
 CLine MyLine;
}

// this '}' ends the section of the program where MyLine is
// valid. ~CLine() will be called. (MyLine goes out of 'scope')
```

For our class, ~CLine() doesn't need to do anything. However, sometimes you may want to put your cleanup code here, like deleting any allocated memory in your class. Since we have nothing to do, our function code is empty:

```
CLine::~CLine()
{
 // do nothing
}
```

Let's fill in the other two functions.

```
void CLine::SetPoints(int x1, int y1, int x2, int y2)
{
 m_nX1=x1;
 m_nX2=x2;
 m_nY1=y1;
 m_nY2=y2;

 return;
}

void CLine::Draw()
{
 // psuedo code here, these are operating system
 // functions to draw a line
 MoveTo(m_nX1, m_nY1);
 LineTo(m_nX2, m_nY2);

 return;
}
```

How would I call these functions? Here are a couple of examples, one with pointers and one without:

```
CLine *pLine = new CLine(0,0,10,10);
pLine->Draw();
delete pLine;

CLine MyLine;
MyLine.SetPoints(0,0,10,10);
MyLine.Draw();
```

That's it for the class. Now this class can be used in other classes. You can imagine a CSquare class that has four Cline classes in it:

```
class CSquare
{
 CLine m_LineTop;
 CLine m_LineLeft;
 CLine m_LineBottom;
 CLine m_LineRight;
 //...
}
```

Or better yet, the point of all of this class stuff, you can use the CLine class to make your own class. This is done a ton in Visual C. Let's say you wanted to draw lines in your program, and you thought the line class might be nice, but it is missing an important feature: It doesn't let you set the line color. Instead of writing a whole new class, you can simply inherit the CLine class. It would look like this:

```
class CColorLine : public CLine
{
public:
 void Draw(long color);
};
```

What's going on here? Well, with this class we have all the functionality of our other class, but now we can use this other Draw() function that allows us to set the color. The cpp code would look like this:

```
void CColorLine::Draw(long color)
{
 // psuedo code here, these are operating system
 // functions to draw a line
 SetColor(color);

 CLine::Draw();
 return;
}
```

Now we have all the functionality of the other class, but we added an extra function called Draw. But it's the same name as our other Draw! No matter. Cpp is smart enough to know if you call Draw(color) to use the new function; but if you call Draw() it will use the old function. The strange part of the code may be CLine::Draw(). This just tells our program to call the base class's Draw function. We save ourselves from having to write that LineTo and MoveTo code again. Pretty cool, huh? Now we can do something like this:

```
CColorLine MyLine;
MyLine.SetPoints(0,0,10,10);

// assuming 0 is black, this will draw a black line.
MyLine.Draw(0);
```

Of course I'm leaving out a ton of aspects and things here. Like defining operators, overriding functions, virtual functions, protected and private members.... The list goes on. You have enough to get started though.

Lesson 3: Visual C++ IDE and Workspaces

This article was contributed by Brian Martin.

Windows programming is tricky stuff. Don't let anyone fool you. But Microsoft has blessed us with their IDE called Developer Studio. It handles all the compiling and linking, provides help, fills in tons of code for you, and gives you that "visual" designing environment to make cute little dialogs.

There a few things you must learn to use to get anywhere. First and most importantly, *use the online help.* There are so many Windows functions that you will find yourself in the help 50 percent of the time or more for the first few months. If you have visual C 6.0, you need the MSDN for help. Get it. If you have 4.2 or 5.0, you can use the built-in help.

Next, the single most important key combination is Ctrl+W. This brings up what is called the Class Wizard. This guy will insert a bunch of code in your project for you. It handles all the code for connecting functions up to the messages that Windows posts.

You will also find yourself in the Resource view a bit. It is used to design the dialogs. You can drop buttons on them and whatnot. With a couple of clicks here and there, you can lay out your whole application. Then using the Class Wizard, you can have your project 50 percent finished. All that's left is to fill in the functions the Class Wizard made to handle the button click messages and whatnot.

Now you need to know how to start a new program, and we can begin with the real code. Go to the File menu and select New. Then go to the Projects tab and select MFC AppWizard. Type in a name for your application and press OK. The only important option for now is the first one. This is the type of application you want to build. The simplest is Dialog Based. Try them all, but try Dialog Based first. Just select all the defaults afterwards by pressing Next and OK. You'll end up with a few files, but let's ignore everything.

Go to the Resource view and plop some buttons and stuff on the dialog. Just play around. When you feel like it, build the project from the Build menu and run it. (I always just press Ctrl+F5, which builds the project and runs it.) Everything should build and run. Voila. Application complete and running.

One last tip on the IDE. If you right-click on a menu bar, a dialog will pop up. You can select Customize. This is very useful. You can build one custom menu with all the buttons you need on it by simply dragging the buttons to and from the menu bar. You can even change the menu layout (like by putting the File, New command as a button on the toolbar). One really needed control is under the Build category in the Customize dialog. It is the drop-down list used to select the active configuration. Drag that sucker up to your main toolbar and change its size until it looks good to you. I have only one toolbar on my screen, and it has the following buttons on it: Save, Save All, Compile, Build, Stop Build, Rebuild All, Set Active Configuration, Find, Find in Files, Show View, Show Output Window, Set Break Point, Remove Break Point, Tile Windows, and Find in Help.

Lesson 4: MFC Basics

This article was contributed by Brian Martin.

Are you ready to start programming? No, you are not. You don't want me to teach you a stupid "hello world" application, do you? If you want to make the most of Visual C++, you have to use Microsoft Foundation Classes (MFC). These classes are great because they wrap all of those handles we talked about in the first lesson with easy-to-use classes. The most important to you right now is the class CWnd. This wraps the functions that need a window handle (HWND). Remember that PostMessage function I mentioned?

```
PostMessage(your_HWND, WM_PAINT, 0,0);
```

Well, now we can take our Windows class and call its member function.

```
MyCWnd.PostMessage(WM_PAINT, 0, 0);
```

This does the same thing, but now we don't have to keep track of the window handles. But don't be fooled; they are still there. We can still use them, too. They are now just member variables of the class. The handle to the window that a CWnd is associated with is the member variable m_hWnd. We can call the old post message this way:

```
::PostMessage(MyCWnd.m_hWnd, WM_PAINT, 0,0);
```

Those colons (::) are used to tell MFC that we are calling the old-fashioned versions of the function. You can get away without using them most of the time, but I put them here so that you won't be too confused when you see them in Microsoft's code.

The CWnd class is the base for several other classes like CButton and CDialog, which I hope the names make self-explanatory. From CButton you can access the windows handle also. (You'd be surprised how many things are windows: scroll bars, edit boxes, tree views, the desktop....) Got all that? Great!

The next most important class, though you won't explicitly use it much, is CWinApp. This class is the backbone of all of your future MFC applications. This is the class that does the main dirty work under the hood. Your program will have a CWinApp class, which, when created, starts the program execution. The main function called when the CWinApp is constructed is InitInstance(). In this function, windows are created and the application is set up. Think of the InitInstance() function in CWinApp as the main() section in a C program.

Let's move on to one last very useful MFC that you will surely use: CString. This is one of Microsoft's support classes. It is used to make string manipulation easier. Since CString overrides many of the common operators, like = and +, you can do things like this:

```
CString strMyString;
strMyString="May the Force be with you";
strMyString+=" young Jedi.";
printf("%s", strMyString);
//output will be "May the Force be with you young Jedi.";
```

Lesson 5: Dialog-based Applications

This article was contributed by Brian Martin.

We won't build a dialog application just yet, but I will tell you enough here so that you get the picture of what's going on in dialog applications. Dialog apps are the simplest in my opinion. In the IDE, go to File, New, Projects, MFC AppWizard(exe), and type in a project name. Hit Next. Select Dialog Application as the type of application, and then hit Finish. Next go to the File view. You will see the source files created automagically. You should be able to compile and run the application as it is.

What is going on in all these files? Everything boils down to the CWinApp derived class and the CDialog derived class (which is derived from CWnd). Look in the source file named after your project. You should see the InitInstance() function there. Inside that function you can see that a dialog class is constructed; it is set as the "main window" of the application, and it is displayed with the DoModal() function. Once you exit your dialog app, the DoModal() function returns and your dialog is hidden. InitInstance() returns FALSE and your application ends. Now the question is, "What is DoModal()?"

There are two ways to create a dialog, modal and modeless. A modal dialog suspends the program until you press OK, Cancel, or Close. On the other hand, a modeless dialog can remain open while allowing you to press buttons and whatnot on the rest of the application. An example of a modal dialog is one of those annoying error boxes with an OK button on it. That is the only type of dialog we'll talk about here. To create a modal dialog, you simply need to call the dialog's DoModal() function. It returns either IDOK or IDCANCEL, depending on how you exited the dialog. Internally the DoModal() will call OnInitDialog(), which is a good place to initialize your dialog variables. If you create a dialog app, you will notice that a default dialog class and resource is created for you. The file name for the class will be your project name with a "Dlg" tacked on at the end.

Though we aren't making an application just yet, I have to tell you how to put something useful on the dialog. First open up the Resource view, then open up your dialog in the editor. Right-click on the dialog and select Properties. Make sure the Visible check box is checked. If it isn't, you won't be able to see your dialog. (Remember this.

It will come back to haunt you in the future.) You can change the dialog's caption here as well as other things.

Now drag a button control onto the dialog somewhere. Right-click on it and select Properties. You can change the ID of the button to something more descriptive like IDC_SHOWMESSAGE. You can also change the text on the button to something more descriptive like Show Message. You have a button now. But it does nothing. You can easily fix that. Press Ctrl+W to bring up the Class Wizard. Make sure you are on the first tab. You should see your dialog's name and the button's ID in the list on the left. If you select the dialog's name, you can see all of the functions and messages that the Class Wizard will let you add code for on the right. You can see the WM_PAINT and all the other messages we talked about. If you select the ID of the button, you can see the messages that the button sends. Double-click on the CLICK message and accept the default function name. You see that it appears in the list at the bottom. Now double-click on the function in the bottom list. Shazam; you are transported right to the cpp file where you need to fill in the code. Let's do something easy. Just add the line

```
AfxMessageBox("Stupid Text");
```

Compile, build, and run your application (just press Ctrl+F5). If you press the button, you should see a message box pop up when you press the New button. (There are some Afx functions that are useful. I think the message box is the most useful out of all of them. It is instant feedback.)

That was dead simple. You see how to add message handlers now (like for the button click), but you need at least one more vital bit of information to make a useful dialog box—how to use the automatic data handling stuff in MFC. This is best described by going back to the code again. Bring up the Resource editor one more time, and this time add an Edit box to your dialog. Again right-click on it and give it a nice and friendly ID. Hit Ctrl+W and bring up the Class Wizard. This time go to the second tab. Here is where you add member variables that are associated with the controls on your dialog. Double-click on the Edit box's ID. You now have the choice to add a variable to your project. Give it a name like m_strMessage since it will be a string for our message box. Make sure the data type selected is CString there at the bottom. Press OK. And press it again to get out of the Class Wizard.

When you add a member variable to a dialog like this, you can set the value to that in the control of the dialog by calling

```
UpdateData(TRUE);
```

Likewise, you can change the data displayed in the dialog to represent your variable's value by calling

```
UpdateData(FALSE);
```

Let's put this to use and finish up this lesson. Go toward the end of your OnInitDialog() function and in it put the two lines

```
m_strMessage = "Initial text";
UpdateData(FALSE);
```

Then go to the function that is called when the button is pressed, and replace the AfxMessageBox() line with these two lines:

```
UpdateData(TRUE);
AfxMessageBox(m_strMessage);
```

Ok, we are done. What we just did was set the initial text in the Edit box to "Initial Text" with the UpdateData(FALSE). Then when the button is pressed, the text in the message box is displayed since we get the text from the dialog with UpdateData(TRUE).

By playing around and by reading the Help (or a good book), you will learn how to use the other controls. One of the trickiest to figure out without help is the slider bar. If you use one of these, you will have to handle the dialog's scroll messages. That's just a hint for you.

Lesson 6: SDI and MDI Applications

This article was contributed by Brian Martin.

We are getting to some advanced stuff now. In this lesson, I am not going to go in depth at all. I will just give you the flavor of the structure of a single-document interface (SDI) and a multiple-document interface (MDI) application. In the last lesson we will build an SDI application, and you can see the nitty gritty there.

The SDI application is typically used when you intend to work with only one data set at a time. For instance, the program notepad.exe is an SDI application. Netscape is also an SDI application. At any one time, there is only one document open. Word for Windows and the VC++ Developer Studio are MDI applications. In these you can have several documents open at once. This is particularly useful when you want to cut and paste between documents. Another use for MDI applications is to have one document, but several different views open that view the data differently. A graphing application comes to mind, where in one window you have a spreadsheet-like data list and in another window you have a plot of the data. For small applications, an SDI application will usually be all you need. After you master it, the jump to MDI is a snap. Let's go over the structure of an SDI app.

Remember that in a dialog app, we had just two main classes: CWinApp and CDialog. Here again we have a CWinApp, which serves the same purpose as it did in Lesson 5. The CDialog class, however, is replaced by three other classes: CMainFrame, CDocument, and CView.

CDocument is a class that has no display and typically doesn't react much with the messaging system of Windows. It is used as a class to manage your data. MFC will create the code automatically that handles the event of File, Save; File, SaveAs; File, Close; and File, Open. All you need to do is to fill in the blank functions in the CDocument class.

Next is the CView. Most likely you will spend more time writing code to display and interact with the document's data than you will writing any other code. This is where the CView comes in. The CView is a class derived from CWnd, which is used for displaying your CDocument in some way. It is also one of the places where you can handle events like mouse clicks and whatnot. The heart of the CView is usually a call to get a pointer to your document followed by some drawing routines to display the data in your document.

The CMainFrame acts as a way to bridge the gap between your document/view classes and the rest of the application. Do you see that frame that goes all around the application's borders? That is the main frame window of the application. The title bar, the menu, the scroll bars, the status bar, and the toolbars are all part of the main frame window in an SDI application. You typically put the code to handle these objects in the CMainFrame class. The CMainFrame class is the main window of the application. The CView class is typically a child window of CMainFrame. (For the most part, the child/parent window relations just tell Windows which windows are "stuck" to other windows. If you move a parent window, all of the children will move also. If you destroy a parent window, all of the children will be destroyed, and so on.)

You should have a pretty good idea now of how SDI applications are constructed. MDI applications are similar, but there can be several CDocument classes in existence at the same time, and there is an added class called CChildFrame that acts as a connection between CView and CMainFrame.

Lesson 7: Data Viewer

This article was contributed by Brian Martin.

The moment you have been waiting for—we will finally make a useful application. If you have just skipped the last six lessons, then you will probably be able to follow along, but you may not really understand what you are doing. (But since you are the type of person who skips ahead, you are probably used to this.)

I have decided to make this example a data-viewing application that takes a text file of data, reads it in, and then displays it. If that isn't enough, we are then going to use the timer to animate the data. Let's first assume that we are doing an experiment tracking the random motion of a drunken bug on a table. Every second we will measure its distance from two adjacent sides of the table. These are what we will call the bug's x,y coordinates. Our data file looks as shown in Figure 1.1.

390.789	362.245
386.032	366.429
386.559	369.289
385.557	370.483
384.841	372.370
385.785	371.975
389.348	371.005
377.266	379.550
376.916	382.096
373.959	384.111
373.109	384.387
370.598	382.973
370.067	383.667
369.099	377.171
366.549	379.162
368.245	383.977
366.427	385.877
364.343	388.575
365.326	389.769
368.751	389.556
369.598	386.514
389.381	384.817
387.311	381.979
388.205	382.978
386.632	387.414
385.150	388.393
384.099	390.620
382.926	394.712
385.771	396.611
375.693	393.622
376.697	392.655
394.063	397.035
391.727	401.327
379.119	400.460
381.912	407.491
384.119	407.505
383.090	406.474
384.888	408.943
386.664	409.806
386.207	409.759
388.031	411.599
387.911	411.545

Figure 1.1

Go cut and paste this to a file named BugPosition.dat if you want to follow along. We first fire up Visual C++ Developer Studio and create a new project. In this case I called the project BugTracks. For the app wizard options, select SDI Application. Keep the default settings for the rest of the choices, *except* deselect Printing Preview and Docking Toolbar.

First let's figure out how to get our data into the program. Go to the Class view and double-click on your document class. It should be called CBugTracksDoc if you named your project BugTracks. When you double-click on the class name, the .h file will be opened in the editor. Right before the declaration of the class, let's declare a structure to hold the data.

```
struct SBugData
{
 float x;
 float y;
};
```

Also I want to use one of Microsoft's template classes. Templates are C++ things that allow you to write a function for an arbitrary data type. The one I like to use is the CArray class. Include the afxtempl.h before your structure declaration:

```
#include <afxtempl.h>
```

and then in a public area of your class declare a CArray template class as follows:

```
CArray <SBugData, SBugData> m_BugDataArray;
```

Yeah, it looks funny, but that is the way you want to type it. This is sort of like declaring a data type of CArray, but we have to tell the template class what type of data we want to store in the array. That is done between the brackets <,>. The first thing in the brackets is the type of data we want to put in the array. The second thing is what we will pass to the CArray class when we want to add a new element. Since we have a list of data points, it is obvious that we want to have an array of SBugData. The second parameter is also SBugData, meaning that we will just pass the data to the array. (Alternatively, we could have passed a reference to the data, but that is another lesson.)

Let's go to the .cpp file for the document and add the code now. Expand the CBugTracksDoc in the Class view. You should see the member functions for the document. Double-click on OnNewDocument(). You will jump to the function in the .cpp file. This function is called every time a new document (file) is opened. All we want to do here is to clear out the array so that it will be ready for the new data. Where you see the //TODO comment, add this line of code:

```
m_BugDataArray.RemoveAll();
```

Now to fill up the array, jump to the Serialize() function. This is a function called when a new file is opened or saved. Instead of the good old FILE pointers you use in C with fopen, we are going to use Microsoft's CArchive class. You will notice that a CArchive is passed (by reference) to the Serialize() function. This class has the same functionality that we get with the fread and fwrite functions.

```
void CBugTracksDoc::Serialize(CArchive& ar)
{
 // if not storing the data, read it
 if (!ar.IsStoring())
 {
  SBugData Data;
  CString strOneLine;

  // read data in, one line at a time
  while(ar.ReadString(strOneLine))
  {
   // convert the text to floats
   sscanf(strOneLine,"%g %g\n",&Data.x,&Data.y);

   // add the data to the array
   m_BugDataArray.Add(Data);
  }
 }
}
```

For the very basic display, we just need to add some code to draw the data. Go to the function OnDraw() in the Class view CBugTracksView. This is the function that is called every time the window needs refreshed. All drawing is done through the CDC class. The CDC class has several drawing functions, but here we will only use the MoveTo and LineTo calls.

```
void CBugTracksView::OnDraw(CDC* pDC)
{
 // get a pointer to the document class
 CBugTracksDoc* pDoc = GetDocument();

 // get the total number of data points
 int N=pDoc->m_BugDataArray.GetSize();

 // draw all of the connecting lines
 for(int i=0; i < N-2; i++)
 {
  pDC->MoveTo(pDoc->m_BugDataArray[i].x,   pDoc->m_BugDataArray[i].y);
  pDC->LineTo(pDoc->m_BugDataArray[i+1].x, pDoc->m_BugDataArray[i+1].y);
 }
}
```

Well that is it! Compile and run the program. You will get a few warnings since our data is float, but screen coordinates are int, which is harmless in this case. Once the program is running, go to File, Open and select the data file we created above. It should display the track in the lower-middle part of the window. We could call it quits here, but let's add a couple more features.

First, I hate the File, Open menu. Let's make our application accept files that are dropped on the main window. Go to the InitInstance() function in our CWinApp class CBugTracksApp. Near the end of the function add these lines:

```
// Enable drag/drop open
m_pMainWnd->DragAcceptFiles();
```

Now let's take advantage of the status bar and put some useful text in it. The status bar is managed by the CStatusBar class, which is a protected member of CMainFrame. This means that we can't touch it from other classes. We can either move its declaration to a public part of the class or just move a public member function to CMainFrame to change the status bar text. We will do the latter. Right-click on CMainFrame in the Class view and select Add Member Function. A dialog will pop up to help add the member function. Type in void for the function type (this is the return value of the function), and type in ChangeStatusText(LPCTSTR text) as the function declaration. Make sure that the access is set to public. Press OK. This will automagically add the declaration to the .h file and a blank function to the .cpp file of CMainFrame. The LPCTSTR is one of many Microsoft definitions for data types. We could alternately have typed ChangeStatusText(const char *text). LPCTSTR stands for Long Pointer to a Constant T STRing. A T-string is just a string that will work on computers with different character sets (like Japanese). On computers in the United States, a T-string is just the same as a char *.

Jump to the new function in the CMainFrame .cpp file and add the code to change the text on the status bar. To do this we'll just use the CWnd function SetWindowText. CStatusBar is derived from CWnd, so we can always use any of the CWnd functions with it. A hint on how to find out about all of these strange new functions—use Help and look at the class members for the class, and then look at the class members for all of the base classes from which it was derived. Your function should now look like this:

```
void CMainFrame::ChangeStatusText(LPCTSTR text)
{
 m_wndStatusBar.SetWindowText(text);
}
```

We have to call this function from somewhere, and I'll do it from the document. Go to the File view, which is the view I use most. Under Source Files, double-click on your document file BugTracksDoc.cpp. Go to the top of that file and include the header file for CMainFrame right after the rest of the includes so that we can access the new function we just made.

```
#include "MainFrm.cpp"
```

Next go to our Serialize() function and modify the reading code to spit some text out to the status bar. We first get a pointer to the main window, which is the CMainFrame window in SDI applications. Since the function AfxGetMainWnd() returns a CWnd*, we cast it to a CMainFrame*. Then we use the CString's Format function and CArray's GetSize function to create a text string for the status bar.

```
void CBugTracksDoc::Serialize(CArchive& ar)
{
 if (!ar.IsStoring())
 {
  SBugData data;
  CString line;
  CString strStatus;

  // get a pointer to the main window
  // (which is the mainframe for SDI applications)
  CMainFrame *pMain = (CMainFrame*) AfxGetMainWnd();

  while(ar.ReadString(line))
  {
   sscanf(line,"%g %g\n",&data.x,&data.y);

   // tell the user your reading points
   strStatus.Format("Reading point %d",m_BugDataArray.GetSize());
   pMain->ChangeStatusText(strStatus);

   m_BugDataArray.Add(data);
  }

  // tell the user the total number of points
  strStatus.Format("Loaded %d points.", m_BugDataArray.GetSize());
  pMain->ChangeStatusText(strStatus);
 }
}
```

If you run the app, you'll notice all of the default menu items. We don't need most of these. Let's clean up the menus and add an item for animating the bug track, which we'll code later.

Go to the Resource view. Under the Menu resource, double-click on IDR_MAINFRAME. This is the menu resource for the main window. In the Edit window, click on File, then delete the menu entries for New, Save, and Save As. Also delete the main menu headings for Edit and View. Next, go to the empty box at the end of the menu and add a new heading called Track by selecting the empty box and typing Track. Drag the Track menu heading so that it is between File and Help. Click on the Track menu, and then click on the empty submenu box. Type in &Animate\tAlt+A. The & underlines the A in Animate so that it is the menu hot key. The \t is just the scan code for a tab and the Alt+A will be our hot key to start the animation. For the ID, type in ID_TRACK_ANIMATE, though this will be filled in automatically if you ever forget.

In order to make Alt+A our hot key, go to the Accelerator resource and double-click on IDR_MAINFRAME. In the Edit window, double-click on the empty box at the end of the list. From the drop-down list for the ID, select the ID of your new menu item (ID_TRACK_ANIMATE). Press the Next Key Typed button, and then press Alt+A. Hit Enter to close the dialog.

Before we are done with resources, you should modify the icons to something more suitable for this app. I'm sure you can figure out how to do this. The only hint here is to modify the 32×32-sized icon *and* the 16×16-sized icon. If you want part of the icon to be transparent, use that greenish color with the two borders around it on the color palette.

Now we can get back to coding. It's time to add fancier drawing and animating. We will animate the bug track by drawing more and more segments of the path in red as time increases. The rest of the path will be drawn in black.

In order to keep track of the last segment in the path that is to be drawn in red, we have to add a member variable to our document. Go to the Class view, right-click on the document class, and select Add Member Variable. Type in int as the data type and m_nBugPosition as the variable name. Make sure that it is public and press OK.

Jump to the OnNewDocument() in the document class. Add this line to initialize the new variable to −1. We will use the value −1 to designate that the track is not being animated.

```
m_nBugPosition = -1;
```

Next let's add the message handler for our Animate hot key and menu. Press Ctrl+W to bring up the Class Wizard. In the Class Name drop box, select the View class (CBugTracksView) and in the Object ID list, select the ID of our new menu and hot key command (ID_TRACK_ANIMATE). You'll see the two possible choices in the Messages list. Double-click on COMMAND to add a function to handle our new command. You will be prompted for a function name. Just accept the default one OnTrackAnimate() and press OK. You will see the function appear in the Member Function list near the bottom of the dialog. Double-click on the function to jump directly to the code. We set m_nBugPosition to zero and started a timer that will redraw the bug tracks in intervals of 0.2 seconds.

```
void CBugTracksView::OnTrackAnimate()
{
// get the document
CBugTracksDoc* pDoc = GetDocument();

// set the position to the first data point
pDoc->m_nBugPosition=0;

// create a timer with id=1 and delay of 200 milliseconds
SetTimer(1,200, NULL);
```

Next we need to handle the timer message. Ctrl+W back to the Class view. Make sure you are looking at the View class, select the class as the Object ID, then double-click WM_TIMER in the message list to handle the timer message. Again, double-click on the function name to jump to the code. In the OnTimer function we will first check the ID of the timer to make sure we are responding to the correct timer. In this case we set the timer ID to 1. Then we will invalidate the window so that it will be repainted.

```
void CBugTracksView::OnTimer(UINT nIDEvent)
{
 if(nIDEvent==1)
 {
 // tell windows the view needs redrawn
 // note: the last parameter is the erase flag.
 // if it is TRUE, things will flicker like crazy.
 InvalidateRect(NULL,FALSE);
 }

 CView::OnTimer(nIDEvent);
}
```

All that is left now is to fix up the OnDraw() function in the view class. We need to first draw the red tracks, then the blue ones, then increment the position m_nBugPosition. If m_nBugPosition is larger than the number of positions, we will set it to −1 and kill the timer.

One of the new things in this code is the CPen class, which is needed to change the color of the line. The way these graphical objects work is that you select the object into the CDC class. When you are done with it, you select the old one that was in there previously and delete the one you just used.

```
void CBugTracksView::OnDraw(CDC* pDC)
{
 CBugTracksDoc* pDoc = GetDocument();
 ASSERT_VALID(pDoc);

 // make pens for solid lines of thickness 2
 CPen RedPen(PS_SOLID, 2, RGB(255,0,0));
 CPen BluePen(PS_SOLID, 2, RGB(0,0,255));

 CPen *pOldPen = pDC->SelectObject(&RedPen);

 int i, N=pDoc->m_BugDataArray.GetSize();

 // draw any tracks which need animated
 for(i=0; i < pDoc->m_nBugPosition-1; i++)
 {
 pDC->MoveTo(pDoc->m_BugDataArray[i].x,)pDoc->m_BugDataArray[i].y);
 pDC->LineTo(pDoc->m_BugDataArray[i+1].x,pDoc->m_BugDataArray[i+1].y);
 }
```

```
// change pens
pDC->SelectObject(&BluePen);

// start drawing non animated tracks, but need to check for a
// valid starting postion
int start=pDoc->m_nBugPosition;
if(start<0) start=0;
for(i=start; i < N-2; i++)
{
 pDC->MoveTo(pDoc->m_BugDataArray[i].x,)pDoc->m_BugDataArray[i].y);
 pDC->LineTo(pDoc->m_BugDataArray[i+1].x,pDoc->m_BugDataArray[i+1].y);
}

// deselect pens and delete them
pDC->SelectObject(pOldPen);
RedPen.DeleteObject();
BluePen.DeleteObject();

// move to next position or quit animating
if(pDoc->m_nBugPosition!=-1) pDoc->m_nBugPosition++;
if(pDoc->m_nBugPosition>=N)
{
 pDoc->m_nBugPosition=-1;

 // stop timer 1
 KillTimer(1);

 // redraw and erase so all lines are in initial state (blue)
 InvalidateRect(NULL);
 }
}
```

Ctrl+F5 the program to build and run it. Fix any bugs, and you are done! Of course many improvements can be made, like scaling and centering the path to better fit the view, printing the path, and so on, but I think you have enough to go on. Good luck! (And don't be afraid of that F1 key.)

Comments

Here are some fixes to minor bugs in the sample code:

The line

```
#include "MainFrm.cpp"
```

should be changed to

```
#include "MainFrm.h"
```

And the line

```
pDC->MoveTo(pDoc->m_BugDataArray[i].x,)pDoc->m_BugDataArray[i].y);
```

should be changed to

```
pDC->MoveTo(pDoc->m_BugDataArray[i].x,pDoc->m_BugDataArray[i].y);
```

In other words, the extra ")" should be removed.

—Mike Brown

To fix a problem when opening a second file, make the following changes:

In the document class, add a protected member variable named m_bFileOpened of type bool.

In the document class constructor, initialize this new variable as shown:

```
m_bFileOpened = false;
```

At the beginning of the Serialize routine, add the following code:

```
if (m_bFileOpened)
{
  m_BugDataArray.RemoveAll();
  m_nBugPosition = -1;
}
```

Use the Class Wizard to add the OnOpenDocument member function, then add the following line to it:

```
M_bFileOpened = true;
```

—leizhengdeng

What Are Threads?

This article was contributed by Gopal Mor.

Environment: C++

Introduction

This article tries to explain the conceptual aspect of multithreaded programming. Much of the explanation is in context with Windows NT. Most of the material is derived from MSDN.

What Are Threads?

Windows NT's basic unit of execution is a thread. That means WIN NT does not execute processes; instead, it executes threads. *Threads* are code sequences that run multitasked on individual stacks. A thread has its own sequence of code, which gets executed in a concurrent fashion. So threads help us achieve concurrent processing. WIN NT Scheduler controls the execution of all the threads running in a system. In WIN NT, each thread has its own priority, numbered from 0 to 31, based on which WIN NT schedules the execution of each thread. The higher the priority number, the higher the thread's priority. A process may have a single thread or multiple threads. A single process has to have a minimum of one thread. Processes can spawn threads and can terminate threads. A thread can be in one of three states at any given time:

- Running—The thread is currently running on one of the CPUs.
- Waiting—The thread is in a suspended state and cannot run until a specified event occurs.
- Ready—The thread is ready to run, but no processor is currently available.

Ready and running threads are called *runnable threads*. The runnable threads can utilize available CPU cycles. The number of currently running threads on a system is limited by the number of CPUs available. On a single-processor system, the number of threads running at a given time is one. On a multiple processor system, the number of threads running at a given time is equal to the number of processors.

FROM THE FORUM

Question: ProgressBar in separate thread (from maxcode):

How can I run a ProgressBar in a separate thread using CreateThread, BeginThread, or something similar?

Answer (from Apeiron):

From one of your dialog member functions, call AfxBeginThread to start a new thread that can process its own routine to take care of the ProgressBar.

```
CMyDlg::StartProgress()
{
    m_bRunProgress = TRUE;
    m_cProgress.SetRange(/*MAKE A RANGE*/);
    AfxBeginThread(Progress, (LPVOID*)this, THREAD_PRIORITY_NORMAL);
}

CMyDlg::StopProgress()
{
    m_bRunProgress = FALSE;
}
```

Then, the thread routine should look like this:

```
UINT Progress(LPVOID pParam);    // declaration

UINT Progress(LPVOID pParam)
{
    CMyDlg *pDlg = (CMyDlg *)pParam;

    int iCount = 0;
    while(pDlg->m_bRunProgress)
    {
        //Do some processing
        pDlg->m_cProgress.SetPos(iCount);
        iCount++;
    }
    return 0;
}
```

When a CPU becomes available, the OS finds the highest priority queue with ready threads on it, removes the thread at the head of the queue, and runs it. This process is called a *context switch*. Each context switch adds a little overhead; as a result, the system will get sluggish as the number of threads increases. WIN NT is a pre-emptive multi-tasking system; this means that the amount of time for which a thread keeps running is decided by OS and not by the thread itself. If enough CPU time is available and no other higher priority threads are ready, the OS allows the running thread to complete its quota of time, which is called *thread quantum*. After a thread completes its thread quantum, the OS finds the ready thread at the head of the highest priority queue and runs it. If a thread completes its thread quantum and a higher priority thread is ready, the OS pre-empts the currently running thread and runs the higher priority thread.

Why Multithreading?

There are several reasons you may need to use multithreading; the most important of them is to enhance your application's performance. This includes, for example, any application that has something to do in the background, irrespective of what is going on in the foreground (user interface). In such applications, there can be one worker thread, which performs a background job, and the main thread, which performs activities related to user interface.

FROM THE FORUM

Question: Global versus static thread functions (from Shahzad):

When starting a thread with _beginthread(), it is possible to call the class member as the thread function. Is this same functionality possible when using the MFC AfxBeginThread call to start the thread using a member function of the same class, or does the thread function need to be essentially global?

Answer (from OReubens):

The function doesn't have to be global, but you do have to define it as "static" if you define it inside the class.

Remember that whenever you write a regular class-member function, you always get an implicit first parameter to the function this.

```
CMyClass::MyFunc()
```

to the compiler is the same as

```
static CMyClass::MyFunc(CMyClass* this)
```

In case you were always wondering where the this comes from, it's provided implicitly on nonstatic member functions.

Since the thread function definition doesn't have a this, you need to define the function as static in your class definition.

Sometimes multithreaded application designs are more logical and less complex than the same designs without multithreading. An application that controls temperature receives temperature measurements from two pyrometers (temperature measuring devices) at regular intervals; the application should respond to these measurements in definite time (real time). It is more logical to have two threads running that accept temperature measurements from each pyrometer and send the response back.

So it is an important design criterion to have multiple threads or to go for a single-threaded application. There is not a hard and fast rule available.

Where Are We Going?

In a multithreaded application, if the threads are independent of each other, it's much easier to design, develop, and debug such applications. But in the practical world, the picture is not so rosy. The threads are always dependent on each other and they share common resources. There starts the world of thread synchronization.

FROM THE FORUM

Question: Accessing class members from Thread function (from shahzad):

Since our thread function is static, does it mean we always have to swim in static functions thereafter and be prevented from accessing other nonstatic members and variables within the class?

Answer (from OReubens):

Nope, you don't have to.

One of the parameters you can pass to the AfxBeginThread call is a 32-bit value. This value is passed on to the Thread function itself and can be typecast back to your class, to access member functions and variables.

An example of this is as follows:

```
class MyClass
{
 public:
    MyClass();
    ~MyClass();
    int SomeFunc();
    static UINT ThreadProc( LPVOID pParam );
};


MyClass::MyClass()
{
    AfxBeginThread(ThreadProc, this);
}

UINT MyClass::ThreadProc( LPVOID pParam )
{
    MyClass* pThis = (MyClass*)pParam;
    pThis->SomeFunc();
}
```

2

Arrays and Collections

In this chapter

All Windows applications deal with data. Some store it on disk, some on the Internet. Wherever it is stored, when it comes to using the data, you often need to place it into an array or collection.

In this chapter, you will find some useful ways of dealing with and sorting arrays and collections.

- "Functions for Setting and Retrieving Values from Variant Safe Arrays" provides two helper routines that may be invaluable when dealing with variant safe arrays.

- "Iterating Through List Containers" shows an elegant way to traverse an object container.

- "Sortable CObArray Class" shows an object array that can easily be sorted.

- "Sortable CObList Class" is similar to the CObArray class. This class provides an easy method of sorting objects in an object list, as opposed to an object array.

Functions for Setting and Retrieving Values from Variant Safe Arrays

This article was contributed by Nanda Kishore.

Here are two very easy-to-use functions for setting (FillVariant) and retrieving (GetVariant) values from a variant safe array. All of the instructions that you'll need in order to use these functions can be found in the following comments. Simply copy the code from the CD-ROM into your files and follow these instructions.

```
/////////////////////////////////////////////////////////////////////////
// Kishore:-
// include this pice of code in .h file.
// function for putting values to VARIANT->SAFEARRAY
// function for getting values from VARIANT->SAFEARRAY
//
```

```
// @1 Type of Array
// @2 Actual type contained in the variant
// @3 Variant to read or write
// @4 Actual array to read or write
// @5 VT_BSTR or VT_DATE ...  (FillVariant)
// Usage:-
// BSTRArray someThing; someThing.Add(bstr);
// FillVariant<BSTRArray,BSTR>(&toVariant,someThing,VT_BSTR);
//
// _BSTR_TArray someThing;
// GetVariant<_BSTR_TArray,BSTR>(fromVariant,someThing);
// _bstr_t _bstr=someThing.GetSize(),GetAt(),[n]
//
// GetVariant<DATEArray,DATE>(fromVariant,dt);
// GetVariant<OLEDATETIMEArray,DATE>(fromVariant,dt);
// OleDateTime x=dt.GetAt(n) ...GetSize(),[],.....
/////////////////////////////////////////////////////////////////////////

#include <afxtempl.h>

typedef CArray<BSTR,BSTR> BSTRArray;
typedef CArray<DATE,DATE> DATEArray;
typedef CArray<_bstr_t,_bstr_t> _BSTR_TArray;
typedef CArray<COleDateTime,COleDateTime> OLEDATETIMEArray;
typedef CArray<DWORD,DWORD> DWORDArray;

template <class T,class T1>
void FillVariant(VARIANT* pVariant, T& arrySrc,int iType)
{
 ASSERT(NULL!=pVariant);
 VariantInit(pVariant);
 int iMax = arrySrc.GetSize();

 SAFEARRAY * pSafeArray;
 SAFEARRAYBOUND aDim[1];
 aDim[0].lLbound = 0;
 aDim[0].cElements = iMax;

 pVariant->vt = VT_ARRAY | iType;

 pSafeArray = SafeArrayCreate(iType, 1, aDim);

 T1* dwArray = NULL;
 SafeArrayAccessData(pSafeArray, (void**)&dwArray);

 for(int nCount = 0; nCount < iMax ; nCount++)
 {
  dwArray[nCount] = (T1)arrySrc[nCount];
 }
 SafeArrayUnaccessData(pSafeArray);
 pVariant->parray = pSafeArray;
}
```

```
template <class T,class T1>
void GetVariant(VARIANT variant, T& arrySrc)
{
 long lStartBound = 0;
 long lEndBound = 0;

 SAFEARRAY* pSafeArray  = variant.parray;
 ASSERT(NULL!=pSafeArray);
 SafeArrayGetLBound(pSafeArray, 1, &lStartBound);
 SafeArrayGetUBound(pSafeArray, 1, &lEndBound);

 T1* arrayAccess = NULL;
 SafeArrayAccessData(pSafeArray, (void**)&arrayAccess);

 for(int iIndex = lStartBound; iIndex <= lEndBound; iIndex ++)
 {
  arrySrc.Add((T1)arrayAccess[iIndex]);
 }
 SafeArrayDestroy(pSafeArray);
 SafeArrayUnaccessData(pSafeArray);
}
```

Iterating Through List Containers

This article was contributed by Zoran M. Todorovic.

When using containers in a program, I declare a class that represents an item in a container:

```
// Can also be a struct
class CMyClass : public CObject {
// Program specific
...
};
typedef CTypedPtrList<CPtrList,CMyClass*> TMyList;
```

A separate class (container) has the actual container object:

```
class CMyClassList : public CObject {
private:
TMyList List;
// Maybe some other data members too
public:
// Usual stuff (construction, destruction etc.)
void Flush(void);
BOOL Add(CMyClass *ptr);
CMyClass *Find(...);
BOOL Del(...);
};
```

If the container is associated with a user interface object (tree control, list control, and so on), one must iterate through the container and perform an action for each item (or for those that satisfy some criteria). An easy way to do it is to move a List variable to a public part of the class declaration and then access it directly. This is bad since it violates a data encapsulation principle (in all but trivial examples, class declaration has a lot more member variables and methods, and performs some useful jobs, too).

One approach is to use a public member function and a supplied callback function, which are executed for each item. This is messy since a supplied callback function is usually a member function of another class; so for each different callback function, class CMyClassList must have an overloaded member function. If a callback function is a static nonmember function, one must use a DWORD function argument to pass a "this" pointer to a static callback function. Then from within a callback function, cast a DWORD to point to a class object. Then invoke a method that actually performs some action with a container item.

A much easier and more elegant approach is to use a special iterator class. A new class declaration is slightly modified:

```
class CMyClassListIterator;
class CMyClassList : public CObject {
private:
TMyClassList List;
// Maybe something else
public:
// Usual stuff (construction, destruction etc.)
void Flush(void);
BOOL Add(CMyClass *ptr);
CMyClass *Find(...);
BOOL Del(...);
friend CMyClassListIterator; // New stuff
};
```

A new iterator class is declared as follows:

```
class CMyClassListIterator : public CObject {
private:
CMyClassList& Owner;
POSITION Pos;
public:
CMyClassListIterator(TProcess& obj)
:CObject(),Owner(obj) { Reset(); }
void Reset(void) { Pos = Owner.List.GetHeadPosition(); }
void Next(void) { Owner.List.GetNext(Pos); }
CMyClass *Current(void) { return (CMyClass*)Owner.List.GetAt(Pos); }
BOOL IsDone(void) { return (Pos == NULL) ? TRUE : FALSE; }
};
```

Now, all you need to do to iterate through the list is to implement the following piece of code:

```
CMyClassList MyList;
........
CMyClassListIterator iterator(MyList);
while (!iterator.IsDone()) {
CMyClass *ptr = iterator.Current();
// Use ptr but do not delete it.
// You can modify its contents however.
iterator.Next();
};
```

You can also easily implement a nested iteration. A good side effect of this implementation is that your code for list iteration is focused on the job that must be done since all the code is implemented in one function (no callbacks). Also, data encapsulation is preserved since the List object is not directly visible.

Sortable CObArray Class

This article was contributed by Douglas Peterson.

```
// SortableObArray.h
///////////////////////////////////////////////////////////////

class CSortableObArray : public CObArray
{
public:
    void Sort(int(*CompareFunc)(CObject* pFirst, CObject* pSecond));
    void Sort(int iStartPos, int iElements, int(*CompareFunc)
➥(CObject* pFirst, CObject* pSecond));
};


template< class TYPE >
class CTypedSortableObArray : public CSortableObArray
{
public:
    // Accessing elements
    TYPE GetAt(int nIndex) const
    { return (TYPE)CSortableObArray::GetAt(nIndex); }
    TYPE& ElementAt(int nIndex)
    { return (TYPE&)CSortableObArray::ElementAt(nIndex); }
    void SetAt(int nIndex, TYPE ptr)
    { CSortableObArray::SetAt(nIndex, ptr); }

    // Potentially growing the array
    void SetAtGrow(int nIndex, TYPE newElement)
    { CSortableObArray::SetAtGrow(nIndex, newElement); }
```

```
    int Add(TYPE newElement)
    { return CSortableObArray::Add(newElement); }
    int Append(const CTypedPtrArray< CSortableObArray, TYPE >& src)
    { return CSortableObArray::Append(src); }
    void Copy(const CTypedPtrArray< CSortableObArray, TYPE >& src)
    { CSortableObArray::Copy(src); }

    // Operations that move elements around
    void InsertAt(int nIndex, TYPE newElement, int nCount = 1)
    { CSortableObArray::InsertAt(nIndex, newElement, nCount); }
    void InsertAt(int nStartIndex, CTypedSortableObArray< TYPE >* pNewArray)
    { CSortableObArray::InsertAt(nStartIndex, pNewArray); }

    // overloaded operator helpers
    TYPE operator[](int nIndex) const
    { return (TYPE)CSortableObArray::operator[](nIndex); }
    TYPE& operator[](int nIndex)
    { return (TYPE&)CSortableObArray::operator[](nIndex); }

    void Sort( int(*CompareFunc)(TYPE pFirstObj, TYPE pSecondObj) )
    { CSortableObArray::Sort((int(*)(CObject*,CObject*))CompareFunc); }
    void Sort( int iStartPos, int iElements, int(*CompareFunc)
➥(TYPE pFirstObj, TYPE pSecondObj) )
    { CSortableObArray::Sort(iStartPos, iElements, (int(*)
➥(CObject*,CObject*))CompareFunc); }
};



// SortableObArray.cpp
//////////////////////////////////////////////////////////////////

#define STRIDE_FACTOR 3

void CSortableObArray::Sort(int(*CompareFunc)
➥(CObject* pFirst, CObject* pSecond))
{
    // CompareFunc is expected to return a positive integer if pFirstObj
    // should follow pSecondObj (is greater than)

    // Uses Shell Sort

    // Basically it does a bunch of smaller insertion sorts than insertion
    // sorts the whole thing.  Insertion sorting is much faster on a list
    // that is already mostly sorted.

    // ** NOTE:  Because GetSize() is called to retrieve the number of
    //                   elements, you shouldcall SetSize() with the number
    //                   of valid elements.  An alternative is shown in the
    //                   sort function below.
```

```
    ASSERT_VALID(this);

    BOOL bFound;
    int iElements = GetSize();
    int iInner,iOuter,iStride = 1;
    CObject *pTmp;

    while (iStride <= iElements)
        iStride = iStride * STRIDE_FACTOR + 1;

    while (iStride > (STRIDE_FACTOR - 1))
    {
        iStride = iStride / STRIDE_FACTOR;
        for (iOuter = iStride; iOuter < iElements; iOuter++)
        {
            bFound = 0;
            iInner = iOuter - iStride;
            while ((iInner >= 0) && !bFound)
            {
                if (CompareFunc(m_pData[iInner+iStride],m_pData[iInner]) < 0)
                {
                    pTmp = m_pData[iInner+iStride];
                    m_pData[iInner+iStride] = m_pData[iInner];
                    m_pData[iInner] = pTmp;
                    iInner -= iStride;
                }
                else
                    bFound = 1;
            }
        }
    }
}

void CSortableObArray::Sort(int iStartPos, int iElements, int(*CompareFunc)
➡(CObject* pFirst, CObject* pSecond))
{
    // This variation allows you to sort only a portion of the array

    ASSERT_VALID(this);
    ASSERT( iStartPos >= 0 && iStartPos <= GetUpperBound() );
    ASSERT( GetSize() - iStartPos >= iElements );

    BOOL bFound;
    int iInner,iOuter,iStride = 1;
    CObject *pTmp;
    CObject **pData = &m_pData[iStartPos];

    while (iStride <= iElements)
        iStride = iStride * STRIDE_FACTOR + 1;
```

```
        while (iStride > (STRIDE_FACTOR - 1))
        {
            iStride = iStride / STRIDE_FACTOR;
            for (iOuter = iStride; iOuter < iElements; iOuter++)
            {
                bFound = 0;
                iInner = iOuter - iStride;
                while ((iInner >= 0) && !bFound)
                {
                    if (CompareFunc(pData[iInner+iStride],pData[iInner]) < 0)
                    {
                        pTmp = pData[iInner+iStride];
                        pData[iInner+iStride] = pData[iInner];
                        pData[iInner] = pTmp;
                        iInner -= iStride;
                    }
                    else
                        bFound = 1;
                }
            }
        }
}


// Usage
/////////////////////////////////////////////////////////////

// Create a CObject based class
class CMyObject : public CObject
{
public:
    CString name;
    static int CompBackward(CMyObject* pFirstObj, CMyObject* pSecondObj)
    {
        return -lstrcmp((LPCTSTR)pFirstObj->name,(LPCTSTR)pSecondObj->name);
    }
};

// Create an array object
CTypedSortableObArray< CMyObject* > array;

array.SetSize(10);

// Fill the array with a bunch of objects
for (int i=0; i < 10; i++)
{
    CMyObject * pObj = new CMyObject;
    pObj->name.Format("Object #%d",i);
    array[i] = pObj;
}
```

```
// Sort the array
array.Sort(CMyObject::CompBackward);

// Display the contents of the now sorted array
for (int i=0; i < 10; i++)
{
    TRACE1("%s\n",array[i]->name);
}
```

Sortable CObList Class

This article was contributed by Douglas Peterson.

```
// SortableObList.h
///////////////////////////////////////////////////////////////

class CSortableObList : public CObList
{
public:
    CSortableObList(int nBlockSize = 10) : CObList(nBlockSize) { }

    void Sort(int(*CompareFunc)(CObject* pFirstObj, CObject*pSecondObj));
    void Sort(POSITION posStart, int iElements, int (*CompareFunc)
➡(CObject* pFirstObj, CObject* pSecondObj));
};


template< class TYPE >
class CTypedSortableObList : public CSortableObList
{
public:
// Construction
    CTypedSortableObList(int nBlockSize = 10) : CSortableObList(nBlockSize) { }

    // peek at head or tail
    TYPE& GetHead()
        { return (TYPE&)CSortableObList::GetHead(); }
    TYPE GetHead() const
        { return (TYPE)CSortableObList::GetHead(); }
    TYPE& GetTail()
        { return (TYPE&)CSortableObList::GetTail(); }
    TYPE GetTail() const
        { return (TYPE)CSortableObList::GetTail(); }

    // get head or tail (and remove it) - don't call on empty list!
    TYPE RemoveHead()
        { return (TYPE)CSortableObList::RemoveHead(); }
    TYPE RemoveTail()
        { return (TYPE)CSortableObList::RemoveTail(); }
```

```
    // add before head or after tail
    POSITION AddHead(TYPE newElement)
        { return CSortableObList::AddHead(newElement); }
    POSITION AddTail(TYPE newElement)
        { return CSortableObList::AddTail(newElement); }

    // add another list of elements before head or after tail
    void AddHead(CTypedSortableObList< TYPE >* pNewList)
        { CSortableObList::AddHead(pNewList); }
    void AddTail(CTypedSortableObList< TYPE >* pNewList)
        { CSortableObList::AddTail(pNewList); }

    // iteration
    TYPE& GetNext(POSITION& rPosition)
        { return (TYPE&)CSortableObList::GetNext(rPosition); }
    TYPE GetNext(POSITION& rPosition) const
        { return (TYPE)CSortableObList::GetNext(rPosition); }
    TYPE& GetPrev(POSITION& rPosition)
        { return (TYPE&)CSortableObList::GetPrev(rPosition); }
    TYPE GetPrev(POSITION& rPosition) const
        { return (TYPE)CSortableObList::GetPrev(rPosition); }

    // getting/modifying an element at a given position
    TYPE& GetAt(POSITION position)
        { return (TYPE&)CSortableObList::GetAt(position); }
    TYPE GetAt(POSITION position) const
        { return (TYPE)CSortableObList::GetAt(position); }
    void SetAt(POSITION pos, TYPE newElement)
        { CSortableObList::SetAt(pos, newElement); }

    void Sort( int(*CompareFunc)(TYPE pFirstObj, TYPE pSecondObj) )
        { CSortableObList::Sort((int(*)(CObject*,CObject*))CompareFunc); }
    void Sort( POSITION posStart, int iElements, int(*CompareFunc)
➡(TYPE pFirstObj, TYPE pSecondObj) )
        { CSortableObList::Sort(posStart, iElements, (int(*)
➡(CObject*,CObject*))CompareFunc); }
};


// SortableObList.cpp
/////////////////////////////////////////////////////////////////////

void CSortableObList::Sort(int (*CompareFunc)
➡(CObject* pFirstObj, CObject* pSecondObj))
{
    // CompareFunc is expected to return a positive integer if pFirstObj
    // should follow pSecondObj (is greater than)

    // Uses Insertion Sort
```

```
       // The Shell Sort is much faster than a straight insertion sort, however,
       //  it cannot be performed on a linked list (it COULD, but the resulting
       //  code would probably be much slower as a Shell Sort jumps all around
       //  the reletive positions of elements).

       // An Insertion Sort works by evaluating an item, if that item should
       // precede the item in front of it, than it shifts all the items that
       // should follow that item up one place until it finds the correct position
       // for the item, whereby it then 'inserts' that item.

       ASSERT_VALID(this);

       // If the list contains no items, the HEAD position will be NULL
       if (m_pNodeHead == NULL)
           return;

       CObject *pOtemp;
       CObList::CNode *pNi,*pNj;

       // Walk the list
       for (pNi = m_pNodeHead->pNext; pNi != NULL; pNi = pNi->pNext)
       {
           // Save data pointer
           pOtemp = pNi->data;

           // Walk the list backwards from pNi to the beginning of the list or
           // until the CompareFunc() determines that this item is in its correct
           // position shifting all items upwards as it goes
           for (pNj = pNi; pNj->pPrev != NULL && CompareFunc
➥(pNj->pPrev->data,pOtemp) > 0; pNj = pNj->pPrev)
               pNj->data = pNj->pPrev->data;

           // Insert data pointer into it's proper position
           pNj->data = pOtemp;
       }

}

void CSortableObList::Sort(POSITION posStart, int iElements, int (*CompareFunc)
➥(CObject* pFirstObj, CObject* pSecondObj))
{
       // This variation allows you to sort only a portion of the list

       // iElements can be larger than the number of remaining elements without
       // harm
       // iElements can be -1 which will always sort to the end of the list

       ASSERT_VALID(this);
       ASSERT( AfxIsValidAddress((CObList::CNode*)posStart, sizeof
➥(CObList::CNode)) );
```

```
    // Make certain posStart is a position value obtained by a GetHeadPosition
    // or Find member function call as there is no way to test whether or not
    // posStart is a valid CNode pointer from this list. Ok, there is one way,
    // we could walk the entire list and verify that posStart is in the chain,
    // but even for debug builds that's a bit much.

    // If the list contains no items, the HEAD position will be NULL
    if (m_pNodeHead == NULL)
        return;

    CObject *pOtemp;
    CObList::CNode *pNi,*pNj;

    // Walk the list
    for (pNi = (CObList::CNode*)posStart; pNi != NULL && iElements != 0;
         pNi = pNi->pNext, iElements--)
    {
        // Save data pointer
        pOtemp = pNi->data;

        // Walk the list backwards from pNi to the beginning of the sort or
        // until the CompareFunc() determines that this item is in it's correct
        // position shifting all items upwards as it goes
        for (pNj = pNi; pNj->pPrev != NULL && pNj->pPrev != ((CObList::CNode*)
             posStart)->pPrev && CompareFunc(pNj->pPrev->data,pOtemp)
           > 0; pNj = pNj->pPrev)
            pNj->data = pNj->pPrev->data;

        // Insert data pointer into it's proper position
        pNj->data = pOtemp;
    }

}



// Usage
///////////////////////////////////////////////////////////

// Create a CObject based class
// Create a CObject based class
class CMyObject : public CObject
{
public:
    CString name;
    static int CompBackward(CMyObject* pFirstObj, CMyObject* pSecondObj)
    {
        return -lstrcmp((LPCTSTR)pFirstObj->name,(LPCTSTR)pSecondObj->name);
    }
};
```

```
// Create a list object
CTypedSortableObList< CMyObject* > list;

// Fill the list with a bunch of objects
for (int i=0; i < 10; i++)
{
    CMyObject * pObj = new CMyObject;
    pObj->name.Format("Object #%d",i);
    list.AddTail(pObj);
}

// Sort the list
list.Sort(CMyObject::CompBackward);

// Display the contents of the now sorted list
for (POSITION pos = list.GetHeadPosition(); pos != NULL; )
{
    CMyObject* pObj = list.GetNext(pos);
    TRACE1("%s\n",pObj->name);
}
```

3

Documents and Views

In this chapter

The Document/View architecture is used, with minimal overhead, to provide applications a way to separate data from visualizations of that data in one or more windows.

This is one of the least understood aspects of the Visual Studio framework and often the cause of much debate. Used correctly, however, the Document/View architecture provides a lot of functionality and future expandability to an application.

In this chapter, you will find some practical guides to using this framework effectively, as well as a description of it.

- "MFC Under the Hood: Creating an MFC Application" provides a feet-first approach to building Document/View applications from the ground up, with

some quick information about what's going on.

- "Using Better Tracing to Understand the Doc/View Architecture" gives those wishing to get an in-depth understanding of the structure of the Document/View architecture a clear picture of what makes it tick.

- "Command Routing Beyond a Split Frame" describes a simple technique to enable inactive views to process commands.

- "Replacing a View in a Doc-View Application" is an extremely useful article I find myself referring to on a regular basis. The article describes how to seamlessly swap between various view types at runtime.

MFC Under the Hood: Creating an MFC Application

This article was contributed by Andrew Fenster.

Environment: Visual C++

Most of the time when you are creating a new MFC application, you'll start with the MFC App Wizard. The App Wizard generates a basic skeleton application, which you will flesh out into a full-fledged, useful program.

Even the skeleton application you get from the App Wizard contains a lot of very arcane-looking code, and there's a great deal of hidden code as well. The purpose of this article is to demystify some of that code. I'll show you how to build a simple MFC application without the App Wizard. By the time you are done, the mysterious-looking code that comes from the App Wizard will no longer be so mysterious, and you'll be better prepared to modify it to suit your own purposes.

The Hidden Code First

Every 32-bit Windows application has two essential program elements: WinMain and WndProc. Your program will have one WinMain for the entire program and one WndProc for each window in the program. Although MFC creates these for you, you still need to know a little about them.

WinMain is the function that starts your application. Once your application is running, the Windows operating system will start placing your application's messages in a message queue. WinMain makes three Windows API calls to get these messages from the operating system and to process them. First, it calls GetMessage to retrieve a message. Then, it calls TranslateMessage to perform any necessary conversion of the message. Finally, WinMain calls DispatchMessage, which tells the operating system to send the message to the appropriate WndProc for handling.

Once WndProc receives a message, it looks through its message handlers for instructions on what should be done with the message. Your job as a Windows application programmer is to write the handlers.

A Simple MFC Application: Less than 20 Lines of Code

Next, we'll look at a simple, bare-bones MFC application. MFC provides WinMain and WndProc. We must provide an MFC-derived application class and window management class.

Our application class will be derived from the MFC class CWinApp. CWinApp provides all the member variables and functions to initialize, start, run, and close an application. CWinApp contains a pointer called m_pMainWnd, which will point to an object of our derived window management class. Each MFC application has one and only one object derived directly from CWinApp. In the example below, that class is called "CMyApp."

Our window management class will be derived from CFrameWnd. CFrameWnd has all the member variables and functions to create and manage windows. Note that when you create an object of our derived windows class, you have not created an actual window. The new object uses its Create() function to create windows.

Here's what happens when we start our program. You can follow along in the code:

1. WinMain runs this code: **CMyApp app;**. This creates an object of type CMyApp named "app". app will have all the member variables and functions of CWinApp that are needed to start, run, and close our application.

2. Then WinMain calls app's **InitInstance()** function. InitInstance() creates a new CMyWnd object with **m_pMainWnd = new CMyWnd;**.

3. The CMyWnd constructor calls its **Create()** function, which creates an instance of the window but does not display it.

4. The app's InitInstance() function then displays the window with **m_pMainWnd-> ShowWindow(m_nCmdShow);**.

5. WinMain calls the app's **Run()** function, which dispatches messages to the rest of the application.

Here is the code. Try it—it works!

```
#include <afxwin.h>

//derive my own window class from CFrameWnd
class CMyWin:  public CFrameWnd
{
    public:
    CMyWin( );
    DECLARE_MESSAGE_MAP( )
};

//define my window class' constructor:
CMyWin::CMyWin( )
{
    Create(0, "This Text Will Appear in the Title Bar");
}

//derive my own application class from CWinApp
class CMyApp:  public CWinApp
{
    public:
    virtual BOOL InitInstance( );
};

//define my application class' InitInstance( )
BOOL CMyApp::InitInstance( )
{
    m_pMainWnd = new CMyWin( );
    m_pMainWnd->ShowWindow(m_nCmdShow);
    m_pMainWnd->UpdateWindow();
    return TRUE;
}
```

```
//here is my application's message map
BEGIN_MESSAGE_MAP(CMyWin, CFrameWnd)
    // any messages to be processed by
    // CMyWin get listed here.
END_MESSAGE_MAP( )

//declare an instance of application
//class for WinMain to use.
CMyApp app;
```

Figure 3.1 shows what you get when you compile and run.

Figure 3.1

Your actual window will be bigger.

Single Document Interface Applications

The code from the preceding section creates a simple, bare-bones application. The code that you will find in a single document interface application is more complicated, but it still works along the same lines. You still have an application class derived from CWinApp. You still have a window management class derived from CFrameWnd. In this case, however, the derived window management class is called CMainFrame.

Your derived application class still has an InitInstance() function, but the function looks a lot more complicated. Among other things, it contains something like this:

```
CSingleDocTemplate* pDocTemplate;
pDocTemplate = new CSingleDocTemplate(
    IDR_MAINFRAME,
    RUNTIME_CLASS(CMyDoc),
    RUNTIME_CLASS(CMainFrame),  // main SDI frame window
    RUNTIME_CLASS(CMyView));
AddDocTemplate(pDocTemplate);
```

Here, the application object creates a single document template pointer and points it to a new single document template object. There are four parameters passed to the CSingleDocTemplate constructor. The first is an integer, the resource ID for the IDR_MAINFRAME resource. The next three parameters pass class information for my Document class, Frame class, and View class. Then the pointer to this new CSingleDocTemplate is added to the list of document templates maintained by the application object. (In an SDI application, there's only one template.)

IDR_MAINFRAME is a resource containing

1. The application's icon
2. The application's menu
3. The accelerator table that goes with the menu
4. A document string

The document string contains up to seven pieces of information in substrings separated by "\n" characters:

1. The title that appears in the frame window's title bar.
2. The title assigned to new documents. If omitted, the default is "Untitled."
3. A description of the document type in an MDI application. This substring isn't used in an SDI application.
4. A description of the document type, followed by its default file name extension, for example, "My Big Program(*.mbp)."
5. The three letter extension for the document type, for example, ".mbp."
6. A name with no spaces that identifies the document type in the registry.
7. A descriptive name of the document type, for example, "My Big Program Document."

Here's a sample string:

```
"My Big Program\n\n\nMy Big Program(*.mbp)\n.mbp\nBigProgram\nMBP Document."
```

Conclusion

So there you have it. Now that you know a little more about what your wizard-generated code is doing, you can go in and start modifying it. For example, if you want to change the size and positioning of your application's main window, you can modify the Create() function. Try substituting the following code for the Create() function listed in the previous example. You'll get a much smaller window positioned in the upper left corner of the screen.

```
RECT x;
x.top = 30;
x.left = 30;
x.bottom = 300;
x.right = 300;
Create(NULL, "My New Window", WS_OVERLAPPEDWINDOW, x);
```

There are a lot of settings and functions you can play with. You might be the type who never changes the default code. Even so, the more you know about what's going on, the better your programs will be.

Using Better Tracing to Understand the Doc/View Architecture

This article was contributed by Mark Messer.

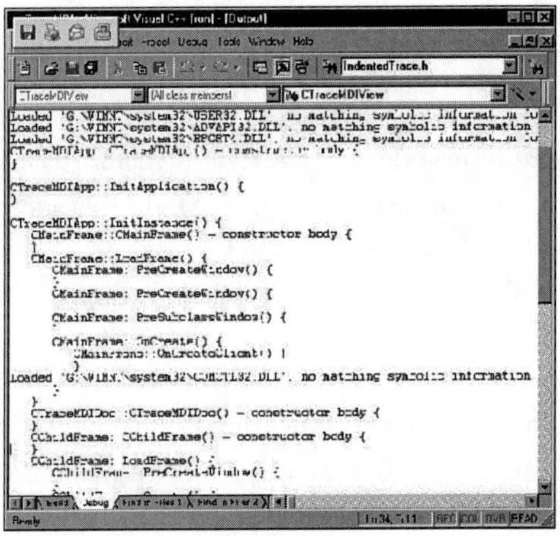

Figure 3.2

Purpose

One of the hard things about learning the Document/View architecture is that it is full of marvelous functions, but nobody tells you which function gets called when. You are supposed to override functions when you want to add functionality, but it is not clear which function is the right one.

One way to find out which function you want to override is to override each function you want to know about and put a TRACE statement in it. Now each time one of your functions is called, a line of text appears in the Debug window. Start the program; see what happens. Click the mouse; see what happens.

This is fine as far as it goes. But to understand the Document/View architecture, you want to see a lot of functions. The Debug window quickly turns into a mess. You don't learn anything. It would help if the Debug window was more readable.

The CIndentedTrace class helps with this. You can use it to make the Debug window look more like C++ code. By adding a line of code to a function like the CMyClass member function MyFunc(), CIndentedTrace prints

```
CMyClass::MyFunc() {
```

when it is called. When the function exits, CIndentedTrace prints

```
}
```

Functions called by MyFunc() can be treated the same way, except that their text will be indented. If MyFunc() calls SubFunc(), the Debug window looks like this

```
CMyClass::MyFunc() {
 CMyClass::SubFunc() {
  }
 }
```

CIndentedTrace can also be used to add lines of text that look like C++ comments. For example,

```
CMyClass::MyFunc() {
 // This explains something that goes on inside MyFunc().
 }
```

CIndentedTrace contains other utility functions for such things as hex dumps of strings and displaying text strings for GetLastError() messages.

TRACE is a macro whose behavior depends on whether _DEBUG is defined. When compiled with a debug configuration, TRACE does its job. When compiled with a release configuration, it disappears. The CIndentedTrace header file contains macros to do the same thing. If you use these macros instead of calling CIndentedTrace yourself, CIndentedTrace will only be called in debug versions of your program.

Running the Demos

You may want to try out the demos before seeing how they work.

The TraceEasy demo shows an easy example of using the CIndentedTrace class without macros. It is for understanding the class.

The TraceMacro demo is an example of how to use all the features of the CIndentedTrace class with macros.

The TraceSDI and TraceMDI demos use CIndentedTrace to make the inner workings of the single and multiple document interface visible.

All demos work only from the development environment with debugging active. No compiled code has been included.

To run the demos:

1. Download and unzip them. Put each one in a separate directory. Each demo should have some source files and three or four files in a res subdirectory.

2. Make sure tracing is enabled. This is done with the Tracer utility found in the VC++ tools (Task bar, Start button, Programs, Microsoft Visual C++, Microsoft Visual C++ Tools, Tracer). The Enable Tracing check box should be checked. You will probably not want any of the other check boxes checked under most circumstances.

3. Use the Visual C++ development environment to open the workspace file (the dsw file). In most cases, this can be done by double-clicking on the file in Windows Explorer.

4. Make sure a debug configuration is selected. Check it on the Build menu, Set Active Configuration option.

5. Compile the demo application. On the Build menu, choose the Build option.

6. If you have just finished compiling, the output window is probably open and displaying 0 error(s), 0 warning(s). If not, on the View menu, select the Output option.

    There is a row of tabs along the bottom of the Output window that say Build, Debug, and so on. When the program runs, TRACE output and other messages go in the Debug window.

7. Run the demo from the development environment. On the Build menu, select the Start Debug option, and the Go suboption.

8. At any time while the program is running or after it has stopped, switch back to the development environment and look in the Debug window.

The SDI and MDI demos trace MFC code through a single document interface application and a multiple document interface application. In each, a vanilla application was created with the App Wizard. The Class Wizard was used to override many functions. The IT_IT() macro was added to each override. This macro uses CIndentedTrace to produce formatted TRACE output.

Some functions were not overridden because they produce too much output. For example, the mouse move message handler produces several messages every time the mouse is touched. The screen drawing functions and idle message handlers are also left out. It is good to trace these to see what they do, even if you don't leave macros in them more than long enough to find out.

Tip: Stepping through the MFC source code is another good way to learn about MFC. Add a breakpoint to the function you want to inspect, run the program, and step into the MFC source code. This works only in MFC code. Microsoft does not supply source code for the C runtime library, SDK functions, or other code. Darn it.

If you do this, be careful about breakpoints in window activation handlers or screen drawing functions. When you are done stepping through such a function, you might continue running the program. The debugger activates the program widows and redraws them. This calls the message handler you just finished stepping through, triggers its breakpoint, and shows you the code you just tried to get out of. To get out of this loop, you must turn off the breakpoint.

Using CIndentedTrace in Your Programs

1. Before beginning to deal with a program, tracing must be enabled. This is done with the Tracer utility found in the VC++ tools (Task bar, Start button, Programs, Microsoft Visual C++, Microsoft Visual C++ Tools, Tracer). The Enable Tracing check box should be checked. You will probably not want any of the other check boxes checked under most circumstances.

2. Make sure you are using a debug configuration. Open your project with Visual Studio. On the Build menu, choose the Set Active Configuration option. Choose the debug configuration. Recompile if needed.

3. Before the class or macros can be used, the IndentedTrace.cpp file must be added to the project (Project, Add to Project, Files...). Just having the file present in the project directory is not enough. The compiler will not compile a source file and the linker will not use the object file unless the source file is part of the project. If the linker doesn't find the CIntendedTrace functions referenced in the code, it will complain with LNK2001 errors.

   The IndentedTrace.h file can be added to the project or not. If not, CIndentedTrace will not appear in the Visual Studio Class View window and IndentedTrace.h will be listed as an external dependency instead of a header file in the File view.

4. Each project cpp file where CIndentedTrace functions or macros are to be used must reference IndentedTrace.h. This can be done by adding

   ```
   #include "IndentedTrace.h"
   ```

   near the top of the cpp file or to a header file that the cpp file includes. Perhaps the best way is to just add it once to stdafx.h.

5. In each function you want to trace, add an IT_IT() macro. It should be the first line so that any code called by the function is properly included inside the function's braces. The IT_IT() macro takes a string argument. The string usually contains the function's class and name. The class should be added because the output window may contain output from many different classes. But you may use any text you want to appear in the output window.

   Within a function, an IT_IT() macro must appear before any other IT_ macro can be used. Only one IT_IT() macro can be used in any function.

6. To add a comment to the output window, add an IT_COMMENT() macro somewhere after the IT_IT().

   Variables can be displayed with a format like TRACE or printf().
   IT_COMMENT1() takes one variable. For two or three variables, use
   IT_COMMENT2() and IT_COMMENT3().

The code you write might look like this:

```
#include "IndentedTrace.h"  // This may go in stdafx.h

CMyClass::MyFunc( int iArg1, double dArg2 )
{
 IT_IT( "CMyClass::MyFunc()" );
 SubFunc( iArg1 );
 IT_COMMENT( "This explains something that goes on inside MyFunc()." );
 // ...
}

CMyClass::SubFunc( int iArg1 )
{
 IT_IT( "CMyClass:: SubFunc()" );
 IT_COMMENT1( "The value of iArg1 is %d", iArg1 );
 ...
}
```

How CIndentedTrace Works

The TraceEasy demo shows how CIndentedTrace works. Only a few CIndentedTrace features are used. No macros are used to make it easy to follow when stepping into CIndentedTrace code.

Look in CTRaceEasyView to find code that uses CIndentedTrace. In OnLButtonUp(), try putting a breakpoint at the CIndentedTrace variable declared. Step into the CIndentedTrace constructor and destructor. To see the destructor, wait until the cursor reaches the closing brace of OnLButtonUp(), and step into the brace.

When a local variable of type CIndentedTrace is created, the CIndentedTrace constructor is called immediately, and the CIndentedTrace destructor is called at the end of the function body when local variables go out of scope. The most important things the constructor does are print its argument and a "{" at the current indent level and increment the indent level. The most important things the destructor does are decrement the indent level and print a "}".

Note that if the CIndentedTrace variable is declared on the first line of a function, it will be constructed before any other local variables. Its destructor will be called last. This is important.

CIndentedTrace keeps track of the indent level with the static member variable ms_iTraceDepth. Because ms_iTraceDepth is static, all CIndentedTrace objects must share a single copy of it. This makes it an ideal way for CIndentedTrace objects to share information about the current indent level. Each time a new CIndentedTrace object is created, ms_iTraceDepth is incremented. Each time one is destroyed, ms_iTraceDepth is decremented.

Each CIndentedTrace object keeps track of the indent level it was created at with m_nLocalTraceDepth. Since this member variable is not static, no other CIndentedTrace object can touch it. It remains fixed for the life of the object that created it.

Other CIndentedTrace functions, such as Comment(), can only be called in functions that have defined a CIndentedTrace variable. This is obvious in TraceEasy, but when macros are used, the variable definition is hidden in a macro.

Comment() just prints "// " and its argument at the local indent level.

The TraceMacro demo shows how to use most CIndentedTrace features, including some explained in the "For More Advanced Users" section that follows. TraceMacro is a little more complex, but it mostly does the same things as TraceEasy.

One difference is that TraceMacro uses macros for all CIndentedTrace variable definitions and function calls. The macros are defined at the end of the IndentedTrace header file.

The IT_IT macro creates a local variable with the unlikely name of _IT_vnirrrdaewu in debug compiles. This name was chosen because, in most programs, it will not already be used by another variable. _IT_vnirrrdaewu stands for "Variable Name I Really, Really, Really Doubt Anyone Else Will Use." If you do not share my doubts, please feel free to rewrite the macros with a name based on a GUID.

Most of the other macros call a CIndentedTrace function. They require that the variable _IT_vnirrrdaewu be defined. This means they can only be used after IT_IT() or IT_EMBEDDED_IT has been used. IT_IT() is intended for the usual local variable case. IT_EMBEDDED_IT is intended for a special case where CIndentedTrace must be a class member variable.

For More Advanced Users

A constructor with an initialization list may need to be handled a little differently. The initialization list is executed before entering the constructor body. An IT_IT() macro in the constructor body makes it look like the initialization list is not part of the constructor. The thing to do is put CIndentedTrace in the initialization list too. This means it has to be a member variable of the class.

Recall that the order of the constructors in an initialization list is set by the order that member variables are declared in the header, *not* the order in the initialization list. If this is not familiar, see *Effective C++* by Scott Meyer. In any case, the CIndentedTrace member variable must be declared first in the class.

CIndentedTrace prints a "{" and indents when constructed, and unindents and prints a "}" when destroyed. This means there will be a "{" when the class is constructed and a "}" when it is destroyed. If you want the class constructor and destructor each bracketed with { and }, you will have to call Entry() and Exit() to put them there yourself. A couple of Comments() may be useful as well.

Macros can be used for all of this. The IT_EMBEDDED_IT macro creates an uninitialized CIndentedTrace member variable named _IT_vnirrrdaewu. This member variable should be initialized in the constructor initialization list with IT_EMBEDDED_INIT(). You will probably want to add IT_EXIT to the constructor body and IT_ENTRY() to the destructor body. You may want to add IT_COMMENT() as well.

Example header file:

```
class CMyClass
{
IT_EMBEDDED_IT;  // Must come before other member variables.
CEmbeddedClass m_EC;

CMyClass();
~CMyClass();
// ...
}
```

Example cpp file:

```
CMyClass::CMyClass()
 : IT_EMBEDDED_INIT("CMyClass::CMyClass - "
                    "beginning of constr init list" ),
                    m_EC( int iSomeArg )
{
IT_COMMENT( "CMyClass::CMyClass - beginning of c'tor body " );
// Other initialization
IT_EXIT();
}

CMyClass::~CMyClass()
{
IT_ENTRY("CMyClass::~CMyClass - beginning of destructor body ")
// Other destruction
IT_COMMENT( "CMyClass::~CMyClass - End of destructor body");
// m_EC will be destroyed after the destructor body is done.
}
```

Note that if the IT_IT() macro is used in a member class, a member variable and a local variable with the same name have been declared. This is okay. The local variable hides the member variable. This means that if you add IT_COMMENT() to the function, it will invoke the local CIndentedTrace and print at the local function's indent level.

If you have any doubts about which instance of CIndentedTrace produces what output, add IT_ENABLE_SERIAL_NUM(bEnable). This calls a static function and so can be used before any CIndentedTrace variables have been defined. The output will identify itself with serial numbers.

CIndentedTrace is not thread safe. It would not be hard to protect the static variables with a critical section. But a multithreaded program may already have thread synchronization code. If CIndentedTrace had a critical section, the program using it could wait on two resources at the same time. This creates a potential for deadlock. The cause of a deadlock can be hard to find, particularly when some of the code is buried in macros. The developer of a multithreaded program should make the decision to add a critical section to CIndentedTrace if he wants it.

In the meantime, CIndentedTrace works after a fashion in multithreaded programs. Sometimes the indentation is messed up. This is not a big problem because indentation is messed up anyway when output from two execution paths are interleaved.

If you are willing to overlook this shortcoming, you can add IT_ENABLE_THREAD_ID(bEnable). This calls a static function and so can be used before any CIndentedTrace variables have been defined.

The output produced outside the main thread will identify itself with a thread ID. This can be used together with serial numbers.

There is another approach to tracing a multithreaded app. IT_EMBEDDED_IT and IT_EMBEDDED_INIT create a CIndentedTrace member variable in a class. The member variable has the right name, so all the macros can be used in any class function. All the output they produce will have the same indent level, but this can be an advantage in a multithreaded application.

FROM THE FORUM

Question: Accessing Doc/View variables (from Salim S):

I am using an SDI application and have three classes (View, Doc, and CTest). In CTest, how can I access variables of View and Doc classes?

Answer (from sounder):

```
CFrameWnd *pWnd= AfxGetApp()->m_pMainWnd;

// To access the view's members:
CUrView *pView= ((CUrView*) pWnd->GetActiveView());
pView->variable; // you can access public data members or functions.

// To access the document's members:
CUrDoc *pDoc= (CUrDoc*) pWnd->GetActiveDocument();
pDoc->variable;
```

Command Routing Beyond a Split Frame

This article was contributed by Bartosz Bien.

Abstract: The article presents a simple method of routing WM_COMMAND messages through a number of views in a split frame window. This simplifies dealing with command routing and UI updates for inactive views.

The standard framework route does not include inactive views, which causes toolbar buttons and menus to gray when their mother view is deactivated. Users are confused. To bring back their happiness, I have overridden the CCmdTarget::OnCmdMsg function in the main frame (obviously derived from CFrameWnd):

```
BOOL CMainFrame::OnCmdMsg(UINT nID, int nCode, void* pExtra,
➡  AFX_CMDHANDLERINFO* pHandlerInfo)
{
    CDocument *pDoc = GetActiveDocument();
    if(pDoc)
    {
    POSITION pos = pDoc->GetFirstViewPosition();
    CView *pView = NULL;
    while(pView = pDoc->GetNextView(pos))
    {
        if(pView != GetActiveView()
        && pView->OnCmdMsg(nID, nCode, pExtra, pHandlerInfo))
        return TRUE;
    }
    }

    return CFrameWnd::OnCmdMsg(nID, nCode, pExtra, pHandlerInfo);
}
```

I used a list of views contained in the active document (if any). The command message is passed to all views but the active one, which had a chance to handle it before it was routed to the frame window. If the message is handled by one of the views (OnCmdMsg indicates it by returning TRUE), no further processing is needed and we can return. Otherwise, the base class member is called to restore the conventional framework route.

Comments

Visual C++ version 5 has a problem compiling the sample code. Here is how to correct this:

Due to some cosmetic changes to the MFC, the function CView::OnCmdMsg is no longer protected in VC6. (Why should it be, while it is public in CCmdTarget?)

In VC5, you can correct this simply by just changing CView★ to CCmdTarget★:

```
if(pDoc)
{
    POSITION pos = pDoc->GetFirstViewPosition();
    CCmdTarget *pCT = NULL;
    while(pCT = pDoc->GetNextView(pos))
    {
        if(pCT != GetActiveView() &&
        pCT->OnCmdMsg(nID, nCode, pExtra, pHandlerInfo))
            return TRUE;
    }
}
```

It's that easy because CView is inherited from CCmdTarget (so you don't need to cast!), and (pCT != GetActiveView()) is just a comparison of pointers.

—Bartosz Bien

Replacing a View in a Doc-View Application

This article was contributed by Jorge Lodos.

Sometimes the way a document is being visualized needs to be significantly changed. For example, in PowerPoint, you can see the slides in a WYSIWYG form or view only the text in a text edit window. In the MFC world, one can find an amazingly large quantity of programs that implement this behavior defining one CView descendant and making it responsible for all visualization changes. This path has several disadvantages:

- Big, difficult-to-manage class definition file.
- Diminished reusability: You could reuse one big CView descendant or nothing.
- Hard to maintain: What if you want to modify or add a new "look" to the document?
- Wasted memory: Some variables (objects) will exist in memory and won't be used.

For an application using the MFC Document-View architecture, it is more appropriate to define different view classes and switch between them when necessary. This shall overcome all the disadvantages listed before. There probably will be some features common to all views for same type of document, so it is a good idea to have a direct CView descendant that implements all the functionality common to all view types. The views used by the document should be descendants of this class ("grandchildren" of CView).

The code needed to implement view switching depends on the frame window containing the view. There are three common cases: The view is contained within a CFrameWnd (SDI application), the view is contained within a CMDIChildWnd (MDI application), and the view is a pane of a splitter window (either in SDI or MDI applications). In all cases what we need is a method in our document class to switch to the desired view. This method should receive the new view type as a parameter and return a success flag. The advantage of having this method in the document class becomes obvious when there are several document types that each can have different view types.

Let's start with an SDI application that doesn't have splitters:

```
BOOL CMyDocument::SwitchToView(CRuntimeClass* pNewViewClass)
{
    CFrameWnd* pMainWnd = (CFrameWnd*)AfxGetMainWnd();
    CView* pOldActiveView = pMainWnd->GetActiveView();

    // If we're already displaying this kind of view, no need to go further.
    if (pOldActiveView->IsKindOf(pNewViewClass))
        return TRUE;

    // Set the child window ID of the active view to AFX_IDW_PANE_FIRST.
    // This is necessary so that CFrameWnd::RecalcLayout will allocate
    // this "first pane" to that portion of the frame window's client
    // area not allocated to control bars.  Set the child ID of
    // the previously active view to some other ID.
    ::SetWindowLong(pOldActiveView->m_hWnd, GWL_ID, 0);

    // create the new view
    CCreateContext context;
    context.m_pNewViewClass = pNewViewClass;
    context.m_pCurrentDoc = this;
    CView* pNewView = STATIC_DOWNCAST(CView, pMainWnd->CreateView(&context));
    if (pNewView != NULL)
    {
        // the new view is there, but invisible and not active...
        pNewView->ShowWindow(SW_SHOW);
        pNewView->OnInitialUpdate();
        pMainWnd->SetActiveView(pNewView);
        pMainWnd->RecalcLayout();

        // destroy the old view...
        pOldActiveView->DestroyWindow();
        return TRUE;
    }

    return FALSE;
}
```

In the case of an MDI application (again without splitters):

```
BOOL CMyDocument::SwitchToView(CRuntimeClass* pNewViewClass)
{
    CMDIFrameWnd* pMainWnd = (CMDIFrameWnd*)AfxGetMainWnd();
    // Get the active MDI child window.
    CMDIChildWnd* pChild = (CMDIChildWnd*)pMainWnd->MDIGetActive();
    // Get the active view attached to the active MDI child window.
    CView* pOldActiveView = pChild->GetActiveView();
    // If we're already displaying this kind of view, no need to go further.
    if (pOldActiveView->IsKindOf(pNewViewClass))
        return TRUE;

    // Set flag so that document will not be deleted when view is destroyed.
    BOOL bAutoDelete = m_bAutoDelete;
    m_bAutoDelete = FALSE;
    // Delete existing view
    pOldActiveView->DestroyWindow();
    // restore flag
    m_bAutoDelete = bAutoDelete;

    // Create new view.
    CView* pNewView = (CView *)pNewViewClass->CreateObject();
    if (pNewView == NULL)
    {
        TRACE1("Warning: Dynamic create of view type %Fs failed\n",
➥pNewViewClass->m_lpszClassName);
        return FALSE;
    }

    // Draw new view.
    CCreateContext context;
    context.m_pNewViewClass = pNewViewClass;
    context.m_pCurrentDoc = this;
    context.m_pNewDocTemplate = NULL;
    context.m_pLastView = NULL;
    context.m_pCurrentFrame = pChild;
    if (!pNewView->Create(NULL, NULL, AFX_WS_DEFAULT_VIEW, CRect(0, 0, 0, 0),
               pChild, AFX_IDW_PANE_FIRST, &context))
    {
        TRACE0("Warning: couldn't create view for frame\n");
        delete pNewView;
        return FALSE;
    }

    pNewView->SendMessage(WM_INITIALUPDATE, 0, 0);  // WM_INITIALUPDATE
➥ is defined in afxpriv.h
    pChild->RecalcLayout();
    pNewView->UpdateWindow();
    pChild->SetActiveView(pNewView);
    return TRUE;
}
```

When the view to replace is a pane of a splitter window, there is also a small difference between SDI and MDI applications, related to the retrieval of the current active view. In the following method you must comment out what you don't need depending on your application type:

```
BOOL CMyDocument::SwitchToView(CRuntimeClass* pNewViewClass)
{
/*    Uncomment this if this is a SDI application

    CFrameWnd* pMainWnd = (CFrameWnd*)AfxGetMainWnd();
    CView* pOldActiveView = pMainWnd->GetActiveView();
*/
/*    Uncomment this if this a MDI application

    CMDIFrameWnd* pMainWnd = (CMDIFrameWnd*)AfxGetMainWnd();
    // Get the active MDI child window.
    CMDIChildWnd* pChild = (CMDIChildWnd*)pMainWnd->MDIGetActive();
    // Get the active view attached to the active MDI child window.
    CView* pOldActiveView = pChild->GetActiveView();
*/
    // If we're already displaying this kind of view, no need to go further.
    if (pOldActiveView->IsKindOf(pNewViewClass))
        return TRUE;

    CSplitterWnd* pSplitter = (CSplitterWnd *)pOldActiveView->GetParent();
    int row, col;
    ASSERT(pSplitter->IsChildPane(pOldActiveView, row, col));
    CRect viewrect;
    pOldActiveView->GetWindowRect(&viewrect);

    // set flag so that document will not be deleted when view is destroyed
    m_bAutoDelete = FALSE;
    // Delete existing view
    pOldActiveView->DestroyWindow();
    // set flag back to default
    m_bAutoDelete = TRUE;

    // Create new view
    CCreateContext context;
    context.m_pNewViewClass = pNewViewClass;
    context.m_pCurrentDoc = this;
    context.m_pNewDocTemplate = NULL;
    context.m_pLastView = NULL;
    context.m_pCurrentFrame = NULL;
    if (!pSplitter->CreateView(row, col, pNewViewClass, viewrect.Size(),
➥&context))
        return FALSE;
```

```
        // Set active
        CView* pNewView = (CView *)pSplitter->GetPane(row, col);
        pSplitter->GetParentFrame()->SetActiveView(pNewView);

        pSplitter->RecalcLayout();
        pNewView->SendMessage(WM_PAINT);
        return TRUE;
    }
```

Now that we have a method in our document class that will replace the current view, let's use it. The new view type should be decided (in response to a menu selection, for instance), and the function must be called as follows:

```
        CRuntimeClass* pNewViewClass = RUNTIME_CLASS(CMyView);
        if (!SwitchToView(pNewViewClass))
            // failed
        else
            // succeeded
```

One final word to the Class Wizard fans. When you have a descendant of a CView descendant, the Class Wizard won't allow you to edit this class. To change this behavior, change all Class Wizard comments, replacing the name of your direct CView descendant with CView. Class Wizard will now work.

Visual Studio

4

Debugging

In this chapter

If your code always works right the first time, you can skip right past this chapter. For everyone else, you will find some useful debugging techniques in this chapter.

- "Some General Debugging Tips" begins by reviewing some of those simple steps that need to be followed when debugging a problem. You may find it useful to refer to them here, as trying to remember them in times of stress can be difficult.

- "Why Doesn't My Project Work in Release Mode?" highlights some of the torments of moving from debug mode into release mode.

- "Extending Visual Studio 6.0 Debugger—The Undocumented Feature" describes some hidden features Visual Studio has, and how to exploit them when debugging.

Some General Debugging Tips

This article was contributed by Tom Moor.

Here are some general tips and tricks that have proven to be useful over the years.

KISS: Keep It Simple, Stupid

Try to reduce the problem by building a sample application. With the new AppWizard, it takes less than a minute to build a running MFC application! So whenever you encounter a problem or start programming in a new area (like OLE automation or owner drawn controls), build a new test application. You can fool around there, and the rebuilds are fast!

Use the "Debug Windows"

There are six Debug Windows in the IDE aside from "Variables" and "Watch." The "Call Stack" and the "Memory" window are the ones I use the most.

If you set your breakpoints well, the "Call Stack" will give you an excellent view of when and where your methods are called and what parameters are used.

You don't have to be an assembler wizard to make use of the "Memory" window. Most times, I use it to view some values that are not shown completely in the "Watch" window.

Try the context menus on the "Debug Windows" (by right mouse clicking). They have some nice features!

Use All Available Resources

There is a ton of useful information available. The resource I use the most is the MSDN (Microsoft Developer Network) CDs. These two CDs are published quarterly by Microsoft and contain a lot of excellent examples and technical information.

You can search the same knowledge base on the Web at http://support.microsoft. com/support. But sometimes it takes quite some time to get a search result, so I prefer the CDs!

To get more information about MSDN, go to http://www.microsoft.com/msdn.

There are a lot of other useful sites on the net. Check them out. Many have a discussion board and free source code!

Chances are good that somebody out there has solved the same problem you're facing. Don't try to reinvent the wheel!

A good place to start is at http://www.codeguru.com/links/links.shtml.

Read, Read, Read

There are many magazines and books regarding MFC/MSVC/Win32. Some of them are excellent, but a lot aren't worth the paper! Check your local bookstore and those on the Web!

To get the latest on debugging, check John Robbins' "Bugslayer" column in the *Microsoft System Journal* at http://www.microsoft.com/msj. He is an expert on debugging, and he also shares tips in his column. You can find some of them adapted in this section.

Why Doesn't My Project Work in Release Mode?

This article was contributed by Keith Rule.

So, you've made a classic developer mistake: You've assumed your working debug mode application will work in release mode, and now you've discovered it doesn't. If you're like me you've probably discovered this after months of development without ever building or testing a release mode version. This leads to our first rule:

> **Rule 1**: Always regularly test *both* the debug and release mode versions of your applications.

Are you absolutely certain your program is working in debug mode? I recently aided in sorting out what appeared to be a debug-vs.-release mode problem that turned out to be something else. So, make sure that the debug version works on the same machines that the release version fails on.

> **Rule 2**: Never classify a problem as a debug-versus-release mode problem unless you've tried both versions on several different machines.

Preprocessor Differences

One of the likely problems is caused by differences during compilation with preprocessor symbols. Try compiling your debug version with the following changes:

- In Project Settings (Alt+F7) under the C++/C tab, set the category to "General" and change the "_DEBUG" preprocessor definition to "NDEBUG."
- Under the C++/C tab, set the category to "Preprocessor" and add the preprocessor definition "_DEBUG" to the "Undefined Symbols" edit field.
- Recompile using "Rebuild All."

If this recreates your problems in your debug version, make the following changes to your code:

- Change all occurrences of ASSERT() to VERIFY().
- Look for any code you've placed inside a "#ifdef _DEBUG" wrapper that might be needed in the release version.
- Look for code in TRACE() that must be executed. TRACEs, like ASSERTs, are compiled out in release mode.

If this fixes your problems in debug mode, try rebuilding the release mode version.

Rule 3: Be very cautious that you don't place code that must be executed in a place where it will be compiled out in release mode.

Variable Initialization Differences

Variables are often initialized differently in debug versions than in the release version of software. If you've assumed that your variables are zeroed when they are declared, that could easily cause strange behavior in release mode on Win9x. You can also introduce bugs that are Win9x-specific. WinNT, for security reasons, zeroes all memory before it is used.

Rule 4: Never assume that your variables are initialized unless you've explicitly initialized them in your code. This includes global variables, automatic variables, malloced data, and newed data.

Are You Ignoring Compiler Warnings?

It's possible that turning up the compiler warning level will expose your problem. I always set compiler warnings to either "Level 3" or "Level 4," depending on how masochistic I'm feeling. Go through and resolve every compiler warning. (This is a very good idea to do before you release your code anyway.) This can expose initialization problems and many other potential errors that may be causing your problem.

Rule 5: When you start a project, turn the warning level to "Level 3" or "Level 4" and make sure your code compiles with no warnings *before* you check your code in.

Have You Removed Any Resources?

If you have references to resources that have been removed from your resource file, your debug version may work, but your release version may crash.

Rule 6: Make sure all references to resources are removed when you delete them from your resource file. This includes references in resource.h.

Debugging in Release Mode

It is possible to debug in release mode. The first step is to turn on symbols:

- In Project Settings (Alt+F2) under the "C++/C tab", set the category to "General" and change the Debug Info setting to "Program Database."
- Under the "Link tab" check the "Generate Debug Info" tab.
- Recompile using "Rebuild All."

This will allow you to see the symbols in the release version. You might want to also consider the following:

- You may want disable your optimization settings when debugging your release version (though this isn't absolutely necessary).
- If you have trouble placing breakpoints, the command "__asm {int 3}" will cause your program to stop at that line. (Be sure to remove these lines from your program when you are done debugging.)

Debugging in release mode has several limitations:

- The most annoying one is that you can't easily see into MFC because you don't have the symbols included for the MFC DLL.
- You must add symbols to the release versions of all libraries and DLLs you wish to debug in your release application.

Comments

There is a possible Microsoft bug when building release mode applications:

Go to the C++ tab of the Project Settings dialog. Then go the Category box and select Optimizations. In debug mode, you should have "Disable(Debug)."

For release mode, make sure you have "Default" selected. Note that the actual default for release mode DLLs is "Maximize Speed."

THIS IS AN MS BUG. A tech rep at Microsoft informed me that "Maximize Speed" Optimizations are *not* fully supported for DLLs in v5.0 and have been known to cause weird memory errors and other crashes.

—Curtiss Murphy

Another potential problem in a multithreaded environment is the following:

There may be an inadvertent optimization problem when creating a multithreaded application.

If you have a variable that has to be accessed from two or more threads, you have to use the *volatile* keyword. Otherwise if one thread changes the variable, a second thread may not notice the change because the variable was optimized and the compiler may use a CPU register.

This is not a problem in debug mode, but you may have a problem in release mode.

—Gevorg Ter-Saakov

Harmful Assert statements:

After following the suggestion in the article of adding source code to the release build and then running that under BoundsChecker, I discovered a huge memory leak that had previously been undetected.

This innocent-looking font code runs beautifully in debug mode:

```
ASSERT(DeleteObject());
```

In release build, a significant resource leak is caused because the code contained in an ASSERT is not even compiled in a release build. If you want an ASSERT on the DeleteObject, a better way to achieve this would be:

```
BOOL bResult = DeleteObject();
ASSERT(bResult==TRUE);
```

The font object will then be properly deleted.

—Matt Chase

Extending Visual Studio 6.0 Debugger— The Undocumented Feature

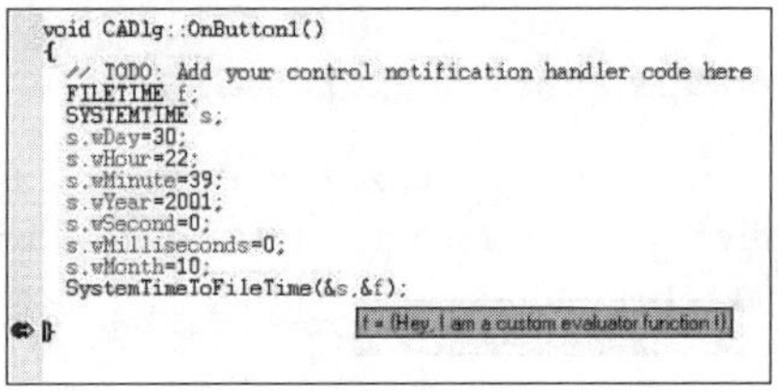

```
void CADlg::OnButton1()
{
    // TODO: Add your control notification handler code here
    FILETIME f;
    SYSTEMTIME s;
    s.wDay=30;
    s.wHour=22;
    s.wMinute=39;
    s.wYear=2001;
    s.wSecond=0;
    s.wMilliseconds=0;
    s.wMonth=10;
    SystemTimeToFileTime(&s,&f);
                                    f = (Hey, I am a custom evaluator function!)
```

Figure 4.1

This article was contributed by Darko Vukoje.

Environment: VC6

Everybody has heard about the autoexp.dat file as a way to show custom data types in Visual Studio 6 Debugger. It is very useful, but sometimes not satisfactory. Say that during a debug session you want to see a variable value of some custom data type, for example, FILETIME. FILETIME is 64-bit value that represents a number of 100-nanosecond units since January, 1st 1601. This value is divided into a struct containing two 32-bit values: Low and high 32-bits of that 64-bit value.

```
typedef struct _FILETIME {
    DWORD dwLowDateTime;
```

```
    DWORD dwHighDateTime;
} FILETIME, *PFILETIME, *LPFILETIME;
```

Using documented autoexp.dat capabilities is simply not possible to show a date time data type (and many other custom data types) in a human-readable form during a debug session. Until I discovered an undocumented autoexp.dat feature, I had used a simple Visual Studio 6.0 add-in that was invoked from my Add-In toolbar button. Of course, such a solution did the job, but it is a little bit annoying to select a variable or set a mouse cursor to it in the source code window and then press the Add-In toolbar button. I thought there was no way to show myself interpreted variable values in a Debugger Tooltip or Watch window.

But, still, there *is* a way to do it. What you need to do is to write a WIN32 DLL that exports a function with the following prototype:

```
HRESULT WINAPI AddIn_SystemTime( DWORD dwAddress,
                                 DEBUGHELPER *pHelper,
                                 int nBase,
                                 BOOL bUniStrings,
                                 char *pResult,
                                 size_t max,
                                 DWORD reserved )
```

I will explain the meaning of the parameters and data types soon. After you write that function that needs to evaluate your custom data type variable value, you just need to add the following line in your autoexp.dat (AutoExpand section) file:

```
MyDataType=$ADDIN(MyLibrary.dll,fCustomDataTypeViewer)
```

Where MyDateType is a data type for which you are writing a custom viewer, MyLibrary.dll is a DLL from which you exported a custom viewer function, and fCustomDataTypeViewer is the name of the exported function. It is best to put a full path to the DLL instead of a DLL name only because Visual Studio sometimes gets confused, and this feature was not working properly when I put just a DLL name without a path.

For the FILETIME example, it should look like this:

```
HRESULT WINAPI FILETIME_Viewer( DWORD dwAddress,
                                DEBUGHELPER *pHelper,
                                int nBase,
                                BOOL bUniStrings,
                                char *pResult,
                                size_t max,
                                DWORD reserved )
{
  FILETIME FileTime;
  SYSTEMTIME SysTime;
  DWORD nGot;
  if (pHelper->dwVersion<0x20000)
  {
```

```
            // This is the way to find out which debugger
            // version is running VC 6.0 version
            if (pHelper->ReadDebuggeeMemory(pHelper,
                dwAddress, sizeof(FileTime), &FileTime,
                &nGot)!=S_OK)
                    return E_FAIL;

            if (nGot!=sizeof(FileTime))
                    return E_FAIL;
        }
        else
        {
            if (pHelper->ReadDebuggeeMemoryEx(pHelper,
                pHelper->GetRealAddress(pHelper),
                sizeof(FileTime), &FileTime,&nGot)!=S_OK)
                    return E_FAIL;
            if (nGot!=sizeof(FileTime))
                    return E_FAIL;
        }
        // convert to SystemTime
        if (!FileTimeToSystemTime( &FileTime, &SysTime ))
            return E_FAIL;

        // and then just call the simple formatting function
        // which will fill the out buffer

        return FormatDateTime( &SysTime, pResult, max );
    }
```

And now, here is the explanation of the types and parameters used:

Each time your mouse cursor is over some variable (or the variable is in a watch or a quick watch window) of FILETIME data type, the debugger will call your DLL's exported function. If it returns S_OK, pResult contents will be shown in a debugger tooltip.

dwAddress is an address of your object in the debugger memory space. Of course, you can't use this address in your custom viewer DLL memory space. You need to read it using a callback function provided with the DEBUGHELPER structure, which is declared in the following way:

```
typedef struct tagDEBUGHELPER
{
  DWORD dwVersion;
  BOOL (WINAPI *ReadDebuggeeMemory)(struct tagDEBUGHELPER *pThis,
                    DWORD dwAddr,
                    DWORD nWant,
                    VOID* pWhere,
                    DWORD *nGot );
  // from here only when dwVersion >= 0x20000
  DWORDLONG (WINAPI *GetRealAddress)( struct tagDEBUGHELPER *pThis );
  BOOL (WINAPI *ReadDebuggeeMemoryEx)( struct tagDEBUGHELPER *pThis,
```

```
                        DWORDLONG qwAddr,
                        DWORD nWant,
                        VOID* pWhere,
                        DWORD *nGot );
    int (WINAPI *GetProcessorType)( struct tagDEBUGHELPER *pThis );
} DEBUGHELPER;

typedef HRESULT (WINAPI *CUSTOMVIEWER)(DWORD dwAddress,
                                       DEBUGHELPER *pHelper,
                                       int nBase,
                                       BOOL bUniStrings,
                                       char *pResult,
                                       size_t max,
                                       DWORD reserved );
```

For the Visual Studio 6.0 debugger version, you are interested only in the ReadDebuggeeMemory callback. This callback reads the object being debugged in memory into the memory structure provided with your custom viewer. It doesn't necessarily need to be the real object as it is in your program. You just need to provide the matching memory layout for the object members that you are interested in.

The next parameter, DWORD nWant, represents the size in bytes that you want to copy. VOID★ pWhere is the memory location where the object or part of the object being debugged will be copied. Finally, DWORD ★nGot is an output value that shows how many bytes were copied successfully.

After you read the memory from the program's debugged memory space, it is up to you to interpret it and return a result to the debugger. The resulting expression should be copied into char ★pResult, watching for the maximum buffer size, which the debugger has sent you through the size_t max parameter. Also, there are additional parameters available:

- int nBase, which is the hex or decimal system base of your current debugger setting
- BOOL bUniStrings, which should be ignored

You should be careful because if your custom evaluator DLL crashes, your Visual Studio session will also crash. Not only can you export a function from this DLL, but you can export as many functions for as many different custom data type viewers as you want to introduce.

As I know, this hidden feature is not documented in Visual Studio 6 companion documentation. It appears for Visual Studio .NET, but I tried it also in Visual Studio 6.0 and it works. You don't even need to have any part of Visual Studio .NET installed on your machine.

Of course, this feature is very suitable to evaluate and show more complex data types, especially classes from your framework. I just gave a single example with a FILETIME object.

5

Add-Ins and Macros

In this chapter

When Microsoft designed the Integrated Development Environment (IDE) for Visual Studio, they designed it in such a way that it could be configured, extended, and enhanced.

Using the macros and add-ins described in this chapter, you will discover not only how the IDE can be enhanced, but also some great examples of how you can very simply add the new features you've always wanted.

- "WM_COMMAND User Message Macro" describes a simple macro that allows you to easily use custom messages within your applications by providing a simple way to add the handler and reference to the message map, saving you a lot of valuable time.

- "Project Line Counter Add-In v1.11" is a sophisticated add-in that does what it suggests—counts the lines in a project, as well as describes several programming techniques.

- "File Dialog Macro" provides a simple way to add the common File dialog to your applications, while relieving you of the task of remembering the various parameters needed to make it work the way you want.

- "Comment/Uncomment and Other Macros" describes a selection of simple macros and shows how easily some macros may be constructed.

WM_COMMAND User Message Macro

These macros were contributed by John Christian Lonningdal.

Here is a nice macro that works well if you are working on an MFC project involving user messages. I always got irritated every time I had to add user messages, and I sometimes forgot what parameters should be used. This macro pops up a dialog box where you just enter your user message (for example, WM_MYMESSAGE). It inserts the message body plus the line in the AFX_MSG_MAP as well as the line in the header file under AFX_MSG.

It creates the name based on the message, so if it finds WM_ in the beginning, this is stripped away and replaced with the word On, which is how all the other MFC messages are defined.

It uses another macro you have on your Web page called ToggleHandCPP. It should probably be refined so that it doesn't spew garbage when it is unable to find the header file.

BTW, you have to be in the cpp file to run the macro; if not, a message box will pop up. (The macro can be extended to do this switch automatically of course.)

I've been using this for awhile and it seems to work just fine. Please report any bugs if you find them.

```
Sub AddMessage()
'DESCRIPTION: Adds user messages to MFC project (WM_COMMAND)

    ext = ActiveDocument.Name
    pos = Instr(ext, ".")
    if pos > 0 then
        Do While pos <> 1
            ext = Mid(ext, pos, Len(ext) - pos + 1)
            pos = Instr(ext, ".")
        Loop
        ext = LCase(ext)
    end if
    If ext = ".cpp" Then
        msg = InputBox ("Write the message ID:")
        If msg <> "" Then
            'func = LCase(msg)
            If Left(msg, 3) = "WM_" Then
                func = "On" + Mid(msg,4,1) + Mid(LCase(msg),5)
            End If

            ActiveDocument.Selection.EndOfDocument
            ActiveDocument.Selection.FindText "AFX_MSG_MAP", dsMatchBackward
            ActiveDocument.Selection.FindText "AFX_MSG_MAP", dsMatchBackward
            ActiveDocument.Selection.CharRight dsMove, 2
            ActiveDocument.Selection.WordRight dsExtend
            ActiveDocument.Selection.Copy
            ActiveDocument.Selection.EndOfLine
            ActiveDocument.Selection.NewLine
            ActiveDocument.Selection = "ON_MESSAGE("+msg+", "+func+")"
            ActiveDocument.Selection.EndOfDocument
            ActiveDocument.Selection.NewLine
            ActiveDocument.Selection = "LONG "
            ActiveDocument.Selection.Paste
            ActiveDocument.Selection = "::"+func+"( UINT uParam, LONG
➥lParam )"
```

```
            ActiveDocument.Selection.NewLine
            ActiveDocument.Selection = "{"
            ActiveDocument.Selection.NewLine
            ActiveDocument.Selection = "return 0;"
            ActiveDocument.Selection.NewLine
            ActiveDocument.Selection.CharLeft
            ActiveDocument.Selection = "}"
            ActiveDocument.Selection.NewLine
            ActiveDocument.Selection.LineUp
            ActiveDocument.Selection.LineUp
            ActiveDocument.Selection.LineUp
            ActiveDocument.Selection.EndOfLine
            ActiveDocument.Selection.NewLine
            ToggleHandCPP
            ActiveDocument.Selection.EndOfDocument
            ActiveDocument.Selection.FindText "AFX_MSG", dsMatchBackward
            ActiveDocument.Selection.LineUp
            ActiveDocument.Selection.EndOfLine
            ActiveDocument.Selection.NewLine
            ActiveDocument.Selection = "afx_msg LONG "+func+"
➥( UINT uParam, LONG lParam );"
            ToggleHandCPP
        End If
    Else
        MsgBox "File is not a .cpp file"
    End If
End Sub
```

Comments

If you prefer capitalizing the first letter of every word without using any underscores
in your function names—for instance, WM_MY_MESSAGE would be
OnMyMessage() instead of OnMy_message()—make the following slight modification
to accommodate this:

```
Sub AddEvent()
'DESCRIPTION: Adds user messages to MFC project (WM_COMMAND)
    ext = ActiveDocument.Name
    pos = Instr(ext, ".")
    if pos > 0 then
        Do While pos <> 1
            ext = Mid(ext, pos, Len(ext) - pos + 1)
            pos = Instr(ext, ".")
        Loop
        ext = LCase(ext)
    end if
    If ext = ".cpp" Then
        msg = InputBox ("Enter the message ID:")
        If msg <> "" Then
            If Left(msg, 3) = "WM_" Then
                func = "On" + Mid(msg,4,1) + Mid(LCase(msg),5)
```

```
                    pos = Instr(func,"_")
                    Do While pos > 0
                        func = Left(func,pos-1) + UCase(Mid(func,pos+1,1))
➥+Mid(func,pos + 2)
                        pos = Instr(func,"_")
                    Loop
                End If
            ActiveDocument.Selection.EndOfDocument
            ActiveDocument.Selection.FindText "AFX_MSG_MAP", dsMatchBackward
            ActiveDocument.Selection.FindText "AFX_MSG_MAP", dsMatchBackward
            ActiveDocument.Selection.CharRight dsMove, 2
            ActiveDocument.Selection.WordRight dsExtend
            ActiveDocument.Selection.Copy
            ActiveDocument.Selection.EndOfLine
            ActiveDocument.Selection.NewLine
            ActiveDocument.Selection = "ON_MESSAGE("+msg+", "+func+")"
            ActiveDocument.Selection.EndOfDocument
            ActiveDocument.Selection.NewLine
            ActiveDocument.Selection = "LONG "
            ActiveDocument.Selection.Paste
            ActiveDocument.Selection = "::"+func+"( UINT uParam, LONG lParam)"
            ActiveDocument.Selection.NewLine
            ActiveDocument.Selection = "{"
            ActiveDocument.Selection.NewLine
            ActiveDocument.Selection = "return 0;"
            ActiveDocument.Selection.NewLine
            ActiveDocument.Selection.CharLeft
            ActiveDocument.Selection = "}"
            ActiveDocument.Selection.NewLine
            ActiveDocument.Selection.LineUp
            ActiveDocument.Selection.LineUp
            ActiveDocument.Selection.LineUp
            ActiveDocument.Selection.EndOfLine
            ActiveDocument.Selection.NewLine
            ToggleHandCPP
            ActiveDocument.Selection.EndOfDocument
            ActiveDocument.Selection.FindText "AFX_MSG", dsMatchBackward
            ActiveDocument.Selection.LineUp
            ActiveDocument.Selection.EndOfLine
            ActiveDocument.Selection.NewLine
            ActiveDocument.Selection = "afx_msg LONG "+func+"
➥( UINT uParam, LONG lParam );"
            ToggleHandCPP
        End If
    Else
        MsgBox "File is not a .cpp file"
    End If
End Sub
```

—Billy Chism

Project Line Counter Add-In v1.11

This article was contributed by Oz Solomonovich.

Figure 5.1

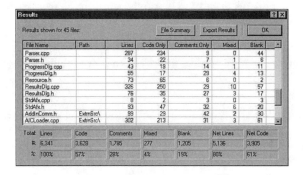

Figure 5.2

Environment: Visual C++ 5 and 6

Description

The Project Line Counter add-in reports statistics about files in your Visual C++ projects. Line Counter was created in order to demonstrate various programming tools and techniques.

Features

- Varied statistical data about your source code, including
    - Number of lines
    - Lines with code
    - Lines with C/C++ style comments
    - Mixed lines (code and comments)

- Reports the distribution of files in your project, by extension
- Can export the statistical data to a text report file
- Automatic scan of your project file
- Single-click activation
- Various parsing options
- Online help
- Full source code

The Source Code

Line Counter is a demo/proof of concept application for demonstrating various technologies:

1. Reusable components from WndTabs (pluggable online help, registry configuration, and so on).
2. The Add-In Communication library.
3. Joshua Jensen's Workspace Whiz! interface is a powerful extension library for DevStudio add-ins.

All of these components are discussed in detail in the add-ins online Help file.

What's New?

Version 1.11 is a maintenance release that adds support for WWhizInterface! v2.10.

The previous version 1.10 was a maintenance release with some new features and a few internal changes:

- Line Counter no longer uses the STL, and dependencies on the various STL runtime libraries (such as MSVCP60.dll) have been removed.
- New feature: A file summary dialog that displays the distribution of files by extension.
- New feature: Ability to export the statistical results as a simple text report.
- The old HTML Help support module (HTMLHelpBase.cpp) has been replaced with a new and much improved support module (HHSupp.cpp). Unlike the old HTMLHelpBase that only handled help for dialogs and property pages, the new support module supports full MFC applications. There have also been improvements in the dialog handling code.

File Dialog Macro

This macro was contributed by Christian Skovdal Andersen.

Too often I have found myself in a situation where I needed to save or open a file through the standard common dialogs. The MFC implementation of the common dialog is quite elegant, but it involves a lot of parameters, which are often hard to remember.

This macro will take you through a few steps in a wizard-like mode and create the right code for you.

FileDialogHandler

```
Sub FileDialogHandler()
'DESCRIPTION: Automatically inserts the statements needed for a
➥file-open/file-save dialog

    dim strExt

    writeln " {// BLOCK - inserted by CFileDialog macro"


    ' Ask for the type of dialog
    dim bSaveDialog
    bSaveDialog = 1
    bAnswer = MsgBox("Do you want to make a save dialog (Yes) or an open
➥ dialog (No)", vbYesNo)

    ActiveDocument.Selection.StartOfLine dsFirstText
    ActiveDocument.Selection = " CFileDialog dlg("
    if bAnswer = vbYes then
    ActiveDocument.Selection = "FALSE"
    else
    ActiveDocument.Selection = "TRUE"
    bSaveDialog = 0
    end if

    ' The extension of the file
    strExt = InputBox("What is the extension of the filetype?",
➥ "Extension", "txt")
    ' The name of the file
    strName = InputBox("What is the name of the filetype?",
➥ "Name", "Text File")

    ' Only apply a default extension if it is a save-as dialog
    if bAnswer = vbYes then
        ActiveDocument.Selection = ","""*." & strExt & """"
    else
        ActiveDocument.Selection = ", """"""
    end if
```

```
        ActiveDocument.Selection = ", "

        ' Only  if it is a save-as dialog should a default filename be provided
        dim strDefaultName
        if bAnswer = vbYes then
        strDefaultName = "Untitled." & strExt
            strDefName = InputBox("What is the default filename?",
➡ "Default Filename", strDefaultName)
            ActiveDocument.Selection = """" & strDefaultName & """, "
        else
            ActiveDocument.Selection = """"", "
        end if

        dim flags
        dim filebuffer
        dim bMultiSelectDlg
        bMultiSelectDlg = 0
        filebuffer = "none"
        if bSaveDialog = 0 then
            ' Spørg om dialog typen
            bAnswer = MsgBox("Do you want a multiple selection dialog?", vbYesNo)

            if bAnswer = vbYes then
                bMultiSelectDlg = 1
                flags = "¦OFN_ALLOWMULTISELECT"
                filebuffer = InputBox("How big should the selection buffer be?",
➡ "Multiple Selection", "10240")
            else
                flags = ""
            end if
        end if

        ActiveDocument.Selection.NewLine

        ActiveDocument.Selection.StartOfLine dsFirstText
        ActiveDocument.Selection = " OFN_HIDEREADONLY¦OFN_OVERWRITEPROMPT"
➡ & flags & ", "
        ActiveDocument.Selection.NewLine

        ActiveDocument.Selection.StartOfLine dsFirstText
        ActiveDocument.Selection = " """ & strName & " (*." & strExt & ")¦*." &
➡ strExt & "¦All Files (*.*)¦*.*¦¦""", this);"
        ActiveDocument.Selection.NewLine
        ActiveDocument.Selection.NewLine

        if filebuffer <> "none" then
            ActiveDocument.Selection.StartOfLine dsFirstText
            ActiveDocument.Selection = " char cbBuffer[" & filebuffer & "];"
            ActiveDocument.Selection.NewLine

            ActiveDocument.Selection.StartOfLine dsFirstText
            ActiveDocument.Selection = " dlg.m_ofn.nMaxFile = " & filebuffer & ";"
            ActiveDocument.Selection.NewLine
```

```
        ActiveDocument.Selection.StartOfLine dsFirstText
        ActiveDocument.Selection = " dlg.m_ofn.lpstrFile = cbBuffer;"
        ActiveDocument.Selection.NewLine

    end if


    ' If you want to use a special caption for your dialog
    dim caption
    if bSaveDialog = 1 then
        szDefCaption = "Save As"
    else
        szDefCaption = "Open"
    end if
    caption = InputBox("What should the caption of the dialog be?
➡(cancel = default)", "Dialog Caption", szDefCaption)
    if caption <> "" then
        ActiveDocument.Selection.StartOfLine dsFirstText
        ActiveDocument.Selection = " dlg.m_ofn.lpstrTitle = " & caption & ";"
        ActiveDocument.Selection.NewLine
    end if


    ' Initial directory to look in
    if bSaveDialog = 1 then
        szDefCaption = "Save As"
    else
        szDefCaption = "Open"
    end if
    caption = InputBox("Initial directory to search for files
➡(cancel = default)? If you're using a string in stead
➡of a variable put the string in quotation marks",
➡"Dialog Caption", "")
    if caption <> "" then
        ActiveDocument.Selection.StartOfLine dsFirstText
        ActiveDocument.Selection = " dlg.m_ofn.lpstrInitialDir =
➡" & caption & ";"
        ActiveDocument.Selection.NewLine
    end if

    ActiveDocument.Selection.NewLine

    ActiveDocument.Selection.StartOfLine dsFirstText
    ActiveDocument.Selection = " if (dlg.DoModal() == IDOK)"
    ActiveDocument.Selection.NewLine

    ActiveDocument.Selection.StartOfLine dsFirstText
    ActiveDocument.Selection = " {"
    ActiveDocument.Selection.NewLine

    ActiveDocument.Selection.StartOfLine dsFirstText
    ActiveDocument.Selection = " // Insert your code here..."

    ActiveDocument.Selection.NewLine
```

```
    if bMultiSelectDlg = 1 then
        ActiveDocument.Selection.StartOfLine dsFirstText
        ActiveDocument.Selection = " // Insert your code here..."

        ActiveDocument.Selection.NewLine

        ActiveDocument.Selection.StartOfLine dsFirstText
        ActiveDocument.Selection = " POSITION pos;"
        ActiveDocument.Selection.NewLine
        ActiveDocument.Selection.StartOfLine dsFirstText
        ActiveDocument.Selection = " for (pos = dlg.GetStartPosition() ;
➡pos != NULL ; )"
        ActiveDocument.Selection.NewLine
        ActiveDocument.Selection.StartOfLine dsFirstText
        ActiveDocument.Selection = " {"
        ActiveDocument.Selection.NewLine
        ActiveDocument.Selection.StartOfLine dsFirstText
        ActiveDocument.Selection = " // Use dlg.GetNextPathName(pos);
➡to extract filename (including path)"

        ActiveDocument.Selection.NewLine
        ActiveDocument.Selection.StartOfLine dsFirstText
        ActiveDocument.Selection = " {"
        ActiveDocument.Selection.NewLine
    else
        ActiveDocument.Selection.StartOfLine dsFirstText
        ActiveDocument.Selection = " // Use dlg.GetPathName() to extract
➡filename (including path);"

        ActiveDocument.Selection.NewLine
    end if

    ActiveDocument.Selection.StartOfLine dsFirstText
    ActiveDocument.Selection = " }"
    ActiveDocument.Selection.NewLine

    ActiveDocument.Selection.StartOfLine dsFirstText
    ActiveDocument.Selection = " } // End block"

    ActiveDocument.Selection.NewLine

    ActiveDocument.Selection.StartOfLine dsFirstText

    'End Recording
End Sub
```

A Note About WriteLn

Because of compatibility reasons (I don't want people to have to copy one macro to use another), I have not used the function below to write text. However, it is pretty handy and will make your code look a lot better. It does the same as WriteLn from Pascal.

This function is not meant to be called by the user, but only from other scripts.

```
sub writeln(line)
    ActiveDocument.Selection.StartOfLine dsFirstText
    ActiveDocument.Selection = line
    ActiveDocument.Selection.NewLine
end sub
```

Comment/Uncomment and Other Macros

These macros were contributed by Adam Solesby.

Here are some macros that I find very useful and that may be useful for others as well. The most useful macro for me is the comment/uncomment macro. Assign this macro to a key (Ctrl+/), and then use it to toggle comments on a single line of code or a block of code. For single lines, the indention level remains; for blocks of code, the comment is placed at the beginning of the line. I think this comment macro is a little more powerful than the existing one on the site. Hope some people find them useful.

```
'............................................................................
'FILE DESCRIPTION: These are useful macros by Adam Solesby <ADAM@SOLESBY.COM
'............................................................................

' This routine has many uses if you are trying to determine the type of
' source file.
' This has been modified from the one included with DevStudio
' Return value:  0 Unknown file type
'                1 C-related file, this includes .c, .cpp, .cxx, .h, .hpp, .hxx
'                2 Java-related file, this includes .jav, .java
'                3 ODL-style file, .odl, .idl
'                4 VBS-style file, .dsm
'                5 VBS-style file, .asp
'                6 HTML-style file, this includes .html, and .htm
'                7 Resource file, .rc, .rc2
'                8 Def-style file, .def
' USE: Pass this function the document that you wish to get information for.
Function FileType (ByVal doc)
    ext = doc.Name
    FileType = 0
    pos = Instr(ext, ".")
    if pos > 0 then
```

```
            Do While pos <> 1
                ext = Mid(ext, pos, Len(ext) - pos + 1)
                pos = Instr(ext, ".")
            Loop
            ext = LCase(ext)
        End If

        If ext = ".rc" Or ext = ".rc2" Then
            FileType = 7
        ElseIf doc.Language = dsCPP Then
            FileType = 1
        ElseIf doc.Language = dsJava Then
            FileType = 2
        ElseIf doc.Language = dsIDL Then
            FileType = 3
        ElseIf doc.Language = dsVBSMacro Then
            FileType = 4
        ElseIf ext = ".asp" Then
            FileType = 5
        ElseIf doc.Language = dsHTML_IE3 Or doc.Language = dsHTML_RFC1866 Then
            FileType = 6
        ElseIf ext = ".def" Then
            FileType = 7
        Else
            FileType = 0
        End If

        'MsgBox "Ext:" + vbTab + ext + vbLf + "Lang:" + vbTab + doc.Language + 
➡ vbLf + "Type:" + vbTab + CStr(FileType)
End Function

' Counts the lines in the document passed
Function FLOC (ByVal doc)
        doc.Selection.SetBookmark     ' Mark place

        doc.Selection.SelectAll
        StartLine = doc.Selection.TopLine
        EndLine = doc.Selection.BottomLine
        If EndLine < StartLine Then
            Temp = StartLine
            StartLine = EndLine
            EndLine = Temp
        End If

        doc.Selection.PreviousBookmark     ' Return to current line
        doc.ClearBookmarks
        FLOC = EndLine
End Function
```

```
Sub LOC ()
'DESCRIPTION: Counts total lines in all open documents
    'msg = "Total Line Count" + vbLf + vbLf
    tloc = 0
    For i = 1 to Documents.Count
    TypeOfFile = FileType(Documents.Item(i))
        If TypeOfFile = 1 Then     ' C or C++ source file
            dloc = FLOC(Documents.Item(i))
            tloc =  tloc + dloc
            msg = msg & Documents.Item(i).Name & ":" & vbTab  & dloc & vbLf
        End If
    Next
    msg = msg & "-------------------------------------------" &
➥  vbLf & "Total:" & vbTab & vbTab & tloc
    MsgBox msg , ,"Total Line Count"
End Sub


' This will comment/uncomment out single lines or blocks. Single lines are
' commented with the same indention level. Blocks are commented at the
' beginning of the line. Assign this to a key (e.g. ctrl-/) and it will toggle
' the current line/block of code. This will handle both "//" and "'" style
' comments

Sub CustomCommentOut ()
'DESCRIPTION: Comments out a selected block of text.
    Dim win
    set win = ActiveWindow
    If win.type <> "Text" Then
      MsgBox "This macro can only be run when a text editor window is active."
    Else
        TypeOfFile = FileType(ActiveDocument)
        '    MsgBox "Type: " + CStr(TypeOfFile)
        If TypeOfFile > 0 And TypeOfFile < 6 Then
            If TypeOfFile > 3 Then
                CommentType = "'"     ' VBShit
                CommentWidth = 1
            Else
                CommentType = "//"     ' C++ and java style comments

                CommentWidth = 2
            End If

            StartLine = ActiveDocument.Selection.TopLine
            EndLine = ActiveDocument.Selection.BottomLine
            If EndLine < StartLine Then
                Temp = StartLine
                StartLine = EndLine
                EndLine = Temp
            End If
```

```
                       ' Single line -- comment at start of text
                       '    have to check for comments at start of line and start of text
                       If EndLine = StartLine Then

                           ActiveDocument.Selection.StartOfLine dsFirstColumn
                           ActiveDocument.Selection.CharRight dsExtend, CommentWidth

                           If ActiveDocument.Selection = CommentType Then
                               ActiveDocument.Selection.Delete
                           Else
                               ActiveDocument.Selection.StartOfLine dsFirstText
                               ActiveDocument.Selection.CharRight dsExtend, CommentWidth

                               If ActiveDocument.Selection = CommentType Then
                                   ActiveDocument.Selection.CharRight dsExtend
                                   ActiveDocument.Selection.Delete
                               Else
                                   ActiveDocument.Selection.StartOfLine dsFirstText
                                   ActiveDocument.Selection = CommentType + vbTab +
➡ ActiveDocument.Selection
                               End If
                           End If

                       ' Multi-line -- comment at start of line
                       Else
                           For i = StartLine To EndLine
                               ActiveDocument.Selection.GoToLine i

                               CommentLoc = dsFirstColumn

                               ActiveDocument.Selection.StartOfLine CommentLoc
                               ActiveDocument.Selection.CharRight dsExtend, CommentWidth

                               If ActiveDocument.Selection = CommentType Then
                                   ActiveDocument.Selection.Delete
                               Else
                                   ActiveDocument.Selection.StartOfLine CommentLoc
                                   ActiveDocument.Selection = CommentType +
➡ActiveDocument.Selection
                               End If

                           Next
                       End If
                   Else
                       MsgBox("Unable to comment out the highlighted text" + vbLf + _
                           "because the file type was unrecognized." + vbLf + _
                           "If the file has not yet been saved, " + vbLf + _
                           "please save it and try again.")
                   End If
               End If
           End Sub
```

```
Sub Duplicate()
'DESCRIPTION: Duplicates the current selected line

    ActiveDocument.Selection.Copy
    ActiveDocument.Selection.CharRight
    ActiveDocument.Selection.Paste
End Sub

Sub RemoveLineFeed()
'DESCRIPTION: Go to end of line and delete line feed

    ActiveDocument.Selection.EndOfLine
    ActiveDocument.Selection.Delete
    ActiveDocument.Selection.LineDown
End Sub

Sub EndOfLinePaste()
'DESCRIPTION: This macro pastes the contents of the clipboard at the end of
'the line and then goes to the next line.

    ActiveDocument.Selection.EndOfLine
    ActiveDocument.Selection.Paste
    ActiveDocument.Selection.LineDown
    ActiveDocument.Selection.EndOfLine
End Sub

Sub StartOfLinePaste()
'DESCRIPTION: This macro pastes the contents of the clipboard at the start of
'the line and then goes to the next line.

    ActiveDocument.Selection.StartOfLine dsFirstText
    ActiveDocument.Selection.Paste
    ActiveDocument.Selection.LineDown
    ActiveDocument.Selection.StartOfLine dsFirstText
End Sub
```

Comments

If you prefer to #if out a bunch of code rather than comment out each line, the following macro will do that for a single line or a selected block of text:

```
Sub IfZeroOut()
    PoundType = "#if 0"

    If FileType(ActiveDocument) <> 1 Then
        MsgBox ("This macro only works on" + vbLf + _
                ".c, .cpp, .cxx, .h, .hpp, or .hxx files")
    Else
        Sel = ActiveDocument.Selection
        For i = 1 To Len(Sel) - 1
```

```
            If Mid(Sel, i, 1) = vbLf Then
                Sel = Left(Sel,i) + vbTab +
                    Right(Sel, Len(Sel)-i)
            End If
        Next
        Sel = vbLf + PoundType + vbLf + vbTab + Sel + _
            vbLf+ "#endif //" + "if zero'd out"
        If Right(Sel,1) <> vbLf Then
            Sel = Sel + vbLf
        End If
        ActiveDocument.Selection = Sel
    End If
End Sub
```

—Bruce

Windows Programming

6

Windows CE

In this chapter

With the advent of more and more portable computing devices, Windows has entered the world of embedded programming with the Windows CE operating system. In this chapter, you will find some articles specifically devoted to this emerging technology.

- "CceButtonST v1.2" allows you to add professional-looking buttons with multicolor icons to your Windows CE applications.

- "CceFileFind—File Finder Class for Windows CE" provides an easy-to-use mechanism for searching the local CE system for files.

- "Memory Leak Detection for WinCE" describes a very useful way of detecting memory leaks in Windows CE applications.

CCeButtonST v1.2

This article was contributed by Davide Calabro.

This is the reference control for MFC flat buttons with text and icons. Give your CE applications a professional look!

Figure 6.1

Figure 6.2

Figure 6.3

Environment: eMbedded VC++ 3.0, Windows CE 3.0

Abstract

CCeButtonST is a class derived from the MFC CButton class. With this class, your CE applications can have standard buttons or new and modern buttons with "flat" style!

The main CCeButtonST features are

- Standard CButton properties.
- Text and icon on the same button.
- Only text or only icon buttons.
- Support for any size icons (max. 256 colors).
- Standard or flat button style.
- Change runtime from flat to standard style.
- Buttons can have two images, one when the mouse is over the button and one when the mouse is outside (only for flat buttons).

- Every color can be customized.
- Can be used via DDX_ calls.
- Can be used in DLLs.
- Can be dynamically created.
- Each button can have its own mouse pointer.
- Button is also highlighted when the window is inactive, as in Internet Explorer.
- Built-in basic support for menus.
- Can be derived to create other button styles not supplied by default.
- Full source code included!
- UNICODE compatible.
- Windows CE v3.0 compatible.
- Cost-less implementation in existing applications.

How to Integrate CCeButtonST in Your Application

In your project, include the following files:

- CeBtnST.h
- CeBtnST.cpp

Create a CCeButtonST Object Statically

With Dialog Editor, create a standard button called, for example, IDOK (you don't need to make it owner drawn), and create a member variable for this button:

```
CCeButtonST m_btnOk;
```

Now attach the button to CCeButtonST. For dialog-based applications, attach it in your OnInitDialog:

```
// Call the base-class method
CDialog::OnInitDialog();

// Create the IDOK button
m_btnOk.SubclassDlgItem(IDOK, this);
```

Or attach it in your DoDataExchange:

```
// Call the base method
CDialog::DoDataExchange(pDX);

// Create the IDOK button
DDX_Control(pDX, IDOK, m_btnOk);
```

Create a CCeButtonST Object Dynamically

In your application, create a member variable for the button. Please note that this variable is a *pointer*.

```
CCeButtonST* m_pbtnOk;
```

Now create the button. For dialog-based applications, attach it in your OnInitDialog:

```
// Call the base-class method
CDialog::OnInitDialog();

// Create the IDOK button
m_pbtnOk = new CCeButtonST;
m_pbtnOk->Create(_T("&Ok"),
                  WS_CHILD | WS_VISIBLE | WS_GROUP | WS_TABSTOP,
                  CRect(10, 10, 200, 100),
                  this,
                  IDOK);
// Set the same font of the application
m_pbtnOk->SetFont(GetFont());
```

Remember to destroy the button, or you will get a memory leak. This can be done, for example, in your class destructor:

```
if (m_pbtnOk) delete m_pbtnOk;
```

Class Methods

SetIcon (Using Resources)

SetIcon assigns icons to the button. Any previous icon will be removed.

```
// Parameters:
//      [IN]    nIconIn
//              ID number of the icon resource to show
//              when the mouse is over the button.
//              Pass NULL to remove any icon from the button.
//      [IN]    sizeIn
//              Size of the icon.
//      [IN]    nIconOut
//              ID number of the icon resource to show when
//              the mouse is outside the button.
//              Can be NULL.
//      [IN]    sizeOut
//              Size of the icon.
//      [IN]    nIconDis
//              ID number of the icon resource to show when
//              the button is disabled.
//              Can be NULL.
```

```
//      [IN]    sizeDis
//              Size of the icon.
//
// Return value:
//      BTNST_OK
//          Function executed successfully.
//
DWORD SetIcon( int nIconIn,
               CSize sizeIn = CSize(32,32),
               int nIconOut = NULL,
               CSize sizeOut = CSize(32,32),
               int nIconDis = NULL,
               CSize sizeDis = CSize(32,32))
```

SetIcon (Using Handles)

SetIcon assigns icons to the button. Any previous icon will be removed.

```
// Parameters:
//      [IN]    hIconIn
//              Handle fo the icon to show when the mouse is
//              over the button.
//              Pass NULL to remove any icon from the button.
//      [IN]    sizeIn
//              Size of the icon.
//      [IN]    hIconOut
//              Handle to the icon to show when the mouse is
//              outside the button.
//              Can be NULL.
//      [IN]    sizeOut
//              Size of the icon.
//      [IN]    hIconDis
//              ID number of the icon resource to show when
//              the button is disabled.
//              Can be NULL.
//      [IN]    sizeDis
//              Size of the icon.
//
// Return value:
//      BTNST_OK
//          Function executed successfully.
//
DWORD SetIcon( HICON hIconIn,
               CSize sizeIn = CSize(32,32),
               HICON hIconOut = NULL,
               CSize sizeOut = CSize(32,32),
               HICON hIconDis = NULL,
               CSize sizeDis = CSize(32,32))
```

SetFlat

Sets the button to have a standard or flat style.

```
// Parameters:
//     [IN]  bFlat
//               If TRUE the button will have a flat style, else
//               will have a standard style.
//     [IN]  bRepaint
//               If TRUE the control will be repainted.
//
// Return value:
//     BTNST_OK
//         Function executed successfully.
//
DWORD SetFlat(BOOL bFlat = TRUE, BOOL bRepaint = TRUE)
```

SetAlign

Sets the alignment type between icon and text.

```
// Parameters:
//   [IN]  byAlign
//             Alignment type.     Can be one of following values:
//             ST_ALIGN_HORIZ      Icon on left, text on right
//             ST_ALIGN_VERT       Icon on top, text on bottom
//             ST_ALIGN_HORIZ_RIGHT Icon on right, text on left
//                                 By default, CCeButtonST buttons
//                                 have ST_ALIGN_HORIZ alignment.
//   [IN]  bRepaint
//             If TRUE the control will be repainted.
//
// Return value:
//     BTNST_OK
//         Function executed successfully.
//     BTNST_INVALIDALIGN
//         Alignment type not supported.
//
DWORD SetAlign(BYTE byAlign, BOOL bRepaint = TRUE)
```

SetCheck

Sets the state of the check box.

If the button is not a check box, this function has no meaning.

```
// Parameters:
//     [IN]  nCheck
//               1 to check the checkbox.
//               0 to un-check the checkbox.
//     [IN]  bRepaint
//               If TRUE the control will be repainted.
//
```

```
// Return value:
//     BTNST_OK
//         Function executed successfully.
//
DWORD SetCheck(int nCheck, BOOL bRepaint = TRUE)
```

GetCheck

Returns the current state of the check box.

If the button is not a check box, this function has no meaning.

```
// Return value:
//     The current state of the checkbox.
//         1 if checked.
//         0 if not checked or the button is not a checkbox.
//
int GetCheck()
```

SetDefaultColors

Sets all colors to a default value.

```
// Parameters:
//     [IN]    bRepaint
//             If TRUE the control will be repainted.
//
// Return value:
//     BTNST_OK
//         Function executed successfully.
//
DWORD SetDefaultColors(BOOL bRepaint = TRUE)
```

SetColor

Sets the color to use for a particular state.

```
// Parameters:
// [IN]   byColorIndex
//        Index of the color to set. Can be one of the
//        following values:
//        BTNST_COLOR_BK_IN     Background color when mouse
//                              is over the button
//        BTNST_COLOR_FG_IN     Text color when mouse is
//                              over the button
//        BTNST_COLOR_BK_OUT    Background color when mouse
//                              is outside the button
//        BTNST_COLOR_FG_OUT    Text color when mouse is
//                              outside the button
//        BTNST_COLOR_BK_FOCUS  Background color when the
//                              button is focused
//        BTNST_COLOR_FG_FOCUS  Text color when the
//                              button is focused
```

```
// [IN]  crColor          New color.
//
// [IN]  bRepaint         If TRUE the control will
//                        be repainted.
// Return value:
//     BTNST_OK
//         Function executed successfully.
//     BTNST_INVALIDINDEX
//         Invalid color index.
//
DWORD SetColor(BYTE byColorIndex, COLORREF crColor, BOOL bRepaint = TRUE)
```

GetColor

Returns the color used for a particular state.

```
// Parameters:
// [IN]  byColorIndex
//         Index of the color to get. Can be one of
//         the following values:
//         BTNST_COLOR_BK_IN     Background color when
//                               mouse is over the button
//         BTNST_COLOR_FG_IN     Text color when mouse is
//                               over the button
//         BTNST_COLOR_BK_OUT    Background color when mouse
//                               is outside the button
//         BTNST_COLOR_FG_OUT    Text color when mouse is
//                               outside the button
//         BTNST_COLOR_BK_FOCUS  Background color when
//                               the button is focused
//         BTNST_COLOR_FG_FOCUS  Text color when the
//                               button is focused
// [OUT]  crpColor
//         A pointer to a COLORREF
//         that will receive the color.
//
// Return value:
//     BTNST_OK
//         Function executed successfully.
//     BTNST_INVALIDINDEX
//         Invalid color index.
//
DWORD GetColor(BYTE byColorIndex, COLORREF* crpColor)
```

SetAlwaysTrack

Sets the highlight logic for the button. Applies only to flat buttons.

```
// Parameters:
// [IN]  bAlwaysTrack
//         If TRUE the button will be hilighted even
//         if the window that owns it, is not the
//         active window.
```

```
//              If FALSE the button will be hilighted only if
//              the window that owns it, is the active window.
//
// Return value:
//    BTNST_OK
//       Function executed successfully.
//
DWORD SetAlwaysTrack(BOOL bAlwaysTrack = TRUE)
```

SetBtnCursor

Sets the cursor to be used when the mouse is over the button.

```
// Parameters:
//    [IN]    nCursorId
//            ID number of the cursor resource.
//            Pass NULL to rem/?ë a previously loaded cursor.
//    [IN]    bRepaint
//            If TRUE the control will be repainted.
//
// Return value:
//    BTNST_OK
//       Function executed successfully.
//    BTNST_INVALIDRESOURCE
//       Failed loading the specified resource.
//
DWORD SetBtnCursor(int nCursorId = NULL, BOOL bRepaint = TRUE)
```

DrawBorder

Sets a border if the button border must be drawn. Applies only to flat buttons.

```
// Parameters:
//    [IN]    bDrawBorder
//            If TRUE the border will be drawn.
//    [IN]    bRepaint
//            If TRUE the control will be repainted.
//
// Return value:
//    BTNST_OK
//       Function executed successfully.
//
DWORD DrawBorder( BOOL bDrawBorder = TRUE,
                  BOOL bRepaint = TRUE)
```

DrawFlatFocus

Sets whether the focus rectangle must be drawn for flat buttons.

```
// Parameters:
//    [IN]    bDrawFlatFocus
//            If TRUE the focus rectangle will be
//            drawn also for flat buttons.
```

```
//     [IN]    bRepaint
//             If TRUE the control will be repainted.
//
// Return value:
//     BTNST_OK
//         Function executed successfully.
//
DWORD DrawFlatFocus( BOOL bDrawFlatFocus,
                     BOOL bRepaint = TRUE)
```

GetDefault

Returns whether the button is the default button.

```
// Return value:
//     TRUE
//         The button is the default button.
//     FALSE
//         The button is not the default button.
//
BOOL GetDefault()
```

SetURL

Sets the URL that will be opened when the button is clicked.

```
// Parameters:
//     [IN]    lpszURL
//             Pointer to a null-terminated string that
//             contains the URL.
//             Pass NULL to removed any previously specified URL.
//
// Return value:
//     BTNST_OK
//         Function executed successfully.
//
DWORD SetURL(LPCTSTR lpszURL = NULL)
```

SetMenu

Associates a menu to the button. The menu will be displayed by clicking the button.

```
// Parameters:
//     [IN]    nMenu
//             ID number of the menu resource.
//             Pass NULL to remove any menu from the button.
//     [IN]    hParentWnd
//             Handle to the window that owns the menu.
//             This window receives all messages from the menu.
//     [IN]    bRepaint
//             If TRUE the control will be repainted.
//
```

```
// Return value:
//     BTNST_OK
//         Function executed successfully.
//     BTNST_INVALIDRESOURCE
//         Failed loading the specified resource.
//
DWORD SetMenu( UINT nMenu,
               HWND hParentWnd,
               BOOL bRepaint = TRUE)
```

OnDrawBackground

This function is called every time the button background needs to be painted. This is a virtual function that can be rewritten in CCeButtonST-derived classes to produce a whole range of buttons not available by default.

```
// Parameters:
//     [IN]   pDC
//            Pointer to a CDC object that indicates
//            the device context.
//     [IN]   pRect
//            Pointer to a CRect object that indicates the
//            bounds of the area to be painted.
//
// Return value:
//     BTNST_OK
//         Function executed successfully.
//
virtual DWORD OnDrawBackground(CDC* pDC, LPCRECT pRect)
```

OnDrawBorder

This function is called every time the button border needs to be painted. This is a virtual function that can be rewritten in CCeButtonST-derived classes to produce a whole range of buttons not available by default.

```
// Parameters:
//     [IN]   pDC
//            Pointer to a CDC object that indicates
//            the device context.
//     [IN]   pRect
//            Pointer to a CRect object that indicates
//            the bounds of the area to be painted.
//
// Return value:
//     BTNST_OK
//         Function executed successfully.
//
virtual DWORD OnDrawBorder(CDC* pDC, LPCRECT pRect)
```

GetVersionI

Returns the class version as a short value.

```
// Return value:
//     Class version. Divide by 10 to get actual version.
//
static short GetVersionI()
```

GetVersionC

Returns the class version as a string value.

```
// Return value:
//     Pointer to a null-terminated string
//     containig the class version.
//
static LPCTSTR GetVersionC()
```

Remarks

The demo application shows nearly all the features of the CCeButtonST class. It includes project settings for all the emulators included in Visual C++ eMbedded Tools v3.0 plus settings to compile and run on the Advantech PCM-4823 single board computer. CCeButtonST architecture makes it possible to produce a whole range of buttons not available by default. If someone implements new button styles, I will be happy to include that code in the next CCeButtonST demo application.

Comments

Unfortunately the DDX_Check does not work with CCeButtonST because it is not a real check box. The problem lies in the DDX asking for the check box's internal check/uncheck state, which is not used in CCeButtonST. The DDX uses two messages to get (BM_GETCHECK) and set (BM_SETCHECK) the check box state.

To add this functionality, modify the code as shown here:

.h additions:

```
:private
    LRESULT MsgGetCheck(WPARAM wParam, LPARAM lParam);
    LRESULT MsgSetCheck(WPARAM wParam, LPARAM lParam);
```

.cpp additions:

In the BEGIN_MESSAGEMAP section add

```
ON_MESSAGE(BM_GETCHECK, MsgGetCheck)
ON_MESSAGE(BM_SETCHECK, MsgSetCheck)
```

And add the following functions:

```
LRESULT CCeButtonST::MsgGetCheck(WPARAM wParam, LPARAM lParam)
{
    ASSERT(m_bIsCheckBox);  // only for checkboxes
    return (GetCheck() );
}

LRESULT CCeButtonST::MsgSetCheck(WPARAM wParam, LPARAM lParam)
{
    ASSERT(m_bIsCheckBox); // only for checkboxes
    SetCheck(wParam);
    return 0;
}
```

—Attila Dobozi

FROM THE FORUM

Question (brucemack):

How can I create an animated hour glass that runs in the background on Windows CE?

Answer (Indian_Techie):

Use the CWaitCursor class, which is not an hour glass but Windows CE's default wait cursor. When the CWaitCursor object is instantiated, the animation starts; then when the object is destroyed or goes out of scope, it stops.

```
CWaitCursor* waitCur = NULL;

void OnStart()
{
    waitCur = new CWaitCursor; //Animation starts..
}

void OnStop()
{
    delete waitCur; //Animation gets stoped..
}
```

CCeFileFind—File Finder Class for Windows CE

This article was contributed by Waseem Anis.

Figure 6.4

Environment: VC6 SP2, NT4 SP3, CE 2.0/2.01/2.11

Class CCeFileFind performs local file searches on a Windows CE system. CCeFileFind includes member functions that begin a search, locate a file, and return the name, path, or size of the file. The following code will enumerate all the files in the current directory, printing the name of each file:

```
CCeFileFind finder;

BOOL bWorking = finder.FindFile("*.*");

while (bWorking)
{
 bWorking = finder.FindNextFile();
 AfxMessageBox( finder.GetFileName() );
}
```

After calling FindFile to begin the file search, call FindNextFile to retrieve subsequent files. You must call FindNextFile at least once before calling any of the attribute member functions.

FROM THE FORUM

Question (Chris Richardson):

How can I get information about the owner of a PocketPC device running Windows CE, such as the one shown on the Today screen.

Answer (Chris Richardson):

I found the answer myself. The information can be found as follows:

```
// Get the name of the Device Owner from the registry.
CString a_sOwnerName;
CRegKey a_oControlPanel;
```

```
if( a_oControlPanel.Open( HKEY_CURRENT_USER, _T("ControlPanel") ) == ERROR_
➥SUCCESS )
{
    CRegKey a_oOwner;
    if( a_oOwner.Open( a_oControlPanel, _T("Owner") ) == ERROR_SUCCESS )
    {
        TCHAR a_aucData[1024] = {0};
        DWORD a_dwType = 0;
        DWORD a_dwDataLen = 1024;

        if( RegQueryValueEx( a_oOwner, _T("Owner"), NULL, &a_dwType,
➥(unsigned char*)a_aucData, &a_dwDataLen ) == ERROR_
➥SUCCESS )
        {
            // We've got it!
            // The owner's name is the first field, and
            // from what I've seen is null terminated.
            a_sOwnerName = a_aucData;
        }
    }
}
```

Memory Leak Detection for WinCE

This article was contributed by Ciprian Miclaus.

Environment: WinCE

Introduction

This code detects memory leaks in embedded VC++ almost the same way crtdbg does in VC++. At the end of program execution, it will display in the debug window if there were any memory leaks. It will also display how the memory looks so you can identify where your memory leak occurred. It will display in the debug window a message saying "no memory leaks detected" if there were no memory leaks. In addition, it displays the amount of free store memory that your program uses.

The code detects memory leaks generated with calls to new and delete operators in C++. The code doesn't detect memory leaks generated with C functions malloc, calloc, or free, but that can be done in the future. Let me know and I will program it.

There are three simple steps that will enable memory leak detection:

1. Define _DEBUG

```
#define _DEBUG
```

2. Include "crtdbg.h"

```
#include "crtdbg.h"
```

3. Let your first line in the code be

```
_CrtSetDbgFlag (ON);
```

Tips on Debugging

Tip 1:

Although it doesn't display the line where the memory leak occurred (read Tip 2), the utility displays the address in hex, and you can add a small code to the operator new function, just after the malloc:

```
if (retPtr == (void*)0x76DA0)
    dumb instruction; <- place a breakpoint on
                          this one, or just use DebugMsg
```

so you can easily detect which line of your code called the operator new to allocate memory at the specified address and wasn't freed.

Tip 2:

Here's a trick that allows you to get the correct line and file name where the memory leak occurred. Define the following line in every file, or define it in a header file and include it in every file where you want an accurate line and file name:

```
#define new new(_T(__FILE__), __LINE__)
```

How It Works

What the code actually does is override the global operator new that, besides allocating memory, retains the pointer to the allocated memory in a list. The operator delete simply releases memory and deletes the reference to that memory from the list. In the end of the program execution, all the pointers still in the list simply mean memory leaks, and they are displayed in the debug window.

The macro _CrtSetDbgFlag (ON); simply declares an instance of garbageCollector. It has to be the first line of your code to ensure that it is the last variable in your program to be destroyed, as in its destructor it performs checking of the pointer list and displays memory leaks. So its destructor must be the last destructor called. Remember this when you have static variables; you must give a global scope to the instance of garbageCollector. You can do that by placing the macro at the global scope. However, the C++ standard does not provide an order of initialization for static variables, which means you cannot ensure that garbageCollector will be initialized first. Therefore, in case of static or global variables, it will report memory leaks for variables initialized after garbageCollector has been initialized.

Comments

When using the suggestions with MFC, you may experience problems. The CObject class has already defined operator new, which hides the other operator new member described in the text. To resolve this problem, try the following:

Replace

```
#define new new(_T(__FILE__),__LINE__)
```

with

```
#define new ::new(_T(__FILE__),__LINE__)
```

Note the global scope specifier.

—sung-joo byun

FROM THE FORUM

Question (waxkeonz):

Which API function can I use to obtain the time or elapsed time in Windows CE?

Answer (jwycoff):

If you are trying to evaluate how long your thread has been running, use the GetThreadTimes() call.

If you are simply interested in a high-precision timer, use QueryPerformanceCounter().

7

Clipboard

In this chapter

Armed with no more than a pocket protector and clipboard, what more could the modern programmer need? To find out more about using the clipboard, keep reading. To find out more about the pocket protector, visit www.pocketprotectors.com.

- "Basic Copy/Paste and Drag/Drop Support" introduces

techniques for serializing object data into and out of the clipboard.

- "Advanced Copy/Paste and Drag/Drop Support" describes methods of interacting with the Microsoft Office family of products using the clipboard.

Basic Copy/Paste and Drag/Drop Support

This article was contributed by Keith Rule.

Overview

The clipboard is used to transfer data between windows or applications. It is used either during a Drag/Drop operation or during a Cut/Copy/Paste operation. Whether you are using Drag/Drop or Cut/Copy/Paste, the code used to place data on the clipboard is very similar. This article will show you the basics for accessing the clipboard.

Placing Data on the Clipboard

Writing to the clipboard is straightforward. By following a few simple steps, you can place nearly any supported clipboard format onto the clipboard:

1. Create a new COleDataSource.
2. Create a new CSharedFile (see the initialization in the example below).
3. Write info to the CSharedFile instance.

4. Detach the memory associated with the CSharedFile.

5. Pass the detached memory and format info to CacheGlobalData().

6. Place the data on the clipboard using SetClipboard().

Example 1—Source for Writing to the Clipboard

```
void CClipExamView::OnEditCopy()
{
    COleDataSource*    pSource = new COleDataSource();
    CSharedFile        sf(GMEM_MOVEABLE¦GMEM_DDESHARE¦GMEM_ZEROINIT);
    CString            text = _T("Testing 1... 2... 3...");

    sf.Write(text, text.GetLength()); // You can write to the clipboard as
➡you would to any CFile

    HGLOBAL hMem = sf.Detach();
    if (!hMem) return;
    pSource-CacheGlobalData(CF_TEXT, hMem);
    pSource-SetClipboard();
}
```

Serializing to the Clipboard

Often it is useful to be able to serialize your data to the clipboard so that you can create a custom clipboard for your application. This can be done by registering a custom clipboard format and serializing to a CSharedFile. The following source code illustrates how to serialize a CObject to the clipboard.

Example 2—Serializing to the Clipboard

```
void SerializeToClipboard(CObject* obj, CString formatname )
{
    COleDataSource*    pSource = new COleDataSource();
    CSharedFile        sf(GMEM_MOVEABLE¦GMEM_DDESHARE¦GMEM_ZEROINIT);
    UINT               format = RegisterClipboardFormat(formatname);
    CArchive           ar(&sf, CArchive::store);

    obj-Serialize(ar);
    ar.Close();

    HGLOBAL hMem = sf.Detach();
    if (!hMem) return;
    pSource-CacheGlobalData(format, hMem);
    pSource-SetClipboard();
}
```

Reading Data from the Clipboard

Reading data from the clipboard is nearly the inverse of placing data on the clipboard.

1. Create a COleDataObject instance.
2. Check to see if the format you want is available.
3. Place the data associated with the clipboard into a CMemFile.
4. Read the data out of the CMemFile.
5. Release the global memory.

Example 3—Reading Data from the Clipboard

```
void CClipExamView::OnEditPaste()
{
    COleDataObject    obj;

    if (obj.AttachClipboard()) {
        if (obj.IsDataAvailable(CF_TEXT)) {
            HGLOBAL hmem = obj.GetGlobalData(CF_TEXT);
            CMemFile sf((BYTE*) ::GlobalLock(hmem), ::GlobalSize(hmem));
            CString buffer;

            LPSTR str = buffer.GetBufferSetLength(::GlobalSize(hmem));
            sf.Read(str, ::GlobalSize(hmem));
            ::GlobalUnlock(hmem);

            // Do something with the data in 'buffer'
            TRACE("Paste received = '%s'\r\n", buffer);
        }
    }
}
```

Serializing from the Clipboard

Serializing from the clipboard is only a slight modification of the previous example.

Example 4—Reading Serialized Data from the Clipboard

```
void SerializeFromClipboard(COleDataObject* obj, CObject* cobj,
➥CString formatname)
{
    UINT        format = RegisterClipboardFormat(formatname);

    if (obj-IsDataAvailable(format)) {
        HGLOBAL hmem = obj-GetGlobalData(format);
        CMemFile sf((BYTE*) ::GlobalLock(hmem), ::GlobalSize(hmem));
```

```
        CArchive ar(file, CArchive::load);
        cobj-Serialize(ar);
        ar.Close();
        ::GlobalUnlock(hmem);
    }
}
```

FROM THE FORUM

Question (NetGhost):

How can I get a message from the clipboard when something has been copied to it?

Answer (BlackWind):

Your program needs to become a clipboard viewer and must process the WM_DRAWCLIPBOARD and WM_CHANGECBCHAIN messages. Your program also needs to keep a pointer to the next window in the clipboard chain.

Here is the code you will need:

```
int CMainFrame::OnCreate(LPCREATESTRUCT lpCreateStruct)
{
    // put other stuff here
    m_hwndNextClipboard = SetClipboardViewer();
    return 0;
}

// get your program to process those cb messages...
void CMainFrame::OnDrawClipboard()
{

    // Clipboard has changed... see if it has text
    if (m_bClipboardStarted)
    {
        CString ClipText = GetClipboardText();
        if (ClipText.GetLength() > 0)
        {
        // Got the text... see if it's what you want
        }

        if (::IsWindow(m_hwndNextClipboard))
            ::SendMessage(m_hwndNextClipboard, WM_DRAWCLIPBOARD, 0, 0);
    }
    else
        m_bClipboardStarted = true;
}

void CMainFrame::OnChangeCbChain(HWND hWndRemove, HWND hWndAfter)
{

    if (hWndRemove == m_hwndNextClipboard)
        m_hwndNextClipboard = hWndAfter;
```

```
        if (::IsWindow(m_hwndNextClipboard))
            ::SendMessage(m_hwndNextClipboard, WM_DRAWCLIPBOARD,
➥(WPARAM)hWndRemove, (LPARAM)hWndAfter);
    }

    CString CMainFrame::GetClipboardText()
    {
        CString Ret;

        if (IsClipboardFormatAvailable(CF_TEXT))
        {
            // Text is on the clipboard
            ::OpenClipboard(AfxGetMainWnd()-&gt;GetSafeHwnd());
            HANDLE hText = GetClipboardData(CF_TEXT);
            if (!hText)
                CloseClipboard();
            else
            {
                Ret = (LPCSTR)GlobalLock(hText);
                GlobalUnlock(hText);
                CloseClipboard();
            }
        }

        return Ret;
    }
```

Drag/Drop Support

All of the examples thus far are placing the data on the clipboard as if a copy operation had been invoked. Enabling Drag/Drop is a simple change to the code from the preceding section.

Sourcing a Drag/Drop

The code for the origination of a Drag/Drop is identical to examples for placing data on the clipboard, with one little modification. Rather than executing the SetClipboard() command, you should execute the DoDragDrop() command.

Example 5—Sourcing a Drag/Drop

```
// Initiate the Drag/Drop
void CClipExamView::OnLButtonDown(UINT nFlags, CPoint point)
{
    COleDataSource*    pSource = new COleDataSource();
    CSharedFile        sf(GMEM_MOVEABLE¦GMEM_DDESHARE¦GMEM_ZEROINIT);
    CString            text = _T("Testing 1... 2... 3...");
```

```
    sf.Write(text, text.GetLength()); // You can write to the clipboard as
➡you would to any CFile

    HGLOBAL hMem = sf.Detach();
    if (!hMem) return;
    pSource-CacheGlobalData(CF_TEXT, hMem);
    pSource-DoDragDrop();
}
```

Accepting a Drag/Drop

Example 6—Accepting a Drag/Drop

```
// OnDragOver - Called when mouse moves over window during a Drag/Drop
DROPEFFECT CClipExamView::OnDragOver(COleDataObject* pDataObject, DWORD
➡dwKeyState, CPoint point)
{
    if (pDataObject-IsDataAvailable(CF_TEXT)) {
        return DROPEFFECT_COPY;
    }
    return DROPEFFECT_NONE;
}

// OnDrop - Called when drop occurs
BOOL CClipExamView::OnDrop(COleDataObject* pDataObject, DROPEFFECT
➡dropEffect, CPoint point)
{
    if (pDataObject-IsDataAvailable(CF_TEXT)) {
        HGLOBAL hmem = pDataObject-GetGlobalData(CF_TEXT);
        CMemFile sf((BYTE*) ::GlobalLock(hmem), ::GlobalSize(hmem));
        CString buffer;

        LPSTR str = buffer.GetBufferSetLength(::GlobalSize(hmem));
        sf.Read(str, ::GlobalSize(hmem));
        ::GlobalUnlock(hmem);

        // Do something with the data in 'buffer'
        TRACE("OnDrop received = '%s'\r\n", buffer);
        return TRUE;
    }
    return FALSE;
}
```

Housekeeping Issues

A few additional housekeeping things must be done to make Drag/Drop work correctly:

1. Make sure that your application's InitInstance() member function calls the AfxOleInit() function.

2. The view must be registered as a Drag/Drop target. If you don't do this, you won't be able to accept a Drag/Drop. See Example 7.

3. Several includes must be added to stdafx.h to ensure that your code will compile. See Example 8.

Example 7—Initializing the View as a Drop Target

```
// Enable view as a drop target. Assumes COleDropTarget m_DropTarget is
➥defined in view object.
void CClipExamView::OnInitialUpdate()
{
    CView::OnInitialUpdate();
    m_DropTarget.Register(this);
}
```

Example 8—Include to Add to stdafx.h

```
#include <afxole.h>      // MFC OLE classes
#include <afxodlgs.h>    // MFC OLE dialog classes
#include <afxdisp.h >    // MFC OLE automation classes
#include <afxpriv.h>
```

Comments

To add UNICODE support, make the following changes:

```
sf.Write(text, (text.GetLength()*sizeof(TCHAR)));
```

You should also replace CF_TEXT with CF_UNICODETEXT.

—Barry Hurt

Advanced Copy/Paste and Drag/Drop Support

This article was contributed by Keith Rule.

Introduction

One of the intentions of the clipboard infrastructure in MS Windows is to allow nearly seamless interaction between applications. However, neither Microsoft nor the reams of programming books available seriously discuss the issue of seamless interchange of data with MS Office products. I personally feel this is an unfortunate omission that requires developers to spend a fair amount of time hunting for information and/or doing trial-and-error experiments.

This article addresses several issues around interchanging data with MS Office products. The major topics addressed are

- Placing multiple formats on the clipboard
- Delayed rendering
- A survey of common clipboards
- The preference of several common target applications (MS Word, MS Excel, and MS PowerPoint)

This article assumes a basic understanding of using the clipboard with MFC. If you are unfamiliar with the basic use of the clipboard, please read the article "Basic Copy/Paste and Drag/Drop Support" (at the beginning of the chapter).

Placing Multiple Formats on the Clipboard

A fundamental issue when initiating a drag/cut/copy is that there is no way to know what target application will be the destination. This is a problem when the information you would like MS Word to accept is different from the information you would like MS Excel to accept.

This issue is resolved in two ways:

- The application that initiates the drag/cut/copy may place more than one clipboard format on the clipboard.
- The target often accepts more than one format but has a preference (meaning an acceptance order) for the formats it accepts.

Figure 7.3 shows the acceptance order for Cut/Copy/Paste and Drag/Drop in MS Excel, MS Word, and MS PowerPoint. MS Excel accepts the format "Csv," while neither MS Word nor MS PowerPoint accept that format.

If you would like MS Word to accept data that is different from what you would like MS Excel to accept, all you need to do is place both an RTF representation and a Csv representation on the clipboard. Since MS Excel doesn't accept RTF, it will get the Csv data, and since MS Word doesn't accept Csv, it will get the RTF data. You can often exploit these differences to get the Cut/Copy/Paste and Drag/Drop behavior you desire.

The code example in Listing 7.1 shows how both RTF and Csv formats can be placed on the clipboard at once. Figures 7.1 and 7.2 show the result of using this code when this data is dragged to MS Word and MS Excel.

Listing 7.1 Source for Initiating RTF and Csv Clipboard Formats

```
void CClipExamView::Word2Clipboard(COleDataSource * pSource)
{
    UINT format = ::RegisterClipboardFormat(_T("Rich Text Format"));
    CSharedFile         sf(GMEM_MOVEABLE¦GMEM_DDESHARE¦GMEM_ZEROINIT);
    CString             text = _T("{\\rtf1 {1\\tab 2\\tab 3\\par 4\\tab }
➥{\\b\\i 5}{\\tab 6\\par}}");

    sf.Write(text, text.GetLength());

    HGLOBAL hMem = sf.Detach();
    if (!hMem) return;
    pSource->CacheGlobalData(format, hMem);
}

void CClipExamView::Excel2Clipboard(COleDataSource * pSource)
{
    UINT format = ::RegisterClipboardFormat(_T("Csv"));
    CSharedFile      sf(GMEM_MOVEABLE¦GMEM_DDESHARE¦GMEM_ZEROINIT);
    CString          text = _T("6,5,4\n2,=1+1,1");

    sf.Write(text, text.GetLength());

    HGLOBAL hMem = sf.Detach();
    if (!hMem) return;
    pSource->CacheGlobalData(format, hMem);
}

void CClipExamView::OnEditCopy()
{
    COleDataSource    source;
    Excel2Clipboard(&source);
    Word2Clipboard(&source);
    source.SetClipboard();
}

void CClipExamView::OnLButtonDown(UINT nFlags, CPoint point)
{
    COleDataSource*    pSource = new COleDataSource();
    Excel2Clipboard(pSource);
    Word2Clipboard(pSource);
    pSource->DoDragDrop();
}
```

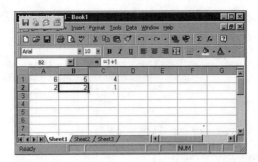

Figure 7.1   Excel as the drop target.

Figure 7.2   Word as the drop target.

It's obvious from looking at the screen shots that the text placed in Word was different than the text placed in Excel. You can exploit the clipboard format preferences of the target applications to get the behavior you wish on a drop.

Delayed Rendering

Delayed rendering does what the name implies. It defers creating the data that goes on the clipboard until it is specifically asked for by the destination application.

The code examples shown so far have placed the entire format on the clipboard when the source application initiates the cut/copy or drag. This can needlessly consume a larger amount of shared memory and can consume time creating unused data that is placed on the clipboard.

If you plan to use the clipboard to move large amounts of data, you should use delayed rendering. This will make the performance of Cut/Copy/Paste and Drag/Drop appear much better to the user.

Modifying COleDataSource for Delayed Rendering

To use delayed rendering, you need to override one or more member functions in the COleDataSource class. By overriding the OnRenderGlobalData() member function, you can intercept the target application's request for data and return whatever data you wish.

You check the requested format by looking at the lpFormatEtc->cfFormat item. If you find a format you accept, you simply write your data to shared memory and place the handle in *phGlobal. Return TRUE if you honored the request for data and FALSE if you didn't.

To specify the supported format when you initiate the cut/copy/drag, you replace the CacheGlobalData() call with the DelayRenderData() call. This specifies the supported format without having to place the data for that format on the clipboard until requested by the target application.

Listing 7.2 A Derived COleDataSource Class That Supports Delayed Rendering

```
class CMyOleDataSource : public COleDataSource
{
public:
    // Called when target application requests data
    BOOL OnRenderGlobalData(LPFORMATETC lpFormatEtc, HGLOBAL* phGlobal)
    {
        if (lpFormatEtc->cfFormat == ::RegisterClipboardFormat("Csv")) {
            // Handle Csv format
            CSharedFile sf(GMEM_MOVEABLE¦GMEM_DDESHARE¦GMEM_ZEROINIT);
            CString      text = _T("Excel2Clipboard\n6,5,4\n3,2,1");
            sf.Write(text, text.GetLength());
            HGLOBAL hMem = sf.Detach();
            *phGlobal = hMem;
            return (hMem != NULL);
        } else if (lpFormatEtc->cfFormat ==
➡::RegisterClipboardFormat(CF_RTF)) {
            // Handle Rich Text Format
            CSharedFile sf(GMEM_MOVEABLE¦GMEM_DDESHARE¦GMEM_ZEROINIT);
            CString      text = _T("{\\rtf1
➡{Word2Clipboard\\par 1\\tab 2\\tab 3\\par 4\\tab 5\\tab 6}}");
            sf.Write(text, text.GetLength());
            HGLOBAL hMem = sf.Detach();
            *phGlobal = hMem;
            return (hMem != NULL);
        }

        return FALSE;
    }

    void SetClipboard()
    {
        // Place available formats on the clipboard
        DelayRenderData(::RegisterClipboardFormat("Csv"));
        DelayRenderData(::RegisterClipboardFormat(CF_RTF));
```

Listing 7.2 Continued

```
        // Initiate a cut/copy to the clipboard
        COleDataSource::SetClipboard();
    }

    DROPEFFECT DoDragDrop(DWORD dwEffects = DROPEFFECT_COPY¦
➥DROPEFFECT_MOVE¦DROPEFFECT_LINK, LPCRECT lpRectStartDrag
➥= NULL, COleDropSource* pDropSource = NULL)
    {
        // Place available formats on the clipboard
        DelayRenderData(::RegisterClipboardFormat("Csv"));
        DelayRenderData(::RegisterClipboardFormat(CF_RTF));

        // Initiate a drag to the clipboard
        return COleDataSource::DoDragDrop(dwEffects,
➥lpRectStartDrag, pDropSource);
    }
};
```

In the example in Listing 7.2, I've chosen to override the SetClipboard() and DoDragDrop() member functions so that I can specify the supported formats. This isn't necessary, but it simplifies the usage of this class, as can be seen in Listing 7.3.

Listing 7.3 An Example Using CMyOleDataSource

```
void CClipExamView::OnEditCopy()
{
    CMyOleDataSource source;
    source.SetClipboard();
}

void CClipExamView::OnLButtonDown(UINT nFlags, CPoint point)
{
    CMyOleDataSource source;
    source.DoDragDrop();
}
```

Common Clipboard Formats

This section describes several commonly used clipboard formats. This is not intended to be an exhaustive list. However, it should be enough to get you started if you are not already familiar with these formats.

CF_TEXT

The CF_TEXT format is probably the most used of the clipboard formats commonly used by developers. This format simply defines a text string that is placed on the clipboard.

See the section "Basic Copy/Paste and Drag/Drop Support" for a simple example of how to read and write CF_TEXT from the clipboard.

If you plan to use the format with MS Excel, keep in mind that tabs ("\t") separate the columns and new lines ("\n") start a new row. In MS Word new lines denote the beginning of a new paragraph.

Csv

The "Csv" format stands for comma-separated values. "Csv" files are easy to export from an application, and most spreadsheets and databases can import this format.

When using the "Csv" format with MS Excel, remember that commas (",") separate columns and new lines ("\n") start a new row.

The actual format value is found using the following code:

```
UINT csvformat = ::RegisterClipboardFormat("Csv");
```

Other than the special format value, this format is a text string and can be created in the same manner as the CF_TEXT format.

Rich Text Format (CF_RTF)

This rich text format is intended as an interchange format for word-processing applications. Because of that, it is a rather large and feature-rich file format. Luckily, it is possible to describe a minimal RTF command set for creating simple formatted documents.

An RTF document consists of a group with the following format:

```
{\rtf1  document contents }
```

The document content is one or more groups that contain plain text and control words. There are many more control words than can be documented here, but I will hit the high points:

- **\par**—Starts a new paragraph
- **\tab**—A tab
- **\b**—Enable bold (scoped within a group)
- **\i**—Enable italics (scoped within a group)
- **\ul**—Enable underline (scoped within a group)

For example, the RTF string

```
{\rtf1 {1 \tab 2 \tab 3 \par 4 \tab {\b\i 5} \tab 6}}
```

would produce the following formatted text:

```
1    2    3
4    5    6
```

That might not be terribly exciting, but it does give you more formatting options than CF_TEXT.

Don't forget that when you embed the backslash ("\") character in a C++ string, you need to prepend it with another backslash.

The actual format value is found using the following code:

```
UINT rtfformat = ::RegisterClipboardFormat(CF_RTF);
```

CF_BITMAP

Randy More's article "Place a Bitmap Image on the Clipboard" (http://www.codeguru.com/clipboard/bitmap_to_clipboard.shtml) discusses how to create and place a CF_BITMAP object on the clipboard. I won't revisit that here, but Listing 7.4 shows how to use the technique Randy described with delayed rendering.

Listing 7.4   Delayed Rendering of a CBitmap

```
BOOL OnRenderData(LPFORMATETC lpFormatEtc, LPSTGMEDIUM lpStgMedium)
    {
        if (lpFormatEtc->cfFormat == CF_BITMAP) {
            CBitmap bitmap;
            CClipExamView*    pView =  (CClipExamView*) ((CFrameWnd*)
➡(AfxGetApp()->m_pMainWnd))->GetActiveView();

            TRACE("Output CF_BITMAP\r\n");
            if (pView != NULL) {
                CClientDC cdc(pView);
                CDC dc;
                dc.CreateCompatibleDC(&cdc);

                CRect bounds;

                pView->GetClientRect(&bounds);

                bitmap.CreateCompatibleBitmap(&cdc, bounds.Width(),
➡bounds.Height());
                CBitmap* oldBitmap = dc.SelectObject(&bitmap);

                CBrush fill(RGB(255, 255, 255));
                dc.FillRect(bounds, &fill);
```

Listing 7.4 Continued

```
                dc.TextOut(0, 0, CString(_T("Bitmap")));
                pView->OnDraw(&dc);

                lpStgMedium->tymed = TYMED_GDI;
                lpStgMedium->hBitmap = HBITMAP(bitmap);

                bitmap.Detach();

                dc.SelectObject(oldBitmap);
                return TRUE;
            }
            return FALSE;
        }
        return COleDataSource::OnRenderData(lpFormatEtc, lpStgMedium);
    }
```

CF_ENHMETAFILE

Randy More's article "Place an Enhanced Metafile on the Clipboard" (http://www.
codeguru.com/clipboard/emf_to_clipboard.shtml) discusses how to create and place a
CF_ENHMETAFILE object on the clipboard. I won't revisit that here, but Listing 7.5
shows how to use the technique Randy described with delayed rendering.

Listing 7.5 Delayed Rendering of a Metafile

```
    BOOL OnRenderData(LPFORMATETC lpFormatEtc, LPSTGMEDIUM lpStgMedium)
    {
        if (lpFormatEtc->cfFormat == CF_ENHMETAFILE) {
            CClipExamView*    pView = (CClipExamView*) ((CFrameWnd*)
➡(AfxGetApp()->m_pMainWnd))->GetActiveView();
            TRACE("Output CF_ENHMETAFILE\r\n");
            if (pView != NULL) {
                CClientDC dcRef(pView);
                CMetaFileDC dcMeta;

                CRect lmbr;
                pView->GetClientRect(lmbr);

                dcMeta.CreateEnhanced(&dcRef, NULL,
➡NULL,"Metafile\0Copy\0\0" );
                dcMeta.SetMapMode(MM_TEXT);

                CBrush fill(RGB(255, 255, 255));
                dcMeta.FillRect(lmbr,&fill);
                dcMeta.TextOut(0, 0, CString(_T("Metafile")));

                pView->OnDraw(&dcMeta);
```

Listing 7.5 Continued

```
            lpStgMedium->hEnhMetaFile = dcMeta.CloseEnhanced();
            lpStgMedium->tymed = TYMED_GDI;

            return TRUE;
        }
        return FALSE;
    }
    return COleDataSource::OnRenderData(lpFormatEtc, lpStgMedium);
}
```

FROM THE FORUM

Question (Melissa Paine):

How can I programmatically copy the text of a CEdit located on a dialog to the clipboard?

Answer 1 (Wing Man):

```
CString txt;
GetDlgItemText(IDC_WHATEVER, txt);
OpenClipboard();
EmptyClipboard();
SetClipboardData (CF_TEXT, txt);
CloseClipboard ();
```

Answer 2 (Kevin Cook):

CEdit has a method called Copy that will copy the text it contains to the clipboard.

```
m_edEdit.SetSel(0, -1);
m_edEdit.Copy();
```

This code will set the current selection of the edit control to the entire contents of the control and then will copy the selection to the clipboard.

Clipboard Preference

Figure 7.3 shows the preference order for the five most popular clipboard formats in MS Office applications. Please notice that the preferences are often different between a Drag/Drop and a Cut/Copy/Paste.

Format	MS-Word 97 (To a blank page)		MS-Excel 97 (To a blank workbook)		MS-PowerPoint 97 (To a blank slide)	
	Drag/Drop	Cut/Copy/Paste	Drag/Drop	Cut/Copy/Paste	Drag/Drop	Cut/Copy/Paste
CF_BITMAP	3	4	-	4	-	2
CF_ENHMETAFILE	-	3	-	3	-	1
CF_DIF	1	1	-	-	1	3
CF_TEXT	2	2	1	1	2	4
Csv	-	-	2	2	-	-

Figure 7.3 MS Office clipboard preferences.

8

Dynamic Link Libraries (.DLLs)

In this chapter

The name Dynamic Link Libraries conjures up images of a librarian storming around campus wearing a bright red cape. Sadly, this visualization does little to improve the often tarnished image of the humble DLL.

In this chapter, you will find a three-part tutorial-style overview of DLLs and their uses within the MFC framework.

- "MFC .DLL Tutorial, Article 1" describes the various types of DLLs and why they can be useful.
- "MFC .DLL Tutorial, Article 2" addresses some common DLL-related compatibility issues with MFC and the compiler.
- "MFC .DLL Tutorial, Article 3" builds upon the above articles to provide some practical examples of DLLs in use.

MFC .DLL Tutorial, Article 1

This article was contributed by Andrew Fenster.

Environment: Visual C++

At one point in time, before COM, before ATL, programmers used ordinary .DLLs instead. You could do a lot with a .DLL. If you had several programs that used the same functions or other resources, you could save space by putting those resources in a .DLL. Putting code used by multiple programs in a single .DLL often saved maintenance time because the code was all in one place. Fixes and other modifications would only have to be done one time. If you had a program that needed to run different routines at different times, you could put those routines into .DLLs and have the application load the appropriate .DLL when it was needed. There were lots of good reasons to use .DLLs.

There are still a lot of good reasons to use .DLLs. They haven't gone away. Sure, whatever you can do with a .DLL, you can probably do with a COM object. Granted, there are a number of shortcomings to .DLLs, some of them serious, which is why we ended up with COM in the first place. Still, .DLLs remain a very useful tool. Compared to COM and ATL, they are much easier to make. Learning COM or ATL requires a serious investment of time and effort. Making a .DLL is relatively easy. Modifying one is easy too. If you know some C++ and MFC, you could be making .DLLs today.

This article will review the types of .DLLs you can make with MFC, including when to use each type and how to make them. In the next article, there will be a discussion of the limitations of .DLLs (which led to the rise of COM and ATL) and how these can be partially avoided. In the third article, there will be more coding details and examples.

Different Types of .DLLs

There are two kinds of .DLLs you can make using MFC: an MFC extension .DLL or a regular .DLL. Regular .DLLs in turn come in two varieties: dynamically linked or statically linked. Visual C++ also allows you to make a generic Win32 .DLL, but in this article I'm only going to discuss the MFC-based .DLL types.

MFC Extension .DLLs

Every .DLL has some kind of interface. The interface is the set of the variables, pointers, functions, or classes provided by the .DLL that you can access from the client program. They are the things that allow the client program to use the .DLL. An MFC extension .DLL can have a C++-style interface. That is, it can provide "export" C++ functions and entire C++ classes to be used by the client application. The functions it exports can use C++ or MFC data types as parameters or as return values. When it exports a class, the client will be able to create objects of that class or derive new classes from it. Inside the .DLL, you can also use MFC and C++.

The MFC code library used by Visual C++ is stored in a .DLL. An MFC extension .DLL dynamically links to the MFC code library .DLL. The client application must also dynamically link to the MFC code library .DLL. As the years have gone by, the MFC library has grown. As a result, there are a few different versions of the MFC code library .DLL out there. Both the client program and the extension .DLL must be built using the same version of MFC. Therefore, for an MFC extension .DLL to work, both the extension .DLL and the client program must dynamically link to the same MFC code library .DLL, and this .DLL must be available on the computer where the application is running.

Note: If you have an application that is statically linked to MFC and you wish to modify it so that it can access functions from an extension .DLL, you can change the application to dynamically link to MFC. In Visual C++, select Project, Settings from the menu. On the General Settings tab, you can change your application to dynamically link to MFC.

MFC extension .DLLs are very small. You can build an extension .DLL that exports a few functions or small classes and has a size of 10–15KB. Obviously, the size of your .DLL depends on how much code you store in it, but in general MFC extension .DLLs are relatively small and quick to load.

Regular .DLLs

The MFC extension .DLL only works with MFC client applications. If you need a .DLL that can be loaded and run by a wider range of Win32 programs, you should use a regular .DLL. The downside is that your .DLL and your client application cannot send each other pointers or references to MFC-derived classes and objects. If you export a function, it cannot use MFC data types in its parameters or return values. If you export a C++ class, it cannot be derived from MFC. You can still use MFC *inside* your .DLL, but not in your interface.

Your regular .DLL still needs to have access to the code in the MFC code library .DLL. You can dynamically link to this code or statically link to it. If you dynamically link, that means the MFC code your .DLL needs in order to function is not built into your .DLL. Your .DLL will get the code it needs from the MFC code library .DLL found on the client application's computer. If the right version of the MFC code library .DLL is not there, your .DLL won't run. Like the MFC extension .DLL, you get a small .DLL (because the .DLL doesn't include the MFC code), but you can only run it if the client computer has the MFC code library .DLL.

If you statically link to the MFC code library, your .DLL will incorporate within itself all the MFC code it needs. Thus, it will be a larger .DLL, but it won't be dependent on the client computer having the proper MFC code library .DLL. If you can't rely on the host computer having the right version of MFC available, this is the way to go. If your application users are all within your own company and you have control over what versions of the MFC .DLLs are lurking on their computers, or if your installation program also loads the right MFC .DLL, this might not be an issue.

Building a .DLL

You can make an MFC-based .DLL with the AppWizard. Select File, New from the menu. On the Projects tab, select MFC AppWizard (.DLL). Pick a name for your new project and click OK. On the next screen, you will have the choice to create an MFC extension .DLL, a regular .DLL using shared MFC .DLL (a regular .DLL dynamically linked to MFC), or a regular .DLL statically linked to MFC. Pick the one you want and click Finish.

AppWizard builds a .DLL that doesn't do anything. The new .DLL will compile, but since it doesn't export any classes or functions yet, it is still essentially useless. You now have two jobs: (1) add functionality to make your .DLL useful; and (2) modify your client application to use your .DLL.

Exporting a Class

Once you're done with the AppWizard, you can add classes to your .DLL by adding the .cpp and .h files from another project, or you can create them from scratch within your current project. To export a class, you add "__declspec(dllexport)" to the class declaration so that it looks like this:

```
class __declspec(dllexport) CMyClass
{
    //class declaration goes here
};
```

If you are making an MFC extension .DLL, you can instead use the AFX_EXT_CLASS macro:

```
class AFX_EXT_CLASS CMyClass
{
    //class declaration goes here
};
```

There are other ways to export a class, but this is the easiest. If your exported class requires a resource that is located in the .DLL, for example a class derived from CDialog, the process is more involved. I'll cover this subject in Article 3. In the following section, I'll discuss what to do to the client application so that it can use your exported class.

Exporting Variables, Constants, and Objects

Instead of exporting a whole class, you can have your .DLL export a variable, constant, or object. To export a variable or constant, you simply declare it like this:

```
__declspec(dllexport) int   MyInt;
__declspec(dllexport) extern const COLORREF MyColor =
                               RGB(50,50,50);
```

When you want to export a constant, you must use the "extern" specifier. Otherwise you will get a link error.

You can declare and export a class object in the exact same manner:

```
__declspec(dllexport) CRect MyRect(30, 30, 300, 300);
```

Note that you can only export a class object if the client application recognizes the class and has its header file. If you make a new class inside your .DLL, the client application won't recognize it without the header file.

When you export a variable or object, each client application that loads the .DLL will get its own copy. Thus, if two different applications are using the same .DLL, changes made by one application will not affect the other application.

It's important to remember that you can only export objects and variables that are of *global* scope within your .DLL. Local objects and variables cease to exist when they go out of scope. Thus, if your .DLL included the following code, it wouldn't work:

```
MyFunction( )
{
    __declspec(dllexport) CSomeClass SomeObject;
    __declspec(dllexport) int SomeInt;
}
```

As soon as the object and variable go out of scope, they will cease to exist.

Exporting a Function

Exporting functions is similar to exporting objects or variables. You simply tack "__declspec(dllexport)" onto the beginning of your function prototype:

```
__declspec(dllexport) int SomeFunction(int);
```

If you are making an MFC regular .DLL that will be used by a client application written in C, your function declaration should look like this:

```
extern "C" __declspec(dllexport) int SomeFunction(int);
```

and your function definition should look like this:

```
extern "C" __declspec(dllexport) int SomeFunction(int x)
{
    //do something
}
```

If you are building a regular .DLL that is *dynamically linked* to the MFC code library .DLL, you must insert the AFX_MANAGE_STATE macro as the first line of any exported function. Thus, your function definition would look like this:

```
extern "C" __declspec(dllexport) int AddFive(int x)
{
    AFX_MANAGE_STATE(AfxGetStaticModuleState( ));
    return x + 5;
}
```

It doesn't hurt to do this in every regular .DLL. If you switch your .DLL to static linking, the macro will simply have no effect.

That's all there is to exporting functions. Remember, only an MFC extension .DLL can export functions with MFC data types in the parameters or return value.

Exporting a Pointer

Exporting an uninitialized pointer is simple. You do it the same way you export a variable or object:

```
__declspec(dllexport) int* SomeInt;
```

You can also export an initialized object this way:

```
__declspec(dllexport) CSomeClass* SomePointer =
                                new CSomeClass;
```

Of course, if you declare and initialize your pointer, you need to find a place to delete it.

In an extension .DLL, you will find a function called DllMain(). This function gets called when the client program attaches your .DLL and again when it detaches. So here's one possible way to handle your pointers in an extension .DLL:

```
#include "SomeClass.h"

_declspec(dllexport) CSomeClass* SomePointer = new CSomeClass;

DllMain(HINSTANCE hInstance, DWORD dwReason, LPVOID lpReserved)
{
    if (dwReason == DLL_PROCESS_ATTACH)
    {

    }
    else if (dwReason == DLL_PROCESS_DETACH)
    {
        delete SomePointer;
    }
}
```

A regular .DLL looks more like an ordinary MFC executable. It has an object derived from CWinApp to handle opening and closing your .DLL. You can use the Class Wizard to add an InitInstance() function and an ExitInstance() function.

```
int CMyDllApp::ExitInstance()
{
    delete SomePointer;
    return CWinApp::ExitInstance();
}
```

Using the .DLL in a Client Application

A .DLL can't run on its own. It requires a client application to load it and use its interface. Making a client application that can do so is not difficult.

When you compile your .DLL, the compiler creates two important files: the .DLL file and the .lib file. Your client application needs both of these. You must copy them into the project folder of your client application. Note that the .DLL and .lib files that are

created when you build in Debug are different than those created when you build in
Release. When you are building your client application in Debug, you need the Debug
versions of the .DLL and .lib files, and when you are building in Release, you need
the Release .DLL and .lib files. The easiest way to handle this is to put the Debug
.DLL and .lib files in your client application's Debug folder and the Release .DLL and
.lib files in the Release folder.

The next step is to go into your client project settings and tell the linker to look
for your .lib file. You must tell the linker the name of your .lib file and where it can
be found. To do this, open Project Settings, go to the Link tab, and enter your file
name and path in the Object/Library Modules box. It should look something like
Figure 8.1.

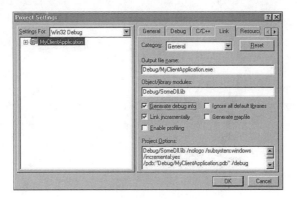

Figure 8.1

In addition to the .DLL and .lib files, your client application needs a header file for
the imported classes, functions, objects, and variables. When we were exporting, we
added "__declspec(dllexport)" to our declarations. Now when we are importing,
we will add "__declspec(dllimport)." So if we wanted to import the variable, object,
and function used in our previous examples, our header file would contain the
following:

```
__declspec(dllimport) int SomeFunction(int);
__declspec(dllexport) CSomeClass SomeObject;
__declspec(dllexport) int SomeInt;
```

Remember, if you used the **extern "C"** specifier in the .DLL, you must also use it in
the client application:

```
extern "C" __declspec(dllimport) int SomeFunction(int);
```

To make things more readable, we might write it like this instead:

```
#define DLLIMPORT __declspec(dllimport)

DLLIMPORT int SomeFunction(int);
DLLIMPORT CSomeClass SomeObject;
DLLIMPORT int SomeInt;
```

Now that you have declared your object, variable, and function in a header file inside your client application, they are available for use.

To import an entire class, you must copy the entire .h header file into the client application. The .DLL and the client application will thus have identical header files for the exported class, except one will say "class __declspec(dllexport) CMyClass" and one will say "class __declspec(dllimport) CMyClass." If you are making an MFC extension .DLL, you could instead say "class AFX_EXT_CLASS CMyClass" in both places.

Once you are done building your client application and you are ready to turn it over to the actual users, you should give them your Release executable and the Release .DLL. You do not need to give the users the .lib file. The .DLL can go in the same directory as the executable, or it can go in the Windows System directory. As discussed above, you may also have to provide your users with the correct MFC code library .DLL. This .DLL was loaded onto your computer when you installed Visual C++. Your users, however, may not have it. It does not come standard with Windows.

A Word of Caution

This article should provide you with enough information to start building your own .DLLs. A word of caution is needed, however. As mentioned at the beginning of this article, there are several serious shortcomings to .DLLs. These shortcomings are the reason that we now have COM and ATL. There are two main problems. First, a .DLL built with one brand of compiler may not be compatible with a client application built with a different compiler. Second, when you modify the .DLL, you may have to recompile the client application, even though you aren't changing any code in the client application. You may still have to copy in a new .DLL and .lib file and recompile.

There are ways to avoid this problem under some circumstances. I'll discuss the problem in more detail in the next article.

MFC .DLL Tutorial, Article 2

This article was contributed by Andrew Fenster.

Environment: Visual C++

As I discussed in the previous article, .DLLs are a useful tool for any MFC programmer. They are subject to a number of important limitations, however, and anyone who is making .DLLs should be aware of these.

MFC Issues

This was discussed in the previous article, but it is worth mentioning again briefly. An MFC extension .DLL can only be used if the client application dynamically links to the same version of MFC and the correct MFC code library .DLL is available on the client computer. A regular .DLL that dynamically links to MFC will only work if the correct MFC code library .DLL is available.

Compiler Incompatibility Issues

One of the biggest problems with C++-based .DLLs arises when a .DLL is built on one brand of compiler and called by an application built on another brand of compiler. Often it won't work without a great deal of effort.

ANSI sets the standards for the C and C++ languages. That is, it specifies the C and C++ functions and data types that should be supported by a compiler. It does not, however, provide a complete standard as to how these functions and data types should be implemented on a binary level. As a result, compiler vendors are free to implement language features in their own proprietary ways.

Most C/C++ programmers know that different compilers handle data types differently. One compiler will allocate two bytes for an int and another will allocate four bytes. One will use four-byte doubles and another will use eight bytes. An even bigger difference with C++ compilers arises from their implementation of function and operator overloading. The differences between compilers go far beyond this, however. The same C or C++ code may be compiled very differently by different compilers. These differences may keep your .DLL from running with someone else's application.

Of course, if you are building an MFC extension .DLL, this is not an issue for you. MFC extension .DLLs are made with a Microsoft compiler. As discussed in the previous article, they can only be used by applications that are dynamically linked to MFC. These applications are also made with a Microsoft compiler.

Compiler incompatibility problems can be fixed by inserting pragmas and other precompile instructions into your code, but this is hard to do and unreliable. There will always be the chance that someone else is using a compiler that's still incompatible.

Recompiling

Let's say you built a .DLL that exports a class called CMyClass. You provide a copy of
the header file for CMyClass to be used by the client application. Suppose that a
CMyClass object is 30 bytes in size.

Now let's suppose you modify the .DLL to change CMyClass. It still has the same
public functions and member variables, but now CMyClass has an additional private
member variable, an int. So now, when you create an object of type CMyClass, it's 34
bytes in size. You send this new .DLL to your users and tell them to replace the old
.DLL. Now you have a problem. The client application is expecting a 30-byte object,
but your new .DLL is creating a 34-byte object. The client application is going to get
an error.

Here's a similar problem. Suppose that instead of exporting CMyClass, your .DLL
exports several functions that use CMyClass references or pointers in their parameters
or return values. You have provided a CMyClass header file that now resides in the
client application. Again, if you change the size of the CMyClass object without
rebuilding the client application, you will have problems.

At this point, the only way to fix the problem is to replace the CMyClass header file
in the client application and recompile it. Once recompiled, the client application will
start looking for a 34-byte object.

This is a serious problem. One of the goals of having a .DLL is to be able to modify
and replace the .DLL without modifying the client application. However, if your .DLL
is exporting classes or class objects, this may not be possible. You may have to recompile the client application. If you don't have the source code for the client application,
you simply can't use the new .DLL.

Solutions

If there were a perfect fix for these problems, we might not have COM. Here are a
few suggestions:

MFC extension .DLLs don't have compiler incompatibility problems. They simply
can't be used by applications built on non-Microsoft compilers. As for regular .DLLs,
you can avoid many compiler problems by only exporting C-style functions and using
the extern "C" specifier. Exporting C++ classes and overloaded C++ functions leaves
you much more vulnerable to compiler incompatibility.

As for having to recompile your client application when you modify the .DLL, there
are relatively easy ways to avoid the problem. I will describe two of them: (1) an interface class and (2) static functions used to create and destroy your exported class.

Using an Interface Class

The goal of an interface class is to separate the class you want to export from the interface to that class. The way to do this is to create a second class that will serve as the interface for the class you want to export. Then, even when the export class changes, you will not need to recompile the client application because the interface class remains the same.

Here's an example of how that would work. Suppose you want to export CMyClass. CMyClass has two public functions, int FunctionA(int) and int FunctionB(int). If I simply export CMyClass, I'll have to recompile the client application every time I add a new variable. Instead, I'll create and export an interface class, CMyInterface. CMyInterface will have a pointer to a CMyClass object. Here's the header file for CMyInterface as it looks inside the .DLL:

```
#include "MyClass.h"

class __declspec(dllexport) CMyInterface
{
    //private pointer to CMyClass object
    CMyClass *m_pMyClass;

    CMyInterface( );
    ~CMyInterface( );

    public:
    int FunctionA(int);
    int FunctionB(int);
};
```

Inside the client application, the header file will look slightly different. The #include will be gone. After all, you can't include MyClass.h because the client application doesn't have a copy of it. Instead, you will use a forward declaration of CMyClass. This will allow you to compile even without the CMyClass header file:

```
class __declspec(dllimport) CMyInterface
{
    //Forward declaration of CMyClass
    class CMyClass;

    CMyClass *m_pMyClass;

    CMyInterface( );
    ~CMyInterface( );

    public:
    int FunctionA(int);
    int FunctionB(int);
};
```

Inside the .DLL, you will implement CMyInterface as follows:

```
CMyInterface::CMyInterface( )
{
     m_pMyClass = new CMyClass;
}

CMyInterface::~CMyInterface( )
{
     delete m_pMyClass;
}

int CMyInterface::FunctionA( )
{
     return m_pMyClass->FunctionA( );
}

int CMyInterface::FunctionB( )
{
     return m_pMyClass->FunctionB( );
}
```

Thus, for every public function in CMyClass, CMyInterface will provide its own corresponding function. The client application has no contact with CMyClass. If it wants to call CMyClass::FunctionA, it instead calls CMyInterface::FunctionA. The interface class then uses its pointer to call CMyClass. With this arrangement, you're free to modify with CMyClass. It doesn't matter if the size of the CMyClass object changes. The size of the CMyInterface object will remain the same. If you add a private member variable to CMyClass, the size of CMyInterface will remain unchanged. If you add a public member variable to CMyClass, you can add getter and setter functions for the new variable in CMyInterface without fear. Adding new functions to CMyInterface will not cause recompile problems.

Creating a separate interface class avoids some compiler incompatibility problems and most recompile problems. As long as the interface class doesn't change, there should be no need to recompile. There are still two relatively minor problems with this solution. First, for every public function and member variable in CMyClass, you must create a corresponding function or variable in CMyInterface. In the example there are only two functions, so that's easy. If CMyClass had hundreds of functions and variables, this would be a more tedious, error-prone process. Second, you are increasing the amount of processing that must be done. The client application no longer calls CMyClass directly. Instead, it calls a CMyInterface function that calls CMyClass. If this is a function that will be called thousands of times by the client application, the extra processing time may begin to add up.

Static Functions

A different way to avoid having to recompile uses static functions to create and destroy the exported class. This solution was sent to me by Ran Wainstain in a comment to my previous article.

When you are creating a class that you intend to export, you add two public static functions, CreateMe() and DestroyMe():

```
class __declspec(dllexport) CMyClass
{
    CMyClass( );
    ~CMyClass( );

    public:
    static CMyClass* CreateMe( );
    static void DestroyMe(CMyClass *ptr);
}
```

CreateMe() and DestroyMe() are implemented as follows:

```
CMyClass* CMyClass::CreateMe( )
{
    return new CMyClass;
}

void CMyClass::DestroyMe(CMyClass *ptr)
{
    delete ptr;
}
```

You export CMyClass as you would any other class. In the client application, you must be sure to use the CreateMe() and DestroyMe() functions. When you want to create a CMyClass object, you don't declare it in the usual fashion, which follows:

```
CMyClass x;
```

Instead, you do this:

```
CMyClass *ptr = CMyClass::CreateMe( );
```

When you are done, you must remember to delete the object:

```
CMyClass::DeleteMe(ptr);
```

Using this technique, you can modify the size of CMyClass without having to recompile the client application.

Conclusion

This article is not a complete review of every issue concerning .DLLs, nor does it cover every possible solution. Good discussions of these issues can be found in *Inside COM* by Dale Rogerson and *Essential COM* by Don Box. For a more detailed understanding of the issue, that's where I would go. This article should at least serve to make you aware of the biggest issues and possible fixes and get you started on your way.

MFC .DLL Tutorial, Article 3

This article was contributed by Andrew Fenster.

Environment: Visual C++

In Article 1 of this series, I covered what types of .DLLs you can make with MFC and how to build MFC regular and extension .DLLs. In Article 2, I covered potential problems that can arise when you use .DLLs and suggested several ways to avoid them. In this article, I'll build upon the first two articles by providing more coding examples and technical details.

Exporting Resources from a .DLL

You may wish to create a .DLL that exports resources such as dialog templates, bitmaps, icons, or strings. You may, for example, wish to make your application multi-lingual, with one .DLL for English strings and dialog templates, another with Spanish strings, and so on. Exporting resources is relatively easy to do.

Your first step in building a .DLL that exports resources is (of course) to build a .DLL and give it some resources. You can use a regular or extension .DLL. Use the AppWizard to create your .DLL, as described in Article 1. To add a resource using the Visual C++ menu, select Insert and Resource, and then select the type of resource you wish to add.

Once you've built your .DLL and given it all the resources it is to import, you must build a header file to be used by the client application. You can add a new header file using the Visual C++ menu by selecting File, Add to Project, New, C/C++ Header File. Now open your .DLL's Resource.h file. Assuming you have compiled your .DLL, the top of this file will look something like this:

```
#define IDS_SOME_STRING1          1
#define IDS_SOME_STRING2          2
#define IDS_SOME_STRING3          3
#define IDD_SOME_DIALOG           11000
#define IDB_SOME_BITMAP           11001
```

As you can see, each of these #defines gives one of your resources an identifying integer value. Copy the complete #define for each resource you wish to export into your newly created header file.

At this point, your .DLL is almost ready to go. Only one more step is required. In Articles 1 and 2, I demonstrated how to use a .DLL with implicit linking. When you are using implicit linking, the client application will attempt to connect to your .DLL automatically. If it cannot do so, the client application won't run. When you use implicit linking, it is important to remember that the client application will not attempt to connect to your .DLL unless your .DLL exports at least one class or function that is used by the client. So even if your .DLL's only purpose is to provide resources, you still must export at least one function or class that is used by the client. It doesn't matter whether your exported class or function does anything useful. It simply has to be there in order to force the client to connect to the .DLL. So all that's left to make your .DLL complete is to export a do-nothing function. See Article 1 for an explanation of how to export a function.

Setting Up the Client Application

Article 1 describes how to build a client application that will connect to your .DLL. Remember, your client application must actually call at least one function from your .DLL or create at least one instance of an imported class. If not, your client application will not automatically connect to your .DLL at runtime. Be sure to add a copy of the header file you created earlier to your client application project.

In some respects, an extension .DLL is easier to use when you are importing resources. This is because an extension .DLL will try to find a resource in your .DLL if it cannot find it in its own resources. Suppose your client application included the following code:

```
CString str;
str.LoadString(IDS_SOME_STRING1);
AfxMessageBox(str);
```

The first thing your client application will do is look for a definition of IDS_SOME_STRING1. Suppose the header file you imported defines IDS_SOME_STRING1 as 1. The client application will look in its own resources for resource #1. If it cannot find resource #1 in its own resources, it will next look in the extension .DLL. If you built a regular .DLL, the client application won't take this extra step.

Note that there is a big potential for problems here. If your client application has some other resource that is also defined as resource 1, it will attempt to load its own resource. The client only looks to your extension .DLL if it can't find the properly numbered resource within its own resources. One way to avoid this problem is to renumber your resources to avoid conflicts.

When you use a regular .DLL, the client application must be told explicitly to look to the .DLL to find the resource. Here's how you do it:

```
//Store the current resource handle
HINSTANCE hClientResources = AfxGetResourceHandle();

//Tell the client to use the .DLL's resources
AfxSetResourceHandle(::GetModuleHandle("SomeDll.dll"));

//Do something with the .DLL's resources
CString str;
strRes.LoadString(IDS_SOME_STRING1);

//Restore the client application resource handle
AfxSetResourceHandle(hClientResources);
```

You can use this technique in your client application even if you are using an extension .DLL. With a regular .DLL it is necessary. While not absolutely necessary with an extension .DLL, it gives you the certainty that the right resources will be loaded.

Exporting a CDialog-based Class

Exporting a class derived from the CDialog class is only slightly more complicated than exporting other classes. The extra complication comes from the fact that you must also export the dialog template, which is a resource.

When you export a class, you must provide a copy of the class header file to be used by the client application. When you export a class derived from CDialog, which has a resource, you must also export the #define for the resource ID. So the easiest thing to do is simply tack the #define onto the top of the header file like this:

```
#ifndef IDD_HELLO_DIALOG
    #define IDD_SOME_DIALOG        9000
#endif
```

As with other exported resources, you can run into problems if the client application also has a resource with the same number. Either be careful to avoid conflicts or use the code shown above to tell the client application explicitly where to find the correct resource.

Note that the same technique used with Cdialog-based classes can also be used with any other class you wish to export that uses resources. Be sure to define the resources in the header file you provide for the client application, and take whatever steps are necessary to avoid conflicts.

FROM THE FORUM

Question (DanielVatier):

I am developing a C++ wrapper (as a static-library) for FORTRAN DLL code and need the get the handle/hinstance of the current DLL to pass to a third-party product. The FORTRAN caller cannot pass the handle or the DLL name (it does not know it). The standard SDK has functions like GetModuleHandle() and GetModuleFileName() but I cannot use them as key information is missing.

Is it possible to solve this problem?

Answer (Alex Fedotov):

I use this code:

```
// this function returns the HINSTANCE of the DLL from which it was called
__declspec(naked) HINSTANCE GetCurrentInstance()
{
    __asm mov eax, [esp] // take the return address
    __asm push eax // duplicate it on the stack
    __asm jmp GetInstanceFromAddress // jump to the helper
}

HINSTANCE __stdcall GetInstanceFromAddress(LPVOID pvAddress)
{
    MEMORY_BASIC_INFORMATION bi;

    if (VirtualQuery(pvAddress, &bi, sizeof(bi))
    {
        if (bi.Type == MEM_IMAGE)
            return (HINSTANCE)bi.AllocationBase;
    }

    return NULL;
}
```

FROM THE FORUM

Question (jagadishkumar):

When doing initialization in DllMain() using DLL_PROCESS_ATTACH, if this initialization fails, I return false. This causes the Windows error message to appear.

Is there some way I can catch this error and display my own custom message?

Answer (jagadishkumar):

I found a way myself by calling SetErrorMode(SEM_FAILCRITICALERRORS); inside DllMain.

9

Files and Folders

In this chapter

One question that seems to appear on the various programming forums with regular monotony is "How do I show a Browse button for a folder dialog?"

The answer to this question, as well as the mysteries of shell programming, will be revealed in this chapter.

- "GetFolder: Shell Extension Folder Browser Function" describes a shell extension folder browser to impress your friends with.

- "SHFILEOPSTRUCT and the SHFileOperation" provides an insight into how Windows copies and moves files around, and also how you can do the same without referring to Microsoft's less-than-verbose documentation of this functionality.

- "Tuning SHGetFileInfo for Optimum Performance" documents a simple but very efficient way of accessing system file information that may otherwise be very time consuming.

GetFolder: Shell Extension Folder Browser Function

This article was contributed by Vishal D. Khapre.

Figure 9.1   Folder browser dialog—also enumerates network drives.

Figure 9.2 Demo application shows how easy it is to display a dialog and retrieve a user-selected folder.

Overview

This is a very standard technique used to retrieve folder information from Windows using the Shell extension functions SHBrowseForFolderA, SHGetPathFromIDList, and SHGetDesktopFolder.

The Code

All you need to do is to call my function GetFolder. However, for the more curious among you who want to know more of the details, there are only two functions used here: one to cause the display of the standard folder browser dialog and a callback function that handles the processing of events while the dialog is being displayed. Here are the basic steps in my code.

GetFolder Steps

1. Call SHGetDesktopFolder to get the IShellFolder interface for the desktop folder.

2. Call the IShellFolder.ParseDisplayName to get the identifier list.

3. Allocate and fill out a BROWSEINFOA structure with the desired parameters (for example, pidl from the IShellFolder.ParseDisplayName, a callback function that the shell will call with the folder names, and so on). The callback function is called BrowseCallbackProc.

4. Call SHBrowseForFolderA to display the folder browse dialog (passing it the BROWSEINFOA structure, which defines how that dialog should appear).

5. Upon return from the SHBrowseForFolderA function, I then call the SHGetPathFromIDList function in order to retrieve the name of the user-selected folder.

BrowseCallbackProc Function

In this function, I only need to handle the BFFM_INITIALIZED and the BFFM_SELCHANGED messages. Even then, all I'm doing is updating a field on the dialog to reflect the currently selected folder. This is the text that I retrieve in the last step of the GetFolder function.

Comments

There is a memory leak in the sample code. The following change corrects this:

The pointer returned by the following line is not being freed:

```
lpID = SHBrowseForFolderA(&bi);
```

The following lines should be added to free this memory:

```
If(lpID != NULL)
{
    ...
    LPMALLOC pMalloc = NULL;
    HRESULT hResult = SHGetMalloc(&pMalloc);
    if(hResult == NOERROR && pMalloc)
    {
        pMalloc->Free(lpID);
        pMalloc->Release(); // added by Steve Lewis
    }
}
```

—Gabriel Praino

To have the dialog box display a default directory, you can add another variable to the dialog's constructor, as shown in the following example.

Pass the default path name as a string when the dialog is created. In the constructor, initialize the member variable m_strFolderPath to hold the default path name.

```
CGetFolderDlg::CGetFolderDlg(const char* szDefaultPath /*=NULL*/,
➥CWnd* pParent /*=NULL*/)
    : CDialog(CGetFolderDlg::IDD, pParent)
{
    //{{AFX_DATA_INIT(CGetFolderDlg)
    m_strFolderPath = _T(szDefaultPath);
    //}}AFX_DATA_INIT
}
```

This takes care of displaying the default folder in the dialog box. In order to get the Browse window to start at the selected default folder, modify the code as follows:

```
void CGetFolderDlg::OnGetfolder()
{
    CString strFolderPath;

    if (GetFolder(&strFolderPath,
        "Sample of  getting folder.",
        this->m_hWnd,
        NULL,
        m_strFolderPath ))  // ADD THIS
    {
        if (!strFolderPath.IsEmpty())
```

```
        {
            m_strFolderPath = strFolderPath;
            UpdateData(FALSE);
        }
    }
}
```

—kdurant

FROM THE FORUM

Question (Anarchi):

How can I verify that a folder exists?

Answer (Philip Nicoletti):

This shows how to use GetFileAttributes() to get information about a file or folder:

```
CString szPath("c:\\windows");

DWORD dwAttr = GetFileAttributes(szPath);

if (dwAttr == 0xFFFFFFFF)
{
    DWORD dwError = GetLastError();

    if (dwError == ERROR_FILE_NOT_FOUND)
    {
        // file not found
    }
    else if (dwError == ERROR_PATH_NOT_FOUND)
    {
        // path not found
    }
    else if (dwError == ERROR_ACCESS_DENIED)
    {
        // file or directory exists, but access is denied
    }
    else
    {
        // some other error has occurred
    }
}
else
{
    if (dwAttr & FILE_ATTRIBUTE_DIRECTORY)
    {
        // this is a directory
    }
    else
    {
        // this is an ordinary file
    }
}
```

SHFILEOPSTRUCT and the SHFileOperation

This article was contributed by John Z. Czopowik.

Environment: Windows 9x/NT/2K, Version 4.00 (or later) of Shell32.dll

Introduction

The function SHFileOperation enables you to copy, move, or delete a file system object. As you can see, this function takes as its sole parameter a pointer to a SHFILEOPSTRUCT structure (also shown in the following example).

```
// SHFileOperation syntax
WINSHELLAPI int WINAPI SHFileOperation(LPSHFILEOPSTRUCT lpFileOp);

// SHFILEOPSTRUCT layout
typedef struct _SHFILEOPSTRUCT{
  HWND          hwnd;
  UINT          wFunc;
  LPCSTR        pFrom;
  LPCSTR        pTo;
  FILEOP_FLAGS  fFlags;
  BOOL          fAnyOperationsAborted;
  LPVOID        hNameMappings;
  LPCSTR        lpszProgressTitle;
} SHFILEOPSTRUCT, FAR *LPSHFILEOPSTRUCT;
```

Unfortunately, despite this function's obvious usefulness, the Microsoft documentation is very ambiguous regarding the SHFILEOPSTRUCT structure and how to fill it out. In fact, there are several pitfalls when using this structure. Therefore, in this article, I'll attempt to address these issues so that those of you using this function for the first time can benefit from my experience as to how to take advantage of this very handy function.

Name Collision Resolution and the hNameMappings Member

hNameMappings is (almost always) an input-only member of SHFILEOPSTRUCT. In fact, after the call to SHFileOperation has returned successfully, this value will actually be set to NULL. The only time that this value will be changed by the SHFileOperation function is if you have specified the flags FOF_RENAMEONCOLLISION | FOF_WANTMAPPINGSHANDLE in the FILEOP_FLAGS member. Then if there were files that had to be renamed due to a name collision, assigning a name mapping object will contain their old and new names to the hNameMappings member.

This member can be treated as a void pointer to a continuous memory block. This memory block, in turn, can be treated as some kind of structure with int as a first member. The value of this integer indicates how many SHNAMEMAPPING structures follow. This way you can retrieve needed info.

File Name Retrieval

Another pitfall that you need to know about deals with retrieving the names of files. pszOldPath and pszNewPath members are declared as LPSTR. However, they are laid out as DWORD; not char! Therefore, any string-copying function available fails to successfully copy the path strings.

Sample Code

Here is a code snippet illustrating these issues. It can be done differently and is not posted for the purpose of code review. Treat it, rather, as a suggestion.

```
CString OldPath;
CString NewPath;
SHFILEOPSTRUCT shFileOp;

//after filling other members:
shFileOp.fFlags = FOF_WANTMAPPINGHANDLE
                ¦ FOF_RENAMEONCOLLISION;

shFileOp.lpszProgressTitle = "Test";
shFileOp.fAnyOperationsAborted = FALSE;

SHFileOperation(&shFileOp);

if(!shFileOp.hNameMappings)
 return;    //there is nothing further to do, no file collision

struct TMPMAP
{
int Indx;
SHNAMEMAPPING *pMapping;
};

//this will give you a  pointer to the beginning of the
//array of SHNAMEMAPPING structures
TMPMAP *pTmpMap = (TMPMAP*)shFileOp.hNameMappings;

for(int in = 0; in < pTmpMap->Indx; in++)
{
  SHNAMEMAPPING *pMap = &pTmpMap->pMapping[in];
```

```
//do the same thing for csOldPath
/*********************************************************/
char *buf = csNewPath.GetBufferSetLength(pMap->cchNewPath);

strcpy(buf, (char*)pMap->pszOldPath); //see the result of
this,

for(int dw = 0 ; dw < 2 * pMap->cchNewPath - 1 ; dw+=2)
{
*buf = (pMap->pszNewPath[dw]);
buf++;
}
buf = 0;
csNewPath.ReleaseBuffer();  //and see the result of this.
/*********************************************************/
}

//always free it if requested
SHFreeNameMappings(shFileOp.hNameMappings);
```

FROM THE FORUM

Question (Vinhuard):

If I use GetCurrentDirectory and am launching the application from the Start menu, the result is pointing to the desktop. How can I obtain the folder containing my application?

Answer (Philip Nicoletti):

Use this code to obtain the location of the application:

```
//
TCHAR szFullPath[MAX_PATH];
TCHAR szDir[_MAX_DIR];
TCHAR szDrive[_MAX_DRIVE];

// get applications full path
//
::GetModuleFileName(NULL,szFullPath,MAX_PATH);

// split into components
//
_splitpath(szFullPath,szDrive,szDir,NULL,NULL);

// store just the drive and path
//
CString strLaunched;
strLaunched.Format(_T("%s%s"),szDrive,szDir);
```

Tuning SHGetFileInfo for Optimum Performance

This article was contributed by Michael Harnad.

If you're writing programs to interface with the Windows Shell, chances are you'll eventually want to use the SHGetFileInfo function. This function retrieves information about an object in the file system, such as a file, a folder, a directory, or a drive root. However, this information may come at a heavy price.

Recently, I wrote an Explorer-style Open File dialog that used a CListCtrl. The CListCtrl was populated by enumerating the Windows Shell for a specified directory. I needed to retrieve the icon and the type name for each Shell object. The dialog performed fine, until I enumerated a directory with several thousand files. The total time required to fill the control ranged from 20–40 seconds. The code I used included the following snippet:

```
// get the shell object info.
SHGetFileInfo(path,
              0,
              &sfi,
              sizeof(SHFILEINFO),
              SHGFI_ICON | SHGFI_TYPENAME);
```

After using the Microsoft Profiler (within the development environment), it was obvious that a good majority of the time was spent executing the SHGetFileInfo command, a command I thought would execute fairly quickly. What I discovered is that using the above format of the command forced the program to access each file in the enumeration to obtain the requested information. This can be a performance hit when you're accessing several thousand files over a network. Microsoft's documentation does not clearly explain this.

The resolution to my problem came about after much research and a reading of Dino Esposito's *Visual C++ Windows Shell Programming*. I needed a way of obtaining the required information *without* accessing every file in the enumeration. The resolution required the following change to my code:

```
// get attributes of the shell object using its pidl.
psfFolder->GetAttributesOf(1, (LPCITEMIDLIST*)&pIDL, &dwFileAttr);

// set the SHGetFileInfo attribute based on the type
// of shell object.  We'll use this to force the
// SHGetFileInfo call to NOT access the shell object.
// (all we want is the icon & type name; the
// combination of the SHGFI_USEFILEATTRIBUTES flag
// and the FILE_ attribute will prevent any unnecessary
// access of the shell object).
if ((dwFileAttr & SFGAO_FOLDER) == SFGAO_FOLDER)
```

```
    attr = FILE_ATTRIBUTE_DIRECTORY;
  else
    attr = FILE_ATTRIBUTE_NORMAL;

  //  get the shell object info.
  SHGetFileInfo(path,
                attr,
                &sfi,
                sizeof(SHFILEINFO),
                SHGFI_USEFILEATTRIBUTES ¦ SHGFI_ICON ¦ SHGFI_TYPENAME);
```

By setting the attr variable to a valid FILE_ flag and adding the SHGFI_
USEFILEATTRIBUTES flag, I was able to avoid accessing each file in the
enumeration. By setting the SHGFI_USEFILEATTRIBUTES flag, I forced the
function to assume that the file passed in through the path variable exists. An
undocumented feature allows the function to use the extension and search the
registry for information about the icon and the type name. This simple change
reduced my total access time to 5–6 seconds. Although not up to par with
Explorer, it's a change I can live with.

10
Printing

In this chapter

In this chapter, you will find out how to provide printing support outside the document/view framework, which typically provides an application's printing support. It also shows you how to tweak the Print Preview toolbar to add some flair to your application.

- The article "Producing WYSIWYG Text Output" shows how you can easily display WYSIWYG text output on devices.
- "Improved Print Preview Toolbar" shows how you can easily make your Print Preview screen look like that of a "real" application.

Producing WYSIWYG Text Output

This article was contributed by Pavel Krupets.

Environment: VC6 SP5, WinNT Family, Win9X

Anyone who has ever tried to implement WYSIWYG text output has encountered the problem of how to draw text on different devices and in different resolutions in the same way—especially if they implemented text formatting.

Here is an explanation of how to implement WYSIWYG text output:

1. First of all, we have to retrieve the reference font data:

```
// Allocate memory to store font cached data
*ppFontInfo=new CTLFontInfo();

// Retrieve OUTLINETEXTMETRIC structure size
UINT nSize=GetOutlineTextMetrics(hDC,0,NULL);

if(!nSize)
  throw system_exception();
```

```
pTextMetrics=(OUTLINETEXTMETRIC*)new BYTE[nSize];

// Retrieve OUTLINETEXTMETRIC structure
if(!GetOutlineTextMetrics(hDC,nSize,pTextMetrics))
  throw system_exception();

// Get reference dc
// The best solution is to use device context with
// the largest resolution
if(!m_hReferenceDC)
{
  if(!CreateReferenceDC())
    leave;
}

// Retrieve device resolution
// Note: if you use GetDeviceCaps(LOGPIXELSY) with
// display device context it will return 96 or 120
// (depends on yours display settings). We have
// to calculate display resolution using next formula:
// GetDeviceCaps(HORZRES)/GetDeviceCaps(HORZSIZE)*25.4.
// Where: 25.4 - mm per inch.
double nLogPixelsY=GetDisplayLogPixelsY( m_hReferenceDC,
                                         m_bDisplay);

// Create reference font with height equal to EMSquare.
LOGFONT lReferenceFont=lFont;
lReferenceFont.lfHeight=-MulDiv(pTextMetrics->otmEMSquare,
                                nLogPixelsY,72);
HFONT hReferenceFont=CreateFontIndirect(&lReferenceFont);

if(!hReferenceFont)
  throw system_exception();

if((hOldFont=
   (HFONT)SelectObject(m_hReferenceDC,hReferenceFont))==NULL)
  throw system_exception();

// Retrieve reference font's OUTLINETEXTMETRIC structure size
UINT nSize1=GetOutlineTextMetrics(m_hReferenceDC,0,NULL);

if(nSize!=nSize1)
{
  delete pTextMetrics;
  pTextMetrics=(OUTLINETEXTMETRIC*)new BYTE[nSize1];
}
```

```
// Retrieve reference font's OUTLINETEXTMETRIC structure
if(!GetOutlineTextMetrics(m_hReferenceDC,nSize1,pTextMetrics))
  throw system_exception();

// Store text metrics inside cached object
// NOTE: We have to divide all metrics by nLogPixelsY to
// use them later with another device context
(*ppFontInfo)->FillInTextMetrics(pTextMetrics,nLogPixelsY);

// Retrieve characters widths
int nCharsCount=pTextMetrics->otmTextMetrics.tmLastChar-
            pTextMetrics->otmTextMetrics.tmFirstChar+1;

int* pCharWidths=new int[nCharsCount];

if(!GetCharWidth(m_hReferenceDC,
                 pTextMetrics->otmTextMetrics.tmFirstChar,
                 pTextMetrics->otmTextMetrics.tmLastChar,
                 pCharWidths))
  leave;

(*ppFontInfo)->FillInCharactersWidths(pCharWidths,nCharsCount,
                 pTextMetrics->otmTextMetrics.tmFirstChar,
                 nLogPixelsY);

// Retrieve kerning pairs
DWORD dwSize=GetKerningPairs(m_hReferenceDC,0,NULL);

if(dwSize)
{
  pKerningPairs=
        (KERNINGPAIR*)new BYTE[dwSize*sizeof(KERNINGPAIR)];

  if(!GetKerningPairs(m_hReferenceDC,dwSize,pKerningPairs))
    throw system_exception();

  (*ppFontInfo)->FillInKerningPairs( pKerningPairs,
                                     dwSize,
                                     nLogPixelsY);

  delete pKerningPairs;
  pKerningPairs=NULL;
}

delete pTextMetrics;
pTextMetrics=NULL;
```

2. We have to calculate the distances between letters using our current device context resolution.

```
TL_PAIR Pair(0,0);

long nCount=strlen(szText);

double fKerningValue=0.0;
double fCurrentWidth=0.0;
double fTotalWidth=0.0;

// This coefficient will be used to convert font
// height from EMSquare to required height
double fReferenceFont2LocalFont=m_fFontHeight/
        (double)pFontInfo->m_TextMetrics.otmEMSquare;
double fLogPixelsY=GetDisplayLogPixelsY(hDC,bDisplay);

for(long i=0;i < nCount;i++)
{
  // Do we need to correct distances between characters?
  if(bPerformKerning)
  {
    if(i < nCount-1)
    {
    // Adjust kerning
    Pair.m_nFirst=szText[i];
      Pair.m_nSecond=szText[i+1];
        fKerningValue=pFontInfo->m_KerningPairsArray[Pair];
    }
    else
      fKerningValue=0.0;
  }

  // Make sure we don't use incorrect (zero-sized) characters...
  _ASSERT(pFontInfo->m_CharactersWidthsArray[szText[i]]);

  // Calculate local character width
  fCurrentWidth=
        pFontInfo->m_CharactersWidthsArray[szText[i]]+
            fKerningValue;

  fCurrentWidth*=
        fLogPixelsY*fReferenceFont2LocalFont*fZoomFactor;

  CharactersWidthsArray.push_back(fCurrentWidth);

  fTotalWidth+=fCurrentWidth;
}
```

3. Now we can display our text on any devices we want using the ExtTextOut function.

```
ExtTextOut(hDC,x,y,ETO_CLIPPED,
          &Rect,
          m_TextLines[i]->GetTextLine(),
          m_TextLines[i]->GetTextLineLength(),
          m_TextLines[i]->GetWidthsArray());
```

This method has one disadvantage: We can use only OpenType/TrueType fonts.

I haven't implemented print preview because I didn't have time to do so. Source code has been written for demo purposes only, and I didn't optimize it.

You can find basic information about fonts and text in the book *Windows Graphics Programming: Win32 GDI and DirectDraw* by Feng Yuan.

FROM THE FORUM

Question (Trouble):

How can I determine the orientation of the printer selected by the user just prior to printing something so that I can adjust my printout accordingly?

Answer (BMeister):

In your OnBeginPrinting, you can use the following code to determine, or force, the orientation:

```
//set the orientation to landscape
//
DEVMODE* pDevMode = pInfo->m_pPD->GetDevMode();

if(pDevMode->dmOrientation != DMORIENT_LANDSCAPE)
{
        pDevMode->dmOrientation = DMORIENT_LANDSCAPE;
}
```

Improved Print Preview Toolbar

This article was contributed by Robin J. Leatherbarrow.

Print Preview is an extremely useful part of the MFC Doc/View architecture. However, the appearance of the Print Preview toolbar leaves a lot to be desired and has not been updated since Print Preview was first added to MFC. The usual MFC-supplied preview button bar is shown in Figure 10.1.

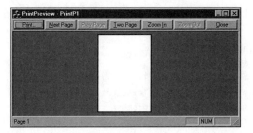

Figure 10.1

Compare this with the replacement toolbar described in this article (see Figure 10.2).

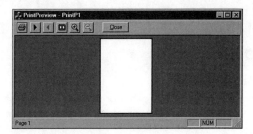

Figure 10.2

The replacement toolbar functions in exactly the same way as the default button bar, but has a more modern appearance. The normal text-based buttons are replaced with owner-drawn ones that use bitmaps for the various actions. ToolTips are available for the bitmapped buttons to help users make their selection.

To use the improved version requires only a few simple steps:

1. Add a few bitmap, string, and dialog resources for the replacement toolbar (see the demo project for details).

2. Add a new CMyPreviewView class to control the preview toolbar and a CMappedBitmapButton class to handle the buttons used. (Source files are CMyPreviewView.cpp and CMappedBitmapButton.cpp.)

3. Add a message handler inside your view class to produce Print Preview using the enhanced toolbar:

```
void CYourView::OnFileImprovedprintpreview()
{
    // need to use CMyPreviewView class
    CPrintPreviewState* pState = new CPrintPreviewState;
```

```
    if (!DoPrintPreview(IDD_PREVIEW, this, RUNTIME_CLASS(CMyPreviewView),
➥pState))
    {
        TRACE0("Error: OnFileImprovedprintpreview failed.\n");
        AfxMessageBox(AFX_IDP_COMMAND_FAILURE);
        delete pState; // preview failed to initialize, delete State now
    }
}
```

The demo project (VC6) shows what needs to be done and includes the various resources that must be added. The demo program allows you to compare the default and improved Print Preview toolbars in a simple application built around a CEditView window.

FROM THE FORUM

Question (cdrom):

When trying to scale my output to the printer, it is appearing at the incorrect scale. How can I correctly print a 40mm×40mm area to the printer?

Answer (Roger Allen):

When printing to the Device Context, make sure you are using the DC->GetDeviceCaps() with LOGICALPIXELSX and LOGICALPIXELSY to get the correct printer limits.

Then you will need to convert the results from imperial inches. In other words, you will need to convert mm->inches->pixels.

11

System

In this chapter

This chapter describes various system-related features not covered in other specific locations, or features relating specifically to the host system on which the application is running.

- "Process and Module Enumeration Class" details a way to enumerate and list all currently executing processes, modules and device drivers on a system.

- "Getting the Module (exe) Filename from an HWND" describes how to determine the name of a running executable from a window handle.

- "A NotQuiteNullDacl Class" deals with some fundamental security issues on NT class operating systems, and a unique way to solve some of these issues.

- "Shared Memory Inter-Process Communication (IPC)" describes a method of inter-process communication using shared memory to pass data very quickly between applications on a local machine.

Process and Module Enumeration Class

This article was contributed by JaeKi Lee.

This article presents a class (CPSAPI) which can be used to enumerate all of the processes, modules, and even device drivers currently executing on either a Windows 9x or Windows NT machine.

As you can see in the provided demo application, this class is extremely easy to use. All you need to do is the following:

- Derive a class from the CPSAPI base class.
- Implement the derived class' OnXXX method that correlates to the desired function:
  - virtual BOOL OnDeviceDriver(LPVOID lpImageBase);

- virtual BOOL OnProcess(LPCTSTR lpszFileName, DWORD ProcessID);
- virtual BOOL OnModule(HMODULE hModule, LPCTSTR lpszModuleName, LPCTSTR lpszPathName);
- Instantiate your object.
- Call the object's Initialize method.
- Call the desired enumeration function:
    - BOOL EnumDeviceDrivers(void);
    - BOOL EnumProcesses(void);
    - BOOL EnumProcessModules(DWORD dwProcessId);

If this sounds a bit difficult, not to worry. A demo application I included with this article illustrates how to do all this.

Getting the Module (exe) Filename from an HWND

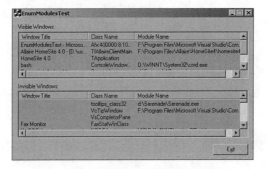

Figure 11.1

This article was contributed by Mike Ryan.

Environment: Windows 2000, Visual C++ 6

After searching for an article on how to find an executable name from an HWND and coming up dry, I decided to write one. First off I would like to say thanks to Jeff Kay for finding the PSAPI stuff on MSDN. :) Also, I would like to say that this code will only work with Windows NT/2000.

In order to compile this project, you must link in PSAPI.lib, which comes on the MSDN CDs. (It also is included in the project zip file, not the source zip file.) If you use this in any projects, PSAPI.dll will need to be supplied with the project since it is not packaged with the OS yet.

I am relatively new to writing for CodeGuru, so here goes... On to the good stuff...

This class will basically use the EnumWindows function to get a handle to all the running windows. This function will be called from the Process() function. The Process function takes an integer called filter. This parameter can be ORed together to create a filter list of windows you do not want to include.

```
#define FILTER_VISIBLEONLY      1 // not compatible with NONVISIBLEONLY
#define FILTER_NONVISIBLEONLY   2 // not compatible with VISIBLEONLY
#define FILTER_PARENTONLY       4 // not compatible with CHILDONLY
#define FILTER_CHILDONLY        8 // not compatible with PARENTONLY
#define FILTER_APPS            16 // filter out programs by class name on
                                  // the exclude list, use AddExclusion
```

The FILTER_VISIBLEONLY will filter out any invisible windows. The FILTER_NONVISIBLEONLY will, of course, filter out any visible windows. The FITLER_PARENTONLY will filter all child windows and get only the parent windows. The FILTER_CHILDONLY will filter out anything that is not a child window. The FILTER_APPS will filter any applications based on their classname. You can add apps to this exclusion list with the function AddExclusion().

The FILTER_VISIBLEONLY is not compatible with FILTER_NONVISIBLEONLY. As well, the FILTER_PARENTONLY is not compatible with the FILTER_CHILDONLY.

Usage

```
CEnumWinModules em;
em.AddExclusion("AFX:400000:8:10011:0:2ed014d"); // msdev's classname

// this will filter all invisible non-parent and the msdev program.
em.Process(FILTER_VISIBLEONLY | FILTER_APPS | FILTER_PARENTONLY);

for (int i=0;i<em.GetWindowCount();i++)
{
 TRACE3("Title: %s\tClass: %s\tExe: %s\n",
  em.GetWindowTitle(i),
  em.GetClassName(i),
  em.GetModuleName(i));
}
```

I hope you guys found this article useful. This is my first attempt at writing for CodeGuru and I apologize if I forgot to do something or this topic was already covered. :)

Comments are definitely welcome.

FROM THE FORUM

Question (cksiow):

How can I get the instance handle from a specified window handle?

Answer (Alex Fedotov):

To get the instance handle of a window, you can use the GetWindowLong call:

```
GetWindowLong(hWnd, GWL_HINSTANCE);
```

Bear in mind that this is only valid for windows belonging to the current process. If you attempt this with a window handle belonging to another process, you will obtain a value, but it will be meaningless outside of the owning process' context, as it essentially refers to a base address at which the module was loaded, which is not valid for external processes.

A NotQuiteNullDacl Class

This article was contributed by Anne Gunn.

Environment: VC6, WinNT4, Win2000, WinXP

Default Security Is Not Always Good Enough

Many of the Win32 API functions, specifically those that create objects such as files, mutexes, and pipes, require a pointer to a SECURITY_ATTRIBUTES structure. Most of us program for a long time before we ever have to code anything other than a NULL for that pointer. The NULL pointer makes the object uninheritable and indicates that the created object should be assigned a default security descriptor. That default security is just the security associated with the creation process, and that is sufficient for most purposes.

However, if you try to share an object created this way between, say, a Service and a regular App, or, now that we have XP, between two logon sessions on the same workstation where the logged on users have different access rights, the objects created with default security begin to fail you right and left.

Take the case of a mutex that you are trying to use to let a Service and an App be aware of each other's existence. Say the App is used to configure the Service. The App needs to work a little differently if the Service is running than if the Service is not. And the Service shouldn't start at all if the App is running, on the theory that its configuration parameters may be in an inconsistent state.

Traditionally each module uses a CreateMutex call to open a handle to a named mutex. If that call succeeds, each module then calls GetLastError to check for ERROR_ALREADY_EXISTS. If the App sees that it is not the original creator of the mutex, it knows the Service is running and modifies its behavior accordingly. If the Service sees that it is not the original creator of the mutex, it just terminates.

The usual code to do this is pretty straightforward. Each module has a section that looks something like

```
HANDLE hMutex = CreateMutex( NULL, FALSE, "MyMutex" );
DWORD dwErr = GetLastError();

if ( hMutex != NULL )
{
   // the call succeeded
   // but is it a new mutex or an existing one?
   if ( dwErr != ERROR_ALREADY_EXISTS )
   {
      // we actually created the mutex
      // free to run in normal mode
   }
   else
   {
      // we got a handle to an existing mutex,
      // take appropriate action
   }
}
else
{
   // call to create the mutex failed
   // use the dwErr value to see why
}
```

This is entirely ordinary code and always works fine between two copies of an App or two different Apps running in the same login session. However, if you test it using a Service and an App, you see that, if the Service is already running, the App's call to CreateMutex fails with a GetLastError result of 5, access denied. A little digging in books or MSDN reveals the problem. The Service is running under the LocalSystem account, so when it creates the mutex with default security, it implicitly denies the App permission to open a handle to the mutex since the App is running under a user logon.

The Null Dacl Solution

This forces you to finally confront the documentation on the SECURITY_ATTRIBUTES structure and the all-important Security Descriptor it points to. After reading a bit and giving your eyes time to stop spinning, the most likely solution you'll hit upon is to build a SecurityDescriptor with a Null Discretionary Access Control List (Dacl). Using a Null Dacl allows anyone any access to the object created and certainly solves the problem at hand. And it is *simple to code*; you can read about it, code it up, and test it in a mortal amount of time.

The code now looks like:

```
// declare and initialize a security attributes structure
SECURITY_ATTRIBUTES MutexAttributes;
ZeroMemory( &MutexAttributes, sizeof(MutexAttributes) );
MutexAttributes.nLength = sizeof( MutexAttributes );
MutexAttributes.bInheritHandle = FALSE; // object uninheritable


// declare and initialize a security descriptor
SECURITY_DESCRIPTOR SD;
BOOL bInitOk = InitializeSecurityDescriptor( &SD,
                          SECURITY_DESCRIPTOR_REVISION );
if ( bInitOk )
{
    // give the security descriptor a Null Dacl
    // done using the  "TRUE, (PACL)NULL" here
    BOOL bSetOk = SetSecurityDescriptorDacl( &SD,
                                      TRUE,
                                      (PACL)NULL,
                                      FALSE );

    if ( bSetOk )
    {
        // Make the security attributes point
        // to the security descriptor
        MutexAttributes.lpSecurityDescriptor = &SD;

        // use the attributes with the Null Dacl to
        // create the mutex
        hMutex = CreateMutex( &MutexAttributes,
                          FALSE,
                          MutexName );
        dwMutexErr = GetLastError();

        ... same logic as before

    }
    else

}
else
    // Initialize failed, use GetLastError to find out why
```

The problem is that using the Null Dacl is bad practice. By allowing anyone any access, it conceivably allows some other process to hijack your object, change its accesses out from underneath you, and disable your application(s) or some part of the file system.

Sound far-fetched? Well, it probably is. And, despite Microsoft's dire warnings, which have gotten louder and more strident with its recent emphasis on secure programming, lots of good programmers have been using the Null Dacl approach for a long time and the sky has not yet fallen.

Still, the danger of just coding up a Null Dacl for your little app-that-no-one-would-bother-to-hijack is that we all borrow code all the time, usually when we are in a hurry. The next time you need to solve this problem, perhaps for a more critical app, or the day the junior programmer down the hall needs an example of how to get around it, the code you write today will get propagated. And generations of code hence, it could just be the centerpiece of an embarrassing incident.

FROM THE FORUM

Question (DGuindon):

I am trying to change the Dacl of all files and folders under a certain folder location. My goal is to set a Null Dacl for all of these files and folders. Is there an easy way to achieve this?

Answer (Alex Fedotov):

Using the SetNamedSecurityInfo call, you can modify both files and folders, simply by passing the path.

NotQuiteNullDacl to the Rescue

So, what we need is an equally easy to use but more secure Dacl, the NotQuiteNullDacl. This Dacl explicitly grants all accesses to the Everyone group (which is essentially what the Null Dacl does) but filters that by first denying Everyone access to the WRITE_DAC and WRITE_OWNER permissions. This means that all users of the object except the original creator get all of the permissions they need to use the object and none of the permissions needed to hijack it.

There are examples of coding for this Dacl lying around, but they are not particularly easy to find. The "Ask Dr. Gui #49" MSDN article has a pretty straightforward discussion and coding. The Richter/Clark *Server-Side Applications* book (see "References") has a much more general discussion and coding in Chapter 10, pp 458–460, but the NotQuiteNullDacl code is pretty well buried in the example.

I've created a wrapper class, called NotQuiteNullDacl, to package the coding and make the better Dacl almost as easy to use as the Null Dacl. The full class is included in the sample code files. The code jumps through some hoops to create a SID for the Everyone group (m_pEveryoneSid) and to initialize the Dacl (m_pDacl). But the critical code is

```
BOOL bAddAce;

// Add an ace that denies WRITE_OWNER and WRITE_DAC to
// 'everyone' which denies everyone but the owner of the
// associated object access to the object's security.
```

```
bAddAce =
  AddAccessDeniedAce( m_pDACL,  // the acl to add the ace to
             ACL_REVISION,     // must be ACL_REVISION
             WRITE_OWNER ¦ WRITE_DAC, // accesses to deny
             m_pEveryoneSid ); // SID to be denied (everyone)
if ( bAddAce )
{
   // Add an ace that gives 'everyone' all accesses
   // to the object. By itself, the bit of code below
   // would be the moral equivalent of a NULL DACL --
   // it gives all rights to everyone.  But, because
   // accesses are evaluating in order of their placement
   // in the DACL the DeniedACE above acts as a filter,
   // before this can be evaluated.
   bAddAce =
     AddAccessAllowedAce( m_pDACL, // the acl to add the ace to
                 ACL_REVISION, // must be ACL_REVISION
                 GENERIC_ALL,  // accesses to allow
                 m_pEveryoneSid ); // SID to be allowed
   if ( bAddAce )
   {
      bAddedOk = true;
   }
}

if ( !bAddedOk )        .
{
   // use GetLastError() to find out why the add failed
}
```

Using the NotQuiteNullDacl Class

Once you've included the class header, using the NotQuiteNullDacl is pretty straight-forward. The setup for the CreateMutex call becomes

```
// create the not-quite-null-dacl
NotQuiteNullDacl Dacl;
bool bDaclOk = Dacl.Create();

if ( bDaclOk)
{
   bool bSetupOk = false;

   // declare and initialize a security attributes structure
   SECURITY_ATTRIBUTES MutexAttributes;
   ZeroMemory( &MutexAttributes, sizeof(MutexAttributes) );
   MutexAttributes.nLength = sizeof( MutexAttributes );
   MutexAttributes.bInheritHandle = FALSE; // object uninheritable

   // declare and initialize a security descriptor
   SECURITY_DESCRIPTOR SD;
   BOOL bInitOk = InitializeSecurityDescriptor( &SD,
```

```
                        SECURITY_DESCRIPTOR_REVISION );
    if ( bInitOk )
    {
        // assign the dacl to it
        BOOL bSetOk = SetSecurityDescriptorDacl( &SD,
                                                 TRUE,
                                                 Dacl.GetPDACL(),
                                                 FALSE );

        if ( bSetOk )
        {
            // Make the security attributes point to
            //the security descriptor
            MutexAttributes.lpSecurityDescriptor = &SD;
            bSetupOk = true;
        }
    }

    if ( bSetupOk )
    {
        // use the security attributes to call CreateMutex
    }
    else
    {
        // the setup failed somehow, use GetLastError()
        // to find out why
    }
}
else
{
    // nqnDacl create failed,
    // use Dacl.GetErr() to find out how
}
```

Side Effects? There Are a Few

Using the NotQuiteNullDacl is not exactly the same as using a Null Dacl. For example, we're used to using CreateMutex either to create a new mutex or to open a handle to an existing mutex. But CreateMutex implicitly asks for MUTEX_ALL_ACCESS on the handle to be opened. If the Mutex was created in one logon session, say by a Service, with the NotQuiteNullDacl, another process won't be able to get MUTEX_ALL_ACCESS since WRITE_DAC and WRITE_OWNER have been explicitly denied. The second process *can* use OpenMutex, asking for SYNCHRONIZE permission, to determine the existence of the mutex.

So now, rather than issuing a CreateMutex call and then having to check the error status when it returns a valid handle, which has always been a little jarring to me, you first try to open the mutex. If you can open it, you know it already exists and can act accordingly. If you can't open it, you can create it. The result is rather more readable code and a much higher level of security in the object created.

References

- Ask Dr. Gui #49

- *Programming Server-Side Applications for Microsoft Windows 2000*, Richter/Clark, Microsoft Press 2000

Shared Memory Inter-Process Communication (IPC)

This article was contributed by Peter Hendrix.

Figure 11.2

Environment: Windows NT 4 SP6, Visual C++ 6 SP3

There are many forms of IPC. I have made extensive use of named pipe communication; however, this is in many cases overkill when you only need IPC within the system. Shared memory can be the solution.

I have made this code as much standard C++ compliant as I could for the simple reason that our company will probably port it to Unix. Another reason is that the code is a little bit faster this way. Porting it to genuine MFC will not be a problem since you only have to change all strings into CStrings, mutexes to Cmutexes, and events to CEvents, this might improve the readability of the code.

The most important feature of this class is that I have tried to make it as much connection oriented as I could. When the "other party" drops the connection, this will be detected by the "current party" as soon as the "Write," "WriteToQueue," or "Read" function is called. When this happens, the "current party" must close its instance and reopen it in order to wait for the "other party" to reconnect.

Another very important feature is that it is duplex. The class creates two shared memory pools to create a duplex connection. It is possible to change the class to use one shared memory pool; however, this would be more time inefficient since we should then have to "mutex" the shared memory access which is now automatically done by a set of named events for each shared memory pool.

FROM THE FORUM

Question (Feng Yuan):

How can I place variables in a shared memory space between several instances of my application?

Answer (Sam Hobbs):

With the following code, when there are two instances of the application running, pressing a key in one process, changes the value of c in the other instance:

```
#include <conio.h>

// - - - - - - - - -
#pragma data_seg(".sdata")
char c='X';
#pragma data_seg()
#pragma comment(linker, "/section:.sdata,rws")
// - - - - - - - - -

int main(int argc, char *argv[], char *envp[])
{
    while (!_kbhit())
    {
        _putch;
    }

    c = _getch();
    _putch(c);
    _putch('\n');

    return 0;
}
```

Shared memory access is controlled by two events for each memory pool: a DataWritten event and a DataRead event.

The "Read" function will wait for the DataWritten event and set the DataRead event; the "Write" function will wait for the DataRead event and set the DataWritten event. This way no simultaneous access to the shared memory is possible.

I have chosen to pack the whole concept into one simple, easy-to-use class that consists of a header file only. There are five public functions in the class:

- CSharedMemory::Open(char* sName, int nDataSize, int nTimeOut = INFINITE)
- CSharedMemory::Close()
- CSharedMemory::Write(void* pData, int nDataSize, DWORD dwTimeOut)
- CSharedMemory::WriteToQueue(void* pData, int nDataSize)
- CSharedMemory::Read(void* pData, int nDataSize, DWORD dwTimeOut)

When you look at the sample code, it will demonstrate the simplicity of the class.

To create a duplex connection between two programs, you must create an instance of the class with the same name in each program. Then you must call the "Open" function for both instances, the order does not matter. Now you can safely use the communication functions "Write," "WriteToQueue," and "Read."

The "WriteToQueue" function was created to provide a nonblocking "Write" function. A thread is created to read the queue and call the CSharedMemory::Write() function. In this way, a program can write to the shared memory without having to wait for the other-party program to process the data that was provided.

Following is the complete source code for the class.

```
#include "process.h"

class CSharedMemory
{
private:
 class CWriteQueue
 {
  // This class is the queue, it contains a pointer to
  // a data block and a pointer to the next queue item.
  friend class CSharedMemory;

  private:
   CWriteQueue(int nDataSize)
   {
    pData = new BYTE[nDataSize];
    pNext = NULL;
   };

   ~CWriteQueue()
   {
    delete [] pData;
   };
   void  *pData;
   CWriteQueue *pNext;
  };

 public:
  enum
  {
   // Return values of the class-functions.
   MEM_ERROR_UNKNOWN  = -1,
   MEM_SUCCESS        = 0,
   MEM_ERROR_CLOSED   = 1,
   MEM_ERROR_TIMEOUT  = 2,
   MEM_ERROR_OTHERPARTY = 3,
   MEM_ERROR_DATASIZE  = 4
```

```
};
CSharedMemory()
{
 m_nOtherInstanceID = 0;
 m_nInstanceID  = 0;
 // Create an event that indicates wether the connection
 // is open or not.
 m_hClosed  = CreateEvent(NULL, TRUE, TRUE, NULL);
 m_hDataWrit[0] = NULL;
 m_hDataWrit[1] = NULL;
 m_hDataRead[0] = NULL;
 m_hDataRead[1] = NULL;
 m_hDataInQueue = NULL;
 m_hQueueMutex = NULL;
};
virtual ~CSharedMemory()
{
 Close();
 CloseHandle(m_hClosed);
};
bool Open(char* sName, int nDataSize, int nTimeOut = INFINITE)
{
 m_pFirst = NULL;

 // The connection must be closed before it can be opened.
 if (WaitForSingleObject(m_hClosed, 0) == WAIT_OBJECT_0)
 {
  // The name may not exceed MAX_PATH, we substract 10
  // because we add some strings to the name in some code.
  if (strlen(sName) != 0 && strlen(sName) < MAX_PATH - 10)
  {
   // The datasize must be larger than 0.
   if (nDataSize > 0)
   {
    // The following mutexes can indicate 4 things:
    // - No instance of this shared memory class was created.
    // - The first instance of this class was created.
    // - The second instance of this shared memory class
    // -    was created.
    // - Both instances were created.
    char sMutex0 [MAX_PATH];
    char sMutex1 [MAX_PATH];
    strcpy(sMutex0 , sName);
    strcpy(sMutex1 , sName);
    strcat(sMutex0 , "Mutex0");
    strcat(sMutex1 , "Mutex1");
    m_hSharedMemoryMutex[0] = CreateMutex(NULL, FALSE, sMutex0);
    m_hSharedMemoryMutex[1] = CreateMutex(NULL, FALSE, sMutex1);
    if (m_hSharedMemoryMutex[0] && m_hSharedMemoryMutex[1])
    {
```

```
// Only two instances of this class (with this name)
// may reside on one system. These will be referred to
// as 'm_nInstanceID and m_nOtherInstanceID'
HANDLE hWait[2] = {m_hSharedMemoryMutex[0],
 m_hSharedMemoryMutex[1]};

DWORD dwResult = WaitForMultipleObjects(2, hWait,
 FALSE, 0);

if (dwResult == WAIT_OBJECT_0
¦¦ dwResult == (WAIT_OBJECT_0 + 1))
{
 if ((m_nInstanceID = dwResult - WAIT_OBJECT_0) == 0)
  m_nOtherInstanceID = 1;
 else
  m_nOtherInstanceID = 0;

 char sName0 [MAX_PATH];
 char sName1 [MAX_PATH];
 strcpy(sName0 , sName);
 strcpy(sName1 , sName);
 strcat(sName0 , "0");
 strcat(sName1 , "1");

 // We will use two shared memory pools to
 // provide duplex communication.
 if ((m_hSharedMemory[0]
 = CreateFileMapping( (HANDLE)0xFFFFFFFF,
            NULL,
            PAGE_READWRITE,
            0,
            sizeof(int) + nDataSize,
            sName0)) != NULL
            &&
  (m_hSharedMemory[1]
 = CreateFileMapping( (HANDLE)0xFFFFFFFF,
            NULL,
            PAGE_READWRITE,
            0,
            sizeof(int) + nDataSize,
            sName1)) != NULL)
 {
  bool bFileMappingAlreadyExists =
   (GetLastError() == ERROR_ALREADY_EXISTS);

  // Now map a pointer to the size tag in
  // the shared memory.
  m_pSize = (int*)MapViewOfFile( m_hSharedMemory[0],
         FILE_MAP_ALL_ACCESS,
         0,
```

```
                  0,
                  sizeof(int));
if (m_pSize)
{
 bool bSharedMemorySizeOk = false;
 if (bFileMappingAlreadyExists)
 {
  // We will check if the size of the memory block
  // is of the same size as the block that was already
  // allocated by another instance of the shared
  // memory class. The size of the memory block is
  // saved in the first integer at the specified shared
  // memory address.
  if (*m_pSize == nDataSize)
   bSharedMemorySizeOk = true;
 }
 else
 {
  // The memory was not allocated by another instance
  // so we have the honors to allocate it. This means
  // also that we should set the size of the memory
  // that we have allocated in the first integer of
  // the shared memory space.
  *m_pSize = nDataSize;
  bSharedMemorySizeOk = true;
 }
 if (bSharedMemorySizeOk)
 {
  m_pSharedMemory[0] =
    (BYTE*)MapViewOfFile(m_hSharedMemory[0],
                         FILE_MAP_ALL_ACCESS,
                         0,
                         0,
                         nDataSize);

  m_pSharedMemory[1] =
    (BYTE*)MapViewOfFile( m_hSharedMemory[1],
                         FILE_MAP_ALL_ACCESS,
                         0,
                         0,
                         nDataSize);

  if (m_pSharedMemory[0] && m_pSharedMemory[1])
  {
   // Move the pointer a little further so that it
   // does not point to the size tag, but to the
   // address of the data that we want to share.
   m_pSharedMemory[0] += sizeof(int);
   m_pSharedMemory[1] += sizeof(int);
```

```
// The following events make sure that data can
// only be read when data was written and
// vise versa.
char sDataWrit0  [MAX_PATH];
char sDataWrit1  [MAX_PATH];
char sDataRead0  [MAX_PATH];
char sDataRead1  [MAX_PATH];
strcpy(sDataWrit0 , sName);
strcpy(sDataWrit1 , sName);
strcpy(sDataRead0 , sName);
strcpy(sDataRead1 , sName);
strcat(sDataWrit0 , "DataWrit0");
strcat(sDataWrit1 , "DataWrit1");
strcat(sDataRead0 , "DataRead0");
strcat(sDataRead1 , "DataRead1");

m_hDataWrit[0] = CreateEvent(NULL,
 FALSE, FALSE, sDataWrit0);

m_hDataWrit[1] = CreateEvent(NULL, FALSE,
 FALSE, sDataWrit1);

m_hDataRead[0] = CreateEvent(NULL, FALSE,
 TRUE, sDataRead0);

m_hDataRead[1] = CreateEvent(NULL, FALSE,
 TRUE, sDataRead1);

if (m_hDataWrit[0]
&& m_hDataWrit[1]
&& m_hDataRead[0]
&& m_hDataRead[1])
{
 m_hSecondInstanceAvailable =
  CreateEvent(NULL, FALSE, FALSE, sName);

 if (m_hSecondInstanceAvailable)
 {
  if (m_nInstanceID == 0)
  {
   // We are the first instance, wait for the second
   // instance to come this far, then we can assume
   // that the connection is fully open.
   if (WaitForSingleObject(m_hSecondInstanceAvailable,
   nTimeOut) == WAIT_OBJECT_0)
   {
    CloseHandle(m_hSecondInstanceAvailable);
    ResetEvent(m_hClosed);
    m_hQueueMutex = CreateMutex(NULL, FALSE, NULL);
```

```cpp
      m_hDataInQueue = CreateEvent(NULL, FALSE,
        FALSE, NULL);

      m_hQueueThread =
        (HANDLE)_beginthread(QueueThread, 0, this);

      return true;
    }
  }
  else if (m_nInstanceID == 1)
  {
    // We are the second instance, signal the other
    // instance that we have come this far.
    // Immediately wait 0 seconds for the event,
    // if it is still signaled we know that the other
    // instance was not waiting, the connection
    // has failed.
    SetEvent(m_hSecondInstanceAvailable);
    if (WaitForSingleObject(m_hSecondInstanceAvailable,0)
    == WAIT_TIMEOUT)
    {
     CloseHandle(m_hSecondInstanceAvailable);
     ResetEvent(m_hClosed);

      m_hQueueMutex = CreateMutex(NULL, FALSE,
        NULL);

      m_hDataInQueue = CreateEvent(NULL, FALSE,
        FALSE, NULL);

      m_hQueueThread =
        (HANDLE)_beginthread(QueueThread, 0, this);

      return true;
    }
  }
   CloseHandle(m_hSecondInstanceAvailable);
  }
  else
  {
   // We could not create the required event.
  }
  }
  else
  {
   // We could not create any event handles.
  }
  UnmapViewOfFile(m_pSharedMemory[0]);
  UnmapViewOfFile(m_pSharedMemory[1]);
}
```

```
      else
      {
        // We could not get a pointer to the actual data.
      }
    }
    else
    {
      // The datasize of the already allocated memory,
      // and the size of this instance do not match.
    }
    UnmapViewOfFile(m_pSize);
  }
  else
  {
    // We could not map to the integer that
    // contains the size of the memory block.
  }
  CloseHandle(m_hSharedMemory[0]);
  CloseHandle(m_hSharedMemory[1]);
}
else
{
  // The memory handles could not be created.
}
}
else
{
  // There was no mutex available, this can mean
  // that there are already two instances of this
  // object with the same name in use on this system.
}
CloseHandle(m_hSharedMemoryMutex[0]);
CloseHandle(m_hSharedMemoryMutex[1]);
}
else
{
  // The mutexes could not be created.
}
}
else
{
  // The datasize is not > 0.
}
}
else
{
  // The name of the shared memory is not valid,
  // or the datasize is not larger than 0.
}
}
else
```

```
 {
  // This instance is already open.
 }
 return false;
};
void Close()
{
 if (WaitForSingleObject(m_hClosed, 0) == WAIT_TIMEOUT)
 {
  // Indicate that this instance is closed
  SetEvent(m_hClosed);

  // Release your own mutex. This will auitomatically signal
  // the other instance of this class that this instance broke
  // the connection.
  ReleaseMutex(m_hSharedMemoryMutex[m_nInstanceID]);

  // The writequeue may still contain elements, empty
  // it.
  EmptyWriteQueue();

  WaitForSingleObject(m_hQueueThread, INFINITE);
  CloseHandle(m_hQueueMutex);
  CloseHandle(m_hDataInQueue);
  m_hQueueMutex = NULL;
  m_hDataInQueue = NULL;

  // Cleanup some stuff.
  CloseHandle(m_hDataWrit[0]);
  CloseHandle(m_hDataWrit[1]);
  CloseHandle(m_hDataRead[0]);
  CloseHandle(m_hDataRead[1]);
  m_hDataWrit[0] = NULL;
  m_hDataWrit[1] = NULL;
  m_hDataRead[0] = NULL;
  m_hDataRead[1] = NULL;

  UnmapViewOfFile(m_pSize);

  m_pSharedMemory[0] -= sizeof(int);
  m_pSharedMemory[1] -= sizeof(int);
  UnmapViewOfFile(m_pSharedMemory[0]);
  UnmapViewOfFile(m_pSharedMemory[1]);

  CloseHandle(m_hSharedMemory[0]);
  CloseHandle(m_hSharedMemory[1]);

  CloseHandle(m_hSharedMemoryMutex[0]);
  CloseHandle(m_hSharedMemoryMutex[1]);
```

```
 }
};
int Write(void *pData, int nDataSize, DWORD dwTimeOut)
{
 // The 'Write' and 'WriteToQueue' functions can be
 // used promiscously.

 // This function writes to the shared memory pool, it
 // can only write to that pool if existing data in the
 // pool has been read by the other instance of this class.
 // If this function returns MEM_ERROR_OTHERPARTY, the
 // calling process should close the connection and re-open
 // it to create a new valid connection.
 HANDLE hWait[3];
 hWait[0] = m_hClosed;
 hWait[1] = m_hSharedMemoryMutex[m_nOtherInstanceID];
 hWait[2] = m_hDataRead[m_nOtherInstanceID];

 DWORD dwWaitResult = WaitForMultipleObjects(3, hWait,
  FALSE, dwTimeOut);

 switch(dwWaitResult)
 {
 case WAIT_OBJECT_0 + 2:
  if (nDataSize > *m_pSize)
   return MEM_ERROR_DATASIZE;
  // Data was read from the shared memory pool,
  // write new data and notify any listener that
  // new data was written.
  memcpy(m_pSharedMemory[m_nOtherInstanceID],
   pData, nDataSize);

  SetEvent(m_hDataWrit[m_nOtherInstanceID]);
  return MEM_SUCCESS;
 case WAIT_OBJECT_0:
  // The close function of this instance was called.
  return MEM_ERROR_CLOSED;
 case WAIT_OBJECT_0 + 1:
  // The other instance closed.
  // Since we locked the mutex by waiting for it, we
  // have to release it again.
  ReleaseMutex(m_hSharedMemoryMutex[m_nOtherInstanceID]);
  return MEM_ERROR_OTHERPARTY;
 case WAIT_ABANDONED_0 + 1:
  // The other instance left without a trace, this
  // means probably that it crashed.
  // Since we locked the mutex by waiting for it,
  // we have to release it again.
  ReleaseMutex(m_hSharedMemoryMutex[m_nOtherInstanceID]);
  return MEM_ERROR_OTHERPARTY;
 case WAIT_FAILED:
  if (!m_hDataRead[m_nOtherInstanceID])
```

```
  return MEM_ERROR_CLOSED;
  // I don't know wat happened, you should
  // call 'GetLastError()'.
  return MEM_ERROR_UNKNOWN;
 case WAIT_TIMEOUT:
  // There was a timeout, the other party has not yet
  // read previous data.
  return MEM_ERROR_TIMEOUT;
 }
 return MEM_ERROR_UNKNOWN;
}
int WriteToQueue(void *pData, int nDataSize)
{
 // The 'Write' and 'WriteToQueue' functions can be
 // used promiscously.

 // This function is somewhat the same as the previous
 // function, however, this function is non-blocking.
 // As long as the connection is valid this function
 // can write new data into a queue. The queue is read
 // by a thread that calls the previous 'Write' function.
 HANDLE hWait[3];
 hWait[0] = m_hClosed;
 hWait[1] = m_hSharedMemoryMutex[m_nOtherInstanceID];
 hWait[2] = m_hQueueMutex;
 switch (WaitForMultipleObjects(3, hWait, FALSE, INFINITE))
 {
 case WAIT_OBJECT_0:
  return MEM_ERROR_CLOSED;
 case WAIT_OBJECT_0 + 2:
  {
   if (nDataSize > *m_pSize)
    return MEM_ERROR_DATASIZE;
   CWriteQueue *pNew = new CWriteQueue(*m_pSize);
   memcpy(pNew->pData, pData, *m_pSize);

   if (!m_pFirst)
    m_pFirst = pNew;
   else
   {
    CWriteQueue *pCurrent = m_pFirst;
    while (pCurrent->pNext)
     pCurrent = pCurrent->pNext;
    pCurrent->pNext = pNew;
   }

   SetEvent(m_hDataInQueue);
   ReleaseMutex(m_hQueueMutex);
  }
  return MEM_SUCCESS;
 case WAIT_OBJECT_0 + 1:
  // The other instance closed.
```

```
    // Since we locked the mutex by waiting for it,
    // we have to release it again.
    ReleaseMutex(m_hSharedMemoryMutex[m_nOtherInstanceID]);
    return MEM_ERROR_OTHERPARTY;
  case WAIT_ABANDONED_0 + 1:
    // The other instance left without a trace, this
    // means probably that it crashed.
    // Since we locked the mutex by waiting for it,
    // we have to release it again.
    ReleaseMutex(m_hSharedMemoryMutex[m_nOtherInstanceID]);
    return MEM_ERROR_OTHERPARTY;
  case WAIT_FAILED:
    // This can happen when the connection was not opened yet.
    // It is caused by an invalid or NULL handle.
    if (!m_hQueueMutex)
     return MEM_ERROR_CLOSED;
    // This must never happen.
    return MEM_ERROR_UNKNOWN;
  }
  return MEM_ERROR_UNKNOWN;
}
int Read(void *pData, int nDataSize, DWORD dwTimeOut)
{
  // This function reads from the shared memory pool, it can
  // only read data when data was written to the pool.
  // It is always a blocking function.

  // It reads data that was written to the shared
  // memory pool by the 'Write' or 'WriteToQueue'
  // functions.
  HANDLE hWait[3];
  hWait[0] = m_hDataWrit[m_nInstanceID];
  hWait[1] = m_hClosed;
  hWait[2] = m_hSharedMemoryMutex[m_nOtherInstanceID];

  DWORD dwWaitResult =
   WaitForMultipleObjects(3, hWait, FALSE, dwTimeOut);

  switch(dwWaitResult)
  {
  case WAIT_OBJECT_0:
    // This happens when data is written into the
    // shared memory pool.
    // It indicates that the data can be copied
    // into a memory buffer.
    if (nDataSize > *m_pSize)
     return MEM_ERROR_DATASIZE;
    memcpy(pData, m_pSharedMemory[m_nInstanceID], nDataSize);
    SetEvent(m_hDataRead[m_nInstanceID]);
    return MEM_SUCCESS;
  case WAIT_OBJECT_0 + 1:
    // This happens when no connection was made yet, or this
```

```
   // instance was closed.
    return MEM_ERROR_CLOSED;
  case WAIT_OBJECT_0 + 2:
    // This happens when the other party closes
    // its connection.
    ReleaseMutex(m_hSharedMemoryMutex[m_nOtherInstanceID]);
    return MEM_ERROR_OTHERPARTY;
  case WAIT_ABANDONED_0 + 2:
    // This happens when the other party gracefully
    // closes its connection.
    // This can be caused by an unexpected termination
    // of the host process of the other instance.
    ReleaseMutex(m_hSharedMemoryMutex[m_nOtherInstanceID]);
    return MEM_ERROR_OTHERPARTY;
  case WAIT_FAILED:
    // This can happen when the connection was not
    // opened yet. It is caused by an invalid or
    // NULL handle.
    if (!m_hDataWrit[m_nInstanceID])
      return MEM_ERROR_CLOSED;
    return MEM_ERROR_UNKNOWN;
  case WAIT_TIMEOUT:
    // This indicates that the maximum wait time
    // (dwTimeOut) has passed.
    return MEM_ERROR_TIMEOUT;
  }
  return MEM_ERROR_UNKNOWN;
}
private:
 void EmptyWriteQueue()
 {
  // This private function avoids memory leaking of
  // items in the send-queue.
  while (m_pFirst && WaitForSingleObject(m_hQueueMutex,INFINITE)
  == WAIT_OBJECT_0)
  {
   if (m_pFirst)
   {
    // First get the first element of the queue
    CWriteQueue *pQueue = m_pFirst;
    m_pFirst = pQueue->pNext;
    delete pQueue;
   }
   ReleaseMutex(m_hQueueMutex);
  }
 }
 static void QueueThread(void *pArg)
 {
  // This thread writes every packet that enteres
  // the queue to the shared memory pool.
  // It ensures that the 'WriteToQueue' function
  // is nonblocking.
```

```
    // The queue access is mutexed to avoid simultaneous
    // access to the queue by this thread and the
    // 'WriteToQueue' function.
    CSharedMemory *pThis = (CSharedMemory*)pArg;
    HANDLE hWait[2] = {pThis->m_hClosed, pThis->m_hDataInQueue};
    bool bQuit = false;
    while (!bQuit)
    {
     switch (WaitForMultipleObjects(2, hWait, FALSE, INFINITE))
     {
     case WAIT_OBJECT_0 + 1:
      {
       BYTE *pData = NULL;
       while (pThis->m_pFirst
       && WaitForSingleObject(pThis->m_hQueueMutex, INFINITE)
        == WAIT_OBJECT_0)
       {
        if (pThis->m_pFirst)
        {
         // First get the first element of the queue
         CWriteQueue *pQueue = pThis->m_pFirst;
         pData = new BYTE[*pThis->m_pSize];
         memcpy(pData, pThis->m_pFirst->pData, *pThis->m_pSize);
         pThis->m_pFirst = pQueue->pNext;
         delete pQueue;
         ReleaseMutex(pThis->m_hQueueMutex);

         pThis->Write(pData, *pThis->m_pSize, INFINITE);
         delete [] pData;
        }
        else
         ReleaseMutex(pThis->m_hQueueMutex);
       }
      }
      break;
     case WAIT_OBJECT_0:
      bQuit = true;
      break;
     }
    }
   }
private:
 // We will use two shared memory pools to create
 // a transparant memory 'pipe'.
 // One pool will be used as destination for one instance,
 // and source for the other instance, the other will be
 // used the other way around.
 // The two mutexes will indicate which instance is
 // already available.
 HANDLE    m_hSharedMemoryMutex[2];
```

```
int     m_nInstanceID;
int     m_nOtherInstanceID;

HANDLE   m_hSharedMemory[2];

BYTE*    m_pSharedMemory[2];

int*    m_pSize;

// This handle indicates wether this instance
HANDLE   m_hClosed;

// is open or closed.
HANDLE   m_hDataWrit[2];
HANDLE   m_hDataRead[2];

HANDLE   m_hSecondInstanceAvailable;

// Queue stuff
HANDLE   m_hQueueThread;
HANDLE   m_hDataInQueue;
CWriteQueue  *m_pFirst;
HANDLE   m_hQueueMutex;
};
```

Comments

There appears to be a memory leak in the sample code. This can be corrected as follows:

The following lines should be changed from

```
m_pSharedMemory[0] = (BYTE*)MapViewOfFile(m_hSharedMemory[0],
➥FILE_MAP_ALL_ACCESS,0,0,nDataSize);

m_pSharedMemory[1] = (BYTE*)MapViewOfFile(m_hSharedMemory[1],
➥FILE_MAP_ALL_ACCESS,0,0,nDataSize);
```

to

```
m_pSharedMemory[0] = (BYTE*)MapViewOfFile(m_hSharedMemory[0],
➥FILE_MAP_ALL_ACCESS,0,0,nDataSize + sizeof(int));

m_pSharedMemory[1] = (BYTE*)MapViewOfFile(m_hSharedMemory[1],
➥FILE_MAP_ALL_ACCESS,0,0,nDataSize + sizeof(int));
```

The original lines may cause problems, for example, when nDataSize is set to 0x10000, which causes memcpy to error.

—David Yeah

IV

Controls

12

Button Controls

In this chapter

Buttons are fun. Users need buttons so that they can click them repeatedly screaming "it doesn't work when I do this…" until someone pulls the mouse out of their hand.

Why make your buttons simple gray rectangles when you could have multicolored works of art, or even buttons that show a character map when clicked?

- The "CStatic-derived Flat Button Class" allows you to use a CStatic control like a regular button, but with pictures.
- If you have you ever wanted more buttons on your caption

bar, the "Caption Bar Interface" could be just what you're looking for.

- If you really want to add some nice buttons to your applications, the "CXPStyleButtonST v1.0" is what you need. With a name like that, you know this class has class.
- If you have ever needed to enter symbols or other characters in an edit box, you know how awkward it is to launch charmap to get what you need. Why not just use the "CCharSetBtn Control" to ensure that symbols are only a click away?

CStatic-derived Flat Button Class

This article was contributed by Kwon Jin-ho.

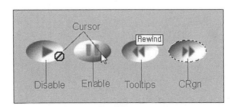

Figure 12.1

Description

CStaticButton is a class derived from the MFC CStatic class. With this class your applications can have standard buttons or new and modern buttons with the "flat" style.

CStaticButton features include

- Standard CStatic properties.
- Only bitmap button—but adding an icon is so easy.
- Not dependent on format, two-color/true-color support.
- Standard or new flat button style.
- Change runtime from Enable-Disable Image.
- Change runtime from ToolTips and CRgn (Default-rect region).
- Can be used via DDX_ calls.
- Can be dynamically created.
- Each button can have its own mouse pointer.
- Full source code included!
- It's free!

Summary

I don't speak English very well. However, I think that the code is simple and easy enough to follow. Just don't forget to change the button image's Notify property.

FROM THE FORUM

Question (Mr Fly):

How can I add a bitmap to a CButton-derived object in my application?

Answer (Narayana Murty):

If you are creating the button at runtime, use this:

```
CButton myButton;

// Create a bitmap button.
myButton.Create(_T("My button"), WS_CHILD¦WS_VISIBLE¦BS_BITMAP,
CRect(10,10,60,50), pParentWnd, 1);

// Set the bitmap of the button to be the system check mark bitmap.
myButton.SetBitmap( ::LoadBitmap(NULL, MAKEINTRESOURCE(OBM_CHECK)) );
```

Or, if you already have a member variable mapped to the button, use this:

```
UINT uStyle = myButton.GetButtonStyle();
uStyle = uStyle ¦ BS_BITMAP;
myButton.SetBitmap( ::LoadBitmap(NULL, MAKEINTRESOURCE(OBM_CHECK)) );
```

Caption Bar Interface

This article was contributed by Anish Mistry of AM Productions.

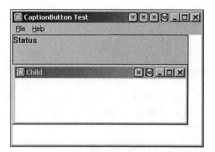

Figure 12.2

Environment: VC6 SP4, W2K SP1—Does not work on Win95 with DirectX because of Transparent Bitmap drawing.

After having this base code for about a year and a half, it has finally matured to the stage where I feel that it can be used in other people's applications. The basis of the CCaptionButton class is to create a button-like interface toolbar in the caption area. My original idea was to create a uniform interface with the existing Windows captions (Minimize, Maximize, and Close), but I decided to go the more creative route and use bitmaps, which would allow me to create a unique interface rather than the same old bland captions. With this, CCaptionButton was born. It uses two bitmaps per caption plus one common mousedown bitmap. You can also pass in HICONs for the captions, but they are then just converted to HBITMAPs.

The features are

- Bitmap image captions
- Icon image captions
- Tooltips
- Dynamic replace
- Dynamic add
- Dynamic delete
- Caption press notification
- Flexible design

As you look through the class, you may notice that some functions that you would expect to see are missing. This is for a simple reason. I did not need to use them during the course of creating programs with this class. They should be quite easy to add, so post an addition in the comments following.

The initialization may seem complex, but it is actually fairly simple. You will probably spend most of your time creating the bitmaps. For the first three captions, I used a technique of combining bitmaps together to create a uniform mouseover effect. This is not necessary, but it saves lots of memory in the .exe since you don't have to store different mouseover bitmaps for every caption.

```
// declare as class variable or global
CCaptionButton cbExtra;

// subclass the window
cbExtra.Init(hWnd);
// set the number of regular captions (Minimize/Maximize/Close)
cbExtra.SetNumOfDefaultCaptions(3);
// set the images transparency color
COLORREF crTransparent = RGB(255,0,255);
cbExtra.SetTransparentColor(crTransparent);
// set the bitmap to be displayed
cbExtra.SetSelectionBitmap((HBITMAP)LoadImage(hInstance,
                            MAKEINTRESOURCE(IDB_SELECTION),
                            IMAGE_BITMAP,
                            0,
                            0,
                            LR_LOADMAP3DCOLORS|LR_DEFAULTCOLOR));

// create our mouseover bitmaps (you could load them directly,
// but this way saves memory)
HBITMAP hMouseOverBitmap = (HBITMAP)LoadImage(hInstance,
                            MAKEINTRESOURCE(IDB_MOUSEOVER),
                            IMAGE_BITMAP,
                            0,
                            0,
                            LR_LOADMAP3DCOLORS|LR_DEFAULTCOLOR);
// caption AM Productions
HBITMAP hCaptionAMBitmap = (HBITMAP)LoadImage(hInstance,
                            MAKEINTRESOURCE(IDB_BITMAP_AM),
                            IMAGE_BITMAP,
                            0,
                            0,
                            LR_LOADMAP3DCOLORS|LR_DEFAULTCOLOR);
HBITMAP hCaptionAMBitmapHilite =
            CCaptionButton::CombineBitmaps(hCaptionAMBitmap,
                    hMouseOverBitmap, crTransparent);
// caption 2
HBITMAP hCaption2Bitmap = (HBITMAP)LoadImage(hInstance,
                            MAKEINTRESOURCE(IDB_BITMAP2),
                            IMAGE_BITMAP,
                            0,
                            0,
                            LR_LOADMAP3DCOLORS|LR_DEFAULTCOLOR);
HBITMAP hCaption2BitmapHilite =
            CCaptionButton::CombineBitmaps(hCaption2Bitmap,
                    hMouseOverBitmap,crTransparent);
```

```
// caption 3
HBITMAP hCaption3Bitmap = (HBITMAP)LoadImage(hInstance,
                             MAKEINTRESOURCE(IDB_BITMAP3),
                             IMAGE_BITMAP,
                             0,
                             0,
                             LR_LOADMAP3DCOLORS|LR_DEFAULTCOLOR);
HBITMAP hCaption3BitmapHilite =
                CCaptionButton::CombineBitmaps(hCaption3Bitmap,
                      hMouseOverBitmap,crTransparent);

// create caption with ID = 1, mouseover effect bitmap of
// hCaptionAMBitmapHilite, normal bitmap of hCaptionAMBitmap,
// and tooltip text of "AM Productions - Visit Now!"
cbExtra.New(1,hCaptionAMBitmapHilite,hCaptionAMBitmap,
                      "AM Productions - Visit Now!");
cbExtra.New(2,hCaption2BitmapHilite,hCaption2Bitmap,"Caption 2");
cbExtra.New(3,hCaption3BitmapHilite,hCaption3Bitmap,"Caption 3");
// just load it directly from the bitmap resources
cbExtra.New(4,
(HBITMAP)LoadImage(hInstance,
                MAKEINTRESOURCE(IDB_BITMAP5),
                IMAGE_BITMAP,
                0,
                0,
                LR_LOADMAP3DCOLORS|LR_DEFAULTCOLOR),
(HBITMAP)LoadImage(hInstance,
                MAKEINTRESOURCE(IDB_BITMAP6),
                IMAGE_BITMAP,
                0,
                0,
                LR_LOADMAP3DCOLORS|LR_DEFAULTCOLOR),
                "Caption 4");
```

At this point you may be saying "That's all great, but how do I know if a caption has been pressed?" Well, here is your answer. When a caption is clicked, a WM_ CBLBUTTONCLICKED message is generated and sent to the window with the captions. The WPARAM of this message contains the ID of the caption that was pressed. The LPARAM contains a POINT structure of the screen coordinates of the cursor when the caption was clicked (which is good for displaying menus).

What is with all those dynamic features? Well, the CCaptionButton class has the ability to add, replace, and delete captions at runtime. To add a caption, simply call the New() function, but as a fifth parameter, specify the zero-based index of where you would like to insert the caption (from right to left). It is not much harder to replace an existing caption.

```
// replacing a caption
cbExtra.Replace(nCurrentCaptionID,
                nNewCaptionID,
                hNewMouseoverBitmap,
                hNewNormalBitmap,
                pNewToolTipText);
```

Deleting a caption may seem difficult, but I'm sure that you will get used to it.

```
// deleting a caption
cbExtra.Delete(nCurrentCaptionID);
```

Known issues include

- Adding significant overhead to a window's message processing
- Flickering during window resize

Updates are

- Removed the SetCaptionType() and SetWindowType() functions and autodetected that information in Init()
- Now works with child windows
- Example shows the use with a child window
- Example shows the use with a modeless dialog

I know that there is a lot of room for improvement, so feel free to post or email comments.

Comments

To make this code work in an MFC child window, make the following changes to the sample code:

Modify the CalculateRect routine as shown:

```
RECT CCaptionButton::CalculateRect(const int &offset,bool toClient) const
// calculate the rectangular area of the caption at the offset
{// begin CalculateRect

RECT windowRect;
SIZE frameSize = GetFrameSize();
SIZE captionSize = GetCaptionSize();
::GetWindowRect(m_hWnd,&windowRect);
RECT captionRect = {NULL};
captionRect.left = windowRect.right-(captionSize.cx*offset+frameSize.cx);
captionRect.top = windowRect.top+frameSize.cy;
captionRect.right = captionRect.left+captionSize.cx;
captionRect.bottom = captionRect.top+captionSize.cy;
// check for partially covered up menu, and compensate
RECT menuRect = {NULL};
HMENU windowMenu = GetMenu(m_hWnd);
if(windowMenu)
{
    GetMenuItemRect(m_hWnd,windowMenu,0,&menuRect);
    // begin ADD CODE
    if(menuRect.bottom != 0) // if it is not a child window
```

```
        {
        captionRect.bottom = menuRect.top-1;
        captionRect.top = captionRect.bottom-captionSize.cy;
        }
    // end ADD CODE
  }
  // ... leave the rest unchanged.
```

—Anish Mistry

CXPStyleButtonST v1.0

This article was contributed by Davide Calabro.

Figure 12.3

Figure 12.4

Environment: VC++ 6.0, XP, Win2k, NT 4.0, Win9x/ME

Abstract

CXPStyleButtonST is a scalable CButtonST-derived control.

If running under Windows XP, the application buttons will be skinned using the currently selected theme (if any), but if running under Windows 9x/ME/NT/2000, the buttons will have the standard, well-known CButtonST flat style. In both cases all CButtonST features are granted! Using CXPStyleButtonST with a zero-cost implementation, your applications running under XP will have the new, smooth and elegant style, but also will run errorless under old Windows versions.

How to Integrate CXPStyleButtonST in Your Application

In your project include the following files:

- BtnST.h
- BtnST.cpp
- XPStyleButtonST.h
- XPStyleButtonST.cpp
- ThemeHelperST.h
- ThemeHelperST.cpp

Create an instance of CThemeHelperST. This class encapsulates all the required APIs to access the currently selected theme (if any) or to run errorless if none is selected or if running under an old Windows version. You need only one instance for all the buttons, so this can be global to the application or only to the current dialog.

```
CThemeHelperST m_ThemeHelper;
```

Create a CXPStyleButtonST Object Statically

With the dialog editor, create a standard button called, for example, IDOK (you don't need to make it owner drawn) and create a member variable for this button:

```
CXPStyleButtonST m_btnOk;
```

Now, attach the button to CXPStyleButtonST. For dialog-based applications, in your OnInitDialog:

```
// Call the base-class method
CDialog::OnInitDialog();

// Create the IDOK button
m_btnOk.SubclassDlgItem(IDOK, this);
```

Or in your DoDataExchange:

```
// Call the base method
CDialog::DoDataExchange(pDX);

// Create the IDOK button
DDX_Control(pDX, IDOK, m_btnOk);
```

Assign the CThemeHelperST instance to the button. This is fundamental, or your button will not have the current theme style even if running under XP!

In your OnInitDialog:

```
// Assign theme helper instance to the button
m_btnOk.SetThemeHelper(&m_ThemeHelper);
```

Create a CXPStyleButtonST Object Dynamically

In your application, create a member variable for the button. Please note that this variable is a *pointer*:

```
CXPStyleButtonST* m_pbtnOk;
```

Now create the button. For dialog-based applications, in your OnInitDialog:

```
// Call the base-class method
CDialog::OnInitDialog();

// Create the IDOK button
m_pbtnOk = new CXPStyleButtonST;
m_pbtnOk->Create(_T("&Ok"),
                 WS_CHILD | WS_VISIBLE | WS_GROUP | WS_TABSTOP,
                 CRect(10, 10, 200, 100),
                 this,
                 IDOK);
// Set the same font of the application
m_pbtnOk->SetFont(GetFont());
```

Assign the CThemeHelperST instance to the button as described in the previous section.

Remember to destroy the button, or you will get a memory leak. This can be done, for example, in your class destructor:

```
if (m_pbtnOk) delete m_pbtnOk;
```

FROM THE FORUM

Question (Erimeier):

I have many CButton-derived objects on my dialog. How can I determine whether a specific one currently has the focus?

Answer (Igor Soukhov):

You can create a simple member function like this:

```
bool CMyDialog::IfButtonHasFocus(CButton * pButton)
{
    return (CWnd::GetFocus() == pButton);
}
```

Class Methods

SetThemeHelper

This assigns a CThemeHelperST instance to the button.

```
// Parameters:
//     [IN]    pTheme
//             Pointer to a CThemeHelperST instance.
//             Pass NULL to remove any previous instance.
//
void SetThemeHelper(CThemeHelperST* pTheme)
```

GetVersionI

This returns the class version as a short value.

```
// Return value:
//     Class version. Divide by 10 to get actual version.
//
static short GetVersionI()
```

GetVersionC

This returns the class version as a string value.

```
// Return value:
//     Pointer to a null-terminated string containing
//     the class version.
//
static LPCTSTR GetVersionC()
```

Remarks

To compile CXPStyleButtonST, you need the Platform SDK (August 2001 or newer). This is not mandatory because at compile time, if not found, it will be emulated. At runtime you don't need any additional SDK or libraries installed.

Credits

CThemeHelperST is based on the CVisualStylesXP code published by David Yuheng Zhao (yuheng_zhao@yahoo.com). Thanks very much!

CCharSetBtn Control

This article was contributed by Thorsten Wack.

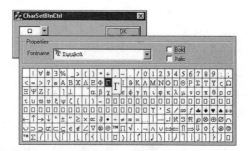

Figure 12.5

Environment: VC6 SP4, NT4 SP3

I needed a control to choose a character from a specific charset and the option to use bold and/or italic font. Therefore, I derived an owner-drawn control from CButton that opens a pop-up dialog as a drop-down window (based on the work of Shekar Narayanan and S. D. Rajan). The dialog itself holds a ComboBox-derived font—ComboBox (which includes some code snippets of Norm Almond) and a custom control that performs the character selection.

To use the control, do the following:

1. Import the header files (included in the source code on the CD) and add the .cpp files (also on the CD) from the section CharSetBtn.

2. Import the resources IDB_GLYPHS (printer images) and IDD_CHARSET_DLG (the pop-up window including the CharSetCtrl).

3. On your dialog insert a button (set style flag owner drawn).

4. Add a CButton control member variable in the Class Wizard. Change the CButton class in the dialog header file to CCharSetBtn, and that's it.

The class CCharSetBtn has got the member variables

```
int      m_nChar;
CString  m_strFaceName;
BOOL     m_bItalic;
BOOL     m_bBold;
```

which perform the data exchange.

With a little modification, you can also use the complete LOFGONT structure.

If you decide to use this code, please do not remove copyright notices from the source and header files and give me a short email.

FROM THE FORUM

Question (gangelo):

How can I capture the BN_CLICKED message both in my CButton-derived class and also in the dialog that is its parent?

Answer (Alex Fedotov):

The BN_CLICKED notification message is sent as a WM_COMMAND message as opposed to a WM_NOTIFY message, so you should use ON_CONTROL_REFLECT_EX and not ON_NOTIFY_REFLECT as you might otherwise expect.

13

ComboBox Controls

In this chapter

Rather than being something you might find on the shelf at your local supermarket, the ComboBox is a strange cocktail containing both a ListBox control and a TextBox control, resulting in one of the more versatile controls in the programmer's toolbox.

Although you may have already seen many examples of how to use this popular control (as it is used in virtually every application), in this chapter you will find details of how to go about extending the regular ComboBox class functionality.

- CHistoryComboEx shows how you can easily add and store the history of previously selected items, displaying them as selection options in the drop-down list.

- The CTooltipComboBox class describes how to add ToolTips to enhance the look and provide better user feedback from your ComboBox controls.

- CComboBoxFolder provides an interesting twist, allowing the use of a drop-down tree control instead of the regular list control.

CComboBoxEx with History!

This article was contributed by Nabil Hussein.

Figure 13.1

Abstract

The CHistoryComboEx class is based on the class (CHistoryCombo) by Paul S. Vickery, which enables you to read and save the items of a ComboBox from and to the Registry. You can also use it to display the contents of a CRecentFileList object.

CHistoryComboEx has the same functions of CHistoryCombo, but instead of the function AddString(), I have added two new implements to the function InsertItem().

How to Use It

1. Copy HistoryComboEx.cpp and HistoryComboEx.h to the folder of your project.

2. Click Project\Add to Project\Files..., and then select the two files of our class and insert them into your project.

3. Add, programmatically or using the Resource Editor, an extended ComboBox control to your dialog.

4. Using the Class Wizard, add a member variable of type CComboBoxEx to your extended ComboBox control. (I'll assume that your variable name is "m_cbeCtrl.")

5. Now open the header file of your dialog box. First, add this line to the top of it:

   ```
   #include "HistoryComboEx.h"
   ```

   Then change the line

   ```
   CComboBoxEx    m_cbeCtrl;
   ```

   to

   ```
   CHistoryComboEx m_cbeCtrl;
   ```

6. Add the following line to the end of your "OnInitDialog()" or "OnInitialUpdate()" function:

   ```
   m_cbeCtrl.LoadHistory("Addresses", "HistoryComboEx");
   ```

   This line will add key names "Addresses" and "HistoryComboEx" to the default key of your application in the Registry. Note: You can change "Addresses" and "HistoryComboEx" to any other values.

7. Add the following line to the handler, which will be running, when your application is going to be closed (OnOK(), for example):

   ```
   m_cbeCtrl.SaveHistory();
   ```

That's all!

Functions

Here, I will write a summary for the functions of CHistoryComboEx. For details please see "HistoryComboEx.cpp." Note: The documentation is the same as for Paul S. Vickery's "CHistoryCombo."

```
CString LoadHistory( LPCTSTR lpszSection,
                     LPCTSTR lpszKeyPrefix,
                     BOOL bSaveRestoreLastCurrent = TRUE,
                     LPCTSTR lpszKeyCurItem = NULL);

CString LoadHistory( CRecentFileList* pListMRU,
                     BOOL bSelectMostRecent = TRUE);

void SaveHistory(BOOL bAddCurrentItemtoHistory = TRUE);

int InsertItem(const COMBOBOXEXITEM *pCBItem)

int InsertItem(CString strItem)

void SetMaxHistoryItems(int nMaxItems);

void ClearHistory(BOOL bDeleteRegistryEntries = TRUE);
```

FROM THE FORUM

Question: Custom Popup for a ComboBox (from lichtf):

I am trying to have a custom pop-up menu be displayed when the user right-clicks on the Edit portion of the ComboBox.

I have added this code to the inherited CComboBox class I made:

```
LRESULT CCustomCombo::WindowProc(UINT message, WPARAM wParam, LPARAM lParam)
{
// TODO: Add your specialized code here and/or call the base class
if(message == WM_CONTEXTMENU){
CMenu* hMenu = new CMenu;
hMenu->LoadMenu(IDR_MENU_COMBO);

CMenu* hSubMenu = hMenu->GetSubMenu(0);

hSubMenu->TrackPopupMenu(TPM_LEFTALIGN | TPM_RIGHTBUTTON,LOWORD(lParam),
➥HIWORD(lParam),(CWnd*)this);

hMenu->DestroyMenu();
}
else{
return CComboBox::WindowProc(message, wParam, lParam);
}
}
```

This works when the user right-clicks on the drop-down arrow or around the edge of the Edit portion of the ComboBox, but not in the Edit portion. Is there any way to capture the messages from this Edit portion of the control? Or is there some other way to go about this?

Answer (from fel):

You could subclass the Edit box in the ComboBox.

One way of doing this would be in the OnCtlColor function of your CCustomCombo. It should look something like this:

```
HBRUSH CCustomCombo::OnCtlColor(CDC* pDC, CWnd* pWnd, UINT nCtlColor)
{
  if (nCtlColor == CTLCOLOR_EDIT)
  {
    if (m_edit.GetSafeHwnd() == NULL)
      m_edit.SubclassWindow(pWnd->GetSafeHwnd());
  }

  HBRUSH hbr = CComboBox::OnCtlColor(pDC, pWnd, nCtlColor);
  return hbr;
}
```

m_edit is your implementation of a CEdit class that shows your menu on WM_RBUTTONUP.

ComboBox with Item ToolTips

This article was contributed by Edward Antonyan.

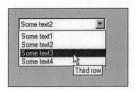

Figure 13.2

Environment: VC6 SP5, NT4 SP6 (not tested on another OS)

To use this ComboBox, follow these steps:

1. Include TooltipComboBox.h, TooltipComboBox.cpp, TooltipListCtrl.h, and TooltipListCtrl.cpp in your project.

2. In the Resource Editor, create a drop-list ComboBox.

3. Create a control member variable for the ComboBox in VC's Class Wizard.

4. Include TooltipComboBox.h and replace CComboBox with CTooltipComboBox in your .h file. Also include afxtempl.h to support CMap.

5. To have your own tips, you can either use SetItemTip and SetComboTip functions or replace the GetItemTip function in CTooltipListCtrl and the GetComboTip function in CTooltipComboBox.

Because this ComboBox uses CComboBox's listbox to store items, it has no special behavior and can be used as a usual CComboBox. It uses Hai Ha's article style to replace the standard drop-down list with a virtual list control. A virtual one is used to prevent having two identical lists. Only the drop-list combo style is currently working like standard CComboBox.

I think the code is simple enough and doesn't need any other comments.

Comments

To add CBN_SELCHANGE notification, add the following code changes:

```
void CTooltipListCtrl::OnKillFocus(CWnd* pNewWnd)
{

 ...

 m_pComboParent->SetCurSel( m_nLastItem );
 m_pComboParent->SetFocus( );

//========================= <--- Added for notification

 m_pComboParent->GetParent()->SendMessage(WM_COMMAND,
 ➥ MAKEWPARAM(GetWindowLong(m_pComboParent->GetSafeHwnd(), GWL_ID),
 ➥ CBN_SELCHANGE), (LPARAM)m_pComboParent->GetSafeHwnd()));

//========================= <---

 CListCtrl::OnKillFocus( pNewWnd );

}
```

—Andrew

To show the selected item in the tooltip, add the following code changes:

```
CString CTooltipListCtrl::GetItemTip(int nRow) const
{
    CString sResult;
    int nWidth;

    sResult = GetItemText( nRow, 0 );
```

```
nWidth = GetStringWidth( sResult );

if ( nWidth + 5 < GetColumnWidth( 0 ) )
    sResult = "";

return sResult;


}
```

—Edward Antonyan

FROM THE FORUM

Question: Read-Only ComboBox (from Mitre):

I have created a ComboBox within a dialog box. The user can only select values to be entered from the combo listbox; he cannot type in any value. Values selected may be int or CString. Besides using the drop list style, is there any other way of preventing the user from typing in values?

Answer (from Emi):

To set the Edit control of a drop-down ComboBox to read-only, modify your code as follows:

```
CComboBox *pCombo = (CComboBox *)GetDlgItem(IDC_COMBO1);
CWnd* pWndChild = pCombo->GetWindow(GW_CHILD);
while (pWndChild)
{
    char szClassName[256];
    int nLenClassName = 256;

    ::GetClassName(pWndChild->m_hWnd, szClassName, nLenClassName);
    if (stricmp(szClassName, "edit") == 0)
    {
        CEdit *pEdit;
        pEdit = new CEdit();
        pEdit->SubclassWindow(pWndChild->m_hWnd);
        pEdit->SetReadOnly();
        pWndChild = pWndChild->GetNextWindow();
        delete pEdit;
    }
    if (pWndChild)
    pWndChild = pWndChild->GetNextWindow();
}
```

ComboBox with Tree Drop Down

This article was contributed by Hai Ha.

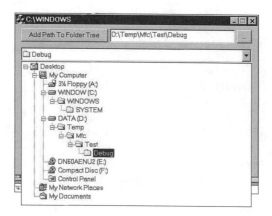

Figure 13.3

Environment: VC6, Win200, ME (has not been tested on other OS)

Using the Class

1. Just as you normally would, place a ComboBox on the dialog. Name it m_comboBoxFolder.

2. Add the files ComboBoxFolder.cpp, ComboBoxFolder.h, TreeCtrlFolder.cpp, TreeCtrlFolder.h, Folder.cpp, and Folder.h to your project.

3. Import the bitmap files to folder0.bmp and give them resource Ids of "IDB_FOLDER."

4. In the header file for the dialog, add an include for ComboBoxFolder.h at the top. Manually change the variable from CComboBox m_comboBoxFolder; in step 1 to CComboBoxFolder m_comboBoxFolder;.

5. In the dialog's OnInitDialog() function, call m_comboBoxFolder.Init(0, 300) for setting the dropped width and height of a tree drop down.

   - To add a path to the tree drop down, call

     ```
     m_comboBoxFolder.AddPath("C:\\Windows\\temp");
     ```

- Whenever a user selects an item in the tree drop down, a message, WM_SELECTITEM_CHANGE, will be sent to Dialog:. A small demo that follows shows how to catch the message and get the parameter that has been passed.

```
ON_MESSAGE(WM_SELECTITEM_CHANGE, OnSelectItemChange)

long CTestDlg::OnSelectItemChange(WPARAM w, LPARAM l)
{ CString path = "";
 CFolder* folder = (CFolder*) w;
 if (folder != NULL)
   path = folder->m_path;

 return 0;
}
```

- To get the path selected in the tree drop down, call

```
m_comboBoxFolder.GetSelectedPath()
```

I haven't added too much here as an explanation of the code because the code is included and very easy to understand.

Comments

To receive notifications from the control if your parent class is not a regular dialog box (as would be the case when using a CFormView-derived class), make the following changes:

In CComboBoxFolder.h, replace

```
Init(int w=0, int h=0);
```

with

```
Init(int w=0, int h=0, CWnd* notifyParent=NULL);
```

In CComboBoxFolder.cpp, replace

```
CComboBoxFolder::Init(int w, int h)
```

with

```
CComboBoxFolder::Init(int w, int h, CWnd* notifyParent)
```

Also within the Init routine, replace

```
m_treeCtrl.CreateEx (0, WC_TREEVIEW, NULL, style, rc,
GetParent(), 0, NULL);
```

with

```
m_treeCtrl.CreateEx (0, WC_TREEVIEW, NULL, style, rc,
notifyParent, 0, NULL);
```

Now, whenever you initialize the CComboBoxFolder, pass the pointer of the window that you want to receive the notification.

For example

```
m_comboBoxFolder.Init(0, 300, this);
```

—Hai Ha

To change the control so that the ComboBox and Tree control use the same font, change the Init routine as shown:

```
void CComboBoxFolder::Init(int w, int h)
{
    CRect rc(0, 0, 10, 10);
    UINT style = WS_POPUP ¦ WS_BORDER ¦ TVS_DISABLEDRAGDROP ¦ TVS_HASLINES ¦
➥ TVS_LINESATROOT ¦ TVS_HASBUTTONS    ¦ TVS_FULLROWSELECT;
    m_treeCtrl.CreateEx (0, WC_TREEVIEW, NULL, style, rc, GetParent(), 0,
➥ NULL);
    m_treeCtrl.CreateImageList();
    m_treeCtrl.Init(this);
    m_treeCtrl.SetFont(GetFont()); // Modified by beback 2002/03/02
    GetClientRect(rc);
    if (w <= 0) w = rc.right;
    if (h <= 0) h = 100;
    SetDroppedWidth(w);
    SetDroppedHeight(h);
}
```

—Sangbaek Park

To add more support for NT4, make the following changes to the CtreeCtrlFolder::Init method:

Change

```
SHGetSpecialFolderPath(NULL, szPath, CSIDL_DESKTOP , FALSE);
```

to

```
LPITEMIDLIST itemlist = 0;
SHGetSpecialFolderLocation(NULL, CSIDL_DESKTOP, &itemlist);
strcpy(szPath, (LPCTSTR)itemlist);
```

—Sangbaek Park

CCheckComboBox: A ComboBox with a Checked Tree Drop Down

This article was contributed by Magerusan G. Cosmin.

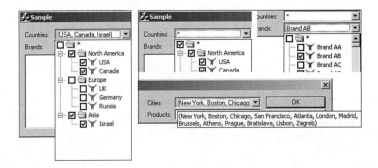

Figure 13.4

Environment: VC6, Windows 98, 2000, NT4

Often programmers encounter situations when it is necessary to filter data based on a number of criteria. A solution is to implement a number of simple combos or checklist boxes. This has the disadvantage of not allowing multiple choices (combos) or of taking a lot of space (checklist boxes).

I wanted a control with the functionality of both a combo and a tree with check boxes. Such a control would act like a combo showing a drop down, but would also allow multiple selections and fast selection or deselection of all items.

I saw on CodeGuru other ideas that are more or less close to what I expected from such a control, but I think they lack functionality in one way or another, so I decided to write my own solution.

The user keys are

- F4 (to drop/close the drop down)
- Up or down (to move the selection up or down)
- Right (to expand current item)
- Left (to collapse current item)
- Space (to check or uncheck the current item)

Using CCheckComboBox, for example, if you want to add the three countries "USA" (ID=5), "Canada" (ID=6), "UK" (ID=7), and their corresponding continents, you would have to write the following code:

```
//## ADD tree items:
m_choCountries.AddString("North America");
  m_choCountries.AddString("USA",    5, ROOT_LEVEL + 2);
```

```
  m_choCountries.AddString("Canada", 6, ROOT_LEVEL + 2);
m_choCountries.AddString("Europe");
  m_choCountries.AddString("UK",     7, ROOT_LEVEL + 2);

//## CHECK all items
m_choCountries.CheckAll(TRUE);

//## UNCHECK the item with ID = 6
m_choCountries.SetCheck(6, FALSE);

//## GET all checked items
CString strCheckedItems = m_choCountries.GetCheckedIDs();
```

FROM THE FORUM

Question: ComboBox dropped listbox height (from Ahmet AKGUN):

After creating a ComboBox dynamically, how can I set the height of the drop down list box?

Answer (from Matt Hauser):

When creating a ComboBox dynamically, such as the following:

```
m_combo.Create(WS_CHILD ¦ WS_VISIBLE ¦ WS_VSCROLL ¦
CBS_SORT ¦ CBS_DROPDOWNLIST ¦ WS_TABSTOP, CRect(320, 10, 580, 280), this, 113);
```

The last parameter of CRect (in this case the 280) represents the drop down dimension of the ComboBox.

FROM THE FORUM

Question: Enter Key in ComboBox (from sebap):

I have a dialog-based application including a ComboBox control. I am having trouble with the Enter Key event because when I press the Enter key when the ComboBox has focus, the application is closing.

Why?

Answer (from Philip Nicoletti):

Normally, in PreTranslateMessage(), to check which control has focus, you would do something like this:

```
//
CWnd *pWnd = GetFocus();
if (pWnd != NULL)
{
    if (pWnd-&gt;GetParent() == GetDlgItem(IDC_EDIT1))
    {
        // IDC_EDIT1 has focus
    }
}
//
```

It appears that ComboBox works differently. It looks like the Edit control of the ComboBox is what has focus, so you need to do this:

```
BOOL CDialog_basedDlg::PreTranslateMessage(MSG* pMsg)
{
    if(pMsg->message==WM_KEYDOWN && pMsg->wParam==VK_RETURN)
    {
        CWnd *pWnd = GetFocus();
        if (pWnd != NULL)
        {
            if (pWnd->GetParent() == GetDlgItem(IDC_COMBO1)) //
➥ change to your ID
            {
                return TRUE;
            }
        }
    }
    return CDialog::PreTranslateMessage(pMsg);
}
```

14

Edit Controls

In this chapter

In this chapter you will find examples of how to extend the simple edit control to provide many needed and interesting features.

- "Auto-Fill Edit Control" is an edit control with a memory, automatically completing entries for you.
- If you need to save some screen real estate, you can use the "Hybrid Edit Control That Combines Prompt Text and Edit Control."
- The "Masked Edit Control (3)" provides an excellent way to limit the user input to expected values.
- The "Numeric Edit and Numeric Spin Controls" extend the functionality of the regular spin control and edit control combination.

Auto-Fill Edit Control

This article was contributed by Massimo Colurcio.

Environment: Windows 98, Visual C++ 5.0

A fine class for lazy operators. :)

This is an enhanced edit class. It allows you to reduce the input time from recording the words previously inserted and showing them when some letters are typed.

This class is generated starting from CEdit and can store up to 128 words (but it's possible to change this limit); it's use is really easy. All you have to do is follow these steps:

1. Design your own CDialog or CFormView (or derived class) inserting the standard Edit box.
2. Include AFEdit.h and AFEdit.cpp in your project.
3. In the CXYZ.h file generated for the dialog (or view), include AFEdit.h and replace all occurrences of CEdit with CAFEdit.
4. In the OnInitDialog (or OnInitialUpdate), add the strings you want to be inserted in the words list for each Edit box.

Every time you insert a new word in a specific Edit box, the relative list will grow if necessary (without duplicating any words). Of course, if the class is deleted, all data is lost. I tested it in a multiline Edit box too, and it works fine.

There is only one known problem: In a multiline Edit box, the pair Ctrl+Tab inserts a tab into the text. The source I wrote still isn't able to intercept that key combination. :(

In debug mode a double-click on an Edit box shows a dialog with the entire list.

Hybrid Edit Control That Combines Prompt Text and Edit Control

This article was contributed by Tom Archer.

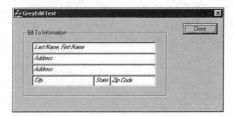

Figure 14.1

Initialized dialog (before user has input any data). Notice the prompts inside the edit controls that relieve the dialog designer of having to place static controls on the dialog (or view).

Introduction

If you've ever used Intuit's Quicken or Peachtree's Accounting for Windows, you may have noticed something called a "grey edit control" on some of the dialogs and views. As you can see in Figure 14.1, a grey edit control is one in which the text is grey and italicized until the control has focus or until data has been entered into the control. This little control becomes useful in situations where there is simply no room on the dialog (or view) for a static control telling the user what information is required. An example might be the address portion of a form where the controls are nestled so closely together that any attempt at placing static controls near the edit controls would look awful. Another great example of where this control is useful is when you want your dialog (or view) to represent (as closely as possible) an actual paper document such as an invoice or purchase order.

Rules for Display

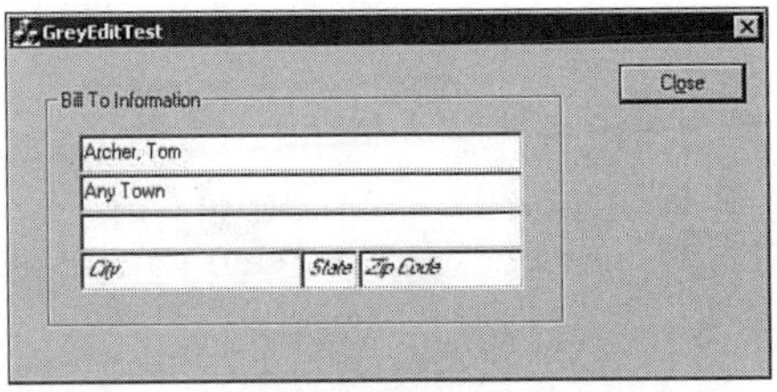

Figure 14.2

Rules are set so that the user can tell a prompt from real data:

- If the field has a value, then display that value.
- If the field has focus and no value, then display a blank.
- If the field does not have focus and has no value, show a prompt (in italics) so that the user knows what is needed.

Using the grey edit control, the programmer can have the control's prompt be displayed in the edit control itself. As you can see in Figure 14.2, the rules that are used for displaying the data are very simple. The grey and italicized font lets the user know that what they are looking at is a prompt and not the data itself. After the control receives focus, the grey text disappears so that the user is not distracted. When the control loses focus, whether or not the grey text returns depends on whether the user typed any information into the control.

Using the CGreyEdit Control

To use the CGreyEdit control, all you need to do is instantiate it and call its Init method function.

```
BOOL CGreyEdit::Init(UINT uiControlId,
                     CWnd *pParent,
                     const char*lpszDefaultText,
                     COLORREF lBackgroundColor,
                     UINT uiAlignment)
```

The Init method function breaks down as follows:

- **uiControlId**: Resource ID of the edit control you want to subclass.
- **pParent**: Parent window of the control.
- **lpszDefaultText**: Default, or prompt text, to be displayed until the control has focus or the user has entered data into the control.

- **lBackgroundColor**: This value defaults to COLOR_WINDOWTEXT and represents the control's background color.
- **uiAlignment**: Valid values include TA_CENTER, TA_LEFT, or TA_RIGHT. Defaults to TA_LEFT.

To use the control, simply create a member variable of type CGreyEdit in your dialog or view class. Then call the object's Init function. Here's an example of doing this:

```
BOOL CGreyEditTestDlg::OnInitDialog()
{
//...
m_editName.Init(IDC_EDT_NAME,
                this,
                _T("Last Name, First Name"),
                RGB(255,0,0));
//...
}
```

Masked Edit Control (3)

This article was contributed by Jeff Knight.

Figure 14.3

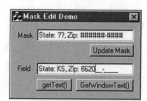

Figure 14.4

We had been using the MSMask.ocx control in our MFC application for almost a year. Recently a 200K memory leak was traced to the setText method (200K each time it was called), so we downloaded another masked edit class from the Web, but it flickered intensely and the code was kind of icky. Anyway, I decided to write my own. Turns out it works better than I could have hoped. It's easy to use, and the source code is very simple, allowing anyone to extend it as necessary.

In ::OnInitDialog():

```
m_maskEdit.SubclassDlgItem(IDC_EDIT_MASK, this);

// Initialize the control to "State: KS, Zip: 66202-1234"
m_maskEdit.setMask("State: ??, Zip: #####-####");
m_maskEdit.setText("KS662021234");
```

In ::OnOk():

```
// getText returns "KS66202123"
CString strTemp = m_maskEdit.getText();

// GetWindowText yields "State: KS, Zip: 66202-1234"
m_maskEdit.GetWindowText(strTemp);
```

Comments

Modified OnUpdate code:

```
void CMaskEdit::OnUpdate()
{
    int nStart, nEnd;
    GetSel(nStart, nEnd);
    CString strEditText;
    GetWindowText(strEditText);

    if (strEditText == m_strSaveText)
        return;

    if (m_bLastKeyWasBackspace)
    {
        m_strSaveText.SetAt(nStart, isMaskChar(nStart) ? m_strMaskText[nStart]
➥: m_cPlaceHolder);
        CWnd::SetWindowText(m_strSaveText);
        int nNext = gotoNextEntryChar(nStart);
        SetSel(nNext, nNext);
    }
    else if (m_bLastKeyWasDelete)
    {
        m_strSaveText.SetAt(nStart, isMaskChar(nStart) ? m_strMaskText[nStart]
➥: m_cPlaceHolder);
        CWnd::SetWindowText(m_strSaveText);
        int nNext = gotoNextEntryChar(nStart + 1);
        SetSel(nNext, nNext);
    }
    else
    {
```

```
            if (nStart - 1 < 0)
                return;
            int nNext = gotoNextEntryChar(nStart - 1);
            char cWanted = strEditText[nStart - 1];
            char cReplace = 0;

            if (getReplacementChar(nNext, cWanted, cReplace))

            {

                if (m_strSaveText.GetLength() < nNext)

                    m_strSaveText.GetBufferSetLength(nNext);

                m_strSaveText.SetAt(nNext, cReplace);

                m_strSaveText.ReleaseBuffer();

                nNext = gotoNextEntryChar(nNext + 1);

            }

            CWnd::SetWindowText(m_strSaveText);
            SetSel(nNext, nNext);
        }
    }
```

—Catalin A. Culiniac

To verify the mask restrictions in the setText method, make the following changes:

```
    void CMaskEdit::setText(LPCTSTR pszText)
    {
        CString strText(pszText);
        m_strSaveText.Empty();
        int nMaskIndex = 0;
        int nTextIndex = 0;

        while (nMaskIndex < m_strMaskText.GetLength())
        {
            if (!isMaskChar(nMaskIndex))
            {
                if (nTextIndex < strText.GetLength())
                {
                    char cWanted = strText[nTextIndex];
                    char cReplace = 0;
                    if (!getReplacementChar(nMaskIndex, cWanted, cReplace))
                        nTextIndex++;
                    else
                    {
```

```
                    m_strSaveText += strText[nTextIndex++];
                    nMaskIndex++;
                }
            }
            else
            {
                m_strSaveText += m_cPlaceHolder;
                nMaskIndex++;
            }
        }
        else
        {
            m_strSaveText += m_strMaskText[nMaskIndex];
            nMaskIndex++;
        }
    }
    CWnd::SetWindowText(m_strSaveText);
}
```

—Catalin A. Culiniac

Numeric Edit and Numeric Spin Controls

This article was contributed by T.VU KHAC.

Figure 14.5

In my application I needed an edit control that accepts only numeric numbers. In many science applications, this is indispensable, but it is actually not implemented in MS Visual C/C++. It is not difficult to implement this control, and I have seen some people implement it. In my own code, some new features were enriched as error messages, range defines, and so on.

Note: To use the CNumEdit class properly, the ES_NUMBER and ES_MULTILINE must not be set.

Another control added in my work is CNumSpinCtrl, which enables you to use a spin control as a numeric one, which is also not implemented in MFC.

Note: To use the CNumSpinCtrl class properly, the ES_AUTOBUDDY and ES_SETBUDDYINTEGER must not be set.

Your suggestions are appreciated. Enjoy!

```
class CNumEdit : public CEdit
{
    DECLARE_DYNAMIC(CNumEdit)
public:
    CNumEdit();
    virtual ~CNumEdit();
    enum {VALID = 0x00, OUT_OF_RANGE = 0x01, INVALID_CHAR = 0x02};
    virtual void ChangeAmount(int step);
    virtual float GetDelta();
    virtual void SetDelta(float delta);
    virtual void GetRange(float &min, float &max)const;
    virtual void SetRange(float min, float max);
    virtual void Verbose(BOOL v);
    virtual BOOL Verbose()const;
    virtual int IsValid()const;
    virtual int IsValid(const CString &str)const;
    virtual BOOL SetValue(float val);
    virtual float GetValue()const;
protected:
    virtual CString& ConstructFormat(CString &str, float num);
    BYTE m_NumberOfNumberAfterPoint;
    BOOL m_Verbose;
    float m_Delta, m_MinValue, m_MaxValue;
    DECLARE_MESSAGE_MAP()
};

class CNumSpinCtrl : public CSpinButtonCtrl
{
    DECLARE_DYNAMIC(CNumSpinCtrl)
public:
    CNumSpinCtrl();
    virtual ~CNumSpinCtrl();
    virtual void SetDelta(float delta);
    virtual float GetDelta();
    virtual void SetBuddy(CNumEdit *edit);
    virtual CNumEdit* GetBuddy() const;
    virtual void GetRange(float &lower, float& upper ) const;
    virtual void SetRange(float nLower, float nUpper );
    virtual float GetPos();
    virtual void SetPos(float val);
};
```

FROM THE FORUM

Question (John Escobar):

How can I limit the characters that may be entered in an edit control to numbers after the control has been created?

Answer (NigelQ):

You can set the ES_NUMBER style to the control as shown:

```
long Style = GetWindowLong(m_EditCtrl.m_hWnd, GWL_STYLE); // Get style
Style |= ES_NUMBER; // apply the new style
SetWindowLong(m_EditCtrl.m_hWnd, GWL_STYLE, Style); // make it so!
```

FROM THE FORUM

Question (link):

How can I easily append to the text in my edit control?

Answer (fogel):

You can add text anywhere you want using RelaceSel. In your case, you will need to use SetSel to select the end of the current text:

```
M_EditCtrl.SetSel(-1, -1); // sets selection to end of document
m_EditCtrl.ReplaceSel("append");
```

FROM THE FORUM

Question (Yudong):

I have a multiline edit control, but it is interpreting my \n characters as some strange code instead of giving me a new line. How can I insert a new line in the text?

Answer (bug_crusher):

You need to use the \r\n combination to specify a new line.

15

ImageList Controls

In this chapter

Use ImageList controls to collect bitmap images for use in other controls or for drawing methods.

- "Loading an 8bpp (256-Color) Bitmap into an ImageList As a 32bpp Bitmap" provides an

explanation of how to deal with 256-color bitmaps as 32bpp bitmaps to provide a richer color set than the normal half-tone palette.

Loading an 8bpp (256-Color) Bitmap into an ImageList As a 32bpp Bitmap

This article was contributed by Joel Schultz.

Environment: MFC, Win32

One thing that always bugged me about ImageLists is that when you load a 256-color bitmap into them, they use the half-tone palette, which likely could screw up your bitmap's colors. Yet, Windows Explorer is magically able to display icons in its right-pane list control (coming from an ImageList) in full color. So how does it do this?

Listing 15.1 Won't Work (MFC)

```
BOOL CImageList::Create( UINT nBitmapID,
                         int cx,
                         int nGrow,
                         COLORREF crMask)
BOOL CImageList::Create( LPCTSTR lpszBitmapID,
                         int cx,
                         int nGrow,
                         COLORREF crMask)
```

Listing 15.1   Continued

(Win32)

```
HIMAGELIST ImageList_LoadBitmap( HINSTANCE hi,
                                 LPCTSTR lpbmp,
                                 int cx,
                                 int cGrow,
                                 COLORREF crMask)
HIMAGELIST ImageList_LoadImage( HINSTANCE hi,
                                LPCSTR lpbmp,
                                int cx,
                                int cGrow,
                                COLORREF crMask,
                                UINT uType,
                                UINT uFlags)
```

None of the methods shown in Listing 15.1 will do the trick. They will use the half-tone palette since they seem to detect the 8bpp nature of the bitmap and create an "ILC_COLOR8" ImageList, and ImageLists with the ILC_COLOR8 flag always use the half-tone palette.

To get around this, you can create the ImageList in one step, and then add the bitmap in a second step. In Listings 15.2 and 15.3, I assume that you will be using a COLORREF mask for transparency—but nothing requires this to be the case; you could just as easily use a mask bitmap. The key to this technique is the two-step construction and loading of the ImageList.

Listing 15.2   Will Work (MFC)

```
// Create the full-color image list
// cx, cy = your icon width & height
// You could also use ILC_COLOR24 rather than ILC_COLOR32
CImageList imgl;
imgl.Create(cx, cy, ILC_MASK | ILC_COLOR32, 0, 0);

CBitmap bmp;
// Load your imagelist bitmap (bmp) here, however
//    you feel like (e.g. CBitmap::LoadBitmap)

COLORREF rgbTransparentColor;
// Set up your transparent color as appropriate

// Add the bitmap into the image list
imgl.Add(&bmp, rgbTransparentColor);
```

Listing 15.3   Will Work (Win32)

```
// Create the full-color image list
// cx, cy = your icon width & height
// You could also use ILC_COLOR24 rather than ILC_COLOR32
HIMAGELIST himgl = ImageList_Create(cx,
                                    cy,
                                    ILC_MASK ¦ ILC_COLOR32,
                                    0,
                                    0);

HBITMAP hbmp;
// Load your imagelist bitmap (hbmp) here, however
//    you feel like (e.g. LoadImage)

COLORREF rgbTransparentColor;
// Set up your transparent color as appropriate

// Add the bitmap into the image list
ImageList_AddMasked(himgl, hbmp, rgbTransparentColor);
```

FROM THE FORUM

Question (SKULK):

I want to display files in my CListCtrl object. How can I get the same images that explorer uses?

Answer (STT):

You can use the following code to attach the system ImageList to your CListCtrl, then use SHGetFileInfo with the SHGFI_ICON flag to retrieve the appropriate icon index:

```
//image list setup
HIMAGELIST hSystemSmallImageList;
SHFILEINFO ssfi;
CImageList m_smallImageList;

//get a handle to the system small icon list
hSystemSmallImageList = (HIMAGELIST) SHGetFileInfo ((LPCTSTR)_T("C:\\"),
➥ 0, &ssfi, sizeof(SHFILEINFO),SHGFI_SYSICONINDEX
➥ ¦ SHGFI_SMALLICON);

//attach it to the small image list
m_smallImageList.Attach(hSystemSmallImageList);

//Set the list control image list
GetListCtrl().SetImageList(&m_smallImageList, LVSIL_SMALL);

// detach the system image list
m_smallImageList.Detach();
```

FROM THE FORUM

Question (wigg):

How can I display icons in any column of a list control instead of just the left column?

Answer (wigg):

I found the answer myself:

```
LV_ITEM lvitem;
...
lvitem.mask = LVIF_TEXT ¦ LVIF_IMAGE ¦ LVIF_STATE ¦ LVIF_PARAM;
lvitem.iItem = <your row id>;
lvitem.lParam = <your lParam value>; // If you need it
lvitem.iSubItem = <the column number: zero based>;
lvitem.stateMask = LVIS_STATEIMAGEMASK;
lvitem.state = INDEXTOSTATEIMAGEMASK(<image number>);
lvitem.iImage = <image number>;

// szField was already allocated above.
lvitem.pszText = szField;

// insert new item
iActualItem = m_ListCtrl.InsertItem(&lvitem);

// Now set the icon!
m_ListCtrl.SetItemText(0, 4, szField);
```

16

ListBox Controls

A Dual ListBox Selection Manager

This article was contributed by Steve Aube.

I have seen many applications that provide the user with the ability to select an item from one list and put it into another. One example is the NT User Manager Group Memberships screen. This is commonly done by placing two ListBoxes side by side. Then buttons are generally used to add, add all, remove, remove all, and move items up and down in the list of chosen items. Figure 16.1 is a screen shot from my demo application.

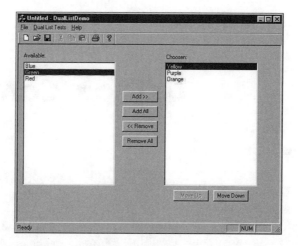

Figure 16.1

I created a class named CDualListManager that handles all of the drudgery of moving items between the two lists. One list represents the list of available items, and the other represents the list of chosen items. (I use the word *chosen* instead of *selected* to avoid any confusion with the highlighted item in a list.) This class is intended to be a member of the CDialog, CformView, or CpropertyPage class. All the parent class has to do is properly initialize this class and call a couple of member functions for CDualListManager to take care of the following things:

- If the Add button is pressed, the selected item(s) are moved from the available list to the chosen list.
- If the Add All button is pressed, all of the items in the available list are moved to the chosen list.
- If the Remove button is pressed, the selected item(s) are moved from the chosen list to the available list.
- If the Remove All button is pressed, all of the items in the chosen list are moved to the available list.
- If the Move Up button is pressed, the selected item(s) in the chosen list are moved up in the list by one. This button can be pressed repeatedly until all of the selected items have reached the top of the list. When that occurs, the button is disabled.
- If the Move Down button is pressed, the selected item(s) in the chosen list are moved down in the list by one.
- Double-clicking on an item moves it to the opposite list.

- When item(s) are moved from one list to another, the item that was moved is selected in the list to which it was moved. The list from which the item was removed selects the item that is at the location of the previous item. If the item at the bottom of the list is moved, the item immediately above it is selected. If the last item in the list is removed, there is no selection.

- When items are moved between lists and up and down in the chosen list, the availability of buttons changes. For instance, if an item is moved to the top of the chosen list the Move Up button doesn't make sense, so when this occurs the Move Up button is automatically disabled.

- Disabling a button that has the focus causes problems for keyboard users. This code checks to see whether a button has the focus before it disables it. If it does, the focus is forwarded to the next available control.

To use this class, follow these steps:

1. Add a member variable of this class type to the dialog box, property page, or form view where you want to use it.

2. From the initialization method (OnInitDialog() for a dialog box or property page and OnInitialUpdate() for a view), do the following things in this order:

   - Add the items to the available and chosen lists with the calls AddItemToAvailableList(…) and AddItemToChosenList(…). The first parameter is the name of the item and the second parameter is a unique identifier for the item.

   - Call InitializeControls(…) with a pointer to the parent window and the IDs of all of the controls.

   - Override OnCmdMsg(…).

Notes:

- If you don't need certain features (like the capability to move an item up or down in the chosen list), simply provide a NULL value for that ID. The rest of the class will continue to work correctly. The IDs for the two lists are required because a dual list manager doesn't make sense unless it has two lists to work with.

- This code will work with single, multiple, and extended ListBoxes.

- The order of the controls doesn't matter. You can put the chosen list on the left, right, top, or bottom of the selected list. Just make sure you supply the control IDs in the right order.

The demo application uses this dual list manager in a form view, a dialog box, and a property page. This code will show how to use it in a form view.

Make the following changes to OnInitialUpdate:

```
void CDualListDemoView::OnInitialUpdate()
{
... // Normal processing
// ADDED TO THE DEFAULT LISTS.
// This code will need to be replaced with your
// application-specific code that knows what belongs
// in each list.
m_DualListManager.AddItemToAvailableList(_T("Red"), 0);
m_DualListManager.AddItemToAvailableList(_T("Green"), 1);
m_DualListManager.AddItemToAvailableList(_T("Blue"), 2);
m_DualListManager.AddItemToChoosenList(_T("Yellow"), 3);
m_DualListManager.AddItemToChoosenList(_T("Purple"), 4);
m_DualListManager.AddItemToChoosenList(_T("Orange"), 5);

// ADDED TO INITIALIZE THE MANAGER CLASS
m_DualListManager.InitializeControls(this,
 IDC_FV_LIST_AVAILABLE,
 IDC_FV_LIST_CHOOSEN,
 IDC_FV_ADD,
 IDC_FV_ADD_ALL,
 IDC_FV_REMOVE,
 IDC_FV_REMOVE_ALL,
 IDC_FV_MOVE_UP,
 IDC_FV_MOVE_DOWN);
}
```

Override the OnCmdMsg method and add a call to the ProcessCmdMsg on the DualListManager Object:

```
BOOL CDualListDemoView::OnCmdMsg(UINT nID, int nCode,
void* pExtra, AFX_CMDHANDLERINFO* pHandlerInfo)
{
// ADDED TO INTERCEPT MESSAGE THAT THE DUAL
// LIST MANAGER NEEDS
m_DualListManager.ProcessCmdMsg(nID, nCode);

// NOW CALL THE BASE CLASS
return CFormView::OnCmdMsg(nID, nCode, pExtra, pHandlerInfo);
}
```

Add the following member to your header file:

```
CDualListManager m_DualListManager;
```

A Visual Studio–Like ListBox Class

This article was contributed by Stefano Passiglia.

Figure 16.2

Environment: VC6 SP1, NT4 SP5, WIN 95/98

This article presents an extended ListBox control. Its look and feel resembles the one that you can find in the Tools, Options dialog of the Visual Studio environment.

As you can see from Figure 16.2, this new ListBox allows in-place item editing, and also adds the possibility to show a Browse button near the Edit field.

Moreover, because the new ListBox control is derived from a drag ListBox, it is also possible to reorder items by dragging and dropping them or via the Alt+Up/ Alt+Down keys.

I also wrote a simple "buddy" class, which you can see in the upper part of Figure 16.2, that makes the control even easier to use.

How to Use It

To use this ListBox class, simply drop a normal ListBox on a dialog and associate it with a CListBoxEx class:

```
// This class overrides the OnBrowseButton method.
class CMyListBoxEx: public CListBoxEx
{
public:

 virtual void OnBrowseButton( int iItem )
 {
  iItem;
  CSHBrowseDlg dlgBrowse;
  if ( dlgBrowse.DoModal() ) SetEditText( dlgBrowse.GetFullPath() );
 };
};

class CListBoxExDemoDlg : public CDialog
{
// Construction
public:
 // standard constructor
 CListBoxExDemoDlg(CWnd* pParent = NULL);

// Dialog Data
 //{{AFX_DATA(CListBoxExDemoDlg)
 enum { IDD = IDD_LISTBOXEXDEMO_DIALOG };
 CMyListBoxEx     m_ListBoxEx;
 //}}AFX_DATA
};
```

It's as easy as that! The OnBrowseButton() is called synchronously when the user clicks the "…" button. Other events that are called are OnBeginEditing() and OnEndEditing().

If you also want to use the buddy class, drop a button on the dialog, change its properties, and make it owner drawn with a client edge.

Then, in your dialog OnInitDialog(), subclass the button control like this:

```
// Add the ListBox buddy
m_ListBoxExBuddy.SubclassDlgItem( IDC_LISTBUDDY, this );
m_ListBoxExBuddy.SetListbox( &m_ListBoxEx );
```

Other Improvements

I added a lot of (I think) useful methods that add quite a bit of functionality to the raw ListBox and make it a bit more user friendly:

```
// Editing and dragging are anabled by default
void AllowEditing( BOOL bAllowEditing = TRUE )
{
m_bAllowEditing = bAllowEditing;
};

void AllowDrag( BOOL bAllowDrag = TRUE )
{
m_bAllowDrag = bAllowDrag;
};

// Editing methods
void BeginEditing( int iItem );
void EndEditing( BOOL fCancel );

// Add a new empty string and begin editing
void EditNew();

void SetEditStyle( DWORD dwEditStyle );

HWND GetEditHandle() const;

void SetEditText( const CString & strNewText ) const;

// Item methods
int MoveItemUp( int iItem );
int MoveItemDown( int iItem );
void SwapItems( int iFirstItem, int iSecondItem );

void SetItem( int iItem, LPCTSTR szItemText, DWORD dwItemData );
void SetItemText( int iItem, LPCTSTR szItemText );

// Virtual (overridables) events
virtual BOOL OnBeginEditing( int iItem );
virtual BOOL OnEndEditing( int iItem, BOOL fCanceled );

virtual void OnBrowseButton( int iItem );
```

Comments

A minor assertion failure exists within the code when using the debug build. To correct this functionality, modify the code as follows:

```
int CListBoxEx::MoveItemUp( int iItem )
{
    ASSERT( iItem >= 0 );

    if (!(iItem > 0))
        return iItem;

    if ( iItem > 0 )
    {
        SwapItems( iItem, iItem-1 );
        SetCurSel( iItem - 1 );
    }

    return iItem;
}
```

—Sok Woo, Lim

If you wish to use the control with an Edit control, but without the Browse button, make the following changes to the sample code:

In the CMyListBoxEx constructor, remove the following statement:

```
SetEditStyle( LBEX_EDITBUTTON );
```

This will prevent the browse button from being displayed. Also, change the CListBoxEx constructor as set m_dwEditStyle to 0 as follows:

```
m_dwEditStyle = 0;
```

—Abhi

The F2 and Delete keys only work with the last item selected with the mouse. If you are using the up/down arrows, you might begin editing the wrong item. To correct this, change the OnKeyDown handler routine as follows to make use of the currently selected item, as opposed to the cached item:

```
void CListBoxEx::OnKeyDown( UINT nChar, UINT nRepCnt, UINT nFlags )
{
    CDragListBox::OnKeyDown( nChar, nRepCnt, nFlags );

    if(nChar == VK_F2)
    {
        m_iSelected = GetCurSel();
```

```
            if( (m_iSelected != -1) && m_bAllowEditing &&
                 (OnBeginEditing( m_iSelected ) != FALSE) )
            {
                // Begin Editing
                BeginEditing( m_iSelected );
            }
    }
    else if( nChar == VK_DELETE )
    {
        m_iSelected = GetCurSel();

        if( m_iSelected != -1 )
            DeleteString( m_iSelected );
    }


} // CListBoxEx::OnKeyDown
```

—Paul McLachlan

The buddy's icons can remain raised if the mouse exits the CWnd too quickly. Use SetCapture() when the button is highlighted, and then ReleaseCapture() when it is invalidated to solve this problem. The problem arises because the control does not get a WM_MOUSEMOVE message when the mouse is outside of the client area. Make the following changes to the sample code to correct this:

1. Add the following member variable to the CListBoxExBuddy class (.h):

   ```
   BOOL m_captured
   ```

2. In the constructor, set m_captured to FALSE.

3. Modify the following methods:

   ```
   void CListBoxExBuddy::InvalidateButton( int  iIndex, BOOL bUpdateWindow
   ➥/*= TRUE */ )
   {
       if ( iIndex < __BMP_NUMBTN )
       {
           InvalidateRect( &m_arcButtons[ iIndex ], FALSE );
           if( !m_captured )
           {
               SetCapture();
               m_captured = TRUE;
           }
       }

       if ( bUpdateWindow ) UpdateWindow();
   ```

```
    } // CListBoxExBuddy::InvalidateButton
    void CListBoxExBuddy::OnMouseMove( UINT    nFlags, CPoint point )
    {
        if ( !m_bButtonPressed )
        {
            UINT iIndex = FindButton( point );

            // If found a button, update info
            if ( iIndex != m_iButton )
            {
                InvalidateButton( m_iButton, FALSE );
                m_iButton = iIndex;
                InvalidateButton( m_iButton, TRUE );
                if( m_iButton == __BMP_NUMBTN && m_captured )
                {
                    ReleaseCapture();
                    m_captured = FALSE;
                }
            }
        }

        // Relay tooltip events
        //m_ToolTip.RelayEvent( const_cast<MSG *>( GetCurrentMessage() ) );
        //m_ToolTip.Activate( TRUE );

        CWnd::OnMouseMove(nFlags, point);

    } // CListBoxExBuddy::OnMouseMove
```

—Paul McLachlan

FROM THE FORUM

Question (Saeed):

How can I get the horizontal scroll to work correctly when the text in the ListBox control exceeds the width of the box?

Answer (Dmitry Zemskov):

Use the following code to set the width of the horizontal scroll based upon the widest string:

```
    void SetHorizontalExtent( CListBox& rListBox )
    {
        int nIdx = rListBox.GetCount();

        if ( nIdx == LB_ERR )
            return;
```

```
        int nHExtent = 0;

        if ( nIdx )
        {
            CDC* pDC = rListBox.GetDC();
            ASSERT( pDC );
            CFont* pOldFont = pDC -> SelectObject( rListBox.GetFont() );

            CString S;
            SIZE TextExt;
            LONG nMaxExt = 0;

            while( nIdx-- )
            {
                rListBox.GetText( nIdx, S );
                TextExt = pDC -> GetOutputTextExtent( S );
                if ( TextExt.cx > nMaxExt )
                    nMaxExt = TextExt.cx;
            }

            TextExt.cx = nMaxExt;
            pDC -> LPtoDP( &TextExt );
            nHExtent = TextExt.cx + 2;

            pDC -> SelectObject( pOldFont );
            rListBox.ReleaseDC( pDC );
        } // if ( nIdx )

        rListBox.SetHorizontalExtent( nHExtent );

    } // void SetHorizontalExtent( CListBox& rListBox )
```

17

ListView Controls

Select an Item Programmatically

Unlike a ListBox control, the ListView control does not have a SetCurSel() or SetSel() function. To achieve that kind of functionality, use the following statement:

```
m_listctrl.SetItemState( rownum,LVIS_SELECTED | LVIS_FOCUSED ,
➥LVIS_SELECTED | LVIS_FOCUSED);
```

If you don't use the LVIS_FOCUSED flag and the control allows multiple selection, then you will likely end up with two items highlighted—one that has the focus and one that you just selected.

Another gotcha is that if you do not set the LVS_SHOWSELALWAYS style for the ListView control, you don't see the highlighting until the control gets focus.

Comments

In addition to the sample code, an easy way to deselect all of the items in a ListView control would be to pass -1 as the index parameter, as shown in the following code:

```
// -1 changes the state of all items in the list.
m_listCtrl.SetItemState(-1, ~LVIS_SELECTED, LVIS_SELECTED);
```

—Sasha Aickin

To programmatically scroll an item into view, use the following code:

```
m_listCtrl.EnsureVisible( nItem, FALSE );
```

—Sacha Saxer

Sort a List (Numeric/Text) Using Callback

This article was contributed by Iuri Apollonio.

This is a small class that permits the sorting of list controls. It works by substituting every original item's data with a small class (preserving the value), sorting it using the standard (fast!) list control way, and then putting everything back the way it was.

Step 1: Implementing the Class

The class will contain two subclasses to manage numeric and text column data. The numeric is provided to avoid such problems as the sorting of 11 before 2, which would occur with string comparison. There also are four comparing routines (for ascending and descending text and integer columns).

The header file of the class should be like this:

```
class CSortClass
{
public:
    CSortClass(CListCtrl * _pWnd, const int _iCol, const bool _bIsNumeric);
    virtual ~CSortClass();

    int iCol;
    CListCtrl * pWnd;
    bool bIsNumeric;
    void Sort(const bool bAsc);

    static int CALLBACK CompareAsc(LPARAM lParam1, LPARAM lParam2,
➥LPARAM lParamSort);
    static int CALLBACK CompareDes(LPARAM lParam1, LPARAM lParam2,
➥LPARAM lParamSort);
```

```
    static int CALLBACK CompareAscI(LPARAM lParam1, LPARAM lParam2,
➥LPARAM lParamSort);
    static int CALLBACK CompareDesI(LPARAM lParam1, LPARAM lParam2,
➥LPARAM lParamSort);

public:
    class CSortItem
    {
    public:
        virtual  ~CSortItem();
        CSortItem(const DWORD _dw, const CString &_txt);
        CString txt;
        DWORD dw;
    };
    class CSortItemInt
    {
    public:
        CSortItemInt(const DWORD _dw, const CString &_txt);
        int iInt ;
        DWORD dw;
    };
};
```

The CPP file will implement the header file:

```
//////////////////////////////////////////////////////////////////////
// CSortClass

CSortClass::CSortClass(CListCtrl * _pWnd, const int _iCol,
➥const bool _bIsNumeric)
{
    iCol = _iCol;
    pWnd = _pWnd;
    bIsNumeric = _bIsNumeric;

    ASSERT(pWnd);
    int max = pWnd->GetItemCount();
    DWORD dw;
    CString txt;
    if (bIsNumeric)
    {
        for (int t = 0; t < max; t++)
        {
            dw = pWnd->GetItemData(t);
            txt = pWnd->GetItemText(t, iCol);
            pWnd->SetItemData(t, (DWORD) new CSortItemInt(dw, txt));
        }
    }
    else
    {
        for (int t = 0; t < max; t++)
        {
```

```
                dw = pWnd->GetItemData(t);
                txt = pWnd->GetItemText(t, iCol);
                pWnd->SetItemData(t, (DWORD) new CSortItem(dw, txt));
            }
        }
    }

CSortClass::~CSortClass()
{
    ASSERT(pWnd);
    int max = pWnd->GetItemCount();
    if (bIsNumeric)
    {
        CSortItemInt * pItem;
        for (int t = 0; t < max; t++)
        {
            pItem = (CSortItemInt *) pWnd->GetItemData(t);
            ASSERT(pItem);
            pWnd->SetItemData(t, pItem->dw);
            delete pItem;
        }
    }
    else
    {
        CSortItem * pItem;
        for (int t = 0; t < max; t++)
        {
            pItem = (CSortItem *) pWnd->GetItemData(t);
            ASSERT(pItem);
            pWnd->SetItemData(t, pItem->dw);
            delete pItem;
        }
    }
}

void
CSortClass::Sort(const bool bAsc)
{
    if (bIsNumeric)
    {
        if (bAsc)
            pWnd->SortItems(CompareAscI, 0L);
        else
            pWnd->SortItems(CompareDesI, 0L);
    }
    else
    {
        if (bAsc)
            pWnd->SortItems(CompareAsc, 0L);
        else
            pWnd->SortItems(CompareDes, 0L);
    }
}
```

```
int CALLBACK CSortClass::CompareAsc(LPARAM lParam1, LPARAM lParam2,
➥LPARAM lParamSort)
{
    CSortItem * i1 = (CSortItem *) lParam1;
    CSortItem * i2 = (CSortItem *) lParam2;
    ASSERT(i1 && i2);
    return i1->txt.CompareNoCase(i2->txt);
}

int CALLBACK CSortClass::CompareDes(LPARAM lParam1, LPARAM lParam2,
➥LPARAM lParamSort)
{
    CSortItem * i1 = (CSortItem *) lParam1;
    CSortItem * i2 = (CSortItem *) lParam2;
    ASSERT(i1 && i2);
    return i2->txt.CompareNoCase(i1->txt);
}

int CALLBACK CSortClass::CompareAscI(LPARAM lParam1, LPARAM lParam2,
➥LPARAM lParamSort)
{
    CSortItemInt * i1 = (CSortItemInt *) lParam1;
    CSortItemInt * i2 = (CSortItemInt *) lParam2;
    ASSERT(i1 && i2);
    if (i1->iInt == i2->iInt) return 0;
    return i1->iInt > i2->iInt ? 1 : -1;
}

int CALLBACK CSortClass::CompareDesI(LPARAM lParam1, LPARAM lParam2,
➥LPARAM lParamSort)
{
    CSortItemInt * i1 = (CSortItemInt *) lParam1;
    CSortItemInt * i2 = (CSortItemInt *) lParam2;
    ASSERT(i1 && i2);
    if (i1->iInt == i2->iInt) return 0;
    return i1->iInt < i2->iInt ? 1 : -1;
}

CSortClass::CSortItem::CSortItem(const DWORD _dw, const CString & _txt)
{
    dw = _dw;
    txt = _txt;
}

CSortClass::CSortItem::~CSortItem()
{
}

CSortClass::CSortItemInt::CSortItemInt(const DWORD _dw, const CString & _txt)
{
    iInt = atoi(_txt);
    dw = _dw;
}
```

Step 2: Using It

The class is designed to be easy to use. In answer to a column click message in a list control, write something like this:

```
void CMyListCtrl::OnColumnclick(NMHDR* pNMHDR, LRESULT* pResult)
{
    NM_LISTVIEW* pNMListView = (NM_LISTVIEW*)pNMHDR;

    // bAscending will be used to order from lower to higher or higher to lower
    bool bAscending = true;

    CSortClass csc(this, pNMListView->iSubItem, bAscending);
    csc.Sort(bAsc);

    *pResult = 0;
}
```

Comments

The following is a possible improvement to the column click handler routine:

```
void xxx::OnColumnclicklistxxx(NMHDR* pNMHDR, LRESULT* pResult)
{

    NM_LISTVIEW* pNMListView = (NM_LISTVIEW*)pNMHDR;

    static bool bAscending = false;
    CListCtrl* p_clist = &m_listxxx;
    CSortClass csc( p_clist, pNMListView->iSubItem, false); // false =
➡for string items
    bAscending = !bAscending;
    csc.Sort(bAscending);

    *pResult = 0;

}
```

—iztok

CreateDragImage for (Unlimited) Multiple Selected Items

This article was contributed by Hao (David) TRAN.

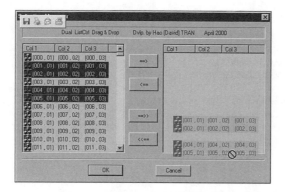

Figure 17.1

Environment: NT4 VC5 (also tested on WIN98 VC6)

This is based on the article "CreateDragImage for Multiple Selected Items in CListCtrl" by Frank Kobs. Thanks, Frank, for the idea!

I have some suggestions for modifications to Frank's CreateDragImageEx() with the following advantages:

- You can use the code in VC 5 (of course, it can also be used in VC 6).

- You can select as many items to drag and drop as you want. (When I selected 500 items to drag and drop, Frank's CreateDragImageEx() didn't work. In fact, for the items selected out of the ListCtrl's ClientRect, called CreateDragImage(), it returned a blank rectangle. Thus, it is not necessary to create a big bitmap with blank rows.

- You can make better use of the optional service. (At the end of Frank's CreateDragImageEx(), if you press the mouse button and then quickly move the hot point, the cursor will have a certain distance from the hot point of DragImage. That's because the GetMousePos() will have a different position then the GetMessagePos().)

Here is my version of CreateDragImageEx():

```
CImageList* CMyList::CreateDragImageEx(LPPOINT lpPoint)
{
 if (GetSelectedCount() <= 0)
  return NULL; // no row selected

 CRect rectSingle;
 CRect rectComplete(0,0,0,0);

 // Determine List Control Client width size
 GetClientRect(rectSingle);
 int nWidth = rectSingle.Width();

 // Start and Stop index in view area
 int nIndex = GetTopIndex() - 1;
 int nBottomIndex = GetTopIndex() + GetCountPerPage() - 1;
 if (nBottomIndex > (GetItemCount() - 1))
 nBottomIndex = GetItemCount() - 1;

 // Determine the size of the drag image (limited for
 // rows visible and Client width)
 while ((nIndex = GetNextItem(nIndex, LVNI_SELECTED)) != -1)
 {
  if (nIndex > nBottomIndex)
   break;

  GetItemRect(nIndex, rectSingle, LVIR_BOUNDS);

  if (rectSingle.left < 0)
  rectSingle.left = 0;

  if (rectSingle.right > nWidth)
  rectSingle.right = nWidth;

  rectComplete.UnionRect(rectComplete, rectSingle);
 }

 CClientDC dcClient(this);
 CDC dcMem;
 CBitmap Bitmap;

 if (!dcMem.CreateCompatibleDC(&dcClient))
  return NULL;

 if (!Bitmap.CreateCompatibleBitmap(&dcClient,
     rectComplete.Width(),
     rectComplete.Height()))
  return NULL;
```

```
CBitmap *pOldMemDCBitmap = dcMem.SelectObject(&Bitmap);
// Use green as mask color
dcMem.FillSolidRect(0, 0,
                    rectComplete.Width(),
                    rectComplete.Height(),
                    RGB(0,255,0));

// Paint each DragImage in the DC
nIndex = GetTopIndex() - 1;
while ((nIndex = GetNextItem(nIndex, LVNI_SELECTED)) != -1)
{
 if (nIndex > nBottomIndex)
  break;

 CPoint pt;
 CImageList* pSingleImageList = CreateDragImage(nIndex, &pt);

 if (pSingleImageList)
 {
  GetItemRect(nIndex, rectSingle, LVIR_BOUNDS);

  pSingleImageList->Draw(&dcMem,
   0,
   CPoint(rectSingle.left - rectComplete.left,
   rectSingle.top - rectComplete.top),
   ILD_MASK);

  pSingleImageList->DeleteImageList();
  delete pSingleImageList;
 }
}

dcMem.SelectObject(pOldMemDCBitmap);
CImageList* pCompleteImageList = new CImageList;
pCompleteImageList->Create(rectComplete.Width(),
                           rectComplete.Height(),
                           ILC_COLOR | ILC_MASK,
                           0, 1);

// Green is used as mask color
pCompleteImageList->Add(&Bitmap, RGB(0, 255, 0));
Bitmap.DeleteObject();

if (lpPoint)
{
 lpPoint->x = rectComplete.left;
 lpPoint->y = rectComplete.top;
}

return pCompleteImageList;
}
```

I use my CreateDragImageEx to create the commonly dual ListCtrl selection manager. The CreateDragImageEx in the demo is situated on the Dialog level in order to demonstrate another way to use CreateDragImageEx.

You can double-click, use the Move button, or drag and drop single or multiple items from one list to another. All items moved to another list are selected and placed at the top of the list automatically, allowing the user to move back and forth to Undo.

Comments

A one-time flicker is caused by referencing screen coordinates instead of local window coordinates. You can correct this by replacing this line

```
m_pDragImage->DragEnter(NULL, pNMListView->ptAction);
```

with

```
CRect rect;
::GetWindowRect(pList->m_hWnd, &rect);
CPoint pt = pNMListView->ptAction;
pt.Offset(rect.left, rect.top);
m_pDragImage->DragEnter(NULL, pt);
```

—1st.app

In CreateDragImageListEx the ImageList is only created with the default color depth (ILC_COLOR). In order to display high color icons, this should be ILC_COLOR32, as shown in the following code:

```
pCompleteImageList->Create(rectComplete.Width(), rectComplete.Height(),
➥ILC_COLOR32 ¦ ILC_MASK, 0, 1);
```

—Tim Kosse

There is a problem with the image mask when dragging. Correct this by changing the last parameter of the Draw call from ILD_MASK to ILD_NORMAL. Replace the line

```
pSingleImageList->Draw( &dcMem, 0, CPoint(rectSingle.left -
➥rectComplete.left, rectSingle.top - rectComplete.top), ILD_MASK);
```

with

```
pSingleImageList->Draw( &dcMem, 0, CPoint(rectSingle.left -
➥rectComplete.left, rectSingle.top - rectComplete.top), ILD_NORMAL);
```

—Tim Kosse

Adaptable Property List Control

This article was contributed by Stefan Belopotocan.

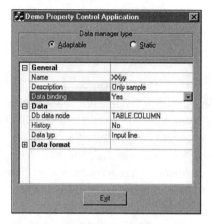

Figure 17.2

Environment: VC6 SP4, NT5 SP5

In an application I was developing, there was a need to implement some kind of user interface for changing object properties for different types of objects. Some object properties are static, but there are objects whose properties change according to their actual state. So I have decided to create a control like in Microsoft Visual Basic with the feature of adapting the context of property items to an object's current state. Take a look at a simple example. I need to describe the individual items of a form. An item can display simple text but also a concrete representation from a database. If this item displays only simple text, I do not need to enter other parameters (object properties) for describing and formatting data.

How It Works

The CPropertyListCtrl class implements necessary utilities for presenting property items and for user interaction.

The CInPlaceEditImp and CInPlaceComboBox classes implement in-place controls for editing item values. CInPlaceEditImp is for string values and CInPlaceComboBox is for list items or enumerations.

At the end, the CPropertyItemString, CPropertyItemList, CPropertyItemCategory, CPropertyItemManager, and CPropertyItemManagerAdaptable classes exist for the manipulation of property data items. The CPropertyItemString and CPropertyItemList classes are for the basic editing of property data values. The CPropertyItemCategory class contains property items of one category, and CPropertyItemManager is a container for all property categories of an object. The CPropertyItemManagerAdaptable class supports a mechanism for adaptability.

How to Use It

Follow these steps:

1. Include the source files in your project.
2. If you need to, you can either define your own property list item values (enumerations) derived from the class CPropertyItemList or implement your own custom property item value derived from the base class CPropertyItem.
3. Implement your property item manager, which describes the property items of your object. In cases where the property items change according to the object's state, derive your property item manager from the class CPropertyItemManagerAdaptable.
4. Use the CPropertyListCtrl control in your dialog or view and set its property item manager by using the SetPropertyItemManager method.

How to Implement Your Own Property Item Value Class

Derive the new class from the base class CPropertyItem and implement its get/set methods and its virtual methods:

- virtual void DrawValue(CDC* pDC, CRect& rect), for drawing a property item value into the CPropertyListCtrl dc context.
- virtual void CreateInPlaceControl(CWnd* pWndParent, CRect& rect, CWnd*& pWndInPlaceControl), for creating its own suitable in-place control for editing its value.
- virtual void SetData(CWnd* pWndInPlaceControl), for setting its value after the end of editing by an in-place control.

```
// CMyPropertyItem

class CMyPropertyItem : public CPropertyItem
{
 CMyPropertyItem(const CMyPropertyItem& d);
 CMyPropertyItem& operator=(const CMyPropertyItem& d);

protected:
 DECLARE_DYNAMIC(CMyPropertyItem)
```

```
public:
 CMyPropertyItem(MyDataType myData = INI_VALUE);
 virtual ~CMyPropertyItem();

 // Attributes
 MyDataTyp& GetData() const;
 void SetData(MyDataType& myData);

 // Operations
 virtual void DrawValue(CDC* pDC, CRect& rect);
 virtual void CreateInPlaceControl(CWnd* pWndParent,
                                   CRect& rect,
                                   CWnd*& pWndInPlaceControl);
 virtual void SetData(CWnd* pWndInPlaceControl);

 // Data
private:
 MyDataType m_myData;
};
```

Also, define its GET_ITEM... and SET_ITEM... macros, which are used in conjunction with BEGIN_ITERATE_PROPERTY_ITEMS macros. For a better understanding of this, look at how the CPropertyItemString or CPropertyItemList classes are implemented.

How to Define Your Own Property List Item Value Class

Use predefined macros for implementing property list item values. This example defines the CMyCustomPropertyItemList with two property items:

```
// CMyCustomPropertyItemList

BEGIN_LIST_ITEM_DATA_TYPE(CMyCustomPropertyItemList)
 LPCTSTR_STRING_ITEM_DATA(_T("A string value here")),
 ID_STRING_ITEM_DATA(IDS_STRING_VALUE_FROM_RESOURCES)
END_LIST_ITEM_DATA_TYPE(CMyCustomPropertyItemList)
```

Or you can implement your own class, derived from the CPropertyItemList class, declaring its virtual LPCTSTR GetItemData(int nItem) const function:

```
// CMyOwnPropertyItemList
class CMyOwnPropertyItemList : public CPropertyItemList
{
//....
public:
 virtual LPCTSTR GetItemData(int nItem) const;
}
```

How to Implement Your Own Property Item Manager Class

In order that the CPropertyListCtrl control knows which items to display, you have to implement your own property item manager describing the property items of your object. If your object property items are static, you simply derive your property item manager from the class CPropertyItemManager and declare the following items in the constructor using predefined macros:

```
// CMyStaticPropertyItemManager
CMyStaticPropertyItemManager::CMyStaticPropertyItemManager()
{
 // General
 BEGIN_PROPERTY_TAB(_T("General"), true)
  PROPERTY_ITEM(ID_PD_NAME, CPropertyItemString,
               _T("Name"), true)

  PROPERTY_ITEM(ID_PD_DESCRIPTION, CPropertyItemString,
               _T("Description"), true)

  PROPERTY_ITEM(ID_PD_BIND_DATA, CPropertyItemListYesNo,
               _T("Data binding"), true)
 END_PROPERTY_TAB()

 // Data
 BEGIN_PROPERTY_TAB(_T("Data"), true)
  PROPERTY_ITEM(ID_PD_DB_NODE, CPropertyItemString,
               _T("Db data node"), true)

  PROPERTY_ITEM(ID_PD_HISTORY, CPropertyItemListYesNo,
               _T("History"), true)
 END_PROPERTY_TAB()
}
```

Also, implement get/set methods for accessing the property item values of your object. For simple reference access, you can use predefined macros:

```
bool CMyStaticPropertyItemManager::SetData(const CObject* pData)
{
 const CMyData* pMyData = static_cast< const CMyData* >(pData);

 BEGIN_ITERATE_PROPERTY_ITEMS()
  SET_ITEM_STRING(ID_PD_NAME, pMyData->m_strName)
  SET_ITEM_STRING(ID_PD_DESCRIPTION, pMyData->m_strDescription)
  SET_ITEM_LIST(ID_PD_BIND_DATA, pMyData->m_bBindDatabaseData)
  SET_ITEM_STRING(ID_PD_DB_NODE, pMyData->m_strDbTableColumn)
  SET_ITEM_LIST(ID_PD_HISTORY, pMyData->m_bCreateHistoryData)
 END_ITERATE_PROPERTY_ITEMS()
```

```
 return true;
}

bool CMyStaticPropertyItemManager::GetData(CObject* pData) const
{
 CMyData* pMyData = static_cast< CMyData* >(pData);

 BEGIN_ITERATE_PROPERTY_ITEMS()
  GET_ITEM_STRING(ID_PD_NAME, pMyData->m_strName)
  GET_ITEM_STRING(ID_PD_DESCRIPTION, pMyData->m_strDescription)
  GET_ITEM_LIST(ID_PD_BIND_DATA, pMyData->m_bBindDatabaseData)
  GET_ITEM_STRING(ID_PD_DB_NODE, pMyData->m_strDbTableColumn)
  GET_ITEM_LIST(ID_PD_HISTORY, pMyData->m_bCreateHistoryData)
 END_ITERATE_PROPERTY_ITEMS()

 return true;
}
```

If you want to implement an adaptable property item manager, derive it from the class CPropertyItemManagerAdaptable and define a virtual void OnDataChanged (CPropertyItem* pPropertyItem, CPropertyListCtrl* pWndPropertyListCtrl, int nIndex) method for changing a property item's state:

```
void CMyAdaptablePropertyItemManager::OnDataChanged(CPropertyItem*
➥pPropertyItem,
                                        CPropertyListCtrl* pWndPropertyListCtrl,
                                        int nIndex)
{
 bool bDoChecking = false;

 switch(pPropertyItem->GetPropertyID())
 {
  case ID_PD_BIND_DATA:
  {
   // Yes/No item
   bool bEnableTabs;
   static_cast<CPropertyItemList*>(pPropertyItem)->GetData(bEnableTabs);

   // Enable/Disable tabs 1
   CPropertyItemCategory* pPropertyItemTab = GetCategoryTab(1);

   if(pPropertyItemTab->SetEnabled(bEnableTabs))
    bDoChecking = true;

   // Enable/Disable tabs 2
   int nItemType;

   static_cast<CPropertyItemList*>
   (pPropertyItemTab->GetPropertyItem(ID_PD_DATA_TYPE))->GetData(nItemType);

   pPropertyItemTab = GetCategoryTab(2);
```

```
     if(pPropertyItemTab->SetEnabled(bEnableTabs && nItemType < 4))
       bDoChecking = true;
   }
   break;

   case ID_PD_DATA_TYPE:
   {
     // Enumerate item
     int nItemType;
     static_cast<CPropertyItemList*>(pPropertyItem)->GetData(nItemType);

     For items 4 (Form) and 5 (Macro) disable tab #2, for others enable
     CPropertyItemCategory* pPropertyItemTab = GetCategoryTab(2);
     bDoChecking = pPropertyItemTab->SetEnabled(nItemType < 4);
   }
   break;

   default:
   return;
 }

 if(bDoChecking)
   CheckState(pWndPropertyListCtrl, nIndex, pPropertyItem->GetPropertyID());
}
```

Things to Improve

Eliminate flicker, meanwhile showing in-place controls. Add further edit controls.

If you have any other suggested improvements, please let me know so that I can incorporate them into the next release. If you want to see how I have used this control in my projects, take a look at http://welcome.to/StefanBelopotocan.

Comments

To correct the minor problem with the height of the drop-down list, modify the sample code as follows:

```
#define DEFAULT_IPLISTBOX_HEIGHT (13+1) * 8 // 13+1: common itemheight with
➡margin times 8 items

void CInPlaceComboBoxImp::ResetListBoxHeight()
{
    CRect rect;

    GetClientRect(rect);
    rect.right -= 1;
```

```
    int nItems = m_wndList.GetCount();
    int nListBoxHeight = nItems > 0 ? m_wndList.GetItemHeight(0)+1) * nItems
➥: DEFAULT_IPLISTBOX_HEIGHT;

    if(nListBoxHeight > DEFAULT_IPLISTBOX_HEIGHT)
        nListBoxHeight = DEFAULT_IPLISTBOX_HEIGHT;

    m_wndList.SetWindowPos(NULL, 0, 0, rect.Width(), nListBoxHeight,
➥SWP_NOZORDER¦SWP_NOMOVE);

}
```

—Sander van Woensel

Flickering seen when using the control can be eliminated with the following modification:

```
void CInPlaceComboBoxImp::ResetListBoxHeight()
{
    ...

    // Replace this line
    m_wndList.SetWindowPos(NULL, 0, 0, rect.Width(), nListBoxHeight,
➥SWP_NOZORDER¦SWP_NOMOVE);

    // With this one
    m_wndList.MoveWindow(rect.top, rect.left, rect.Width(),
➥nListBoxHeight, FALSE);

}
```

—Andreas Grau

FROM THE FORUM

Question (jase jennings):

How can I make the text background for icons in a ListView control appear transparent so that the color behind is visible?

Answer (Redllar):

The following example works with the desktop icons and can be modified for your own ListView controls. You can also change the text colors via the command-line switches:

```
#include <windows.h>
#include <commctrl.h>
#include <stdio.h>

WINAPI WinMain( HINSTANCE hInstance, HINSTANCE hPrevInstance, LPSTR
➥lpCmdLine,int nCmdShow )
{
```

```
        HWND hWnd;
        COLORREF crTextColor;

        crTextColor = RGB(0, 0, 0);

        if( *lpCmdLine )
        {
            char cC=0;
            int iR=0, iG=0, iB=0, iA=0;
            sscanf(lpCmdLine, "%d %d %d %d %c", &iR, &iG, &iB, &iA, &cC);
            crTextColor = RGB(max(0, min(255, iR+iA)), max(0, min(255,
                     iG+iA)), max(0, min(255, iB+iA)));

            if( cC )
                crTextColor = ~crTextColor;
        }
        else
        {
            crTextColor = ~GetSysColor(COLOR_BACKGROUND);
        }

        if( hWnd = FindWindowEx(NULL, NULL, "Progman", NULL) )
        {
            if( hWnd = FindWindowEx(hWnd, NULL, "SHELLDLL_DefView", NULL) )
            {
                if(hWnd = FindWindowEx(hWnd, NULL, "SysListView32", NULL) )
                {
                    ListView_SetBkColor (hWnd, CLR_NONE);
                    ListView_SetTextBkColor(hWnd, CLR_NONE);
                    ListView_SetTextColor (hWnd, crTextColor);
                    ListView_RedrawItems (hWnd, 0,
                        ListView_GetItemCount(hWnd) - 1);
                }
            }
        }

    return 0;

    }
```

FROM THE FORUM

Question (rajasekar.s):

I have two ListView controls that I need to synchronize. Scrolling one should scroll the other at the same time. How can this be done?

Answer (rajasekar.s):

I found the solution myself:

```
// Message map entry maps to this member. So use this to sync the other view...
void CAssignListView::OnVScroll(UINT nSBCode, UINT nPos, CScrollBar*
➡pScrollBar)
{
    CListCtrl::OnVScroll(nSBCode, nPos, pScrollBar);

    CAtListView & refAnotherView = GetAttributeView( );
    CSize sz( 0, (GetTopIndex() - refAnotherView.GetTopIndex()) *
        m_iRowHeight );
    refAnotherView.Scroll (sz);

}
```

I also made these changes to the other ListView control.

FROM THE FORUM

Question (jonhsv):

I have a ListView control with check boxes enabled. It works well, but when a check box is clicked and its state changes, I need to write these changes to a database. How can I do this?

Answer (wayside):

The following example shows how to catch the check box change notification messages:

Add this to the header:

```
afx_msg void OnItemchangedVersionsFileList(NMHDR* pNMHDR, LRESULT* pResult);
```

Add this to the message map:

```
ON_NOTIFY(LVN_ITEMCHANGED, IDC_VERSIONS_FILE_LIST, OnItemchangedList)
```

Here's the message handler routine:

```
void CMyDlg::OnItemchangedList(NMHDR* pNMHDR, LRESULT* pResult)
{
    NM_LISTVIEW* pNMListView = (NM_LISTVIEW*)pNMHDR;

    *pResult = 0;
```

```
        if (pNMListView->uOldState == 0 && pNMListView->uNewState == 0)
            return; // No change

        BOOL bPrevState = (BOOL)(((pNMListView->uOldState &
        LVIS_STATEIMAGEMASK)>>12)-1); // Old check box state

        if (bPrevState < 0) // On startup there's no previous state
            bPrevState = 0; // so assign as false (unchecked)

        // New check box state
        BOOL bChecked=(BOOL)(((pNMListView->uNewState &
            LVIS_STATEIMAGEMASK)>>12)-1);

        if (bChecked < 0) // On non-checkbox notifications assume false
            bChecked = 0;

        if (bPrevState == bChecked) // No change in check box
            return;

        // Now bChecked holds the new check box state
        // pNMListView->iItem contains which item was clicked
        ...

    }
```

18

Menus

In this chapter

Menus provide one of the primary interfaces between user and application. In many applications, menus are simply such a necessity that they attract little attention from developers or users. A professional-looking menu, however, can significantly enhance the user experience.

- "Owner-drawn Menu with Icons (3)" describes an outstanding owner-drawn menu class to add a professional look and feel to any application.

Owner-drawn Menu with Icons (3)

This article was contributed by Brent Corkum.

Figure 18.1

Figure 18.2

What's New in Version 3.0

As you can see I've added the new Office XP drawing style for the menus. I just got a machine with Windows XP on it and I noticed that the menus in all our applications looked terrible. So I decided to do something about it and after two years of not looking at the class, added the new menu drawing style, as well as lots of fixes and user requests. Now the new drawing style isn't exactly like Microsoft's, but I got it so that it looks good enough to me. For people who use the old class, it's a simple matter of exchanging the old BCMenu .cpp and .h files with the new ones.

The class currently uses the new style on XP and the old style on Win9x/NT and 2000. However, if you like the new style and you want to use it on all Windows platforms, just change the following line at the top of the BCMenu.cpp file from

```
UINT BCMenu::original_drawmode=BCMENU_DRAWMODE_ORIGINAL;
```

to

```
UINT BCMenu::original_drawmode=BCMENU_DRAWMODE_XP;
```

Likewise, if you think I did a terrible job, you can change the drawing style to the original one on all the platforms.

Other additions include support for images with greater than 16 colors. The example contains images with both 256 and 16 million colors. There is also an option for how to draw disabled options. In XP mode they are not selected, but you can change this. I also fixed the problem of multiple menu items with the same command ID not getting images (only the first one did!). See the end of this chapter for more information on updates.

Introduction

This class, **BCMenu**, implements owner-drawn menus derived from the CMenu class, the purpose of which is to mimic the menu style used in Visual C++ 5 and MS Word. I can't take credit for all the code; some portions of it were taken from code supplied by Ben Ashley and Girish Bharadwaj. The difference between their code and mine is quite simple: This one makes it very easy to build those cool menus with bitmaps into your application. I've removed the icon-loading stuff and replaced it with bitmaps. The bitmaps allow you to use the 16×15 toolbar bitmaps directly from your toolbars in the Resource editor. As well, there is no scaling of the bitmaps, so they always look good. You also can load Bitmap resources and define bitmaps for your check marks. I've also added the default check mark drawing stuff, separators, proper alignment of keyboard accelerator text, keyboard shortcuts, proper alignment of pop-up menu items, proper system color changes when the Display Appearance changes, plus bug fixes to the Ben Ashley's LoadMenu function for complex submenu systems. I made quite a few other modifications as well, too many to list or remember. I also use Jean-Edouard Lachand-Robert's disabled bitmap dithering function to create the disabled state bitmaps. I must admit, it does a much better job than the DrawState() function. If you find any bugs, memory leaks, or just better ways of doing things, please let me know. I used Visual C++ 5.0 and I have not tested compatibility with earlier VC versions. I've tested it on Win 95/NT at various resolutions and color palette sizes.

Installation (MDI Application)

Well, enough of the boring stuff, lets talk about implementation. To make it easy, I'm first going to list step by step the method for implementing the menus into a MDI application:

1. Create your MDI application using the AppWizard.

2. Insert the BCMenu.cpp and BCMenu.h files into your workspace.

3. Add the following public member functions to your CMainFrame class in the MainFrm.h header file:

   ```
   HMENU NewMenu();
   HMENU NewDefaultMenu();
   ```

4. Add the following public member variables to your CMainFrame class in the MainFrm.h header file:

   ```
   BCMenu m_menu,m_default;
   ```

5. Add the line

   ```
   #include "BCMenu.h"
   ```

   to the top of the MainFrm.h header file.

6. Open the MainFrm.cpp implementation file and add the NewMenu and
   NewDefaultMenu member functions as follows. **IMPORTANT:** Replace the
   IDR_MYMENUTYPE menu ID in the following LoadMenu call with the
   menu ID associated with the menus in your application. Look in the menus
   folder of the Resources view:

```
HMENU CMainFrame::NewMenu()
{
    static UINT toolbars[]={
        IDR_MAINFRAME
    };

    // Load the menu from the resources
    // ****replace IDR_MENUTYPE with your menu ID****
    m_menu.LoadMenu(IDR_MYMENUTYPE);
    // One method for adding bitmaps to menu options is
    // through the LoadToolbars member function.This method
    // allows you to add all the bitmaps in a toolbar object
    // to menu options (if they exist). The first function
    // parameter is an array of toolbar IDs. The second is
    // the number of toolbar IDs. There is also a function
    // called LoadToolbar that just takes an ID.
    m_menu.LoadToolbars(toolbars,1);

    return(m_menu.Detach());
}

HMENU CMainFrame::NewDefaultMenu()
{
    m_default.LoadMenu(IDR_MAINFRAME);
    m_default.LoadToolbar(IDR_MAINFRAME);
    return(m_default.Detach());
}
```

7. Edit the InitInstance() member function of your CwinApp-derived class and add
   the following code in the position noted:

```
// create main MDI Frame window
CMainFrame* pMainFrame = new CMainFrame;
if (!pMainFrame->LoadFrame(IDR_MAINFRAME))
    return FALSE;
m_pMainWnd = pMainFrame;

// This code replaces the MFC-created menus with
// the Ownerdrawn versions
pDocTemplate->m_hMenuShared=pMainFrame->NewMenu();
pMainFrame->m_hMenuDefault=pMainFrame->NewDefaultMenu();
```

```
// This simulates a window being opened if you don't have
// a default window displayed at startup
pMainFrame->OnUpdateFrameMenu(pMainFrame->m_hMenuDefault);

// Parse command line for standard shell commands,
// DDE, file open
CCommandLineInfo cmdInfo;
ParseCommandLine(cmdInfo);
```

8. Add the message handlers for the WM_MEASUREITEM,
    WM_MENUCHAR, and WM_INITMENUPOPUP messages to your
    CMainFrame class. Do this by right-clicking on the CMainFrame class in the
    Class view and selecting Add Windows Message Handler. Choose the Window
    option from the Filter for Messages Available to Class combo box. Select the
    message and add the handler. Then edit the handler and add the following code:

```
//This handler ensures that the popup menu items are
// drawn correctly
void CMainFrame::OnMeasureItem(int nIDCtl,
 LPMEASUREITEMSTRUCT lpMeasureItemStruct)
{
  BOOL setflag=FALSE;
  if(lpMeasureItemStruct->CtlType==ODT_MENU){
    if(IsMenu((HMENU)lpMeasureItemStruct->itemID)){
      CMenu* cmenu =
      CMenu::FromHandle((HMENU)lpMeasureItemStruct->itemID);

      if(m_menu.IsMenu(cmenu)||m_default.IsMenu(cmenu)){
        m_menu.MeasureItem(lpMeasureItemStruct);
        setflag=TRUE;
      }
    }
  }

  if(!setflag)CMDIFrameWnd::OnMeasureItem(nIDCtl,
                                          lpMeasureItemStruct);
}

//This handler ensures that keyboard shortcuts work
LRESULT CMainFrame::OnMenuChar(UINT nChar, UINT nFlags,
 CMenu* pMenu)
{
  LRESULT lresult;
  if(m_menu.IsMenu(pMenu)||m_default.IsMenu(pMenu))
    lresult=BCMenu::FindKeyboardShortcut(nChar, nFlags, pMenu);
  else
```

```
    lresult=CMDIFrameWnd::OnMenuChar(nChar, nFlags, pMenu);
  return(lresult);
}

//This handler updates the menus from time to time
void CMainFrame::OnInitMenuPopup(CMenu* pPopupMenu,
 UINT nIndex, BOOL bSysMenu)
{
  CMDIFrameWnd::OnInitMenuPopup(pPopupMenu, nIndex, bSysMenu);
  if(!bSysMenu){
    if(m_menu.IsMenu(pPopupMenu)¦¦m_default.IsMenu(pPopupMenu))
      BCMenu::UpdateMenu(pPopupMenu);
  }
}
```

9. If you are debugging or you are mixing standard menus with the BCMenus (maybe you have different document templates using the standard menus), then you should turn on RTTI in the project settings.

Well, that's it. Compile the program and look in the File menu. You should see the bitmaps. I've tried the menus with context menus and they seem to work fine. I also have a small sample program (source+exe) that also uses bitmaps for check marks and a few menu options, and has a context menu when you right-click in a view.

FROM THE FORUM

Question (curtiswon):

I have an MDI application to which I am trying to add a context menu. Using the RButtonDown message works, but why am I not receiving the context menu message?

Answer (JohnCz):

The problem is that WM_CONTEXTMENU is sent to the parent of the window that received the mouse click.

In your case you are dealing with an MDI app, so the view has a parent (CChildFrame), and the child frame is a child of the client area of the main frame.

Placing the handler there requires some work since it is not an MFC window.

Instead, use the following code (substituting menu indexes as necessary):

```
    void CREditVDerived::OnRButtonUp(UINT nFlags, CPoint point)
    {
        BOOL bLeft;
        CMenu menu, *pMenu = NULL;

        ClientToScreen(&point);
```

```
     menu.LoadMenu(IDR_MAINFRAME);
     ::SystemParametersInfo(SPI_GETMENUDROPALIGNMENT, 0, &bLeft, 0);

     UINT uiAlignment = 0;
     bLeft ? uiAlignment = TPM_LEFTALIGN ¦ TPM_LEFTBUTTON : TPM_LEFTALIGN ¦
         TPM_LEFTBUTTON;

     pMenu = menu.GetSubMenu(0);

     pMenu->TrackPopupMenu(uiAlignment, point.x, point.y, this);
}
```

Installation (SDI Application)

Follow these steps to install the SDI application:

1. Create your SDI application using the AppWizard.

2. Insert the BCMenu.cpp and BCMenu.h files into your workspace.

3. Add the following public member function to your CMainFrame class in the MainFrm.h header file:

   ```
   HMENU NewMenu();
   ```

4. Add the following public member variables to your CMainFrame class in the MainFrm.h header file:

   ```
   BCMenu m_menu;
   ```

5. Add the line

   ```
   #include "BCMenu.h"
   ```

   to the top of the MainFrm.h header file.

6. Open the MainFrm.cpp implementation file and add the NewMenu and NewDefaultMenu member functions as follows. **IMPORTANT:** Replace the IDR_MAINFRAME menu ID in the following LoadMenu call with the menu ID associated with the menus in your application. Look in the menus folder of the Resources view:

   ```
   HMENU CMainFrame::NewMenu()
   {
     // Load the menu from the resources
     // ****replace IDR_MAINFRAME with your menu ID****
     m_menu.LoadMenu(IDR_MAINFRAME);
     // One method for adding bitmaps to menu options is
     // through the LoadToolbar member function.This method
     // allows you to add all the bitmaps in a toolbar object
     // to menu options (if they exist). The function parameter
   ```

```
// is the toolbar ID. There is also a function called
// LoadToolbars that takes an array of IDs.
 m_menu.LoadToolbar(IDR_MAINFRAME);

 return(m_menu.Detach());
}
```

7. Edit the InitInstance() member function of your CwinApp-derived class and add the following code in the position noted:

```
// Dispatch commands specified on the command line
if (!ProcessShellCommand(cmdInfo))
    return FALSE;

CMenu* pMenu = m_pMainWnd->GetMenu();
if (pMenu)pMenu->DestroyMenu();
HMENU hMenu = ((CMainFrame*) m_pMainWnd)->NewMenu();
pMenu = CMenu::FromHandle( hMenu );
m_pMainWnd->SetMenu(pMenu);
((CMainFrame*)m_pMainWnd)->m_hMenuDefault = hMenu;
```

8. Add the message handlers for the WM_MEASUREITEM, WM_MENUCHAR, and WM_INITMENUPOPUP messages to your CMainFrame class. Do this by right-clicking on the CMainFrame class in the Class view and selecting Add Windows Message Handler. Choose the Window option from the Filter for Messages Available to Class combo box. Select the message and add the handler. Then edit the handler and add the MDI code. Replace the references to CMDIFrameWnd with references to CFrameWnd.

9. If you are debugging or mixing standard menus with the BCMenus (maybe you have different document templates using the standard menus), then you should turn on RTTI in the project settings.

Comments

To change the default color of the menu bar, additional functionality must be added. The following code is an example of this, which you can use to lighten the left portion of the menu:

```
void BCMenu::DrawItem_WinXP (LPDRAWITEMSTRUCT lpDIS)
{
    ASSERT(lpDIS != NULL);

    CDC* pDC = CDC::FromHandle(lpDIS->hDC);
```

```
#ifdef BCMENU_USE_MEMDC
    BCMenuMemDC *pMemDC=NULL;
#endif

    CRect rect, rect2;
    UINT state = (((BCMenuData*)(lpDIS->itemData))->nFlags);
    COLORREF m_newclrBack = GetSysColor((IsNewShell()) ? COLOR_3DFACE
➥: COLOR_MENU);

    COLORREF m_clrBack=GetSysColor(COLOR_MENU);

    BOOL XPflag = m_newclrBack == m_clrBack ? FALSE : TRUE;

    if(!XPflag)
    {
        m_newclrBack=LightenColor(m_newclrBack, 0.35);
        m_clrBack = RGB(255, 255, 255);
    }

    CBrush m_newbrBackground,m_brBackground;
    m_brBackground.CreateSolidBrush(m_clrBack); // m_clrBack is the edge
➥around the right part of the item rect
    m_newclrBack = LightenColor(m_newclrBack, 0.60); // Jase added this line
    m_newbrBackground.CreateSolidBrush(m_newclrBack); // m_newclrBack is
➥the bk clr of the left portion of menu

    ...
}
```

—Jase Jennings

FROM THE FORUM

Question (rohit1024):

How can I create a menu with bitmaps to the left of the text?

Answer (Darl444):

Here is an example of how to display a pop-up menu in a view that has bitmaps
associated with the items:

```
void CMenuBitmapV3View::OnRButtonDown(UINT nFlags, CPoint point)
{
    ClientToScreen(&point);

    BOOL loadok;
    //Get default size of system bitmap for the normal checkmark
    int cx = GetSystemMetrics(SM_CXMENUCHECK);
    int cy = GetSystemMetrics(SM_CYMENUCHECK);
    CBitmap aBitmap, bBitmap, cBitmap;
```

```
loadok = aBitmap.LoadBitmap(IDB_BITMAP1);
loadok = bBitmap.LoadBitmap(IDB_BITMAP2);
loadok = cBitmap.LoadBitmap(IDB_BITMAP3);
CSize bSize;
bSize = aBitmap.SetBitmapDimension(cx, cy);
bSize = bBitmap.SetBitmapDimension(cx, cy);
bSize = cBitmap.SetBitmapDimension(cx, cy);

CMenu aMenu;
aMenu.LoadMenu(IDR_MENU1);

aMenu.SetMenuItemBitmaps(ID_DUMMY_ITEMONE,MF_BYCOMMAND, &aBitmap,
    &aBitmap);
aMenu.SetMenuItemBitmaps(ID_DUMMY_ITEMTWO,MF_BYCOMMAND, &bBitmap,
    &bBitmap);
aMenu. SetMenuItemBitmaps(ID_DUMMY_ITEMTREE,MF_BYCOMMAND,
    &cBitmap, &cBitmap);

CMenu* pPopup = aMenu.GetSubMenu(0);
pPopup->TrackPopupMenu(TPM_LEFTALIGN | TPM_RIGHTBUTTON, point.x, point.y,
    this);

CView::OnRButtonDown(nFlags, point);
}
```

19
Dialogs

Changing the Background Color of Edit Controls

This article was contributed by Duncan Weir.

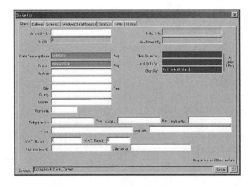

Figure 19.1

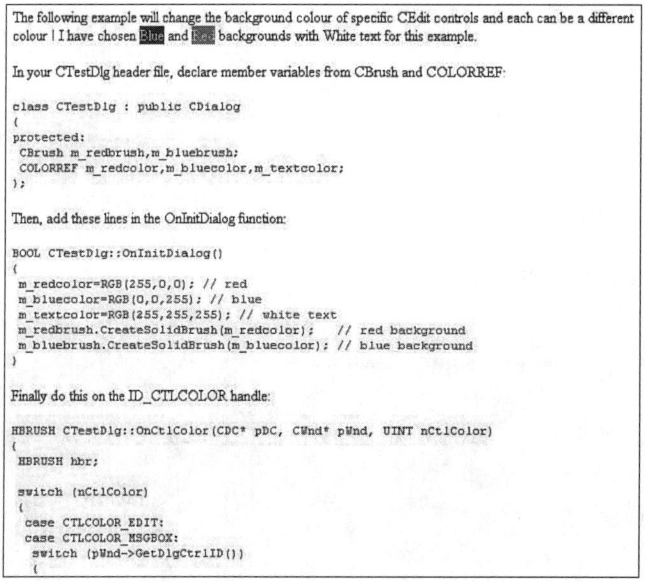

The following example will change the background colour of specific CEdit controls and each can be a different colour I I have chosen Blue and Red backgrounds with White text for this example.

In your CTestDlg header file, declare member variables from CBrush and COLORREF:

```
class CTestDlg : public CDialog
{
protected:
 CBrush m_redbrush,m_bluebrush;
 COLORREF m_redcolor,m_bluecolor,m_textcolor;
};
```

Then, add these lines in the OnInitDialog function:

```
BOOL CTestDlg::OnInitDialog()
{
 m_redcolor=RGB(255,0,0); // red
 m_bluecolor=RGB(0,0,255); // blue
 m_textcolor=RGB(255,255,255); // white text
 m_redbrush.CreateSolidBrush(m_redcolor);   // red background
 m_bluebrush.CreateSolidBrush(m_bluecolor); // blue background
}
```

Finally do this on the ID_CTLCOLOR handle:

```
HBRUSH CTestDlg::OnCtlColor(CDC* pDC, CWnd* pWnd, UINT nCtlColor)
{
 HBRUSH hbr;

 switch (nCtlColor)
 {
  case CTLCOLOR_EDIT:
  case CTLCOLOR_MSGBOX:
   switch (pWnd->GetDlgCtrlID())
   {
```

Figure 19.2

It is very simple for you to change the background color of CEdit controls on your dialog. The following example will change the background color of specific CEdit controls. Each can be a different color! I have chosen blue and red backgrounds with white text for this example.

In your CTestDlg header file, declare member variables from CBrush and COLORREF:

```
class CTestDlg : public CDialog
{
protected:
 CBrush m_redbrush,m_bluebrush;
 COLORREF m_redcolor,m_bluecolor,m_textcolor;
};
```

Then, add these lines in the OnInitDialog function:

```
BOOL CTestDlg::OnInitDialog()
{
 m_redcolor=RGB(255,0,0); // red
 m_bluecolor=RGB(0,0,255); // blue
 m_textcolor=RGB(255,255,255); // white text
 m_redbrush.CreateSolidBrush(m_redcolor);   // red background
 m_bluebrush.CreateSolidBrush(m_bluecolor); // blue background
}
```

Finally, do this on the ID_CTLCOLOR handle:

```
HBRUSH CTestDlg::OnCtlColor(CDC* pDC, CWnd* pWnd, UINT nCtlColor)
{
 HBRUSH hbr;

 switch (nCtlColor)
 {
  case CTLCOLOR_EDIT:
  case CTLCOLOR_MSGBOX:
   switch (pWnd->GetDlgCtrlID())
   {
    case IDC_MYCONTROLNAME1: // first CEdit control ID
     // put your own CONTROL ID here
     pDC->SetBkColor(bluecolor); // change the background color
     pDC->SetTextColor(textcolor); // change the text color
     hbr = (HBRUSH) m_bluebrush; //  apply the brush
    break;

    case IDC_MYCONTROLNAME2: // second CEdit control ID
     // put your own CONTROL ID here
     pDC->SetBkColor(redcolor); // change the background color
     pDC->SetTextColor(textcolor); // change the text color
     hbr = (HBRUSH) m_redbrush; // apply the brush
    break;

     // otherwise do default handling of OnCtlColor
     default:
     hbr=CDialog::OnCtlColor(pDC,pWnd,nCtlColor);
     break;
   }
  break;

  // otherwise do default handling of OnCtlColor
  default:
   hbr=CDialog::OnCtlColor(pDC,pWnd,nCtlColor);
 }

 return hbr; // return brush
}
```

I hope this code helps you as much as other articles on CodeGuru have helped me.

Comments

The following code is based on some MSDN code and provides a solution to transparent backgrounds with static controls and read-only edit controls. It should be made clear that, when working with static controls, hbr is assigned the default value at the beginning and not at the end.

Also, if the edit control is set as read-only or is disabled, then it will be called under CTLCOLOR_STATIC case and not under the CTLCOLOR_EDIT case.

```
// This OnCtlColor handler will change the color of a static control
// with the ID of IDC_MYSTATIC. The code assumes that the CMyDialog
// class has an initialized and created CBrush member named m_brush.
// The control will be painted with red text and a background
// color of m_brush.

HBRUSH CMyDialog::OnCtlColor(CDC* pDC, CWnd* pWnd, UINT nCtlColor)
{

    // Call the base class implementation first! Otherwise, it may
    // undo what we're trying to accomplish here.

    HBRUSH hbr = CDialog::OnCtlColor(pDC, pWnd, nCtlColor);

    // Are we painting the IDC_MYSTATIC control? We can use
    // CWnd::GetDlgCtrlID() to perform the most efficient test.

    if (pWnd->GetDlgCtrlID() == IDC_MYSTATIC)
    {
        // Set the text color to red
        pDC->SetTextColor(RGB(255, 0, 0));

        // Set the background mode for text to transparent
        // so that the background will show through.
        pDC->SetBkMode(TRANSPARENT);

        // Return handle to our CBrush object
        hbr = m_brush;
    }

    return hbr;
}
```

—Snakebyte

Change the background color of a multilane-style edit control in the WM_ ERASEBKGND message handler, as shown in the following code:

```
BOOL CMyEdit::OnEraseBkgnd(CDC* pDC)
{
    CRect rcClient;
    GetClientRect(&rectClient);
    pDC->FillSolidRect(rectClient, m_crColor);
    return (TRUE);
}
```

—Stephan Roth

A Pinnable Dialog Base Class

This article was contributed by David Hill.

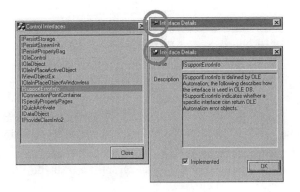

Figure 19.3

Introduction

This class enables you to have a dialog where the user can dynamically switch between modeless and modal behavior by toggling its pinned state. This is similar to the Properties dialog in Developer Studio where you can display the properties of one file or class, pin the dialog, and then select another file or class and see its properties displayed automatically in the Properties dialog. This feature was simpler to implement than I thought it was going to be. Essentially, a pinnable dialog is a modeless dialog. When the dialog is unpinned (that is, when it is to behave as a modal type dialog), it is hidden whenever it loses focus. When the dialog is pinned, it behaves as a standard modeless dialog.

The CPinnableDialog base class handles the switching between the pinned and unpinned states. You just derive your dialog class from CPinnableDialog, create an instance of it in the parent window or frame class, and then hide and show it as appropriate. The pinnable dialog sends a message to the parent window when it is to close. The pinned state simply dictates whether it closes when it is deactivated. The class allows the developer to dictate whether a deactivation closure is treated as a cancel or as if the OK button was pressed.

The CPinnableDialog class uses the dialog's icon in the top-left corner to display the pin instead of using a bitmapped button as Developer Studio does. I think this looks a lot neater and allows the dialog's client area to be completely utilized. When the dialog is closed, it sends a user-defined WM_PINUPCLOSE message to the parent window. Usually the parent handles this message by simply hiding the dialog. The parent window can also determine how the dialog was closed (for example, whether the OK or Cancel buttons were pressed) so that it can retrieve any values that the user has created and validate them if necessary before allowing the dialog to close.

Usage

To implement this behavior in one of your own dialogs, follow these steps:

1. Create your dialog resource as normal and get Class Wizard to generate a dialog class and data members for you. The dialog should have the Title Bar and System Menu styles enabled.

2. Add two icons to your project's resources, one for the pinned state and one for the unpinned state. I "borrowed" the ones from Developer Studio!

3. Change the base class of the dialog to CPinnableDialog. Make sure you change all occurrences of CDialog to CPinnableDialog, especially in the BEGIN_ MESSAGE_MAP macro block.

4. When you call CPinnableDialog's constructor, pass the resource IDs for the dialog template and the two icons as well as the parent CWnd pointer.

5. Add a public function to your dialog class, which can be called to set the dialog's contents when it is to be shown.

6. In the parent window class, add a data member to hold a pointer to your dialog class. In the constructor, create a new dialog object using New and delete it in the destructor.

7. Add a message handler to the parent window class to handle the WM_ PINUPCLOSE message, which the dialog will send when it is to be closed. In the handler, call the dialog's Hide function.

8. Whenever you want to display the dialog, set the dialog's data (using the function you added earlier) and call its Show function.

9. Whenever you might want to update the data that the dialog is displaying (for example, when the user selects another item), check to see whether the dialog is visible (that is, it is pinned) and if it is, call your Refresh function.

The Sample Project

I have included a sample project that illustrates how the CPinnableDialog class can be used. It is a very simple dialog-based application that displays a list of interfaces implemented by a typical ActiveX control. The user can display the properties of any particular interface by either double-clicking on its entry in the list box or by selecting Properties from the Context menu. When the Properties dialog is displayed, the user can pin it and select another interface to see its properties automatically displayed. The name and description fields are read-only, but the user can toggle the implemented flag.

Irregularly Shaped Bitmap Dialog

This article was contributed by David Forrester.

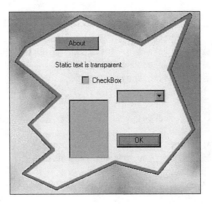

Figure 19.4

The CBitmapDialog class allows you to create a dialog that has a bitmap background, and to have a specified color in the background be transparent. This allows the dialog to be in other shapes than a box, like the one shown in Figure 19.4.

Usage

Use this class like CDialog, but there are several extra functions that you can use:

```
// ** Constructors **

// Use the normal CDialog constructors plus the following
// as the last four parameters:
//
// LPCTSTR       lpszResourceName
// UINT          nIDResource
// LPCTSTR       lpszFilename
// CBitmap       *pBitmap
//
// Example:
// CDialog(int,CWnd*)):CBitmapDialog(IDD_MAINDIALOG,
                                     this,
                                     NULL,
                                     IDB_BITMAP,
                                     NULL,
                                     NULL);
```

```
//
// Use at most one of these parameters and leave the rest
// NULL or 0. If you do not want to set a bitmap in the
// constructor, look below.

// ** Bitmap Setting **

// Loads a bitmap from a resource string or filename.
//  Leave either lpszResourceName or lpszFilename NULL.
BOOL LoadBitmap (LPCTSTR lpszResourceName,
                 LPCTSTR lpszFilename);

// Loads a bitmap from a resource ID
BOOL LoadBitmap (int nIDResource);

// Makes a copy of a given bitmap and uses the copy.
// This is like SetBitmap but you are not responsible
// for handling the bitmap.
BOOL CopyBitmapFrom (CBitmap *pBitmap);

// Uses the bitmap you specify.  NOTE: You are responsible
// for handling the bitmap.
void SetBitmap (CBitmap *pBitmap);

// ** Transparency **

// Specifies whether the window should use transparency.
//  TRUE for transparent, FALSE for opaque. (default is
//  FALSE)
void SetTransparent (BOOL bTransparent);
BOOL GetTransparent ();

// Specifies the color that you want to be transparent.
void SetTransColor (COLORREF col);
COLORREF GetTransColor ();

// Specifies whether static (text) controls have a
// transparent background.
//  TRUE for transparent, FALSE for opaque. (default
//  is TRUE)
void SetStaticTransparent (BOOL bTransparent);
BOOL GetStaticTransparent ();

// ** Dragging **

// With a transparent dialog, you usually won't have a
// caption (like my example).
//  These functions make it so that you can drag anywhere
//  on the dialog to move it.  TRUE is on and FALSE is off.
//  (default is FALSE)
void SetClickAnywhereMove (BOOL bMove);
BOOL GetClickAnywhereMove ();
```

Tips

- In the Resource editor, you can't tell exactly how big the dialog will need to be to hold the entire bitmap. You could either try out different sizes, or if you don't have the Show Window Contents While Dragging Windows option enabled, you could drag the dialog and see how much extra dialog you have on the edge when it shows you the frame.
- Dialogs that use transparency usually look best without a caption or a border. In the Resource editor for your dialog, uncheck Title Bar and set Border to None.

How It Works

It overrides CWnd::OnEraseBackground() to draw the bitmap as the background.

It overrides CWnd::OnCtlColor() to make static controls transparent.

It makes parts of the window transparent by combining many small window regions. (Look at CBitmapDialog::MakeWindowRgn().)

It allows you to drag anywhere by making Windows think that you clicked on the caption (even if there is no caption bar).

Comments

There is a problem using the irregularly shaped dialog class with child dialogs. To correct this, make the following changes to the sample code:

```
void CBitmapDialog ::MakeWindowRgn ()
{
    if (!m_bTransparent || m_bmBitmap == NULL)
    {
        // Set the window region to the full window
        CRect rcWnd;
        GetWindowRect (rcWnd);

        CRgn rgn;
        rgn.CreateRectRgn (0, 0, rcWnd.Width(), rcWnd.Height());
        SetWindowRgn (rgn, TRUE);
    }
    else
    {
        //The whole window rect
        CRect rcWnd;
        GetWindowRect (rcWnd);

        // The client Rect
        CRect rcClient;
        GetClientRect (rcClient);
        ClientToScreen (rcClient);
```

```
// Since the coordinates are with respect to the screen
// Let's make the upper-left of the whole window to (0,0)
// This is the solution to the problem of the of the original code
// By: Prime :)
//===================================
//Adjust the client rectangle
//===================================
rcClient.right  -= rcWnd.left;
rcClient.left   -= rcWnd.left;
rcClient.bottom -= rcWnd.top;
rcClient.top    -= rcWnd.top;


//===================================
//Adjust the window Rectangle
//===================================
rcWnd.right     -= rcWnd.left;
rcWnd.left      -= rcWnd.left;
rcWnd.bottom    -= rcWnd.top;
rcWnd.top       -= rcWnd.top;
//===================================


CRgn rgn;
rgn.CreateRectRgn (rcWnd.left, rcWnd.top, rcWnd.right, rcWnd.bottom);
CRgn rgnClient;
rgnClient.CreateRectRgn (rcClient.left, rcClient.top,
➡rcClient.right,rcClient.bottom);

// Subtract rgnClient from rgn
rgn.CombineRgn (&rgn, &rgnClient, RGN_XOR);

// Get a DC for the bitmap
CDC dcImage;
dcImage.CreateCompatibleDC (NULL);
CBitmap *pOldBitmap = dcImage.SelectObject (m_bmBitmap);

// Get the bitmap for width and height information
BITMAP bm;
m_bmBitmap->GetBitmap (&bm);

// Get window width and height
// Use the minimum width and height
int width = min (bm.bmWidth, rcClient.Width());
int height = min (bm.bmHeight, rcClient.Height());

// Use RLE (run-length) style because it goes faster.
// Row start is where the first opaque pixel is found.  Once
// a transparent pixel is found, a line region is created.
// Then row_start becomes the next opaque pixel.
int row_start;
```

```
        // Go through all rows
        for (int y = 0; y < height; y++)
        {
            // Start looking at the beginning
            row_start = 0;

            // Go through all columns
            for (int x = 0; x < width; x++)
            {
                // If this pixel is transparent
                if (dcImage.GetPixel(x, y) == m_colTrans)
                {
                    // If we haven't found an opaque pixel yet, keep searching
                    if (row_start == x) row_start ++;
                    else
                    {
                        // We have found the start (row_start) and end (x) of
                        // an opaque strip.  Add it to the region.
                        CRgn rgnAdd;
                        rgnAdd.CreateRectRgn (rcClient.left+row_start,
➥rcClient.top+y, rcClient.left+x, rcClient.top+y+1);
                        rgn.CombineRgn (&rgn, &rgnAdd, RGN_OR);
                        row_start = x+1;
                    }
                }
            }
             // If the last pixel is still opaque, make a region.
            if (row_start != x)
            {
                //Create a region of the remaining strip. (if any)
                CRgn rgnAdd;
                rgnAdd.CreateRectRgn (rcClient.left+row_start, rcClient.top+y,
➥rcClient.left+x, rcClient.top+y+1);

                rgn.CombineRgn (&rgn, &rgnAdd, RGN_OR);
            }
        }

        dcImage.SelectObject(pOldBitmap);
        dcImage.DeleteDC();

        //Set the region
        SetWindowRgn (rgn, TRUE);
    }
}
```

—Jeune Prime Origines

20

Property Sheets

In this chapter

Property sheets are types of dialog boxes, and have some very specific requirements. In this chapter we will explore one of those requirements, and how to work around it.

- "Using ON_UPDATE_COMMAND_UI in Property Pages" provides a solution to a difficult and poorly documented command routing problem encountered when using property sheets.

Using ON_UPDATE_COMMAND_UI in Property Pages

This article was contributed by Tim McColl.

Using ON_UPDATE_COMMAND_UI message maps in property pages is the same as in dialogs except that one extra step is required for property pages.

You need to derive a class from CPropertySheet and intercept the WM_KICKIDLE messages:

1. Use Class Wizard to create a new class called CMyPropSheet with a base class of CPropertySheet.

2. In the header add the message function:

    ```
    afx_msg LRESULT OnKickIdle(WPARAM wParam, LPARAM lParam);
    ```

3. In the source file #include afxpriv.h.

4. Add the message map

    ```
    ON_MESSAGE(WM_KICKIDLE, OnKickIdle)
    ```

5. Implement the function

    ```
    LRESULT CMyPropSheet::OnKickIdle(WPARAM, LPARAM)
    {
        SendMessageToDescendants(WM_WM_KICKIDLE, 0, 0, FALSE, FALSE);
        return 0;
    }
    ```

The property sheet now passes all WM_KICKIDLE messages to its property pages.

In the property page class, just add a message map for WM_KICKIDLE and call UpdateDialogControls:

```
LRESULT CMyPropPage::OnKickIdle(WPARAM, LPARAM)
{
    UpdateDialogControls(this, FALSE);
    return 0L;
}
```

Then all you need is ON_UPDATE_COMMAND_UI message maps.

This does not work for modeless property sheets. You need to trap the WM_IDLEUPDATECMDUI message in the property sheet's owner window and send it WM_KICKIDLE messages.

Comments

To limit the number of descendents receiving the update messages, make the following modifications to the sample code. Instead of using SendMessageToDescendents, the currently active property page can be found by using the following code:

```
CPropertyPage *pActivePage = GetActivePage();

if(pActivePage == NULL)
    return lParam <= 2;

return pActivePage->SendMessage(WM_KICKIDLE, wParam, lParam);
```

—Jonathan Schafer

FROM THE FORUM

Question (dennisvr):

How can I pass data between two pages of my property sheet?

Answer (not a doofus):

CPropertyPage has a member function QuerySiblings(WPARAM,LPARAM). The two generic parameters can be used by your application as required. QuerySiblings() generates a PSM_QUERYSIBLINGS message that is passed on to all siblings (other property pages on the sheet).

I generally create an enum that is visible to all pages like this:

```
enum{ QUERY_MY_STRING, QUERY_SOMETHING_ELSE, ... };
```

Then, when one of my pages needs information from another, I do this:

```
CString myString;
if(1L==QuerySiblings(QUERY_MY_STRING,(LPARAM)&myString))
{
    // got my string
}
```

The page that supplies the string handles the PSM_QUERYSIBLINGS message:

```
LRESULT CPageThatHasString::OnQuerySiblings(WPARAM wParam,LPARAM lParam)
{
    if(QUERY_MY_STRING == wParam)
    {
        *((CString *)lParam) = _T("Here's your string");
        return 1L;
    }
    else
        return 0L;
}
```

FROM THE FORUM

Question (AnOnYmOuS):

I want to hide the title (caption) bar of my CPropertySheet. I have tried using ModifyStyle(WINDOW_CAPTION, 0) without effect. How can this be done?

Answer (Dominic Holmes):

You can create your own CpropertySheet-derived class, and override the OnInitDialog. After passing to the default, use ModifyStyle to remove the WS_CAPTION flag.

FROM THE FORUM

Question (frei):

How can I create a property sheet control that has two rows of tabs instead of one?

Answer (ChrisD):

Derive your own class from CPropertySheet, add a handler for PreCreateWindow, and then add the following line before the call to the base class:

```
cs.style |= TCS_MULTILINE;
```

21

Status Bars

In this chapter

Status bars are those things running along the bottom of many applications. They are used primarily to show current status information to users at runtime.

In this chapter you will find some extended functionality that can be placed into the status bar to enhance your applications.

- "Displaying Cursor Position in the Status Bar" shows how to provide visual feedback to the user regarding the current cursor position.
- "Showing the Progress Bar in a Status Bar Pane" allows you to add a very convenient progress control to the status bar.

Displaying Cursor Position in the Status Bar

This article was contributed by Edward Duffy.

Figure 21.1

In many applications in which you use CEditView and CRichEditView classes, it might be convenient to let the user know the position of the cursor, much like the IDE in Visual C++. After some quick searching through MSDN and the CG discussion forums, I found out how easy it would be to add this feature.

Add a new entry to your string table with an ID of ID_INDICATOR_CURPOS and a caption of "Ln %d, Col %d ". The extra spaces are to give you a little bit more room in the panel so that when you get over 100 lines, the text doesn't get clipped.

Add ID_INDICATOR_CURPOS to your indicators[] array in the MainFrm.cpp file. In the message map in the class declaration for CMainFrame, add the following function signature:

```
afx_msg void OnUpdateCurPosIndicator(CCmdUI *pCmdUI);
```

Now go to the actual message map in the MainFrm.cpp file and add the following macro call:

```
ON_UPDATE_COMMAND_UI(ID_INDICATOR_CURPOS,
                    OnUpdateCurPosIndicator)
```

Lastly, create the function body in the MainFrm.cpp file:

```
void CMainFrame::OnUpdateCurPosIndicator(CCmdUI *pCmdUI)
{
 CString strCurPos;
 int nLineNum, nColNum;
 int nSelStart, nSelEnd;

 // you're going to have to get a pointer
 // to the edit control in the view
 m_wndEditCtrl->GetSel(nSelStart, nSelEnd);

 nLineNum = m_wndEditCtrl->LineFromChar(nSelStart);

 nColNum = nSelStart - m_wndEditCtrl->LineIndex(nLineNum);

 strCurPos.Format(ID_INDICATOR_CURPOS,
                 nLineNum+1,
                 nColNum+1);

 m_wndStatusBar.SetPaneText(
  m_wndStatusBar.CommandToIndex(ID_INDICATOR_CURPOS),
  strCurPos);
}
```

That's about it. You can download the sample project if you wish, although there's nothing special in it, really. The only thing that might be of any use is getting that pointer to the edit control.

Comments

To add this functionality to an MDI application, make the following changes to the sample code. Add the ID_INDICATOR_??? to the CMainFrame class. Add the following handler to the CChildFrame class:

```
void CChildFrame::OnUpdateCurPos( CCmdUI *pCmdUI )
{
    CEditView *pView = (CEditView *)GetActiveView();
```

```
    if (pView != NULL)
    {
        CEdit& rEdit = pView->GetEditCtrl();
        int pos = rEdit.CharFromPos( GetCaretPos());
        CString txt;
        txt.Format( "Ln %d Col %d", HIWORD( pos ) + 1, LOWORD( pos )
➥·  rEdit.LineIndex() + 1 );
        pCmdUI->SetText( txt );
    }
}
```

—Sok Woo, Lim

FROM THE FORUM

Question (Tamer Omari):

How can I add a button to my status bar and handle its click events?

Answer (sudheer MG):

Create a new class called CMyBtn derived from CButton.

Add a member variable of type CMyBtn to your main frame class, and then in the main frame's OnCreate function, add the following to create the button and associate it with the status bar as its parent:

```
    m_MyBtn.Create("MyBtn", WS_CHILD | WS_VISIBLE, CRect(0,0,60,20),
    &m_wndStatusBar, 0);
```

Any click notification messages can be processed in your CMyBtn class by handling the BN_CLICKED messages.

Showing a Progress Bar in a Status Bar Pane

This article was contributed by Brad Mann.

This code creates a progress bar anywhere in the status window, and the control is created only once.

1. From the View menu, choose Resource Symbols. Press the New button and assign the symbol a name. (In this example we'll be using ID_INDICATOR_PROGRESS_PANE.) It's probably best if you let the computer assign a value for it.

2. In MainFrm.cpp, find the indicators array (located under the message map section) and type the ID of the resource (ID_INDICATOR_PROGRESS_PANE) in the section. Put it under all the rest of the IDs, unless you don't want the bar in the far right corner. (Placing the ID at the beginning of the array puts the pane in the far left, where the program messages usually go.)

3. Open the string table in the resource editor, and from the Insert menu, choose New String.

4. Double-click the string and select the ID. For the message, just type a bunch of spaces (the more spaces, the larger the progress bar).

Now that we've created the pane, it's time to put a progress bar in it.

1. Declare a public variable in MainFrm.h of type CProgressCtrl. (In this example we'll call it m_Progress.)

2. Declare a protected variable in MainFrm.h of type BOOL. (In this example we'll call it m_bCreated.)

3. In the OnCreate() function in MainFrm.cpp, initialize m_bCreated to FALSE:

```
m_bCreated = FALSE;
```

4. Now, when we need to use the progress bar, we check to see if it's created, and if it isn't, we make a new one:

```
CMainFrame::OnSomeLongProcess()
{
    RECT MyRect;
    // substitute 4 with the zero-based index of your status bar pane.
    // For example, if you put your pane first in the indicators array,
    // you'd put 0, second you'd put 1, etc.
    m_wndStatusBar.GetItemRect(4, &MyRect);

    if (m_bCreated == FALSE)
    {
        //Create the progress control
        m_Progress.Create(WS_VISIBLE|WS_CHILD, MyRect, &wndStatusBar, 1);

        m_Progress.SetRange(0,100); //Set the range to between 0 and 100
        m_Progress.SetStep(1); // Set the step amount
        m_bCreated = TRUE;
    }

    // Now we'll simulate a long process:
    for (int I = 0; I < 100; I++)
    {
        Sleep(20);
        m_Progress.StepIt();
    }
}
```

If the window is resized while the progress bar is created, the progress control doesn't reposition correctly, so we have to override the WM_SIZE event of class CMainFrame:

```
void CMainFrame::OnSize(UINT nType, int cx, int cy)
{
    CMDIFrameWnd::OnSize(nType, cx, cy);
    RECT rc;
    m_wndStatusBar.GetItemRect(4, &rc);

    // Reposition the progress control correctly!
    m_Progress.SetWindowPos(&wndTop, rc.left, rc.top, rc.right - rc.left,
        rc.bottom - rc.top, 0);

}
```

That's the way to implement a progress control into a status bar pane! Although the process is long, it is relatively simple.

FROM THE FORUM

Question (Narva):

How can I add a status bar to my dialog-based application?

Answer (-manu-):

Add this member variable to your dialog class:

```
CStatusBar m_statusBar;
```

In your dialog cpp file, add the following:

```
static UINT indicators[] =
{
    ID_INDICATOR_PROGRESS_PANE,
    ID_STATUSBAR_TEXT
};
```

Add as many panes as you want, and for each of them add a line in the string table and associate with it a string of the length you want for the pane in the status bar. In this example, create two strings, ID_INDICATOR_PROGRESS_PANE and ID_STATUS-BAR_TEXT, with some text ("xxxxxx" for example).

In your OnInitDialog function, do the following:

```
// create status bar
m_statusBar.Create(this);
m_statusBar.SetIndicators(indicators,sizeof(indicators)/sizeof(UINT));

RepositionBars(AFX_IDW_CONTROLBAR_FIRST, AFX_IDW_CONTROLBAR_LAST, 0);

CString csText = "whatever";
// write it in the status bar
m_statusBar.SetPaneText(1, csText);
```

22

Toolbars

In this chapter

Toolbars offer convenient access to important functionality within your applications.

In this chapter, you will discover ways to make your toolbars look better and appear more professional.

- "Toolbar with 16M Color Images" shows a very easy way to use high-color bitmaps on your toolbars without having to make many changes to your application.

- "Full-featured 24-bit Color Toolbar" describes a more comprehensive way of using color bitmaps on a toolbar, showing how to attach image lists to the toolbar.

- "Docking Toolbars Side by Side" documents the often misunderstood way of controlling the layout of multiple toolbars.

Toolbar with 16M Color Images

This article was contributed by Fulop Miklos.

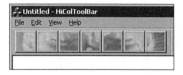

Figure 22.1

I tried Kevin Bentley's trick to use 256 colors, but it didn't work.

I needed to have more than 256 colors, so fortunately I was able to find an alternative way. The following example will show how you can use high-color bitmaps on your toolbars.

First, create your toolbar in Developer Studio—no matter what you do to draw on buttons. Make a high-color bitmap with a bitmap editor (for example, Paint Shop Pro). This new bitmap must be the same size as Toolbar.bmp in your project's \res folder. Then, import the resource into your application as a bitmap and name it IDB_TOOLBARHI. Here's what you must do:

1. Make a CBitmap-type global variable m_bmToolbarHi in your CMainFrame class

2. Include these lines in the function CMainFrame::OnCreate() after initializing the toolbar:

```
if (!m_wndToolBar.Create(this) ¦¦
    !m_wndToolBar.LoadToolBar(IDR_MAINFRAME))
{
    TRACE0("Failed to create toolbar\n");
    return -1; // fail to create
}

// ===========================================================
    m_bmToolbarHi.LoadBitmap( IDB_TOOLBARHI );
    m_wndToolBar.SetBitmap( (HBITMAP)m_bmToolbarHi );
// ===========================================================
```

3. Include this line in the destructor of CMainFrame:

```
CMainFrame::~CMainFrame()
{
// ===========================================================
    m_bmToolbarHi.DeleteObject();
// ===========================================================
}
```

That's all.

Full-featured 24-bit Color Toolbar

This article was contributed by Peter Lee.

Figure 22.2

Environment: VC 6.0 SP4, Win95/NT 3.51 or later

Creating a CToolbar with 16– or 24–bit buttons is easy if you aren't worried about disabled buttons and your buttons don't have any pixels that should be set to the toolbar's background color. Things quickly get more complicated if you want to handle those other cases correctly. This sample program attaches 24–bit images to the standard MFC main frame toolbar and handles both disabled and hot buttons as well as transparent button backgrounds. It can be extended easily to handle 16–bit images or different toolbar configurations.

If your application can be run with the display set to fewer than 16 bits per pixel, you should add code to check the display depth and not load the high-color toolbars in those cases because they won't look good.

Specifying separate bitmaps for the enabled, disabled, and hot buttons isn't too hard. CToolbar::GetToolbarCtrl() gets the toolbar control, and then CToolbarCtrl::SetImageList(), CToolbarCtrl::SetDisabledImageList(), and CToolbarCtrl::SetHotImageList() assign the bitmaps.

Making the image lists 24–bits deep requires that you create the CImageLists with no images, load the images as CBitmaps, and then copy the CBitmaps into the CImageLists.

Loading the bitmaps as 24 bits per pixel even when the user's screen is set to a different bit depth requires extra work, too. CBitmap::LoadBitmap() converts the bitmap to the screen's bit depth, so the Win32 function ::LoadImage() is used instead to create a 24–bit DIBSECTION, which then is attached to a CBitmap so that it can be passed to CImageList::Add().

When a toolbar is created in the Visual Studio toolbar editor, any pixel that is light gray (RGB 192, 192, 192) is replaced with the user's chosen button color at runtime, making those pixels effectively transparent. For some reason this doesn't happen to 24–bit CImageLists. Specifying a mask color when the CImageList is created just ends up replacing that color with black, not with the system button color. This code does that color substitution manually. Before a bitmap is added to an image list, the code iterates over the pixels in the bitmap, replacing each RGB (192, 192, 192) pixel with the system button color (::GetSysColor (COLOR_BTNFACE)). Because the bitmaps are DIBSECTIONs, the code can access the pixels directly for maximum efficiency.

Because the Visual Studio graphics editor can't handle 24–bit images, you must edit the images in another program that can, such as GIMP or Adobe Photoshop. Save them as 24–bit .bmp files in the project's res folder. You can then import them into the project using the Import command in the Developer Studio Resource tab.

```
// these constants represent the dimensions and number of buttons in
// the default MFC-generated toolbar. If you need something different,
// feel free to change them. For extra credit, you can load the
// toolbar's existing image list at runtime and copy the parameters from
// there.
```

```
static const int       kImageWidth (16);
static const int       kImageHeight (15);
static const int       kNumImages (8);

static const UINT      kToolBarBitDepth (ILC_COLOR24);

// this color will be treated as transparent in the loaded bitmaps --
// in other words, any pixel of this color will be set at runtime to
// the user's button color. The Visual Studio toolbar editor defaults
// to 192, 192, 192 (light gray).
static const RGBTRIPLE  kBackgroundColor = {192, 192, 192};


int CMainFrame::OnCreate(LPCREATESTRUCT lpCreateStruct)
{
 if (CFrameWnd::OnCreate(lpCreateStruct) == -1)
  return -1;

 if (!m_wndToolBar.CreateEx(this, TBSTYLE_FLAT, WS_CHILD | WS_VISIBLE
➡| CBRS_TOP
 | CBRS_GRIPPER | CBRS_TOOLTIPS | CBRS_FLYBY | CBRS_SIZE_DYNAMIC) ||
 !m_wndToolBar.LoadToolBar(IDR_MAINFRAME))
 {
  TRACE0("Failed to create toolbar\n");
  return -1; // fail to create
 }

 // attach the high-color bitmaps to the toolbar
 AttachToolbarImages (IDB_HICOLOR_TOOLBAR,
 IDB_HICOLOR_TOOLBAR_DISABLED,
 IDB_HICOLOR_TOOLBAR_HOT);

 // the rest of your CMainFrame::OnCreate() code goes here
}

// find every pixel of the default background color in the specified
// bitmap and set each one to the user's button color.
static void    ReplaceBackgroundColor (CBitmap& ioBM)
{
 // figure out how many pixels there are in the bitmap
 BITMAP       bmInfo;

 VERIFY (ioBM.GetBitmap (&bmInfo));

 // add support for additional bit depths if you choose
 VERIFY (bmInfo.bmBitsPixel == 24);
 VERIFY (bmInfo.bmWidthBytes == (bmInfo.bmWidth * 3));

 const UINT    numPixels (bmInfo.bmHeight * bmInfo.bmWidth);

 // get a pointer to the pixels
 DIBSECTION  ds;
```

```
VERIFY (ioBM.GetObject (sizeof (DIBSECTION), &ds) == sizeof (DIBSECTION));

RGBTRIPLE*     pixels = reinterpret_cast<RGBTRIPLE*>(ds.dsBm.bmBits);
VERIFY (pixels != NULL);

// get the user's preferred button color from the system
const COLORREF        buttonColor (::GetSysColor (COLOR_BTNFACE));
const RGBTRIPLE          userBackgroundColor = {
GetBValue (buttonColor), GetGValue (buttonColor), GetRValue (buttonColor)};

// search through the pixels, substituting the user's button
// color for any pixel that has the magic background color
for (UINT i = 0; i < numPixels; ++i)
{
 if (pixels [i].rgbtBlue == kBackgroundColor.rgbtBlue
 && pixels [i].rgbtGreen == kBackgroundColor.rgbtGreen
 && pixels [i].rgbtRed == kBackgroundColor.rgbtRed)
 {
  pixels [i] = userBackgroundColor;
 }
 }
}


// create an image list for the specified BMP resource
static void    MakeToolbarImageList (UINT inBitmapID,
                                CImageList&     outImageList)
{
CBitmap         bm;

// if we use CBitmap::LoadBitmap() to load the bitmap, the colors
// will be reduced to the bit depth of the main screen and we won't
// be able to access the pixels directly. To avoid those problems,
// we'll load the bitmap as a DIBSection instead and attach the
// DIBSection to the CBitmap.
VERIFY (bm.Attach (::LoadImage (::AfxFindResourceHandle(
MAKEINTRESOURCE (inBitmapID), RT_BITMAP),
MAKEINTRESOURCE (inBitmapID), IMAGE_BITMAP, 0, 0,
(LR_DEFAULTSIZE ¦ LR_CREATEDIBSECTION)))));

// replace the specified color in the bitmap with the user's
// button color
::ReplaceBackgroundColor (bm);

// create a 24-bit image list with the same dimensions and number
// of buttons as the toolbar
VERIFY (outImageList.Create (
kImageWidth, kImageHeight, kToolBarBitDepth, kNumImages, 0));

// attach the bitmap to the image list
VERIFY (outImageList.Add (&bm, RGB (0, 0, 0)) != -1);
}
```

```
// load the high-color toolbar images and attach them to m_wndToolBar
void CMainFrame::AttachToolbarImages (UINT inNormalImageID,
                                      UINT inDisabledImageID,
                                      UINT inHotImageID)
{
   // make high-color image lists for each of the bitmaps
   ::MakeToolbarImageList (inNormalImageID, m_ToolbarImages);
   ::MakeToolbarImageList (inDisabledImageID, m_ToolbarImagesDisabled);
   ::MakeToolbarImageList (inHotImageID, m_ToolbarImagesHot);

   // get the toolbar control associated with the CToolbar object
   CToolBarCtrl&   barCtrl = m_wndToolBar.GetToolBarCtrl();

   // attach the image lists to the toolbar control
   barCtrl.SetImageList (&m_ToolbarImages);
   barCtrl.SetDisabledImageList (&m_ToolbarImagesDisabled);
   barCtrl.SetHotImageList (&m_ToolbarImagesHot);
}
```

Comments

A problem exists where changing the background color of the toolbar from the default color causes the bitmaps to be drawn incorrectly. To resolve this problem, make the following changes to the ReplaceBackgroundColor member function:

Replace

```
if (pixels[i].rgbtBlue == m_kBackgroundColor.rgbtBlue
    && pixels[i].rgbtGreen == m_kBackgroundColor.rgbtGreen
    && pixels[i].rgbtRed == m_kBackgroundColor.rgbtRed)
{
    pixels[i] = userBackgroundColor;
}
```

with

```
/////////////////
// Use Multiply
    pixels[i].rgbtRed= (BYTE)MulDiv(pixels[i].rgbtRed,
➥userBackgroundColor.rgbtRed, 255);
    pixels[i].rgbtGreen=(BYTE)MulDiv(pixels[i].rgbtGreen,
➥userBackgroundColor.rgbtGreen, 255);
    pixels[i].rgbtBlue=    (BYTE)MulDiv(pixels[i].rgbtBlue,
➥userBackgroundColor.rgbtBlue, 255);
```

Also, remember to draw the images with a white background that you want to load into the image list.

—Vincent Yu

Docking Toolbars Side by Side

This article was contributed by Kirk Stowell.

Figure 22.3

There are several articles about docking toolbars, however, I felt that this was important enough to mention here. The same information can be found at Microsoft's MSDN site; here it is in a nutshell:

Add the following method to your CMainFrame class:

```
void CMainFrame::DockControlBarLeftOf(CToolBar* Bar, CToolBar* LeftOf)
{
    CRect rect;
    DWORD dw;
    UINT n;

    // get MFC to adjust the dimensions of all docked ToolBars
    // so that GetWindowRect will be accurate
    RecalcLayout(TRUE);

    LeftOf->GetWindowRect(&rect);
    rect.OffsetRect(1,0);
    dw=LeftOf->GetBarStyle();
    n = 0;
    n = (dw&CBRS_ALIGN_TOP) ? AFX_IDW_DOCKBAR_TOP : n;
    n = (dw&CBRS_ALIGN_BOTTOM && n==0) ? AFX_IDW_DOCKBAR_BOTTOM : n;
    n = (dw&CBRS_ALIGN_LEFT && n==0) ? AFX_IDW_DOCKBAR_LEFT : n;
    n = (dw&CBRS_ALIGN_RIGHT && n==0) ? AFX_IDW_DOCKBAR_RIGHT : n;

    // When we take the default parameters on rect, DockControlBar will dock
    // each toolbar on a separate line. By calculating a rectangle, we
    // are simulating a toolbar being dragged to that location and docked.
    DockControlBar(Bar,n,&rect);
}
```

Now, in your CMainFrame::OnCreate, instead of using DockControlBar, use DockControlBarLeftOf:

```
m_wndToolBar1.EnableDocking(CBRS_ALIGN_ANY);
m_wndToolBar2.EnableDocking(CBRS_ALIGN_ANY);
EnableDocking(CBRS_ALIGN_ANY);
DockControlBar(&m_wndToolBar1);
DockControlBarLeftOf(&m_wndToolBar2,&m_wndToolBar1);
```

This will dock m_wndToolBar2 left of m_wndToolBar1.

Comments

To use the same functionality with CDialogBar-derived classes as well as CToolBar-derived classes, replace all instances of CToolBar with CDialogBar (the base class) throughout the code.

—BC

In order to control the docking order of vertical toolbars, make the following small change. Replace

```
rect.OffsetRect(1,0);
```

with

```
rect.OffsetRect(1,1);
```

—Uwe Kotyczka

FROM THE FORUM

Question (yhwork):

How can I determine whether a toolbar is horizontal or vertical?

Answer (irona20):

The following code will indicate the current state of the toolbar:

```
if ( ((m_ToolBar.GetBarStyle () & CBRS_ALIGN_LEFT) == CBRS_ALIGN_LEFT) ¦¦
((m_ToolBar.GetBarStyle () & CBRS_ALIGN_RIGHT) == CBRS_ALIGN_RIGHT))
    AfxMessageBox ("vertical");
else
    AfxMessageBox ("horizontal");
```

FROM THE FORUM

Question (Alpena Michigan):

How can I programmatically toggle the visibility of my toolbar buttons?

Answer (-manu-):

Use the following to toggle the toolbar button visibility:

```
m_bHide = !m_bHide;
DWORD but_style = m_wndToolBar.GetButtonStyle(nIndex);
if(m_bHide)
    m_wndToolBar.SetButtonStyle(nIndex, but_style & ~WS_VISIBLE);
else
    m_wndToolBar.SetButtonStyle(nIndex, but_style | WS_VISIBLE);
```

23

TreeView Controls

In this chapter

TreeView controls are used to display structured hierarchical lists of items. This type of display is often described as a tree, where branches and leaves stem from the root, or base, of the tree.

- "Finding an Item (Matching Any Member of TV_ITEM)" shows how to traverse through a tree searching for a specific matching item using specified criteria.

- "Drag-and-Drop Enhancement—Auto-Expand While Hovering" indicates a way to add an auto-expand capability to a TreeView control when dragging over it.

Finding an Item (Matching Any Member of TV_ITEM)

This article was contributed by Donovan L. Brown.

FindNextItem traverses a tree searching for an item matching all the item attributes set in a TV_ITEM structure. In the TV_ITEM structure, the mask member specifies which attributes make up the search criteria. If a match is found, the function returns the handle, otherwise it returns NULL. This function uses the function GetNextItem, seen in various CodeGuru.com articles regarding ListView and TreeView controls. The function only searches in one direction (down) and if hItem is NULL, it starts from the root of the tree:

```
HTREEITEM CTreeCtrlEx::FindNextItem(TV_ITEM* pItem, HTREEITEM hItem)
{
    ASSERT(::IsWindow(m_hWnd));

    TV_ITEM hNextItem;

    //Clear Item data
    ZeroMemory(&hNextItem, sizeof(hNextItem));
```

```
//The mask is used to retrieve the data to compare
hNextItem.mask = pItem->mask;
hNextItem.hItem = (hItem) ? GetNextItem(hItem) : GetRootItem();

//Prepare to compare pszText
//Testing pItem->pszText protects the code from a client setting the
//TVIF_TEXT bit but passing in a NULL pointer.
if((pItem->mask & TVIF_TEXT) && pItem->pszText)
{
    hNextItem.cchTextMax = strlen(pItem->pszText);

    if(hNextItem.cchTextMax)
        hNextItem.pszText = new char[++hNextItem.cchTextMax];
}

while(hNextItem.hItem)
{
    if(Compare(pItem, hNextItem))
    {
        //Copy all the information into pItem and return
        memcpy(pItem, &hNextItem, sizeof(TV_ITEM));

        //Free resources
        if(hNextItem.pszText)
            delete hNextItem.pszText;

        return pItem->hItem;
    }

    //The mask is used to retrieve the data to compare and must be
    //reset before calling Compare
    hNextItem.mask = pItem->mask;
    hNextItem.hItem = GetNextItem(hNextItem.hItem);
}

//Set hItem in pItem
pItem->hItem = NULL;

//Free resources
if(hNextItem.pszText)
    delete hNextItem.pszText;

return NULL;
}

BOOL CTreeCtrlEx::Compare(TV_ITEM* pItem, TV_ITEM& tvTempItem)
{
    //This call uses the .mask setting to just retrieve the values
    //that the client wants to compare.
    //Get all the data passed in by pItem
    GetItem(&tvTempItem);
```

```
//Reset the mask so I can keep track of the matching attributes
tvTempItem.mask = 0;

if((pItem->mask & TVIF_STATE) &&
   (pItem->state == tvTempItem.state))
    tvTempItem.mask |= TVIF_STATE;

if((pItem->mask & TVIF_IMAGE) &&
   (pItem->iImage == tvTempItem.iImage))
    tvTempItem.mask |= TVIF_IMAGE;

if((pItem->mask & TVIF_PARAM) &&
   (pItem->lParam == tvTempItem.lParam))
    tvTempItem.mask |= TVIF_PARAM;

if((pItem->mask & TVIF_TEXT) &&
   pItem->pszText && tvTempItem.pszText && //Don't compare if either is NULL
   !strcmp(pItem->pszText, tvTempItem.pszText))
    tvTempItem.mask |= TVIF_TEXT;

if((pItem->mask & TVIF_CHILDREN) &&
   (pItem->cChildren == tvTempItem.cChildren))
    tvTempItem.mask |= TVIF_CHILDREN;

if((pItem->mask & TVIF_SELECTEDIMAGE) &&
   (pItem->iSelectedImage == tvTempItem.iSelectedImage))
    tvTempItem.mask |= TVIF_SELECTEDIMAGE;

//If by this point these two values are the same
//tvTempItem.hItem is the desired item
return (pItem->mask == tvTempItem.mask);
}
```

FROM THE FORUM

Question (rial9):

How can I go about searching through all of my TreeView control's root items so that I can retrieve their lParam values?

Answer (Igor Soukhov):

Use CTreeCtrl::GetNextItem if you are using MFC, or the TreeView_GetNextItem macro if you are dealing directly with the API or ATL. This will allow you to iterate through all items.

Drag-and-Drop Enhancement— Auto-Expand While Hovering

This article was contributed by Pete Peterson.

I used the code from CodeGuru to implement drag-and-drop processing in my tree control. I wanted to modify this slightly so that a node would expand automatically when I dragged a node over a drop target and hovered over it. This is similar to what occurs in Windows Explorer.

The following code snippet could be used in conjunction with the drag-and-drop code offered previously in CodeGuru.

The first step is to add two new variables to your class definition, a hover timer ID and a hover point. The timer ID identifies the timer that is started when you are dragging a tree node and you hover over a drop node for a certain period of time. The hover point stores the current point of the hover. This value needs to be stored, as it is not available in the OnTimer event handler.

You must define two events, OnTimer and OnMouseMove, if you have not done so already. I used the Class Wizard to create them. The following code chunk is from the header file for the tree control. The only items that I included are those that need to be added:

```
class CMyTree : public CTreeCtrl
{
        .
        . // Definition
        .
private:
    UINT          m_nHoverTimerID;
    POINT          m_HoverPoint;

        .
        .     // Other definition
        .
protected:
    // Generated message map function
    //{{AFX_MSG(CMyTree
    afx_msg void OnTimer(UINT nIDEvent);
    afx_msg void OnMouseMove(UINT nFlags, CPoint point);
    //}}AFX_MS
    DECLARE_MESSAGE_MAP()
}
```

In the .cpp file, you need to add code to two functions: OnMouseMove and OnTimer. In OnMouseMove, the hover timer is constantly checked for existence, and if it exists, it is deleted. You only want the OnTimer event to be called when the mouse pointer is still for a certain period of time. The SetTimer will create a timer,

and after the expiration of the selected time period, will send a message triggering the
OnTimer event. In the OnTimer event handler, it is a simple matter to kill the timer,
get the item currently being hovered over, and issue an expand node command:

```
BEGIN_MESSAGE_MAP(CMyTree, CTreeCtrl)
    //{{AFX_MSG_MAP(CMyTree
    ON_WM_TIMER()
    ON_WM_MOUSEMOVE()
    //}}AFX_MSG_MA
    END_MESSAGE_MAP()

void CMyTree::OnMouseMove(UINT nFlags, CPoint point)
{
    HTREEITEM        hitem;
    UINT             flags;

    if ( m_nHoverTimerID )
    {
        KillTimer( m_nHoverTimerID );
        m_nHoverTimerID = 0;
    }

    if (m_bDragging)
    {
        ASSERT(m_pImageList != NULL);
        m_pImageList->DragMove(point);

        m_nHoverTimerID = SetTimer(2, 750, NULL);
        m_HoverPoint = point;

        if ((hitem = HitTest(point, &flags)) != NULL)
        {
            m_pImageList->DragLeave(this);
            SelectDropTarget(hitem);
            m_hitemDrop = hitem;
            m_pImageList->DragEnter(this, point);
        }

        m_pImageList->DragShowNolock(TRUE);
    }

    CTreeCtrl::OnMouseMove(nFlags, point);
}

void CMyTree::OnTimer(UINT nIDEvent)
{
    if ( nIDEvent == m_nHoverTimerID )
    {
        KillTimer( m_nHoverTimerID );
        m_nHoverTimerID = 0;
```

```
        HTREEITEM    trItem    = 0;
        uint         uFlag     = 0;

        trItem = HitTest(m_HoverPoint, &uFlag);

        if ( trItem )
        {
            SelectItem( trItem );
            Expand(trItem,TVE_EXPAND);
        }
    }
    else
    {
        CTreeCtrl::OnTimer(nIDEvent);
    }
}
```

FROM THE FORUM

Question (rekha1976):

I am creating a pop-up menu in my TreeView. My call to TrackPopupMenu requires x and y values. How can I get these values to display the menu in the correct location?

Answer (weiye):

Use the GetCursorPos routine to find the current location of the mouse, and then convert this value to client coordinates:

```
    CPoint oPos;

    // Get current cursor coordinates
    GetCursorPos(&oPos);

    // Convert this to client coordinates
    ScreenToClient(&oPos);
```

You can use oPos.x and oPos.y now with the call to TrackPopupMenu.

24

Splitter Controls

In this chapter

Splitter controls can be implemented within both SDI and MDI frame windows to separate views from other views.

In this chapter, you will find details on some extended functionality of splitter controls beyond their regular use.

- "Minimum Size Splitter" allows you to control the minimum size of a view when hosted within a splitter control.
- "CSplitterWnd Extension That Allows Switching Views in Any Pane" provides a way to switch views within panes of static

splitters without deleting and re-creating those views.

- "Implementing Rulers Inside Splitter Panes" describes a way to show scaled rulers to help indicate the current cursor position within the view.
- "Toolbar Within Splitter Windows" is similar to implementing rulers within a splitter pane, with some extended functionality to provide buttons and text in a similar way to a toolbar. This can be used to provide an effective and professional finish to an application.

Minimum Size Splitter

This article was contributed by Graham Lyus.

For my latest project, we needed splitter panes that had proper minimum sizes—the user couldn't physically resize the splitter pane smaller than a specified amount. The standard MFC splitter class allows you to set minimum sizes, but these only affect what is displayed, not how small the panes can be. CMinSplitterWnd is a drop-in replacement for (and is derived from) CSplitterWnd.

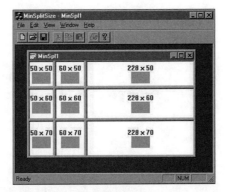

Figure 24.1

Instructions:

1. Add MinSplitterWnd.cpp and MinSplitterWnd.h to your current project (Menu Project, Add to Project, Add Files).

2. Where you currently use CSplitterWnd, replace with CMinSplitterWnd. (Note: Remember to include MinSplitterWnd.h.)

```
#include "MinSplitterWnd.h" // Minimum size splitter.
....
class CMyWnd : public CMDIChildWnd
{
    ....
    CMinSplitterWnd m_wndSplitter;
    ....
};
```

3. Call SetRowInfo and SetColumnInfo as necessary, specifying the required minimum row and column sizes. (This is normally done in the parent window's OnCreateClient function.)

```
....
m_wndSplitter.CreateStatic( this, 2, 2 );
➡// Create with 2 rows and 2 columns.
m_wndSplitter.SetRowInfo( 0, 100, 100 );
➡// Set ideal and minimum size to 100.
m_wndSplitter.SetRowInfo( 1, 100, 100 );
➡// Set ideal and minimum size to 100.
m_wndSplitter.SetColumnInfo( 0, 100, 100 );
➡// Set ideal and minimum size to 100.
m_wndSplitter.SetColumnInfo( 1, 100, 100 );
➡// Set ideal and minimum size to 100.
....
```

4. In the splitter's parent window, add a message handler for
OnWindowPosChanging (to prevent the user from sizing the window
too small) and add the following code to it:

```
void CMyWnd::OnWindowPosChanging(WINDOWPOS FAR* lpwndpos)
{
    //    Don't do anything if minimized.
    if ( IsIconic() )
    {
        CMDIChildWnd::OnWindowPosChanging( lpwndpos );
        return;
    } // if

    //    Calculate the window rect if we have no client area.
    CRect rc( 0, 0, 0, 0 );
    CalcWindowRect( rc );

    //    Add on the minimum client width
    and height from the splitter.
    int nMinWidth    = rc.Width() +
    m_wndSplitter.GetMinClientWidth();
    int nMinHeight   = rc.Height() +
    m_wndSplitter.GetMinClientHeight();

    //    Get the current window size.
    CRect rcWindow;
    GetWindowRect( rcWindow );
    GetParent()->ScreenToClient( rcWindow );

    //    If trying to size too small...
    if ( lpwndpos->cx < nMinWidth )
    {
        //    If dragging left border right...
        if ( rcWindow.left < lpwndpos->x )
        {
            //    How much over are we?
            int nOver = nMinWidth - lpwndpos->cx;

            //    Adjust left coord.
            lpwndpos->x -= nOver;

        } // if

        //    Fix width.
        lpwndpos->cx = nMinWidth;
    } // if
```

```
      //    If trying to size too small...
    if ( lpwndpos->cy < nMinHeight )
    {
        //    If dragging top border down...
        if ( rcWindow.top < lpwndpos->y )
        {
            //    How much over are we?
            int nOver = nMinHeight - lpwndpos->cy;

            //    Adjust left coord.
            lpwndpos->y -= nOver;
        } // if

        //    Fix height.
        lpwndpos->cy = nMinHeight;
    } // if
}
```

5. That's it!

Limitation:

If the minimum sizes exceed the initial frame window size, the window will snap when the window is first resized.

FROM THE FORUM

Question (rz5b):

How can I specify the minimum width of the panes in my splitter window?

Answer (Philip Nicoletti):

Use CSplitterWnd::SetColumnInfo:

```
    void SetColumnInfo( int col, int cxIdeal, int cxMin );
```

The parameters for this are

- **col:** Specifies a splitter window column
- **cxIdeal:** Specifies an ideal width for the splitter window column in pixels
- **cxMin:** Specifies a minimum width for the splitter window column in pixels

You might also need to call RecalcLayout() after the call to SetColumnInfo(...).

CSplitterWnd Extension That Allows Switching Views in Any Pane

This article was contributed by Caroline Englebienne, Aniworld Inc.

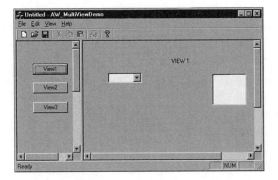

Figure 24.2

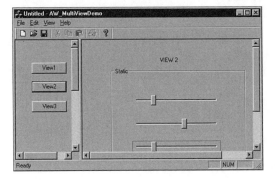

Figure 24.3

This article explains how to switch between multiple views in a splitter window pane *without* deleting and re-creating views. It is inefficient to create and destroy views, and it often disrupts an application's design, yet the only examples of switching views I have found are doing just that! I have created a CSplitterWnd replacement class that adds the multiple-views-per-pane functionality in a lightweight and easy-to-use way. Note: This class is intended for static splitters only, not dynamic ones.

How to Use My Code

I derived a class (AW_CMultiViewSplitter) from CSplitterWnd. You can simply include the files AW_CMultiViewSplitter.h and AW_CMultiViewSplitter.cpp to your project, use an AW_CMultiViewSplitter instead of a classic splitter window, and call the following two functions:

- **int AddView(int nRow, int nCol, CRuntimeClass * pViewClass, CCreateContext* pContext)**

    This function should be called where you would usually call CreateView() but you want more than one view for the pane. If you only need a single view, just call CreateView(), as usual. AddView() returns an int, which is the ID of the newly created view. This ID is used in the function ShowView() if you want to make this new view visible.

- **void ShowView(int viewID)**

    This function takes a viewID as its only parameter. This function takes care of hiding the previously visible view and showing the requested one.

Points of Interest

I will skip the detailed code here and just explain the basic idea that makes it work. For the details, you can download the little sample I wrote to illustrate the use of my splitter window.

The two points of interest are

- How to create multiple views in the same pane
- How to switch between views

How to Create Multiple Views in the Same Pane

In a classic splitter window, when a view is created in a pane, its window identifier is set to an ID that is computed from the row and column numbers corresponding to the pane. Therefore, when you have multiple views for a pane, you must set all but one to ID zero as well as hide all the nonvisible views.

The following code block demonstrates how to add a new view to a pane when one is currently assigned to the pane:

```
HideCurrentView(nRow, nCol)
{
 CWnd * pView  = GetCurrentView(pane.row, pane.col);
 pView->SetDlgCtrlID(0);
 pView->ShowWindow(SW_HIDE);
}

CreateView(nRow, nCol, pViewClass, CSize(10,10), pContext);
```

```
SetCurrentView(nRow, nCol, newViewID)
{
 CWnd * pView  = GetView( viewID);
 pView->SetDlgCtrlID(IdFromRowCol(pane.row, pane.col));
 pView->ShowWindow(SW_SHOW);
}
```

How to Switch Between Views

The window that is displayed is the one whose identifier is the ID computed from the row and column numbers. Then, to switch views, you just need to get the visible one, set its ID to something else, hide it, get the window you want to see, set its ID to the good one (obtained by calling IdFromRowCol), show it, and refresh the splitter.

```
GetPaneFromViewID(viewID);
HideCurrentView(pane.row, pane.col);
SetCurrentView(pane.row, pane.col, viewID);
```

Comments

The use of dynamic_cast within the sample code may cause the compiler to issue Warning C4541 due to the absence of runtime-type information. To resolve this, either enable RTTI in the project settings, or use the code shown next to obtain a pointer to the CMainFrame parent object:

```
CMainFrame *pFrm = (CMainFrame *)AfxGetMainWnd();
```

—brick luo

Implementing Rulers Inside Splitter Panes

This article was contributed by Stefan Ungureanu.

Figure 24.4

Introduction

Many applications that display images or documents show rulers on both sides of the view to indicate your position within the page and allow a more accurate positioning of the cursor. Implementing rulers can be difficult since we must reserve a space for them inside the view. (This gets more difficult on a CScrollView-derived class.) Another solution is to use fixed splitters (ones that cannot be resized). The example that follows demonstrates how to build such rulers.

The Code

The code implementing the ruler splitter window and views used for the rulers themselves can be found in ruler.h and ruler.cpp. Following is a sample of how to use them.

Inside the frame window (which can be either a CFrameWnd or CMDIChildWnd-derived class)

```
// class definition
class CMainFrame : public CFrameWnd
{
[...]
protected:
    DECLARE_FX_RULER(CMainFrame)
```

The next step is to create the splitter and the views. The code that follows matches an SDI application that accommodates the preceding code inside a splitter pane, but you can easily adjust it to fit your needs. In the OnCreateClient member of the CMainFrame class, add code to create the splitter inside the right pane:

```
// class definition
IMPLEMENT_FX_RULER_SPLITTER(<className>, <parentSplitter>,
➥ 0, 1, pContext->m_pNewViewClass);
```

What you have to do next is send notifications to the rulers to let them know about the scroll position change or zoom change. The rulers can also display the mouse position as the cursor moves; this is done by sending notifications to the rulers with just a few lines of code like this:

```
// class definition
GetDocument()->UpdateAllViews(this, VW_VSCROLL, (CObject*)
➥(GetScrollPosition().y));
```

Available hint types are (hint parameters are passed as INTs using a cast to CObject*)

- **VW_HSCROLL**: View is scrolled horizontally
- **VW_VSCROLL**: View is scrolled vertically
- **VW_HPOSITION**: Cursor position changed on the x axis
- **VW_VPOSITION**: Cursor position changed on the y axis

The code is quite easy to follow and change to meet your needs, but if you need assistance, send an email to stefanu@usa.net. Also, please send me bugs or updates to keep this solution up-to-date. For more details on the sample application, contact me at stefanu@usa.net.

Toolbar Within Splitter Windows

This article was contributed by Stefan Ungureanu.

Figure 24.5

Introduction

Has anyone ever wondered how to dock a toolbar inside a splitter pane? Normally, you cannot do that, but you can alter your splitter pane so that it will look just like you placed a toolbar on one of its sides. The trick is to create a two-pane splitter where your initial pane was. We will use our own splitter, which does not allow resizing and has different border settings. There is one additional view to create, and we will derive a class from CFormView since features provided by this class are closer to our goal.

The Code

First goes the custom splitter window:

```
// class definition
classCSmartSplitterWnd :public CSplitterWnd
{
public:
    CSmartSplitterWnd();
    virtual ~CSmartSplitterWnd();
    intHitTest(CPoint pt)const;
protected:
    DECLARE_MESSAGE_MAP()
};
```

```
// class implementation
CSmartSplitterWnd::CSmartSplitterWnd()
{
    m_cxSplitter=3;       // put your own values here to make the
➥splitter fit your needs
    m_cySplitter=3;
    m_cxBorderShare=0;
    m_cyBorderShare=0;
    m_cxSplitterGap=3;
    m_cySplitterGap=3;
}

CSmartSplitterWnd::~CSmartSplitterWnd()
{
}

BEGIN_MESSAGE_MAP(CSmartSplitterWnd, CSplitterWnd)
    //{{AFX_MSG_MAP(CSmartSplitterWnd)
    //}}AFX_MSG_MAP
END_MESSAGE_MAP()

intCSmartSplitterWnd::HitTest(CPoint pt)const
{
    ASSERT_VALID(this);
    // do not allow caller to see mouse hits
    return 0;
}
```

Next, we must create a simple CFormView using the Resource editor and Class Wizard. You can add any controls to your form view, but you must keep in mind that handling the WM_SIZE message may help you improve the look of your view. There are several ways to update your buttons and other controls inside the view; you may need to implement one of them to update, enable, or disable the controls.

The last step is to create the splitter and the views. The code that follows matches an SDI application that accommodates the preceding code inside a splitter pane, but you can easily adjust it to fit your needs.

First, add a member to the CMainFrame class of type CSmartSplitterWnd:

```
classCMainFrame :public CFrameWnd
{
[...]
public:
    CSmartSplitterWnd m_barSplitter;
```

In the OnCreateClient member of the CMainFrame class, add code to create the splitter inside the right pane:

```
// create the splitter window
if (!m_barSplitter.CreateStatic(&m_parentSplitter, 2, 1,
➥WS_CHILD¦WS_VISIBLE¦WS_BORDER,
    m_parentSplitter.IdFromRowCol(1, 0))) returnfalse;

// create the views
m_barSplitter.CreateView(0, 0, RUNTIME_CLASS(CBarView), CSize(0, 0), pContext);
m_barSplitter.CreateView(1, 0, RUNTIME_CLASS(CTheView), CSize(0, 0), pContext);
// then set heights
```

The code is quite easy to follow and change to meet your needs, but if you need assistance, send an email to stefanu@usa.net. Also, please send me bugs or updates to keep this solution up-to-date. For more details on the sample application, contact me at stefanu@usa.net.

FROM THE FORUM

Question (Nigel Merritt):

I have created a splitter view with two rows, both split (separately) into two columns. The lower-right view is a CFormView, and the other three are CViews. The problem is that no matter what sizes I give them in OnCreateClient in CMainFrame, the horizontal split starts at the very top of the frame, so the lower CView and the CFormView take up the whole window, meaning I have to move the horizontal split down every time I run it. Has anyone come across this problem, and how do I solve it?

Answer (Philip Nicoletti):

This always seems to happen when creating multiple splitters in this manner. Just add the following line to the end of OnCreateClient():

```
m_wndSplitter.SetRowInfo(0, 200, 0);   // add this line
```

25

Other Controls

In this chapter

There are many types of controls used within applications. Controls you find in this chapter are those that simply don't fit anywhere else, but are still very useful.

- Many times, you need to view the contents of a specific memory location, showing both ASCII and hexadecimal representations. "A Memory Viewer—With a Powerful Class for Any Kind of Text Editor" provides this functionality.
- The article "System Image List" shows a practical way you can

implement image lists for directories and applications.

- "CMacButton, CMacCheckBox, and CMacRadioButton" shows how to add the Macintosh look and feel to regular CButton-, CCheckBox-, and CRadioButton-derived classes.
- "Macintosh-like Progress Control," from the same author as "CMacButton, CMacCheckBox, and CMacRadioButton," adds the Macintosh look and feel to a regular progress control.

A Memory Viewer—With a Powerful Class for Any Kind of Text Editor

This article was contributed by hou, Jianjun.

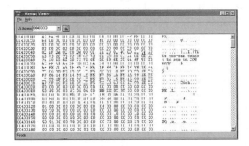

Figure 25.1

Environment: VC6, NT4, Win2000, Win9x/ME

Abstract

The Memory Viewer displays memory contents starting at a specified address (0x00400000, by default). It shows memory contents as the HEX format in a binary editor.

With this viewer, a programmer can watch where Windows runs an application, where it runs a Windows data page, and even where it runs CMOS information (0x000FF5C0).

It shows the memory contents by bytes and explains bytes in ASCII as much as possible. If a memory page is not readable, it shows ? instead.

A toolbar at the top of the window displays the starting address for the memory display. Edit the value in the toolbar and click the Go button to change the starting address. Use the scrollbar at the side of the window to view other memory locations in the system's address space without changing the starting address of the display. The scrollbar can go anywhere in any address without a problem.

The treasure in this program is the class CSW_EditorBase. It is called EditorBase because it can be a basic class for any kind of editor, such as an Information Window or a Binary Viewer. The class has all the necessary frame members for an editor control.

Editors are easily built by deriving just a few members from CSW_EditorBase, and they don't have to take care of flashing, selections, scrollbars, drawing parts, and other boring works that have to be done repeatedly on each kind of editor's job.

If you are looking for a tiny text window, this would be a very nice startup.

In fact, the purpose of the Memory Viewer is just to test this idea and implement the class CSW_EditorBase. It proves well.

How a Common Text Editor Works

To draw text line by line, you have to consider the following:

1. The number of lines, GetTotalLines(), in CSW_EditorBase.

2. The height of a line, which is the maximum height of all characters in a line. GetLineH() in CSW_EditorBase.

3. The line index from a client Y position on pixels. GetLineFromY() in CSW_EditorBase.

4. The number of columns, which should be the maximum columns in all lines. It is used to calculate a scrollbar's range in most situations. GetTotalCols() in CSW_EditorBase.

5. The width of a column. It is important when the font is varied. GetColW() in CSW_EditorBase.

6. The column index from a client X position on pixels. GetColFromX() in CSW_EditorBase.

7. A method to get the string in a line. GetLineStr() in CSW_EditorBase.

8. A method to draw a line. OnDrawItem() in CSW_EditorBase.

9. A method to calculate scrollbar ranges. OnUpdateBars() in CSW_EditorBase.

10. Overriding OnPaint(), MouseMove(), and other CWnd methods.

11. To remove some refresh problems by only drawing the visible lines and moving the whole client area when scrolling.

12. Other work such as how to save all text or draw an image inside.

Class CSW_EditorBase Members

Abstract class CSW_EditorBase derives from CWnd and has the following member functions:

- **Line functions:** A line can be a line of text and its alignment.

```
// Get the number of total lines
virtual UINT    GetTotalLines  (void) = 0;
// Get the height of a line
virtual UINT    GetLineH       (int nLine);
// Get a line number from a position( in pixel)
virtual int     GetLineFromY   (int &Y);
```

- **Column functions:** A column can be a char and its alignment, or an image.

```
// Get the maximum number of columns in all lines
virtual UINT    GetTotalCols   (void) = 0;
// Get the with of a column
virtual UINT    GetColW        (int nCol);
virtual int     GetColFromX    (int &X);


// Cell functions
// Get the line and column index from a point
virtual BOOL    GetLineColFromPt(CPoint &map;Pt,
                                 int &iLine,
                                 int &iCol);


// String functions
// Get the string for a line
virtual void    GetLineStr     (int nLine, CString& str) = 0;
```

```
                    // Paint
                    virtual BOOL     OnDrawItem        ( CDC *pDC,
                                                         UINT nLine,
                                                         LPCTSTR lpStr,
                                                         int FirstSelectedChar = -1,
                                                         int LastSelectedChar = -1);


                    // Scrollbars, update scrollbar's range
                             void     OnUpdateBars      (void);

                    // Don't derive again in subclass, normally.

                    afx_msg BOOL     OnEraseBkgnd      (CDC *pDC);
                    afx_msg void     OnPaint           (void);
                    afx_msg void     OnSize            (UINT nType, int cx, int cy);

                    afx_msg void     OnHScroll         (UINT nSBCode,
                                                         UINT nPos,
                                                         CScrollBar* pScrollBar);
                    afx_msg void     OnVScroll         (UINT nSBCode,
                                                         UINT nPos,
                                                         CScrollBar* pScrollBar);

                    afx_msg void     OnLButtonDown     (UINT nFlags, CPoint point);
                    afx_msg void     OnLButtonDblClk   (UINT nFlags, CPoint point);
                    afx_msg void     OnMouseMove       (UINT nFlags, CPoint point);
                    afx_msg void     OnLButtonUp       (UINT nFlags, CPoint point);
                    afx_msg BOOL     OnMouseWheel      (UINT nFlags,
                                                         short zDelta,
                                                         CPoint pt);
                    ...
```

How to Use Class CSW_EditorBase

Derive a new class from CSW_EditorBase and override some members as necessary.
GetTotalLines(), GetTotalCols(), and GetLineStr() are essential. This class creates an
instance of the new class and puts it inside a view window.

See CSW_TextInfo as a simple example:

```
class CSW_TextInfo : public CSW_EditorBase
{
private:

    // Save all lines here
    CStringArray    m_StrData;
    // Keep the maximum number of columns
```

```
    int           m_MaxColNBR;
    // public members
public:
    CSW_TextInfo   ();
    // Add a line of string
    void    AddLine (LPCTSTR lpStr);
    // Clean all information
    void    Clean   (void);
    // Member overrides from its parent class
protected:
    virtual UINT    GetTotalLines   (void);
    virtual UINT    GetTotalCols    (void);
    virtual void    GetLineStr      (int nLine, CString& str);
};
```

See CSW_BDisplay in the source for a complicated example.

System Image List

This article was contributed by Mark Otway.

A system image list contains each file, folder, shortcut, and so on, which is very handy for creating a custom explorer-type application. I saw Matt Esterly's code for using an image list and noted the comment at the bottom about detaching it from the CImageList; if this isn't done the CImageList destructor frees up the system image list, causing the user to lose all of their desktop icons. Note that this only happens under '95 (haven't tried '98). NT 4 is much more careful and won't let you free its list. There is also the further problem that the CImageList class checks its permanent object list for the handle, and if that handle has already been attached to another instance of CImageList, it Asserts. This means that if you want to use the image list in more than two places at once you'll have a problem.

I had this problem in my app and so wrote a wrapper class, CSystemImageList, to save me having to remember to detach the lists. Basically, the first time an instance of the class is created, it creates two singleton image lists (one for large and one for small icons), which are stored as static members. Every subsequent instance then uses these items, and a simple reference count is used to keep track of their use. When the last CSystemImageList is destroyed, the reference count is zeroed, and the singleton objects are detached from the system image list and then deleted from the heap. This means that you can use the image lists at will without having to worry about multiple instances, asserts, or detaching lists.

Another important difference to Matt's version is that by using the SHGFI_ USEFILEATTRIBUTES flag for SHGetFileInfo, the function doesn't need to open a real file to either get the icon index or the image lists themselves. This is useful, say, if you want to find the image of an object on the Internet, which doesn't actually exist on your local disk.

In order to use the image lists, construct a CSystemImageList and then call

```
CImageList * CSystemImageList::GetImageList( BOOL bSmall = TRUE ) const;
```

which returns a pointer to the required image list (large or small), which can then be passed to, say, CTreeCtrl::SetImageList. Bear in mind that the object must exist for the entire time that the image list is to be used, so it's usually best to make it a member of the window class. A helper function

```
int CSystemImageList::GetIcon( const CString& sName, BOOL bOpen = FALSE, BOOL
➥ bSmall = TRUE ) const;
```

provides a way of getting the particular image index for a filename. The index returned can be from the small or large image list, and in the open or normal state, depending on the parameters passed.

In the demo I've provided is a dialog-based MFC app with a tree control and a list control, each of which is populated with a few items. See below for the code extracts.

The demo code was generated and tested using VC++ v5.0 and has been tested under v6.0.

```
// SysImageListDlg.h - the dialog class

class CSysImageListDlg : public CDialog
{
// Implementation
protected:
    CSystemImageList     m_ImgList;
              :
              :
};


// SysImageListDlg.cpp - OnInitDialog
// Initialise the tree and list controls to use the image

// m_Tree is a CTreeCtrl created from the resources with ClassWizard.
// m_List is a CListCtrl.
m_Tree.SetImageList( m_ImgList.GetImageList(), TVSIL_NORMAL );

// Pass false to GetImageList to get the Large icons
m_List.SetImageList( m_ImgList.GetImageList( FALSE ), LVSIL_NORMAL );

CString sFile;

sFile = "somefile.html";
// Now create an item in each control, setting the icon indices.
// First the tree control - set the index of the icon both closed and open
m_Tree.InsertItem( sFile, m_ImgList.GetIcon( sFile ),
➥m_ImgList.GetIcon( sFile, TRUE ) );

// and the list control - remembering to get the index for the large icon
m_List.InsertItem( 1, sFile, m_ImgList.GetIcon( sFile, FALSE, TRUE ) );
```

CMacButton, CMacCheckBox, and CMacRadioButton

This article was contributed by Paul M. Meidinger.

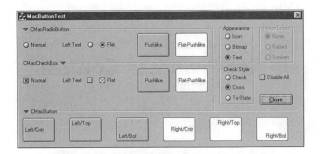

Figure 25.2

Environment: VC6, NT4 SP4

These three classes are my attempt at re-creating the standard buttons on the Macintosh. The normal appearance of the buttons duplicates the 3D look of the more recent MacOS versions, but an old-style flat look can also be used by setting the button's Flat style in the Resource editor.

The following public function is available for CMacButton:

- void SetBold(BOOL bBold = TRUE)
- BOOL GetBold()

The following public functions are available for CMacCheckBox and CMacRadioButton:

- void SetCheck(int nCheck)
- int GetCheck()

Follow these steps to add a CMacXXX button to a dialog:

1. Add the desired files to your project.
2. Add the appropriate include to the header file of your dialog class.
3. Add check boxes/radio buttons/standard buttons to your dialog in the Resource editor.
4. Use Class Wizard to add a member variable of type CMacButton, CMacCheckBox, or CMacRadioButton for the corresponding controls you just added. If the CMacXXX classes are not in the Variable Type list, choose CButton and manually change the types in the header file of your dialog class.

To-do list:

- Add support for bitmaps on buttons.
- Add support for horizontal and vertical alignment.
- Add support for push-like check boxes and radio buttons.
- Add support for tri-state check boxes and radio buttons.

Macintosh-like Progress Control

This article was contributed by Paul M. Meidinger.

Environment: Windows NT4, SP4, Visual C++ 6

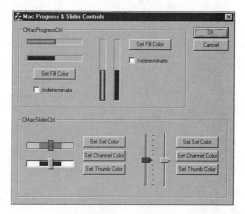

Figure 25.3

This image shows an example of my CMacProgressCtrl and CMacSliderCtrl. For more information on the CMacSliderCtrl, please refer to the article "Macintosh-Like Slider Control" on CodeGuru.com.

This class is my attempt at re-creating the progress control of the Macintosh. This control (CMacProgressCtrl) allows you to change its colors as well as set an *indeterminate state* (similar to the barber-pole look of progress controls on the Mac). This state can be used to indicate to the user that the length of time to finish the current operation is unknown.

Public Member Functions

```
void SetColor(COLORREF crColor)
COLORREF GetColor()
void SetIndeterminate(BOOL bIndeterminate = TRUE)
BOOL GetIndeterminate()
```

Steps to Add a CMacProgressCtrl to a Dialog

Add the desired files to your project. Add the #include directive to the header file of your dialog class, and add a progress control to your dialog in the Resource editor. Use Class Wizard to add a member variable of type CMacProgressCtrl for the corresponding controls you just added. If the CMacProgressCtrl class is not in the Variable Type list, choose CProgressCtrl and manually change the types in the header file of your dialog class.

Comments

There may be color problems when using the release build version of this control due to a problem with the "if" statements in the LightenColor method. It was an unsafe assumption that (b<COLOR> + bIncreaseVal) was to be evaluated and treated as a data type larger than a BYTE. In release mode, the compiler's optimizations treat (b<COLOR> + bIncreaseVal) as a byte, meaning the result is always less than or equal to 255. Using WORDs for these calculations resolves this problem:

```
COLORREF CFingerView::LightenColor(const COLORREF crColor, BYTE bIncreaseVal)
{
    WORD wRed = GetRValue(crColor);
    WORD wGreen = GetGValue(crColor);
    WORD wBlue = GetBValue(crColor);

    if ((wRed + bIncreaseVal) <= 255)
        wRed += bIncreaseVal;
    if ((wGreen + bIncreaseVal)    <= 255)
        wGreen += bIncreaseVal;
    if ((wBlue + bIncreaseVal) <= 255)
        wBlue += bIncreaseVal;

    return RGB(wRed, wGreen, wBlue);
}
```

—Tim Ranker

V

Graphics and Multimedia

26

Bitmaps and Palettes

In this chapter

Bitmaps are digital representations of images. In this chapter, you will find ways to manipulate these bitmaps as well as use other image file formats.

- "A Quick Method to Load a Bitmap File in a CBitmap" describes a simple way to load a bitmap from a file.
- "How to Retain the Aspect Ratio of an Image While Resizing" shows how to correctly scale a bitmap while maintaining its original aspect ratio.
- "Transparent Bitmap: True Mask Method" documents a way to

perform bitmap manipulation in memory instead of onscreen to reduce flickering and increase speed.

- "CPicture: The Yovav (Horror) PictureShow" defines a useful class that can be easily used to display various image file formats.
- "Add GIF Animation to Your MFC and ATL Projects" allows you to add the dynamic element of animated GIFs as well as other image file formats to your applications.

A Quick Method to Load a Bitmap File in a CBitmap

This article was contributed by Ronen Magid.

Here's a quick way to load *.BMP files into a CBitmap object:

1. Create your own CBitmap derived class (say, CMyBitmap).
2. Add a "load from bitmap" method as listed next:

```
BOOL CMyBitmap::LoadBitmap(LPCTSTR szFilename)
{
    ASSERT(szFilename);
    DeleteObject();
```

```
        HBITMAP hBitmap = NULL;
        hBitmap = (HBITMAP)LoadImage(NULL, szFilename, IMAGE_BITMAP, 0, 0,
            LR_LOADFROMFILE ¦ LR_CREATEDIBSECTION ¦ LR_DEFAULTSIZE);
        return Attach(hBitmap);
    }
```

How to Retain the Aspect Ratio of an Image While Resizing

This article was contributed by Michael Hatton.

Figure 26.1

Figure 26.2

Environment: VC6

I needed a way to display images full screen, but I did not want the image to change its aspect ratio since that would distort its shape. If the image were narrow, it would expand to fill up the whole width of the screen, making the image look too wide.

To fix this, I wrote a function that will calculate the rectangle that will be needed. If you stretch the image to fit in the rectangle, it will expand the image to fill as much of the screen as possible without changing the aspect ratio of the picture.

The function has three parameters. The first parameter is the rectangle that you want the image to fill. The second parameter is the size of the picture. The last parameter tells the function whether you want the image to be centered in the rectangle.

The function returns a rectangle that you can use to stretch the image:

```
CRect SizeRectWithConstantAspectRatio( CRect* rcScreen,
                                       CSize sizePicture,
                                       BOOL bCenter)
{
  CRect rect(rcScreen);
  double dWidth = rcScreen->Width();
  double dHeight = rcScreen->Height();
  double dAspectRatio = dWidth/dHeight;

  double dPictureWidth = sizePicture.cx;
  double dPictureHeight = sizePicture.cy;
  double dPictureAspectRatio = dPictureWidth/dPictureHeight;

  //If the aspect ratios are the same, then the screen rectangle
  // will do; otherwise, we need to calculate the new rectangle

  if (dPictureAspectRatio > dAspectRatio)
  {
    int nNewHeight = (int)(dWidth/dPictureWidth*dPictureHeight);
    int nCenteringFactor = (rcScreen->Height() - nNewHeight) / 2;
    rect.SetRect( 0,
                  nCenteringFactor,
                  (int)dWidth,
                  nNewHeight + nCenteringFactor);

  }
  else if (dPictureAspectRatio < dAspectRatio)
  {
    int nNewWidth =  (int)(dHeight/dPictureHeight*dPictureWidth);
    int nCenteringFactor = (rcScreen->Width() - nNewWidth) / 2;
    rect.SetRect( nCenteringFactor,
                  0,
                  nNewWidth + nCenteringFactor,
                  (int)(dHeight));
  }

  return rect;
}
```

This is an example of how to use this function. I used the CPicture class from CodeGuru, but you could use a normal CBitmap class and use CDC::StretchBlt for the same effect.

```
void CMyWnd::OnPaint()
{
  CPaintDC dc(this); // device context for painting
  CString strSize;

  CPicture picture;
  picture.Load(m_strPicturePath);
  // Get picture dimensions in pixels
  picture.UpdateSizeOnDC(&dc);

//Get the dimensions of the screen
  CRect rcScreen( 0, 0,
                  GetSystemMetrics(SM_CXSCREEN),
                  GetSystemMetrics(SM_CYSCREEN));

  //Get dimensions of the image
  CSize sizePicture(picture.m_Width, picture.m_Height);

  //Create a black background
  CBrush backBrush;
  backBrush.CreateSolidBrush(RGB(0,0,0));
  dc.FillRect(&rcScreen, &backBrush);

  CRect rcNewPictureRect =
       SizeRectWithConstantAspectRatio(&rcScreen,
                                       sizePicture,
                                       TRUE);
  picture.Show(&dc, rcNewPictureRect);
}
```

Transparent Bitmap: True Mask Method

This article was contributed by Paul Reynolds.

What Does the Code Do?

This code shows you how to draw a transparent bitmap using memory rather than directly using the screen. This is important because intensive bitmap operations are slow due to the number of bits that are affected, and using the screen makes things even worse because some flicker results. The visual flickering can be eliminated by using memory bitmaps:

1. Copy the section of the screen that is to be affected to a memory bitmap.

2. Carry out the bitmap operation on the memory bitmap instead of on the screen.

3. Copy the memory bitmap back to the screen.

The result is that only one blt affects the screen, so there is no flicker. We may be using two more blt operations, but the operation will probably be perceived as quicker because there is no flicker. (Some device memory blts are faster than blts that have to access the screen.)

MSDN

I had written the source code provided many months ago for a project I was working on. When I decided to submit it to CodeGuru, I had to look at MSDN again to refresh my memory and help me construct a decent explanation for the technique that I use.

One article in particular is called "Bitmaps with Transparency" by Ron Gery (Microsoft Developer Network Technology Group). His explanation of transparent blts is excellent, and I have used this as my reference for constructing the following brief explanation. If you are still a bit unclear, I recommend you read some of the articles that helped this one along.

The True Mask Method

True mask blting does not need modification on the part of the source bitmap to be useful. The masked blt involves a three-step process, with a mask that has all transparent pixels set to 1 and all opaque pixels set to 0:

1. XOR the source bitmap onto the destination (BitBlt with SRCINVERT). This looks a bit funny, but the second XOR restores the destination to its original state.

2. Masking operation: When the mask is ANDed to the destination (BitBlt with SRCAND), all the transparent pixels leave the destination pixels unchanged, whereas the opaque pixels set the destination to black. Now the destination has a blacked-out image of the opaque part of the source and an XORed image of itself in the transparent part.

3. XOR the source to the destination (BitBlt with SRCINVERT). The transparent pixels are restored to their original state, and the opaque pixels are copied directly from the source.

How Do I Use It?

This function takes four parameters:

- The device context that you want to display the bitmap in
- The horizontal position that you want to draw from
- The vertical position that you want to draw from
- The color in the bitmap that is considered to be transparent (as a COLORREF)

```
pBitmap->DrawTransparent(pCDC, xPos, yPos, crTrans);
```

Before I start getting emails on the subject, I should point out that the techniques described in this article specifically target displays and may not necessarily work on some printer devices.

Source Code

```
void CCISBitmap::DrawTransparent(CDC * pDC, int x, int y, COLORREF crColour)
{
    COLORREF crOldBack = pDC->SetBkColor(m_crWhite);
    COLORREF crOldText = pDC->SetTextColor(m_crBlack);
    CDC dcImage, dcTrans;

    // Create two memory dcs for the image and the mask
    dcImage.CreateCompatibleDC(pDC);
    dcTrans.CreateCompatibleDC(pDC);

    // Select the image into the appropriate dc
    CBitmap* pOldBitmapImage = dcImage.SelectObject(this);

    // Create the mask bitmap
    CBitmap bitmapTrans;
    int nWidth = Width();
    int nHeight = Height();
    bitmapTrans.CreateBitmap(nWidth, nHeight, 1, 1, NULL);

    // Select the mask bitmap into the appropriate dc
    CBitmap* pOldBitmapTrans = dcTrans.SelectObject(&bitmapTrans);

    // Build the mask based on transparent color
    dcImage.SetBkColor(crColour);
    dcTrans.BitBlt(0, 0, nWidth, nHeight, &dcImage, 0, 0, SRCCOPY);

    // Do the work - True Mask method - cool if not actual display
    pDC->BitBlt(x, y, nWidth, nHeight, &dcImage, 0, 0, SRCINVERT);
    pDC->BitBlt(x, y, nWidth, nHeight, &dcTrans, 0, 0, SRCAND);
    pDC->BitBlt(x, y, nWidth, nHeight, &dcImage, 0, 0, SRCINVERT);

    // Restore the settings
    dcImage.SelectObject(pOldBitmapImage);
    dcTrans.SelectObject(pOldBitmapTrans);
    pDC->SetBkColor(crOldBack);
    pDC->SetTextColor(crOldText);
}
```

Drawing a Bitmap Transparently by Zafir Anjum

There is a similar article on this subject that uses a slightly different technique often referred to as the Black Source method.

The True Mask method requires no additional work. The mask is built and the source needs no manipulation. The blts cause onscreen flicker, but there are only three of them.

The Black Source method requires additional work on the source bitmap: The transparent bits need to be made black. The onscreen flashing is less noticeable with this method, and once the source is set up with black in the correct places, transparency looks good. For bitmaps as small as icons, transparency is achieved smoothly. (This mechanism is the one used by Windows to display icons on the screen.)

Direct Transparent blts

Some device drivers support transparent blts directly. You can determine this using the C1_TRANSPARENT bit of the CAPS1 capability word returned by the GetDeviceCaps function. A special background mode, NEWTRANSPARENT, indicates that subsequent blts are transparent blts. The current background color of the destination is the transparent color. When this capability is available on the driver, the basic transparent blt operation can be performed as follows:

```
// Only attempt this if the device supports functionality.
if(GetDeviceCaps(hdcDest, CAPS1) & C1_TRANSPARENT)
{
    // Special transparency background mode
        oldMode = SetBkMode(hdcDest, NEWTRANSPARENT);
        rgbBk = SetBkColor(hdcDest, rgbTransparent);
    // Actual blt is a simple source copy; transparency is automatic.
        BitBlt(hdcDest, x, y, dx, dy, hdcSrc, x0, y0, SRCCOPY);
        SetBkColor(hdcDest, rgbBk);
        SetBkMode(hdcDest, oldMode);
}
```

This code has been compiled and built with Microsoft Visual C++ Version 5.0 SP3.

Comments

If you need to be able to resize the bitmap, make the following changes to the sample code:

```
void CYourView::DrawTransparentBitmap(CDC *pDC, CBitmap *Bitmap, short xStart,
➥short yStart, int nWidth, int nHeight, COLORREF
➥cTransparentColor)
{
    COLORREF crOldBack = pDC->SetBkColor(0x00FFFFFF);
    COLORREF crOldText = pDC->SetTextColor(0x00000000);
    CDC dcImage, dcTrans;

    // Create two memory dcs for the image and the mask
    dcImage.CreateCompatibleDC(pDC);
    dcTrans.CreateCompatibleDC(pDC);
```

```
    // Select the image into the appropriate dc
    CBitmap* pOldBitmapImage = dcImage.SelectObject(Bitmap);

    // Create the mask bitmap
    CBitmap bitmapTrans;
    BITMAP     bm;
    Bitmap->GetBitmap(&bm);
    int bmpWidth = bm.bmWidth;
    int bmpHeight = bm.bmHeight;
    bitmapTrans.CreateBitmap(bmpWidth, bmpHeight, 1, 1, NULL);

    // Select the mask bitmap into the appropriate dc
    CBitmap* pOldBitmapTrans = dcTrans.SelectObject(&bitmapTrans);

    // Build the mask based on transparent color
    dcImage.SetBkColor(cTransparentColor);
    dcTrans.BitBlt(0, 0, bmpWidth, bmpHeight, &dcImage, 0, 0, SRCCOPY);

    // Do the work - True Mask method - cool if not actual display
    pDC->StretchBlt(xStart, yStart, nWidth, nHeight, &dcImage, 0, 0,
➥bmpWidth, bmpHeight, SRCINVERT);
    pDC->StretchBlt(xStart, yStart, nWidth, nHeight, &dcTrans, 0, 0,
➥bmpWidth, bmpHeight, SRCAND);
    pDC->StretchBlt(xStart, yStart, nWidth, nHeight, &dcImage, 0, 0,
➥bmpWidth, bmpHeight, SRCINVERT);

    // Restore settings
    dcImage.SelectObject(pOldBitmapImage);
    dcTrans.SelectObject(pOldBitmapTrans);
    pDC->SetBkColor(crOldBack);
    pDC->SetTextColor(crOldText);
}
```

—Paco Garcia

CPicture: The Yovav (Horror) PictureShow

This article was contributed by Dr. Yovav Gad.

Figure 26.3

Environment: Visual C++, Windows 95/98/2000/NT

After many days of searching (and not finding) a way to load a JPG from a resource and show it on a dialog-based application, I decided to take steps.

I created what I call a simple and useful class. You can easily implement it by adding it to a project. You don't have to be a real JPEG freak and invent all the header reading from the beginning. (It uses the IPicture interface just as Internet Explorer does.)

About the Project

I got a little carried away with this ACDSee Alike picture viewer. Because it was not my main purpose, I didn't have time to make it perfect. If you feel lucky and want to improve it here and there, please share it.

```
~~~~~~~~~~~~~~~~~~~~~~~~~~~~~~~~~~~~~~~~~~~~~~~~~~~~~~~~~~~~~

  Picture (Implementations) Version 1.00

  Routines: 4 Showing Picture Files...
          (.BMP .DIB .EMF .GIF .ICO .JPG .WMF)
~~~~~~~~~~~~~~~~~~~~~~~~~~~~~~~~~~~~~~~~~~~~~~~~~~~~~~~~~~~~~
  COPYFREE (F) - ALL RIGHTS FREE
~~~~~~~~~~~~~~~~~~~~~~~~~~~~~~~~~~~~~~~~~~~~~~~~~~~~~~~~~~~~~


class CPicture
{
public:
  void FreePictureData();
  BOOL Load(CString sFilePathName);
  BOOL Load(UINT ResourceName, LPCSTR ResourceType);
  BOOL LoadPictureData(BYTE* pBuffer, int nSize);
  BOOL SaveAsBitmap(CString sFilePathName);
  BOOL Show(CDC* pDC,
            CPoint LeftTop,
            CPoint WidthHeight,
            int MagnifyX,
            int MagnifyY);
  BOOL Show(CDC* pDC, CRect DrawRect);
  BOOL ShowBitmapResource(CDC* pDC,
                          const int BMPResource,
                          CPoint LeftTop);
  BOOL UpdateSizeOnDC(CDC* pDC);

  CPicture();
  virtual ~CPicture();

  IPicture* m_IPicture; // Same As
            // LPPICTURE (typedef IPicture __RPC_FAR *LPPICTURE)

  LONG      m_Height; // Height (in pixels; ignore what
                      //      current device context uses)
  LONG      m_Weight; // Size of the image object in
                      //      bytes (file or resource)
```

```
    LONG     m_Width;  // Width (in pixels; ignore what
                       //       current device context uses)
};
//~~~~~~~~~~Example and Usage: For Dummies~~~~~~~~~~~~~~
//
//  You need to add "CPicture.CPP" and "CPicture.H" into
//  your project (from FileView) so you will get control
//  over the functions in this class. Then you can create
//  a picture object and show it on a device context
//
//  CPicture m_Picture;  // Create a picture object
//                       //   (an instance of this class)
//  #include "Picture.h" // Make sure you include this
//                       //    where you are going to create the object...
//
//  Load picture data into the IPicture interface (.BMP
//                        .DIB .EMF .GIF .ICO .JPG .WMF)
//  ~~~~~~~~~~~~~~~~~~~~~~~~~~~~~~~~~~~~~~~~~~~~~~~~~~~~~~~~~~~~
//  m_Picture.Load("Test.JPG"); // Load from a file -
//                         //   Just load it (show later)
//  m_Picture.Load(IDR_TEST, "JPG"); // Load from a resource
//                         //   Just load it (show later)
//  (You must include the IDR_test in your resources under a custom
//        name, for example - "JPG")
//
//  When you're using DC object on a dialog-based application
//                                  (CPaintDC dc(this);)
//  ~~~~~~~~~~~~~~~~~~~~~~~~~~~~~~~~~~~~~~~~~~~~~~~~~~~~~~~
//  m_Picture.UpdateSizeOnDC(&dc); // Get picture dimensions
//                         //   in pixels
//  m_Picture.Show(&dc,
//                 CPoint(0,0),
//                 CPoint(m_Picture.m_Width, m_Picture.m_Height),
//                 0,0);
//  // Change original dimensions:
//  m_Picture.Show(&dc, CRect(0,0,100,100));
//  // Show bitmap resource:
//  m_Picture.ShowBitmapResource(&dc, IDB_TEST, CPoint(0,0));
//
//  Or when using a pointer on a "regular" MFC application (CDC* pDC)
//  ~~~~~~~~~~~~~~~~~~~~~~~~~~~~~~~~~~~~~~~~~~~~~~~~~~~~~~~~~~~~~~~~~
//  m_Picture.UpdateSizeOnDC(pDC); // Get picture dimensions in pixels
//  m_Picture.Show(pDC,
//                 CPoint(0,0),
//                 CPoint(m_Picture.m_Width, m_Picture.m_Height),
//                 0,0);
//  // Change original dimensions:
//  m_Picture.Show(pDC, CRect(0,0,100,100));
//  // Show bitmap resource:
//  m_Picture.ShowBitmapResource(pDC, IDB_TEST, CPoint(0,0));
//
//  Show picture information
//  ~~~~~~~~~~~~~~~~~~~~~~~~~
```

```
//  CString S;
//  S.Format("Size = %4d\nWidth = %4d\nHeight = %4d\nWeight = %4d\n",
//          m_Picture.m_Weight,
//          m_Picture.m_Width,
//          m_Picture.m_Height,
//          m_Picture.m_Weight);
//  AfxMessageBox(S);
//
//~~~~~~~~~~~~~~~~~Cut the bull here~~~~~~~~~~~~~~~~~~~~~~
```

FROM THE FORUM

Question (itzikel):

I would like to know if there is any way to get the BITMAPINFO object (or the color data from it) while I only have the handle to the bitmap HBITMAP?

Answer (Alex Fedotov):

An HBITMAP can represent either a DDB or a DIB section. In the former case, the color format of the bitmap always matches the format of the compatible device (usually, the screen). In the latter case, the color format can be any allowed formats.

The following code fills a BITMAPINFO structure according to the color format of the specified bitmap. (Error checking is omitted for clarity.)

```
HBITMAP hBitmap = ...;

// this structure is an equivalent of BITMAPINFO except it contains
// a full-sized color table
struct {
    BITMAPINFOHEADER bmiHeader;
    RGBQUAD bmiColors[256];
} bmi;

memset(&bmi, 0, sizeof(bmi));
bmi.bmiHeader.biSize = sizeof(BITMAPINFOHEADER);

HDC hDC = GetDC(NULL);  // any DC will work

GetDIBits(hDC, hBitmap, 0, 1, NULL, (BITMAPINFO *)&bmi,
            DIB_RGB_COLORS);

// now bmi.bmiHeader contains information about the bitmap's
// color format; check whether this is a palletized image and retrieve
// the palette if necessary

if (bmi.bmiHeader.biBitCount <= 8)
{
    GetDIBits(hDC, hBitmap, 0, 1, NULL, (BITMAPINFO *)&bmi,
                DIB_RGB_COLORS);
}

ReleaseDC(NULL, hDC);
```

Add GIF Animation to Your MFC and ATL Projects

This article was contributed by Oleg Bykov.

Figure 26.4

Environment: VC6, SP5, W95, W98, NT4, Win2000

Class CPictureEx was written for an MFC project that required support for banners in JPEG and GIF formats. Static banners weren't hard to display using the OleLoadPicture function and the IPicture interface, but dealing with animated GIFs was a whole different story.

Having rummaged through numerous Internet links, I discovered that there's only one free option available: a COM object by George Tersaakov on CodeGuru. Unfortunately, it had problems with displaying some of my test GIFs. Of course, I could buy a third-party library, but in that case, I would be paying for an extra functionality that I didn't actually need. I decided to give it a try and write my own class. The basic idea was to split a GIF into separate frames and display the frames with the familiar combination of OleLoadPicture and IPicture. After thoroughly reading through specifications of GIF87a and GIF89a, I wrote the class that I bring to your attention. Note that CPictureEx can display not only GIFs (including animated GIFs) but also JPEG, BMP, WMF, ICO, and CUR (that is, everything that OleLoadPicture knows of). Later on, I wrote an ATL version of the class.

Here's how to use the MFC version (CPictureEx):

1. Add a Static text or a Picture control to your dialog. (A group box will do the trick as well.)

2. Change the ID of that control to something like IDC_MYPICTURE.

3. Use the Class Wizard to associate a member variable (for example, m_Picture) with the control added, such as Category: Control, Variable Type: CStatic.

4. In your dialog's header file, change the variable type from CStatic to CPictureEx. (Don't forget to #include "PictureEx.h" and add PictureEx.h and PictureEx.cpp to your project.)

5. In OnInitDialog (or anywhere you fancy), add these lines:

```
if (m_Picture.Load(_T("mypicture.gif")))
    m_Picture.Draw();
```

6. Enjoy the animation!

You can also treat CPicture as a standard CStatic and manually create it (you'll have to, if your host window is not a dialog) by calling CPictureEx::Create(), and then CPictureEx::Load() and CPictureEx::Draw().

To use the ATL version (CPictureExWnd), follow the same steps, but instead of using Class Wizard, manually add a variable of type CPictureExWnd in your class and add the following code to your WM_INITDIALOG handler function:

```
HWND hWnd = GetDlgItem(IDC_MYPIC);
if (hWnd) m_wndBanner.SubclassWindow(hWnd);
```

After that, you can call CPictureExWnd::Load() and CPictureExWnd::Draw(). Of course, you can also call CPictureExWnd::Create directly. CPictureExWnd is just an ordinary window with some extra functionality in its window procedure.

The following interface functions are available:

- **BOOL Load(...):** This loads a GIF and prepares an object for drawing.
- **BOOL Draw():** This draws the picture or continues animation.
- **void Stop():** This stops animation.
- **void UnLoad():** This stops animation and releases all resources.
- **void SetBkColor(COLORREF):** This sets the fill color for transparent areas.
- **COLORREF GetBkColor():** This gets the current fill color.
- **BOOL IsGIF():** This is TRUE if the current picture is a GIF.
- **BOOL IsAnimatedGIF():** This is TRUE if the current picture is an animated GIF.
- **BOOL IsPlaying():** This is TRUE if an animation is being shown for the current picture.
- **SIZE GetSize():** This returns the picture's dimensions.
- **int GetFrameCount():** This returns the number of frames in the current picture.
- **int GetFrameCount():** This returns the number of frames in the current picture.
- **BOOL GetPaintRect(RECT *lpRect):** This returns the current painting rectangle.
- **BOOL SetPaintRect(const RECT *lpRect):** This sets the current painting rectangle.

CPictureEx[Wnd]::Load is available in three versions:

- **BOOL Load(LPCTSTR szFileName):** This version loads a picture from the file szFileName. The function's return type indicates the success of the loading.

- **BOOL Load(HGLOBAL hGlobal, DWORD dwSize):** This load gets a handle to the global memory block, allocated with GlobalAlloc with a GMEM_MOVEABLE flag. The function *does not* free the memory, so don't forget to GlobalFree it. The return value indicates the success of the loading.

- **BOOL Load(LPCTSTR szResourceName,LPCTSTR szResourceType):** The function gets a name for the resource with a picture and a name for the type of that resource. For example:

```
m_Picture.Load(MAKEINTRESOURCE(IDR_MYPIC),_T("GIFTYPE"))
```

After loading a picture, display it with the CPictureEx[Wnd]::Draw() function. If the picture is an animated GIF, the function will spawn a background thread to perform the animation. If it's a still picture, it will be displayed right away with OleLoadPicture/IPicture. You can stop the spawned thread any time with the CPictureEx[Wnd]::Stop() function. If you want not only to stop the animation but also to free all its resources, use CPictureEx[Wnd]::UnLoad() (CPictureEx[Wnd]::Load() calls UnLoad() automatically).

By default, the picture's background is filled with COLOR_3DFACE (the background color of dialog windows). If you need to change the picture's background, call CPictureEx[Wnd]::SetBkColor(COLORREF) after calling CPictureEx[Wnd]::Load().

Comments

To use GIF resources within the application, use the CPictureEx[Wnd]::Load member function as shown next (and as shown in the demo projects):

```
Load(MAKEINTRESOURCE(IDR_MYPIC),_T("GIFTYPE"));
```

—Oleg Bykov

FROM THE FORUM

Question (Chuck Bruce):

I am not able to use the CPalette::GetNearestColorIndex routine. How can I get a good algorithm to find the nearest color available in a 256-color palette?

Answer (Wade):

The following two functions together work really well. We have a math wiz on our team who gave me this to use once, and it is great:

```
double CYourClass::ComputeColorDistance(double r1, double g1, double b1,
➥double r2, double g2, double b2)
{
    double x1 = .412453*r1/255+.357580*g1/255+.180423*b1/255;
    double y1 = .212671*r1/255+.715160*g1/255+.072169*b1/255;
    double z1 = .019334*r1/255+.119193*g1/255+.950227*b1/255;
    double x2 = .412453*r2/255+.357580*g2/255+.180423*b2/255;
    double y2 = .212671*r2/255+.715160*g2/255+.072169*b2/255;
    double z2 = .019334*r2/255+.119193*g2/255+.950227*b2/255;

    double cl1 = 116*pow(y1,1.0/3)-16;
    if (y1 <= .008856) cl1 = 903.3*y1;
    double ca1 = 500*(Fcn(x1)-Fcn(y1));
    double cb1 = 200*(Fcn(y1)-Fcn(z1));
    double cl2 = 116*pow(y2,1.0/3)-16;
    if (y2 <= .008856) cl2 = 903.3*y2;
    double ca2 = 500*(Fcn(x2)-Fcn(y2));
    double cb2 = 200*(Fcn(y2)-Fcn(z2));

    double ld = (cl1-cl2);
    double ad = (ca1-ca2);
    double bd = (cb1-cb2);

    double dist = ld*ld+ad*ad+bd*bd;
    dist = dist / 10100; //4 .05

    return dist;
}

double CYourClass::Fcn(double x)
{
    if (x > .008856)
        return pow(x,1.0/3);
    else
        return 7.787*x+16.0/116;
}
```

FROM THE FORUM

Question (Martin Speiser):

I need to have a function like GetNearestColor. The reason I can't use GetNearestColor is that it is using the current palette, whereas the function I need should always work without depending on the color resolution of the system.

Can anyone give me a hint about the algorithm?

Answer (DanielK):

To find the distance (difference) between rgb1 and rgb2, use the following equation:

```
Distance = (R2 - R1) ^ 2 + (G2 - G1) ^ 2 + (B2 - B1) ^ 2
```

27

DirectX

In this chapter

DirectX represents an emerging and developing technology from Microsoft for the control of and interaction with multimedia components.

- "Using Direct3D8: The Basics" provides a comprehensive insight into this new multimedia world describing the 3D rendering functionality of DirectX 8.0.

Using Direct3D8: The Basics

This article was contributed by Alexandrov Alex.

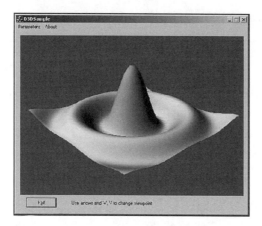

Figure 27.1

Environment: VC6, SP5, Windows 2000, SP2, DirectX 8.0a SDK

Introduction (or #include <windows.h>)

Computer graphics has always been one of the most interesting things in computer programming. In the beginning, no one could even imagine a game like the real world. But time was going by, computers' power was growing, and now it is really hard to surprise anyone with 3D graphics.

There are two 3D libraries in the Microsoft Windows world: OpenGL and Direct3D (a part of DirectX). They are different, but at the same time, they are very much alike. OpenGL is more consistent, and Direct3D is changing permanently. The last release of DirectX was version 8, and I doubt it will be the last.

This article introduces the use of Direct3D8 for building powerful 3D applications. As a sample task, I chose plotting a 3D surface. The sample application and its source code can be found on the accompanying CD and used in your applications:

- DirectX 8.0a SDK
- An English version of DirectX 8.0a Runtime for Windows 95, Windows 98, Windows 98 SE, and Windows ME
- An English version of DirectX 8.0a Runtime for Windows 2000
- A localized version of DirectX 8.0a Runtime

About Sample Application

Every article author has to face a difficult question: Which framework should be used to demonstrate an idea? There are four possible choices for creating a simple Windows application:

- **Pure-API application:** This is simple, small, and easily portable (theoretically).
- **MFC application:** This is the most common choice.
- **WTL application:** This is great, but not everybody has WTL installed.
- **ATL application:** This has little code, but the wizard doesn't support non-COM applications.

Every framework has its advantages and disadvantages. For this article, I chose the ATL framework because I wanted to make my code as clear as possible, without overhead. To me, ATL is clearer than MFC. If you hate ATL, you can stop reading this article now!

In Figure 27.2, you can see a class diagram for the sample application (Booch notation).

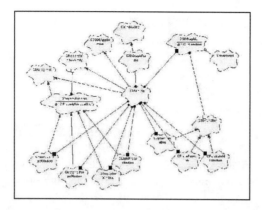

Figure 27.2

Here is the brief description of the most important classes:

- **CMainDlg:** This is the main application class. It's inherited from CDialogImpl and created in WinMain as a nonmodal dialog. It owns one C3DGraphic object, one C3DGraphFrame object, four nonmodal properties windows (CMaterialPropsWindow, CLightPropsWindow, CBackColorWindow, and CFunctionTypeWindow), and three 3D functions objects (CSplashFunction, CPlaneFunction, and CParaboloidFunction).

- **CPropertyWindow:** This is the root class for all properties windows. It's inherited from CDialogImpl.

- **C3DFunction:** This is an abstract class. It exposes functions that are necessary for getting information about a particular 3D function.

- **CPropertyWindowNotify:** This is an abstract class interface for getting notifications from properties windows.

- **CD3D8Application:** This is a wrapper class for managing the lifetime of an IDirect3D8 object.

- **C3DGraphFrame:** This is a window where a 2D image of a 3D function will be displayed (that is, view class for 3D document).

- **C3DGraphic:** This is the most complex class. It renders a given 3D function into a C3DGraphFrame window and sets the light, materials, and other interesting stuff.

From a general point of view, the sample application is ATL EXE server without COM support. All COM-related stuff was removed, so it is just a Windows app. I could tell you how to do all this from scratch, but that is a topic for another article.

What the Heck Is Direct3D8 (or Direct3D8=2*(Direct3D7+DirectDraw7))

There is no more DirectDraw—only Direct3D! This is the greatest change that DirectX programmers have ever seen. Plenty of changes were brought into Direct3D8—many more than were brought into Direct3D7. There were 48 methods of IDirect3DDevice7 versus 94 methods of IDirect3DDevice8.

Back buffering is now supported automatically without those nasty flip chains. Initialization of Direct3D has become as simple as i++, and many of the low-level details are now inaccessible for programmers. The latter is not always good. For example, with Direct3D8, you are not allowed to write something on a primary surface directly. Moreover, you shouldn't read anything directly from a primary surface.

Many programmers still use DirectDraw 7 for specific tasks. But what about those people who have never dealt either with Direct3D7 or Direct3D? For these people, I will try to give a brief explanation of Direct3D8 and what it is:

- Direct3D8 provides a hardware-independent way to use the 3D capabilities of video cards.
- The standard 3D transformation pipeline—world matrix, view matrix, and projection matrix—is supported.
- Support is available for rasterizing geometric primitives such as points, lines, and triangles. High-order primitives are also supported, but only in a hardware way, not in software emulation.
- Direct3D8 has a powerful lighting subsystem (materials and lights).
- The application also has 3D texturing, so you can do amazing things such as put a photo of your ex-girlfriend on a 3D shape (such as a lavatory pan).
- For details, look at the DirectX 8.0a SDK.

Initialization (or How to Start)

For the creation of a Direct3D8 application, you must include all necessary header files in your program and link your program with all necessary libraries. There are two useful header files and two necessary libraries:

- **d3d8.h:** This is a header file with core Direct3D8 interface declarations.
- **d3d8.lib:** This is a library file for linking your program with Direct3D8 DLL.
- **d3dx8.h:** This is a header file with some useful tool functions and interfaces.
- **d3dx8.lib:** This is a library for d3dx8.h.

In the sample project's directory, you can find two files: D3D8Include.h and D3DX8Include.h. Just put them in your project for including necessary headers and linking your program with respective libraries.

Now you have all the stuff that you need. What's next?

You now need to create an IDirect3D8 object. This object provides 3D device creation, checking device capabilities, enumerating and retrieving display adapter modes, and other useful operations. My sample project uses a wrapper class CD3D8Application for creating an IDirect3D8 object. To use this wrapper, you just inherit your application's class from CD3D8Application. In an initialization function (in OnInitDialog, for instance), call function CD3D8Application::Direct3DInitOK to check whether IDirect3D8 was created successfully. IDirect3D8 object is created with the Direct3DCreate8() method. It is a pretty good function because it takes only one parameter that must always be D3D_SDK_VERSION. It is enough to do the following:

```
pDirect3DObject = Direct3DCreate8(D3D_SDK_VERSION);
if (!pDirect3DObject) {
    // Do something! Error occurred!
}
```

After the IDirect3D8 object is created, you must somehow get something on which you can draw 3D graphics. This something is called IDirect3DDevice8. You can access IDirect3DDevice8 by using IDirect3D8's method CreateDevice(). The sample project calls this method in C3DGraphic::Create.

```
D3DDISPLAYMODE theDisplayMode;
hr = m_p3DApplication->m_pDirect3DObject->GetAdapterDisplayMode(
    D3DADAPTER_DEFAULT, &theDisplayMode);
    if (FAILED(hr)) {
    return hr;
}

D3DPRESENT_PARAMETERS thePresentParams;
ZeroMemory(&thePresentParams, sizeof(thePresentParams));
thePresentParams.Windowed    = TRUE;
thePresentParams.SwapEffect = D3DSWAPEFFECT_DISCARD;
thePresentParams.BackBufferFormat = theDisplayMode.Format;
thePresentParams.EnableAutoDepthStencil = TRUE;
thePresentParams.AutoDepthStencilFormat = D3DFMT_D16;

hr = m_p3DApplication->m_pDirect3DObject->CreateDevice(
    D3DADAPTER_DEFAULT, D3DDEVTYPE_HAL,
    m_hwndRenderTarget,
    D3DCREATE_SOFTWARE_VERTEXPROCESSING,
    &thePresentParams,
    &m_p3DDevice);

if (FAILED(hr)) {
    return hr;
}
```

We created a 3D device with the following parameters:

- A 3D device is created for a default video adapter (D3DADAPTER_ DEFAULT).

- The 3D device has one back buffer. The color format of the back buffer is the same as the current display mode.

- The device is not full screen but windowed. All rendering will be performed on the m_hwndRenderTarget window. (This is a handle to our C3DGraphFrame window, if you still remember what that is.)

- The device has automatically created a depth buffer. The format of the depth buffer is 16 bits per point. Today, almost all video adapters support this type of depth buffer. Direct3D uses the depth buffer (also known as the Z buffer) internally to determine which pixels are visible.

- The device should use hardware capabilities for rendering. If a particular capability is not supported by hardware, Direct3D will try to emulate it on a software level. If you change the desired device type from D3DDEVTYPE_HAL to D3DDEVTYPE_REF, all operations will be performed on the software emulation level. Note that such emulation is very slow; moreover, hardware capability cannot be emulated.

- Vertexes should be processed on a software level. We chose it with parameter D3DCREATE_SOFTWARE_VERTEXPROCESSING. It also can be D3DCREATE_MIXED_VERTEXPROCESSING or D3DCREATE_ HARDWARE_VERTEXPROCESSING, but not every adapter supports these modes.

From f(x, y) = x + y + z to 2D Picture

Life would be easy if IDirect3DDevice8 had some function named PleaseDrawPretty3DGraphicOnTheScreen. Alas, we have no such function. To draw some primitives using IDirect3DDevice8, you must put their coordinates into a vertex buffer. Discussion of vertex buffers is beyond the scope of this article, so I can only say that the vertex buffer is an abstraction of the memory block. You can lock it (like a DirectX surface) and write something there. Usually before rendering, we want to clear a buffer surface for drawing a new frame. You can do this with the IDirect3DDevice8::Clear() method. In the sample project, you can see it in the C3DGraphic::ReRender function:

```
hr = m_p3DDevice->Clear(0, NULL,
                        D3DCLEAR_TARGET ¦ D3DCLEAR_ZBUFFER,
                        m_dwBackColor, 1.0f, 0);
if (FAILED(hr)) {
   return hr;
}
```

Here we clear an entire back buffer by filling it with the m_dwBackColor color. Also, we clear the depth buffer and fill it with a 1.0 value. 1.0 is the farthest depth value, and 0.0 is the nearest. A drawing on a 3D device always starts with this:

```
m_p3DDevice->BeginScene();
```

and ends with this:

```
m_p3DDevice->EndScene();
```

All calls for updating the contents of a 3D device must be between BeginScene() and EndScene(). Note that the drawing will be done on a back buffer. To blit updated contents, you must call IDirect3DDevice8::Present().

The drawing of a 3D function is performed with the following code:

```
hr = m_p3DDevice->SetStreamSource(0,
                                  m_pDataVB,
                                  sizeof(GRAPH3DVERTEXSTRUCT));
if (FAILED(hr)) {
  return hr;
}

hr = m_p3DDevice->SetVertexShader(D3DFVF_GRAPH3DVERTEX);
if (FAILED(hr)) {
  return hr;
}

hr = m_p3DDevice->DrawPrimitive(D3DPT_TRIANGLESTRIP,
                                0,
                                m_dwElementsInVB - 2);
if (FAILED(hr)) {
  return hr;
}
```

m_pDataVB is a member of the C3DGraphic class; it contains a pointer to the IDirect3DVertexBuffer8 interface. In our case, contents of the vertex buffer are an array of GRAPH3DVERTEXSTRUCT structures:

```
typedef struct {
  FLOAT x, y, z;
  FLOAT nx, ny, nz;
} GRAPH3DVERTEXSTRUCT;
```

where x, y, and z—coordinates of vertex nx, ny, and nz—are components of the normal vector. The normal vector is used in lighting an engine of Direct3D for correct shading of surfaces. Before calling the DrawPrimitive function, we must set the vertex shader and data stream. We set the data stream with the SetStreamSource function. We pass in this function stream number (0 if only one stream is used), pointer to vertex buffer, and size of each element in the data stream (that is, size of [GRAPH3DVERTEXSTRUCT]). Vertex shaders are a pretty new capability of

Direct3D. A vertex shader is an abstract mechanism used to process vertexes. It can be either in an old FVF format or in a custom vertex shader. Programming vertex shaders is a powerful and complex task, but it is enough for us now to use a simple fixed vertex shader D3DFVF_GRAPH3DVERTEX, which is defined as D3DFVF_XYZ | D3DFVF_NORMAL. The vertex engine should treat the first three float numbers of each vertex as vertex coordinates, and the latter three float numbers as vertex normal vectors.

After setting the data stream and vertex shader, we call the DrawPrimitive method, which renders data from the vertex buffer onto the back buffer's surface. The way in which data will be rendered depends on the first parameter of that method. It can be one of the D3DPRIMITIVETYPE enumeration types: D3DPT_POINTLIST, D3DPT_LINELIST, D3DPT_LINESTRIP, D3DPT_TRIANGLELIST, D3DPT_TRIANGLESTRIP, or D3DPT_TRIANGLEFAN. I decided that the most convenient method of 3D function plotting is to use triangle strips because they need low memory. Function triangulating is performed as shown in Figure 27.3.

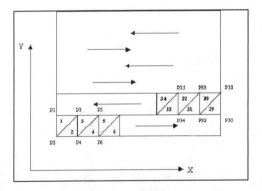

Figure 27.3

This is how strip triangulating works: The vertex buffer contains points P1, P2, P3, P4, and so on. When I call DrawPrimitive with the D3DPT_TRIANGLESTRIP parameter, Direct3D starts to render triangles 1, 2, 3, and so on again. Triangle 1 is defined by points P1, P2, and P3, and triangle 2 is defined by P2, P3, and P4. So N points in the vertex buffer correspond to N–2 triangles. It is pretty nice, but this approach has a drawback: All triangles are linked with each other. That is why even rows are triangulated from the left to the right, and odd rows are triangulated from the right to the left. (Row numeration starts from zero, of course.)

You can find implementation of all this stuff in the C3DGraphic::RecalculateData method. This method uses tool class CGraphGrid, which builds graph grid (X0, Y0, Z0)–(Xn, Yn, Zn).

Light Management, or All Cats Are Gray in the Dark

Direct3D has a powerful lighting engine. It supports several types of light on the scene: directional, point-source light, and spotlight. Directional light has no source—only direction. Directional light is like the sun: All its rays are parallel. Spotlight and point-source light have a point from which all rays shine. For more detailed information, please read MSDN. Maybe soon I will write an article for CodeGuru about Direct3D lighting, but in the meantime, I want to leave you with a problem: All vertexes that are supposed to be lit must have a normal vector included. Normal determination is easy if you still remember school geometry. How do you do it for a 3D graphic? There are at least two ways:

- First, we can find an analytic expression for a normal vector. It will be an accurate result, but for any new 3D function, we will have to make all calculations from the beginning.

- Second, we can calculate the approximate value of a normal vector because we know neighbor points. Although it is an approximate decision, this way doesn't depend on a 3D function. This approach is implemented in my sample project, and you can find it in the C3DGraphic::CalcNormal() function. Here is a brief explanation on finding the normal.

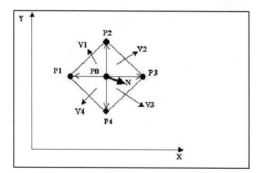

Figure 27.4

Finding four vectors to neighbor points:

$$V01 = P1–P0$$

$$V02 = P2–P0$$

$$V03 = P3–P0$$

$$V04 = P4–P0$$

Finding four normals to face as a cross product of respective vectors:

N1 = [V02,V01]

N2 = [V03,V02]

N3 = [V04,V03]

N4 = [V01,V04]

Finding the resulting normal as an average vector of four faces' normals:

N = (N1 + N2 + N3 + N4) / 4

Material Management, or Why Are They Gray?

Everything in the world has color. Color determines how something looks. An apple is red, the sky is blue. Direct3D treats properties of objects as materials. Materials are described with D3DMATERIAL8 structure:

```
typedef struct _D3DMATERIAL8 {
    D3DCOLORVALUE   Diffuse;
    D3DCOLORVALUE   Ambient;
    D3DCOLORVALUE   Specular;
    D3DCOLORVALUE   Emissive;
    float           Power;
} D3DMATERIAL8;
```

Diffuse, ambient, and specular members of this structure describe how a material reflects respective components of light sources. You can define the power with which specular light is reflected. A nonzero emissive component makes an object shine, but no other object will reflect light that this object emits.

To put a material on an object, you must call the SetMaterial function before calling DrawPrimitive or other drawing functions. You can do it in the following way:

```
hr = m_p3DDevice->SetMaterial(&m_theGraphMaterial);
ATLASSERT(SUCCEEDED(hr));
if (FAILED(hr)) {
    return hr;
}
```

Conclusion, or }

In the end, I want to say a few more words about the sample application. It has four properties windows that you can activate from the Properties menu. Here is the brief description of what you can see on those windows:

- **Material properties:** This property window allows you to edit material parameters, such as diffuse, ambient, emissive, specular color component, and specular power.
- **Light properties:** The scene is illuminated with one directional light source. You can change the diffuse, ambient, and specular color component, as well as light direction.
- **Background color:** This is a color that is used for clearing each frame in a Clear function. You can set red, green, and blue components.
- **Function type:** You can choose one of three 3D functions: splash, plane, and paraboloid.

All values can be changed with trackbars. 0 is a minimum value, and 1 is a maximum value. The minimum value corresponds to the lower position of the trackbar, and the maximum value corresponds to the higher position.

FROM THE FORUM

Question (Jason Teagle):

The samples I've seen so far appear to imply (in windowed mode rather than full screen) that you render your triangles directly to the primary surface (the screen), but surely this is not much faster or smoother than GDI calls to the screen. Isn't it better to render to an off-screen surface, and then flip?

Answer (AnOnYmOuS):

When you're using windowed modes and you want to avoid artifacts, you may create an off-screen buffer and attach it to the primary surface. Then you can draw your triangles on this buffer and blit this to the primary surface. This avoids drawing to the primary surface directly and gets you kind of flipping when you are full screen.

You can't flip when you're in a windowed mode. Flipping switches the entire screen area to another buffer, which would include other windows in this case.

You can also draw directly to the primary surface. This is okay too, but you often get the artifact of partially drawn models appearing. If that's fine with you, it should be okay. Also, when you blit from an offscreen surface to the primary surface, you will get the artifact of tearing in the surface unless you wait for vsync (which no one does).

FROM THE FORUM

Question (Thanh Son):

I tried using MCI, but it would not play movies larger than 3MB. How can I play a big movie?

Answer (Franz):

Use DirectShow:

```
//Code from DirectX SDK Documentation
#include <dshow.h>

int main()
{
    IGraphBuilder *pGraph;
    IMediaControl *pMediaControl;
    IMediaEvent   *pEvent;

    CoInitialize(NULL);

    // Create the filter graph manager and query for interfaces.
    CoCreateInstance(CLSID_FilterGraph, NULL, CLSCTX_INPROC_SERVER,
                        IID_IGraphBuilder, (void **)&pGraph);
    pGraph->QueryInterface(IID_IMediaControl, (void **)&pMediaControl);
    pGraph->QueryInterface(IID_IMediaEvent, (void **)&pEvent);

    // Build the graph. IMPORTANT: Change string to a file on your system.
    pGraph->RenderFile(L"test.avi", NULL);

    // Run the graph.
    pMediaControl->Run();

    // Wait for completion.
    long evCode;
    pEvent->WaitForCompletion(INFINITE, &evCode);

    // Clean up.
    pEvent->Release();
    pMediaControl->Release();
    pGraph->Release();

    CoUninitialize();
    return 0;
}
```

28

GDI

In this chapter

Bitmaps are digital representations of images. In this chapter, you will find ways to manipulate these bitmaps as well as use other image file formats.

- "Detecting the Display Font Size" shows a way to determine the user's selected font settings in their desktop settings. This can be useful when applications need to accommodate different sizes.

- "Drawing an Arrow Line" shows how to draw an arrow line or measuring line as the mouse is being dragged across the window.

- "Streaming an IPicture Object" describes how you can serialize IPicture objects in the Document/View framework.

Detecting the Display Font Size

This article was contributed by Chensu.

Introduction

As you've probably seen, the end user can specify the font size to be Small Fonts, Large Fonts, or Custom Font via the Control Panel's Display applet (see Figure 28.1). Since this setting could adversely affect an application's user interface (UI), there are many times in more advanced applications where the knowledge of which setting the user has chosen would be useful. For example, you can use this information in determining which dialog to present (if you wanted to present a tailor-made dialog for each font size). In addition, knowing the currently selected font size could give your application's end user a warning had the UI been designed with only smaller fonts in mind. Whatever your need, this handy little function will assist you in programmatically determining the selected font size.

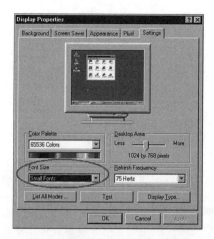

Figure 28.1   Sometimes the end user's choice of font size can wreak havoc with a carefully designed UI.

Function to Detect Font Size

The following code demonstrates how to detect the font size:

```
CDC ScreenDC;
ScreenDC.CreateIC(_T("DISPLAY"), NULL, NULL, NULL);
const int nLogDPIX = ScreenDC.GetDeviceCaps(LOGPIXELSX),
          nLogDPIY = ScreenDC.GetDeviceCaps(LOGPIXELSY);

if (nLogDPIX == 96 && nLogDPIY == 96)
{
 // 96 DPI, Small Fonts
}
else
 if (nLogDPIX == 120 && nLogDPIY == 120)
 {
  // 120 DPI, Large Fonts
 }
 else
 {
  // Otherwise, Custom Font Size
 }
```

Drawing an Arrow Line

This article was contributed by Mayank Malik.

Web site: www.mayankmalik.cjb.net

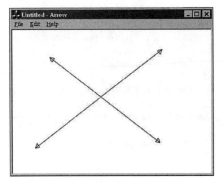

Figure 28.2

Environment: VC 5–6, Windows 95/98/2000/NT/ME

Recently, I had to develop graphics software and wanted to add support for drawing an arrow line/measuring line. This was essential for the software, and I had no option but to go over my trigonometry formulas. After churning for a couple of hours, I came up with this technique for drawing arrowheads at the end of a line.

The lines are drawn when you drag the mouse. The drawing mode used is R2_NOT. As long as the user is dragging the mouse, the line refreshes itself (by redrawing). You need to include "math.h" in your View.cpp file.

This checks when the user starts dragging the mouse:

```
void CPolygonsView::OnLButtonDown(UINT nFlags, CPoint point)
{
  m_Drag = true;   // for mouse drag check
  PointOrigin = point; // value when mouse drag starts
  CView::OnLButtonDown(nFlags, point);
}

void CPolygonsView::OnLButtonUp(UINT nFlags, CPoint point)
{

  m_Drag = false; // for mouse drag check
  MotionFix=0;
  CView::OnLButtonUp(nFlags, point);

}
```

All the drawing is invoked by the MouseMove function. First, the previously drawn line is erased (by drawing over it using R2_NOT), and then the new line is drawn using the new coordinates.

The loop computes all the other coordinates using these elements and draws lines connecting one vertex to the other:

```
void CPolygonsView::OnMouseMove(UINT nFlags, CPoint point)
{
  if (m_Drag && PointOrigin!=point) // for mouse drag check
  {
    CClientDC ClientDC(this);  // graphics
    ClientDC.SetROP2(R2_NOT);
    if (MotionFix) DrawArrow(&ClientDC,PointOrigin,PointOld);
    MotionFix=1;
 // MotionFix is used to prevent redrawing in case it is the
 // First Element
    DrawArrow(&ClientDC,PointOrigin,point);
  }
  PointOld = point;
  CView::OnMouseMove(nFlags, point);
}
```

Okay, that was the easy part. Now the actual computation is done in the DrawArrow function:

```
void DrawArrow(CDC *pdc,CPoint m_One, CPoint m_Two)
{
  double slopy , cosy , siny;
  double Par = 10.0;  //length of Arrow (>)
  slopy = atan2( ( m_One.y - m_Two.y ),
    ( m_One.x - m_Two.x ) );
  cosy = cos( slopy );
  siny = sin( slopy ); //need math.h for these functions

  //draw a line between the 2 endpoints
  pdc->MoveTo( m_One );
  pdc->LineTo( m_Two );

  //here is the tough part - actually drawing the arrows
  //a total of 6 lines drawn to make the arrow shape
  pdc->MoveTo( m_One);
  pdc->LineTo( m_One.x + int( - Par * cosy - ( Par / 2.0 * siny ) ),
    m_One.y + int( - Par * siny + ( Par / 2.0 * cosy ) ) );
  pdc->LineTo( m_One.x + int( - Par * cosy + ( Par / 2.0 * siny ) ),
    m_One.y - int( Par / 2.0 * cosy + Par * siny ) );
  pdc->LineTo( m_One );
  /*/-------------similarly the other end------------/*/
  pdc->MoveTo( m_Two );
  pdc->LineTo( m_Two.x + int( Par * cosy - ( Par / 2.0 * siny ) ),
    m_Two.y + int( Par * siny + ( Par / 2.0 * cosy ) ) );
```

```
pdc->LineTo( m_Two.x + int( Par * cosy + Par / 2.0 * siny ),
  m_Two.y - int( Par / 2.0 * cosy - Par * siny ) );
pdc->LineTo( m_Two );

}
```

FROM THE FORUM

Question (james207):

I am trying to add functionality to my Cview-derived class to allow text to be dragged around the window. What is the best way of doing this?

Answer (Feng Yuan):

The following code allows you to drag text around the view by using the mouse:

```
CTtView::CTtView()
{
    m_cursor_x = 0; m_cursor_y = 0;
    m_first = true;
}

void CTtView::Draw(int x, int y)
{
    CClientDC dc(this);

    CFont font;
    font.CreatePointFont(480, "Times New Roman");
    CFont* pOldFont = dc.SelectObject(&font);

    dc.SetTextAlign(TA_TOP | TA_LEFT);
    dc.SetBkMode(TRANSPARENT);
    dc.BeginPath();

    dc.TextOut(x, y, "Hello", 5);
    dc.EndPath();
    dc.SelectObject(pOldFont);

    dc.SetROP2(R2_XORPEN);
    dc.SelectObject(GetStockObject(WHITE_PEN));

    dc.StrokePath();
}

void CTtView::OnMouseMove(UINT nFlags, CPoint point)
{
    CView::OnMouseMove(nFlags, point);
```

```
        if ( m_first )
            m_first = false;
        else
            Draw(m_cursor_x, m_cursor_y);

        m_cursor_x = point.x;
        m_cursor_y = point.y;

        Draw(m_cursor_x, m_cursor_y);
    }
```

Streaming an IPicture Object

This article was contributed by Eugene Khodakovsky.

Figure 28.3

Environment: VC++ 5–6, NT 4, Win2000, Win95/98

I really like the IPicture object. This COM object works great. However, I had some problem when I was trying to use it in a Document View architecture. The main problem was implementation of serialization. To resolve this problem, I built two classes.

The first class is called CPictureObj, and it is responsible for drawing the picture. The second class, CPictureObjList, is a collection of picture objects. By using both of these classes, it is easy to implement the following functionality:

- Load one or more images into the document (*.bmp, *.jpeg, *.ico, and so on).
- Scale images (zoom in, zoom out).
- Move images by using the cursor.
- Align images.
- Save/load images to/from the compound document file.

Classes

```
class CPictureObj  :
          public CPictureHolder, public CObject
{
  DECLARE_SERIAL(CPictureObj);
public:
  CPictureObj();
  CPictureObj(const CRect position);
  virtual ~CPictureObj();
  void RemoveAndDestroy();

  virtual void Copy( CPictureObj &right);
  virtual HRESULT WriteToStream(IStream* pStream);
  virtual HRESULT ReadFromStream(IStream* pStream);

// Attributes
public:
  HorzAlign GetHorzAlign( void ) const;
  void      SetHorzAlign( HorzAlign eHorzAlign );
  VertAlign GetVertAlign( void ) const;
  void      SetVertAlign( VertAlign eVertAlign );
  BOOL      GetSelected( void ) const;
  void      SetSelected( BOOL bValue );
  void      SetVisible(BOOL bValue);
  BOOL      GetVisible();
  CRect     GetPosition();
  void      SetPosition(const CRect pos);
  CRect     GetStartRect();
  void      SetStartRect(const CRect pos);
  CString   GetPathName();
  void      SetPathName(const CString pathname);

  OLE_HANDLE GetHandle();
  CSize     GetSize();          // in himetric
  CSize     GetSize(CDC*pDC);   // in pixel
  CSize     GetSize(CWnd*pWnd); // in pixel
  BOOL      IsValidPicture();

// Operations
public:

  BOOL Load(LPCTSTR szFile);
  BOOL CreateFromFile(const CPoint pt);
  void ReleasePicture();
  void MoveTo(const CRect& position, CWnd* pView);

  // Drawing picture
  void Draw(CDC* pDC);
  void Draw(CDC* pDC, CRect& rcBounds);
  void Draw(CDC* pDC, const CRect&
          rcPosition, const CRect& rcBounds);
```

```
    void DrawTracker(CDC* pDC);
    void DrawTracker(CDC* pDC, const CRect& rect);
    void ZoomIn();
    void ZoomOut();

protected:

    void CalcZoom();
    void SetZoomToPosition();

protected:

    HorzAlign m_eHorizAlign;
    VertAlign m_eVertAlign;
    BOOL      m_bSelected;
    BOOL      m_bVisible;
    CRect     m_rcPosition; // in pixels
    CRect     m_startRect;  // in pixels
    int       m_trackerStyle;
    int       m_zoomX,m_zoomY;

    // Not serialized
    CString   m_strPathName;

};

class CPictureObjList : public CTypedPtrList{CObList, CPictureObj*}
{
public:
    ~CPictureObjList();

    void RemoveAndDestroy();
    void DeselectAll();

    CSize ComputeMaxSize();          // in himetric
    CSize ComputeMaxSize(CDC* pDC);  // in pixel
    CSize ComputeMaxSize(CWnd* pWnd); // in pixel
    CRect GetRect();                 // in pixel

    CPictureObj* FindSelected();
    CPictureObj* ObjectAt(const CPoint& pt);
    bool Remove(CPictureObj* pObj);
    void Draw(CDC* pDC);

    // Streaming
    HRESULT WriteToStream(IStream* pStream);
    HRESULT ReadFromStream(IStream* pStream);
    BOOL WriteToStorage(LPSTORAGE lpRootStg);
    BOOL ReadFromStorage(LPSTORAGE lpRootStg);

};
```

Using the Classes

To use streaming pictures, create your document object that is derived from COleDocument.

```
class CYourDoc : public COleDocument
```

Inside the document object, define the picture collection like this:

```
CPictureObjList  m_objects;
```

Now you can insert the picture in this simple way:

```
CPictureObj* pObj =  new CPictureObj;
pObj->CreateFromFile(CPoint(10,10));
m_objects.AddHead(pObj);
```

Also, you can load the picture directly from the file:

```
CPictureObj* pObj =  new CPictureObj;
pObj->Load("MyFile.jpg");
m_objects.AddHead(pObj);
```

To scale the picture, you can use the ZoomIn, ZoomOut member functions:

```
CPictureObj* pObj = m_objects.FindSelected();
if(pObj)
{
    pObj->ZoomIn();
}
```

Moving the selected picture is easy. Just use this:

```
CPoint delta = point - c_last;
CPictureObj* pSel = m_objects.FindSelected();
if(pSel)
{
  CRect position = pSel->GetPosition();
  position += delta;
  pSel->MoveTo(position, this);
}
```

Drawing a collection of pictures is also easy:

```
GetDocument()->m_objects.Draw(pDC);
```

You can get an implementation of a picture serialization from here:

```
void CYourDoc::Serialize(CArchive& ar)
{
 CWaitCursor wait;
 COleDocument::Serialize(ar);
 if (ar.IsStoring())
 {
```

```
      m_objects.WriteToStorage(m_lpRootStg);
    }
    else
    {
      m_objects.ReadFromStorage(m_lpRootStg);
      m_objects.DeselectAll();
    }
}
```

FROM THE FORUM

Question (shurangama):

How can I convert a bitmap into an icon?

Answer (Paul Ch):

You can use an image list to convert from a bitmap to an icon:

```
// Where BMPTRANSCLR is the color you want to be transparent
HIMAGELIST hIml = ImageList_LoadBitmap(GetModuleHandle(NULL),
    MAKEINTRESOURCE(IDB_IMAGES), 16, 1, BMPTRANSCLR);

HICON hIcon = ImageList_GetIcon(hIml, 0, ILD_NORMAL);
```

29

Multimedia

In this chapter

The term *multimedia* has grown to cover many things from audio to video hardware and software.

In this chapter, you will find a variety of articles describing the control of different aspects of several multimedia components.

- "Playing MIDI Files Directly from the Resource" describes a convenient way to play MIDI files that are embedded within the application resources.
- "CDR.EXE—Open/Close CD Drive(s) Programmatically" shows how to control the CD drive tray under software control.

- "Transparent Animation Control" documents a way of displaying an AVI file transparently within a dialog.
- "Simple Mixer Control Wrapper" defines a simple-to-use wrapper that encapsulates any Windows multimedia mixer controls.
- "Audio Classes Library with n-Channel Real-Time Mixer Demo" is a comprehensive set of classes that allows the mixing of multiple streaming audio sources. An interesting visual spectrum analyzer is also provided in the sample.

Playing MIDI Files Directly from the Resource

This article was contributed by Joerg Koenig.

Introduction

This class is a slightly modified spinoff from the CGTetris application. It is based on a sample in the DirectX sdk (called mstream). The conversion into a C++ class makes it much easier to use. The CMIDI class makes it easy to play a MIDI file directly from the resource (without copying it into a temporary file). One can use the class to play MIDI files, too. In this case, you have to load the entire file into memory and pass the pointer to the Create() method at the beginning of the buffer.

Public Interface

```
// create the MIDI object. You cannot use a MIDI object before
// you've "Create()"ed one!
BOOL Create(LPVOID pSoundData, DWORD dwSize, CWnd * pParent = 0);
BOOL Create(LPCTSTR pszResID, CWnd * pParent = 0);
BOOL Create(UINT uResID, CWnd * pParent = 0);
// Play the MIDI file. Normally the playback will stop after
// the MIDI plays off.
BOOL Play(BOOL bInfinite = FALSE);
// usually you should never set "bReOpen" to FALSE
// unless you're absolutely sure you will
// not reuse the MIDI object. Normally only the
// destructor of the class should set this flag
BOOL Stop(BOOL bReOpen = TRUE);
BOOL IsPlaying() const;
BOOL Pause();
BOOL Continue();
BOOL IsPaused() const;
// Set playback position back to the start
// normally there is no need to call this method directly.
BOOL Rewind();
// Get the number of volume channels
DWORD GetChannelCount() const;
// Set the volume of a channel in percentage. (default 100%)
// Channels can be addressed from 0 to (GetChannelCount()-1)
void SetChannelVolume(DWORD channel, DWORD percent);
// Get the volume of a channel (in percentage)
DWORD GetChannelVolume(DWORD channel) const;

// Set the volume for all channels in percentage
void SetVolume(DWORD percent);
// Get the average volume for all channels (in percentage)
DWORD GetVolume() const;
// Set the tempo of the playback. (default 100%)
void SetTempo(DWORD percent);
// Get the current tempo (in percentage)
DWORD GetTempo() const;
// You can (un)set an infinite loop during playback.
// Note that "Play()" overrides this setting!
void SetInfinitePlay(BOOL bSet = TRUE);
```

The CMIDI class sends the message WM_MIDI_VOLUMECHANGED to its owner window (if one is set via Create()), if the volume changed during playback in another way than explicitly set by the class. (A MIDI stream can control its volume by itself.) The WPARAM parameter of the message is a pointer to the CMIDI object that sent the message. The LOWORD of the LPARAM parameter describes the channel that changed the volume; HIWORD is the new volume in percentage. The WM_MIDI_VOLUMECHANGED message is #defined as WM_USER+23.

Overridables

```
// NOTE THAT, IF YOU OVERRIDE ONE OF THESE METHODS, YOU MUST CALL
// THE BASE CLASS IMPLEMENTATION, TOO!
// called when a MIDI output device is opened
virtual void OnMidiOutOpen();

// called when the MIDI output device is closed
virtual void OnMidiOutClose();
// called when the specified system-exclusive or stream buffer
// has been played and is being returned to the application
virtual void OnMidiOutDone(MIDIHDR &);
// called when a MEVT_F_CALLBACK event is reached in the MIDI output stream
virtual void OnMidiOutPositionCB(MIDIHDR &, MIDIEVENT &);
```

See the sample for how you could use these overridables. A derived CMyMidi class is inside MidiSampleDlg.h.

Usage

The source consists of two files:

- MIDI.[h|cpp]
- Add a MIDI resource to your application (from the menu Insert, Resource, Import, *.mid, Custom Type MIDI). Create() your CMIDI (derived) object, giving it the resource ID of your MIDI resource. Now you can call Play(), Pause(), Stop(), and so on.

Comments

The Rewind function has a problem when attempting to play certain looped MIDI files. To correct this, make the following simple change to the sample code:

Add the following line to the beginning of the Rewind member function:

```
m_tkCurrentTime = 0;
```

—Vivo Kucha

There appears to be a minor problem every second or so, where a glitch in the playback appears. You can correct this by changing the following line:

```
if( !(m_ptsTrack->fdwTrack & ITS_F_ENDOFTRK) && (m_ptsTrack->tkNextEventDue
➡< m_tkNext) ) {
```

to this:

```
if( !(m_ptsTrack->fdwTrack & ITS_F_ENDOFTRK) && (m_ptsTrack->tkNextEventDue
➥<= m_tkNext) ) {
```

Note the added equal sign toward the end of the second statement.

—Matt Hauser

CDR.EXE—Open/Close CD Drive(s) Programmatically

This article was contributed by Chris Morse Sebrell.

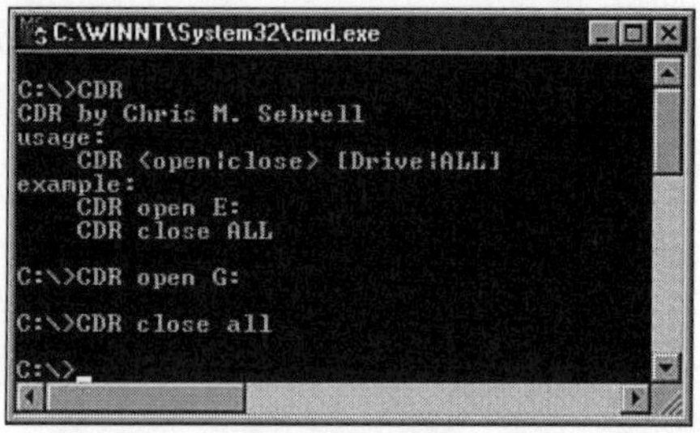

Figure 29.1

In Windows Explorer, you can right-click on a CD drive and select the Eject option to open the CD drive. Unfortunately, there is no Close equivalent to close the drive. This project builds a command-line program that lets you open or close any or all of your CD drives.

To display the program's usage, run the program with no parameters:

```
C:\> CDR
CDR by Chris M. Sebrell
usage:
  CDR [open¦close] [Drive-Letter¦ALL]
example:
  CDR open E:
  CDR close ALL
C:\>
```

To open or close the first logical CD drive, use this:

```
C:\> CDR open
C:\> CDR close
```

If you have more than one CD drive, you can specify a drive letter:

```
C:\> CDR open g:
C:\> CDR close g:
```

If you have more than one CD drive, you can specify all drives:

```
C:\> CDR open all
C:\> CDR close all
```

The main work, routine in the program is CD_OpenClose(BOOL bOpen, TCHAR cDrive):

```
//Open or close CD drive
//cDrive is the drive letter to open, or 0x01 for 'Default' drive
//Examples:
//CD_OpenCloseDrive(TRUE, 'G'); //Open CD door for Drive G:
//CD_OpenCloseDrive(FALSE, 'G'); //Close CD door for Drive G:
//CD_OpenCloseDrive(TRUE, 1);    //Open first logical CD door
void CD_OpenCloseDrive(BOOL bOpenDrive, TCHAR cDrive)
{
MCI_OPEN_PARMS op;
MCI_STATUS_PARMS st;
DWORD flags;

TCHAR szDriveName[4];
strcpy(szDriveName, "X:");

::ZeroMemory(&op, sizeof(MCI_OPEN_PARMS));
op.lpstrDeviceType = (LPCSTR) MCI_DEVTYPE_CD_AUDIO;

if(cDrive > 1)
{
 szDriveName[0] = cDrive;
 op.lpstrElementName = szDriveName;
 flags = MCI_OPEN_TYPE
       ¦ MCI_OPEN_TYPE_ID
       ¦ MCI_OPEN_ELEMENT
       ¦ MCI_OPEN_SHAREABLE;
}
else flags = MCI_OPEN_TYPE
           ¦ MCI_OPEN_TYPE_ID
           ¦ MCI_OPEN_SHAREABLE;

if (!mciSendCommand(0,MCI_OPEN,flags,(unsigned long)&op))
{
 st.dwItem = MCI_STATUS_READY;

 if(bOpenDrive)
  mciSendCommand(op.wDeviceID,MCI_SET,MCI_SET_DOOR_OPEN,0);
 else
  mciSendCommand(op.wDeviceID,MCI_SET,MCI_SET_DOOR_CLOSED,0);

 mciSendCommand(op.wDeviceID,MCI_CLOSE,MCI_WAIT,0);
 }
}
```

Next, to ,facilitate operating on all CD drive doors, add this routine (which calls the CD_OpenCloseDrive() function):

```
void CD_OpenCloseAllDrives(BOOL bOpenDrives)
{
// Determine all CD drives and open (or close) each one
int nPos = 0;
UINT nCount = 0;
TCHAR szDrive[4];
strcpy(szDrive, "?:\\");

DWORD dwDriveList = ::GetLogicalDrives ();

while (dwDriveList) {
 if (dwDriveList & 1)
 {
  szDrive[0] = 0x41 + nPos;
  if(::GetDriveType(szDrive) == DRIVE_CDROM)
  CD_OpenCloseDrive(bOpenDrives, szDrive[0]);
 }
 dwDriveList >>= 1;
 nPos++;
 }
}
```

That's all! The accompanying CD includes source code and the compiled CDR.EXE program. If anyone has additions, corrections, or a whole ,new approach to this, I'd love to hear about it. I'll update this project with any new useful information I receive.

Transparent Animation Control

This article was contributed by Jens Schacherl.

Figure 29.2

Environment: VC6 SP3, NT4 SP4 German (demo application tested with Win98 German)

Because I wanted to put some animations (animated GIFs converted to AVIs) in my application by using the standard CAnimateCtrl, I realized that Microsoft and I interpret the term *transparent* differently.

If you set the flag ACS_TRANSPARENT in CAnimateCtrl, the background of the animation is in no way transparent; instead, it is changed to COLOR_WINDOW, which is not what I expected.

Since my application has a bitmap background, the standard control was useless for me. After staring for some time at the AVIView sample sources, I decided to make my own class that supports real transparency.

The following list shows the public functions of my class CAVICtrl and the flags you can use when loading an animation:

```
// functions

HRESULT Load(UINT nIDResource, DWORD dwFlags = 0L,
 COLORREF clrTransparent = LTGREEN); // load from resource

HRESULT Load(LPCTSTR lpszFile, DWORD dwFlags = 0L,
 COLORREF clrTransparent = LTGREEN); // load from file

BOOL Play(BOOL bOnce = FALSE);
BOOL Stop(BOOL bResetToFirst = FALSE);
void Seek(UINT nTo);
BOOL IsPlaying();

// call this function if the background of the parent
// window changes
void ReinitBackground();

// flags to use with Load()

AVC_HALFSPEED 0x0000001 // plays video with half speed
AVC_DOUBLESPEED 0x0000002 // plays video with double speed

AVC_CENTERAVI 0x0000004 // centers video inside the window
AVC_STRETCHAVI 0x0000008 // stretches video to fit inside the window
AVC_CENTERRECT 0x0000010 // resizes window; center point stays the same

AVC_AUTOPLAY 0x0000020 // starts playing automatically after Load()

// background is COLOR_WINDOW
// instead of transparent (like CAnimateCtrl's
// AVS_"TRANSPARENT")
AVC_MAPWINDOWCOLOR 0x0000040

// ignore clrTransparent parameter and use color of first
// frame's first pixel instead (works only with 8-bit images)
AVC_FIRSTPIXTRANSPRNT 0x0000080
```

If you have a dialog-based application, simply add a static control to your dialog and subclass it with a CAVICtrl in OnInitDialog() before calling one of the loading functions.

I recommend downloading the demo project, which demonstrates the class's usage and the working of some of the flags.

This sample program also uses Joerg Koenig's useful CBitmapDialog class to display the background image.

One great flaw is that the animation function is driven by a timer, so it stops if you click on the parent window to move or resize it.

I'm planning to put the animation code in a different thread for better performance and appearance, but this will be my first travel into the alien world of multithreaded programming, so please be patient.

Comments, suggestions, bug reports, and so on are welcome! Send them directly to me at jschacherl@csi.com.

Enjoy!

Comments

There is a slight problem with the animation when the dialog is moved. This can be corrected.

First, do not call ReinitBackground from the OnWindowPosChanging routine. Instead, call it from the OnSize method:

```
void CAVCDemoDlg::OnSize(UINT nType, int cx, int cy)
{
    m_AviCtrl.ReinitBackground();
    CBitmapDialog::OnSize(nType, cx, cy);
}
```

Next, change the code inside the InitBackground routine as shown.

Change it from this:

```
// calculate position of control in parent
GetWindowRect(&rcAVIWnd);

// border moves window later, so we move it here, too
if (GetExStyle() & (WS_EX_CLIENTEDGE¦WS_EX_DLGMODALFRAME))
{
    rcAVIWnd.OffsetRect(GetSystemMetrics(SM_CXEDGE),
➥GetSystemMetrics(SM_CYEDGE));
}
else if(GetStyle() & WS_BORDER)
{
```

```
        rcAVIWnd.OffsetRect(GetSystemMetrics(SM_CXBORDER),
    ➥GetSystemMetrics(SM_CYBORDER));
    }

    rcParent = rcAVIWnd;
    pParentWnd->ScreenToClient(&rcParent);
```

to this:

```
    GetClientRect(rcParent);
    ClientToScreen(rcParent);
    pParentWnd->ScreenToClient(&rcParent);
```

—Blue Dragon

Simple Mixer Control Wrapper

This article was contributed by Alexander Fedorov.

Environment: VC6, Unicode

This is a small and useful C++ class that can encapsulate any Windows multimedia mixer control. I wrote a simple class, named CAlexfMixer, which can wrap any multimedia mixer control. You can manipulate Master Volume, Mute, or someone else's mixer control with this class if the control supports these operations. You can retrieve information from Peak Meter and other controls like this.

There are some other mixers here, but not all of them are as clear, simple, and universal as my own.

Let's look at class definition:

```
    class CAlexfMixer
    {
    protected:
      HMIXER m_HMixer;
      INT m_iMixerControlID;
      MMRESULT mmr;
      DWORD m_dwChannels;
      BOOL m_bSuccess;
      void ZeroAll();
    public:
      BOOL IsOk() {return m_bSuccess;};
      BOOL On();
      BOOL Off();
      DWORD GetControlValue();
      BOOL SetControlValue(DWORD dw);
      CAlexfMixer(DWORD DstType, DWORD SrcType, DWORD ControlType);
      CAlexfMixer(HWND hwnd, DWORD DstType, DWORD SrcType, DWORD ControlType);
      virtual ~CAlexfMixer();
    };
```

The class has two constructors—with and without a callback window. The class has the member IsOk() to check the manipulation capability of the specified control and members to get and set the control state.

Using the Class

Example 1: Master Volume Control

```
CAlexfMixer mixer(m_hWnd, MIXERLINE_COMPONENTTYPE_DST_SPEAKERS,
                  NO_SOURCE, MIXERCONTROL_CONTROLTYPE_VOLUME);
if (!mixer.IsOk())
    return;
mixer.SetControlValue(500);
```

First, we create an object associated with the Master Volume meter control. The third parameter, NO_SOURCE, is a constant, which is defined in an .h file. This means that control does not have a source line—only a destination line. Second, we check whether this type of control is available. Third, if this control is available, we set the volume to 500.

Example 2: Master Mute

```
CAlexfMixer mixer(MIXERLINE_COMPONENTTYPE_DST_SPEAKERS,
                  NO_SOURCE, MIXERCONTROL_CONTROLTYPE_MUTE );
mixer.Off();
```

Here, we create an object associated with the Master Mute control. Then we switch it off.

Check for the latest versions at http://members.xoom.com/lamer2000/.

Audio Classes Library with n-Channel Real-Time Mixer Demo

This article was contributed by Colin MacKenzie.

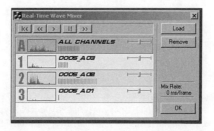

Figure 29.3

Figure 29.4

Environment: Win 98/NT/2000, Visual C++ 6

The AudioClasses library demonstrates the following:

- Loading a wave file manually (thanks to Timothy J. Weber's Rifffile code)
- The Audio Compression Manager API
- Mixing *n*-channels of stereo audio
- Waveform Audio API: Outputting audio data to a sound device
- Implementing a spectrum analyzer and spectrum analyzer (peak-valley) graph
- Fast Fourier Transforms
- Mixer Control: Implementing a custom list box

The AudioClasses library simplifies much of the work involved in playing from a compressed sound source and includes the mixing of many sources at once in real-time into a single sound stream. The library is based on audio streams. You can connect stream objects together like a chain to perform the desired operation.

There are two base types of streams: PlayStream and FilterStream. A PlayStream is meant to be a source of audio data. It's usually from a file, but it can also be from another source, such as a database. A PlayStream class implements the WaveBuffer GetBuffer() virtual method, providing a chunk of audio data (a WaveBuffer) to the requesting object. The requesting object can be another input stream, the player, or a custom object. The WaveStream (which loads a wave file) is an implementation of a PlayStream.

A FilterStream is derived from PlayStream but also accepts an input PlayStream. FilterStreams are used to perform some operation on the input stream before passing its audio data to the requesting object through the WaveBuffer GetBuffer() virtual method. The ConversionStream (which uses the ACM API) is an implementation of a FilterStream. The SpectrumAnalyzer is also a FilterStream that passes the input directly to the output, but performs Fast Fourier Transformation on the audio data so that it can be graphed as a spectrum analyzer. The mixer is also a form of a FilterStream, although it accepts many input streams and is derived from PlayStream.

Derive your own class from PlayStream or FilterStream, and they will be compatible with the library and can be inserted into the stream chain at any point. For example, you can create your own FilterStream to perform echo cancellation on an input stream, or you can create a PlayStream that loads audio data from a database.

In the mixer demo, audio data starts from the wave source stream (WaveStream) into the Audio Compression Manager (ACM) stream (ConversionStream). From there, it goes into the mixer stream (PlayStream), and then the output of the mixer stream is connected to the player. The player requests buffers from its input stream; it is the end of the stream, so it is the consumer. The requests are directed through the stream chain as they are requested from the consumer.

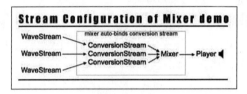

Figure 29.5

NOTICE: Code from the FFTW project has been used in the making of this project. This excellent code is used to generate the Spectrum Analyzer for the AudioClasses library. Here is the introductory statement found on the FFTW Web site:

FFTW is a C subroutine library for computing the Discrete Fourier Transform (DFT) in one or more dimensions, of both real and complex data, and of arbitrary input size. We believe that FFTW, which is free software, should become the FFT library of choice for most applications.

Using the AudioClasses Library

First, you must declare a mixer object to contain the mixing sources and a player to send the mixed audio to the sound device.

```
/* the mixer target : the sound card */
Player    m_player;

/* our mixer control that contains the mixer stream */
CMixerListBox   m_channels;
```

Following is the relevant code in the mixer demo that initializes the mixer:

```
/* set channel listctrl icons */
m_channels.SetVolumeIcon(AfxGetApp()->LoadIcon(IDI_VOLUME),
                AfxGetApp()->LoadIcon(IDI_MUTEDVOLUME));

/* set channels custom listctrl to point to mixer */
m_channels.Popup(IDR_MIXERPOPUP);

/* set the mixer as the play stream */
m_player << m_channels;
```

You can load some files into the mixer with the following, or you can use the AddStream if you have an existing stream:

```
/* load some files into the mixer */
m_channels.Load("c:\\sample1.wav");
m_channels.Load("c:\\sample2.wav");
m_channels.Load("c:\\sample3.wav");
```

Now you can start playing the mix:

```
/* start playing */
player.Play();
```

FROM THE FORUM

Question (Gale):

Is there a way to play a WAV file from the application's resources instead of from a file?

Answer (dizzydave):

Import your WAV file as a resource of type WAVE. Then when you want to play the sound, use the following code:

```
PlaySound(MAKEINTRESOURCE(IDR_WAVE1), GetModuleHandle(NULL), SND_RESOURCE ¦
➡SND_ASYNC);
```

Also, make sure you have the multimedia component included in your project (mmsystem.h and winmm.lib).

FROM THE FORUM

Question (bluesource):

How can I play an AVI movie?

Answer (VGirish):

You can use the CAnimateCtrl to display uncompressed AVI movies without sound:

```
CAnimateCtrl m_ctlAnimate;

m_ctlAnimate.Open("D:\\Test\\ok1.avi");
m_ctlAnimate.Play(0, -1, -1);
```

Or, for more complex AVI files, you can use MCI:

```
HWND hMCI;
TCHAR szFile[] = _T("C:\\Winnt\\Clock.avi");

hMCI = MCIWndCreate(m_hWnd,AfxGetApp()->m_hInstance,
➥MCIWNDF_SHOWNAME¦MCIWNDF_NOMENU, NULL);

if (MCIWndOpen(hMCI,szFile, 0) != 0)
{
    MessageBox("Unable to play AVI!","Error!");
    MCIWndDestroy(hMCI);
}
```

30

OpenGL

In this chapter

OpenGL is a software interface to graphics hardware providing 2D and 3D rendering of objects into a frame buffer.

- "Simple OpenGL Classes" describes some helper classes for use with the OpenGL framework.
- "Starting OpenGL in a Dialog" shows how to create an animated OpenGL object in a dialog box with textures and shading that can be manipulated with the mouse.

- "Starting Rendering Modes" documents the use of an OpenGL object in the document/view framework, demonstrating the use of the various rendering modes.

The contributors of the articles in this chapter briefly describe what their projects do. They let the source code and demos on the CD communicate most of the information.

Simple OpenGL Classes

This article was contributed by Yuantu Huang.

Figure 30.1

Environment: Windows NT4 SP5, Windows 95b/98, Visual C++ 6

In engineering applications it is necessary to have 3D graphics functions that can make visualizations using engineering data. The following simple classes provide such functions and have been implemented using an SDK rather than MFC.

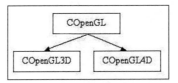

Figure 30.2

Features

- 2D, 3D, and True 3D (4D) display
- Zooming and rotation
- 4D cutting
- Legend and marker
- DIB printing
- Support for some visualization properties such as color selection
- Support for mixed GDI and OpenGL map rendering

History

From 1996 to 1998, I was involved to develop a 3D reservoir modeling package using OpenGL and MFC on Windows NT with interpolation algorithms, such as Kriging, Neural Network, Fuzzy Logic, and genetic and interpolation algorithms. However, the provided classes, which have been rewritten using Win32 API completely, only implement part of the original 3D reservoir modeling package. Due to time constraints, all interpolation algorithms, their binary file outputs, and nonregular 4D map displays are not included in the above classes.

You are free to use or modify these classes in any of your applications. But I make no guarantees about these classes' suitability for use. If there is any problem with anything I wrote, I will certainly try to help solve it.

Source Code

1. OpenGL.h and OpenGL.cpp: property definition, map framework description, zooming, rotation, and so on.
2. OpenGL3D.h and OpenGL3D.cpp: implement the simplest 2D and 3D rendering.
3. OpenGL4D.h and OpenGL4D.cpp: implement the simplest True 3D (4D) rendering.

Support Classes

- ClassArr.h: template-based class similar to MFC CArray, but independent of MFC.
- ColourPicker.h and ColourPicker.cpp: CodeGuru code to implement ColorPicker.
- Hdibapi.h and Hdibapi.cpp: DIB loading and saving.
- Str.h and Str.cpp: The simplest string class.
- TabWindow.h and TabWindow.cpp: MFC CTabCtrl-derived component that contains an implementation of tab views.

Demo Project

The GLDemo, which is an MFC MDI application, demonstrates how to use the classes mentioned above. It uses a splitter window. Most actions are shown in the left window, and rendering is shown in the right window.

From the View menu, click Grid Data to load one of the grid data files (*.grd), where you will find Surfer format files SurfA.grd (ASCII) and SurfB.grd, and other format files (defined by myself and available on request) test3d.grd, test4d.grd, and true3d.grd. For 3D visualization, you can load the maker file (the text file Marker.mrk only for SurfA.grd and SurfB.grd). Please note that Shift+left-click can move the legend. You can find most visualization properties in the left window. In addition, from File, Save to BMP, you can save the active window, client area, and any part of the client area (rectangle) to BMP.

About the Author

I am a senior software engineer for TechComm Simulation Pty Ltd., Sydney, Australia, where I specialize in Client/Server and TCP/IP programming on Unix and Windows NT. My email address is yuantuh@techsim.com.au.

FROM THE FORUM

Question (Rasczak):

I need to draw circles and curves such as Bezier, BSpline. The only references I could find were about calculating and drawing circles with small straight segments. Surely, there must be another way. Is there a derived function in OpenGL to draw a circle easily?

Answer (Philip Nicoletti):

There is no other way. Even if there were a glCircle(), all it would do is join straight segments. OpenGL drawing utilities seem more concerned with 3D (spheres, cylinders, boxes, and so on).

Here is a simple function to draw a circle:

```
void drawCircle (int xc, int yc, int rad)
{
    //
    // draw a circle centered at (xc,yc) with radius rad
    //
    glBegin(GL_LINE_LOOP); // use GL_LINE_STRIP for open figures

    for (int angle=0; angle < 360; angle = angle+5)
    {
        float angle_radians = angle * (float)3.14159 / (float)180;
        float x = xc + rad * (float)cos(angle_radians);
        float y = yc + rad * (float)sin(angle_radians);
        glVertex3f(x, z, y);
    }

    glEnd();
}
```

OpenGL does have direct support of Bezier curves.

Starting OpenGL in a Dialog

This article was contributed by Pierre ALLIEZ.

This is the smallest example to make

- Antialiasing
- Gouraud
- Texture mapping
- Texture lighting
- Texture transparency

This sample creates an OpenGL rendering context in a dialog box and draws a simple cube. We can manipulate the object with the mouse and change texture files with a pop-up menu item. A timer animates a rotation. Texture files are .BMP files (2^n * 2^m * 24 bits).

Figure 30.3

Figure 30.4

Figure 30.5

Figure 30.6

Figure 30.7

Figure 30.8

Starting Rendering Modes

This article was contributed by Pierre ALLIEZ.

Keywords:

- OpenGL rendering context
- MFC
- Rendering mode: wireframe/vertex/faces
- Gouraud shading
- Antialiasing
- Lighting
- Scaling (with sliders)
- Rotation (mouse events)

This sample creates an OpenGL rendering context in a multidocument/view framework and displays the most simple representative object: a sphere. A form view on the left permits us to check rendering options, like rendering modes (vertex, wireframe, and faces), antialiasing, lighting, Gouraud shading (in face and wireframe mode), lighting and background colors, scaling, and animation (rotation). Mouse events permit rotation.

FROM THE FORUM

Question (Lim Say Kiap):

I need to draw a rectangular block, like a cube, using OpenGL. How can I do this?

Answer (Philip Nicoletti):

There are many ways to achieve this. Here is a simple approach:

```
#include <GL/gl.h>
#include <GL/glaux.h>


...
// when you want to draw the cube
//
glPushMatrix(); // save current transformations
glTranslatef(x,y,z); // move to where you want the center of cube

auxSolidCube(length); // draws cube with each side equal to "GLDouble length"
// or, for a non-cube box :
auxSolidBox(width,height,depth); // all parameters are GLDouble

glPopMatrix(); // restore saved transformations
```

VI

Database

31

ADO

In this chapter

ActiveX Data Objects or (ADOs) were developed to provide a single easy-to-use approach to using a wide variety of data sources, programming tools, and platforms.

ADO code can be used in Web pages, Microsoft Office applications, and custom applications with a lot of similarity between the many implementations.

- "ADO Is AOK (a Simple ADO Tutorial)" provides an in-depth explanation of the use of ADO.
- "ADO Is AOK – Part II (or How I Spent My Summer Vacation)" continues the explanation of ADO, showing some practical examples.
- "Creating Database Objects Using ADOX" describes the use of Extended ADO to access databases.

ADO Is AOK (a Simple ADO Tutorial)

This article was contributed by Bob Place.

Environment: Demo written in Visual C++ 6.0

We are all familiar with the CDatabase classes and the CDaoDatabase classes. They are relatively simple to use, they mesh well with our application, and they are easily distributed. Using something like the GenericRecordset class (found here at CodeGuru), makes it even easier to create powerful database applications with little effort on your part.

Now just as you started feeling safe doing database development in C++, Microsoft pushed something on you called UDA (Universal Data Access) and a relatively simple but mostly undocumented object called ADO (ActiveX Data Object). Unfortunately, Microsoft felt that there was little need to show any kind of documentation for Visual C developers. If you search around, you will be hard pressed to find any good examples. Even here at CodeGuru, there is only one other article about ADO.

So after several months of playing around with ADO, I finally felt good about it, and I will probably never use anything but ADO for all future development. When you see how easy it is to use ADO, and how powerful it is (can we say thread safe?), you will probably never go back either. When I wrote the GenericRecordset for DAO, it was to provide a simple way to use dynamic data binding. In other words, it would allow me to base a recordset on a query rather than a table. One of the things I liked about ADO from the start was that this, dynamic data binding, is the default way ADO works.

Getting Started

Before you can use ADO, you have to let your application know you are going to use it. In your stdfx.h file, you need to add the following code:

```
#import "c:\program files\common files\system\ado\msdao15.dll"
➥no_namespaces rename("EOF" adoEOF")
```

This line basically says to use ADO, but not to use namespaces, and change EOF to adoEOF. You have to rename EOF because of a nasty conflict of constants. Once you have done this, there are no include files, and there is nothing else you have to link to your application.

A Look at the Pieces: _ConnectionPtr, _CommandPtr, and _RecordsetPtr

ADO, much like its counterparts DAO and CDatabase, comes in several pieces. Unlike its counterparts, ADO is COM based. An interesting thing about learning ADO is that you are forced to learn a little about COM. (This is a good thing because as a Windows developer you will be headed down that road sooner or later.) The three objects of ADO are the Connection, the Command, and the Recordset.

The Connection object returns a recordset or a NULL. You generally use this to connect to the database and/or to run SQL statements that do not return anything. While the Connection object can return a recordset, that is not the best way to use it. Much like CDaoDatabase, you (for the most part) make this your connection to the database and then use other objects to perform your data I/O.

The Command object returns a recordset and allows you a simple way to run stored procedures or any SQL statement that returns a recordset. You can either use your global connection to the database with this, or you can tell it the connection string when you open your command. This is a nice feature if you are making a one-time connection. But if you are going to create a lot of recordsets, you will want to use the Connection object to connect to the database and Command object to run stored procedures.

And the Recordset object is, well, a recordset. It provides a little more control over the recordset (like locking, cursors, and so on) than the other two methods do. As with the Command object, you do not need to have an open connection. If you include the connection string rather than a pointer to the Connection object, you can use the Recordset object by itself. If you are using multiple recordsets, the best way is to use the Connection object to connect to a database and the Recordset object to make your recordsets. The two parts of ADO I will talk about in this article are the Connection and the Recordset.

_ConnectionPtr

This is the connection interface. It is similar to CDatabase or CDaoDatabase. It basically works the same way they do. You create an instance of it, point it to a database either through ODBC or a provider, and you open it. Look how similar it is to CDaoDatabase:

```
CDaoDatabase MyDb = new CDaoDatabase();
m_DaoServerDB.Open(NULL,FALSE,FALSE,"ODBC;DSN=SAMS_SVR;UID=admin;PWD=admin");
```

Now using ADO:

```
_ConnectionPtr MyDb;
MyDb.CreateInstance(__uuidof(Connection));
MyDb->Open("DSN=SAMS_SVR;UID=admin;PWD=admin","","",-1);
```

_RecordsetPtr

This is the recordset interface. It is similar to CDaoRecordset. Again, when you see how similar it is to CDaoRecordset, you will wonder why you did not use it sooner. Let's see how they work. (We will use the database and the connection above in our example.)

```
CDaoRecordset MySet = new CDaoRecordset(MyDb);
MySet->Open(AFX_DAO_USE_DEFAULT_TYPE,"SELECT * FROM some_table");
```

Now using ADO:

```
_RecordsetPtr MySet;
MySet.CreateInstance(__uuidof(Recordset));
MySet->Open("SELECT * FROM some_table",
    MyDb.GetInterfacePtr(),adOpenDynamic,adLockOptimistic,adCmdText);
```

ADO is slightly more involved. But with some of the added benefits you get with ADO (most of which are beyond the scope of this article), ADO is worth the extra effort here.

Now that we have a Connection and a Recordset, let's get some data out of it. In both cases we are going to fill a list box with information in the recordset (assuming we have a list box called m_List).

DAO:

```
VARIANT *vFieldValue;
COleVariant covFieldValue;
CString Holder;
while(!MySet->IsEOF())
{
```

```
MySet->GetFieldValue("FIELD_1", covFieldValue);
vFieldValue = (LPVARIANT)covFieldValue;
if(vFieldValue->vt!-VT_NULL)
{
Holder.Format("%s",vFieldValue->pbVal);
m_List.AddString(Holder);
}
MySet.MoveNext();
}
```

ADO:

```
_variant_t Holder
while(!MySet->adoEOF)
{
Holder = MySet->GetCollect("FIELD_1");
if(Holder.vt!=VT_NULL)
m_List.AddString((char*)_bstr_t(Holder));
MySet->MoveNext();
}
```

A special note: There is *no* documentation for the GetCollect method. I have searched everywhere, and no one mentioned it.

The other method of retrieving data would be

```
Holder = MySet->GetFields->Field->(_variant_t(FieldNumber))->Value;
```

I like the GetCollect better.

FROM THE FORUM

Question (Vanessa Li):

How can I get the result of "Select Count(*) From MyTable" using ADO?

Answer (Bob Place):

You can use the GetCollect method of a recordset by changing the SQL statement to

```
"SELECT COUNT(*) FROM MyTable AS total_count".
```

Then use the GetCollect method to retrieve the result from the total_count column alias returned by the call:

```
_variant_t Holder = MySet->GetCollect("total_count");
```

Holder.iVal will have the value in it.

Dynamic Binding Versus DFX

Dynamic binding allows you to create a recordset on any legal SQL statement that returns something. For example, imagine trying to create a recordset using DFX that will allow you to sum several fields:

```
SELECT (SUM(field_1) + SUM(field_2)) AS answer FROM some_table
```

Not an easy task (if possible at all). This is one of the advantages of dynamic data binding. Another is the decrease in code. This makes your application smaller and easier to maintain. And last, according to Microsoft, it is the preferred way of retrieving data from a data source. So dynamic binding is more flexible, faster, and easier to maintain. Could we ask for anything more?

With most applications you can have a single (global) connection to a database, and then create recordsets to your heart's content. And if you have written applications with a lot of recordsets, you know the amount of added code that DFX adds to your application. All of this code is gone with dynamic binding.

What the Heck Are _variant_t and _bstr_t?

Unfortunately, our CString class is gone with COM. (Sigh, so is CStringEx.) Because COM had cross-platform development, it needed a more generic way to handle strings and other data. This problem was answered by the VARIANT data type and the BSTR data type. The VARIANT is basically a huge union of every type of data you can think of (except char*). The BSTR is basically a string with a size attached (a replacement for char*).

These can be a royal pain in the fanny to work with. So enter **_variant_t** and **_bstr_t**. Basically (very basically), the _variant_t class wraps the VARIANT data type and allows us to simply cast the data as a type. This simplifies using a VARIANT. The _bstr_t does the same thing with a BSTR. In the example you can see how I get a VARIANT from the Recordset GetCollect method, then I put it into a _bstr_t, and then I cast it to a char*, or I cast the _variant_t as a long, or a double, or whatever....

```
_variant_t Holder;
// first get the VARIANT and put it into the _variant_t
Holder = MySet->GetCollect("FIELD_1");
// now put it into a _bstr_t and cast it to a char*
m_List.AddString((char*)_bstr_t(Holder));
```

Compare that with what you have to do without the _variant_t and _bstr_t:

```
COleVariant covFieldValuel
VARIANT vFieldValue;
CString Holder;
MySet->GetFieldValue("FIELD_1", covFieldValue);
vFieldValue = (LPVARIANT)covFieldValue;
Holder.Format("%s",vFieldValue->pbVal);
m_List.AddString(Holder);
```

Quite a difference.

Update, Insert, and Delete

When I perform an update, insert, or delete, I usually like to use the Connection object or the Command object. The reason for this is that it seems simpler to create the SQL statement in a CString and then use the Execute method. But you can do all three with the Recordset object.

The **Update** method can update based on one of these three parameters:

- Assign values to a Field object's Value property and call the **Update** method.
- Pass a field name and a value as arguments with the **Update** call.
- Pass an array of field names and an array of values with the **Update** call.

The **AddNew** method takes an array of fields and a matching array of values.

The **Delete** method will delete either the current record or the records based on the current filter.

In all three methods, you may need to ReQuery to see the results.

Sample Code

The sample code I have included with this article is a simple MFC application. In CWinApp, I declare the _ConnectionPtr, _CommandPtr, and _RecordsetPtr interfaces.

```
// Global ADO Objects
// connection
_ConnectionPtr    m_pConnection;
_CommandPtr       m_pCommand;
_RecordsetPtr     m_pRecordset;
```

It is interesting to note that (in VC6.0) if you type "m_pConnection.", you will get a list of functions and members, but if you type "m_pConnection->", you get a totally different set of functions and members. This is because you are actually pointing to two different things. If you are looking at the "." methods, you are looking at the smart pointer methods. If you are looking at the "->" methods, you are looking at the ones from whatever you created (_ConnectionPtr, and so on). This is also why you see two lines, one using the "." and one using the "->", right after each other.

```
_ConnectionPtr MyDb;
MyDb.CreateInstance(__uuidof(Connection));
MyDb->Open("DSN=SAMS_SVR;UID=admin;PWD=admin","","",-1);
```

Back to the sample code. In the init instance of the application, I open the connection. It is pointing to a database on my system. You will have to change this to a database (ODBC) on your system or use one of the UDA providers to a database.

```
// When we open the application we will open the ADO connection
m_pConnection.CreateInstance(__uuidof(Connection));
m_pConnection->Open("DSN=ADOTest","","",-1);
```

If you open the About dialog, you will see a list box. You will see a button called Button 1. This is where the meat of the ADO is located. I create instances of the recordset interface, open the recordset based on the query I want to use, and then loop through the records:

```
_variant_t TheValue;
theApp.m_pRecordset.CreateInstance(__uuidof(Recordset));
try
{
    theApp.m_pRecordset->Open("SELECT DISTINCT FLDESC FROM tblFALines",
        theApp.m_pConnection.GetInterfacePtr(),
        adOpenDynamic,
        adLockOptimistic,
        adCmdText);

    while(!theApp.m_pRecordset->adoEOF)
    {
        TheValue = theApp.m_pRecordset->GetCollect("FLDESC");
        if(TheValue.vt!=VT_NULL)
        m_List.AddString((char*)_bstr_t(TheValue));
        theApp.m_pRecordset->MoveNext();
    }
    theApp.m_pRecordset->Close();
}
catch(_com_error *e)
{
    CString Error = e->ErrorMessage();
    AfxMessageBox(e->ErrorMessage());
}
catch(...)
{
    MessageBox("Whoa this is bad");
}
```

Remember to use try and catch. ADO will crash your application in a heartbeat if you don't! You will need to catch _com_error all the time.

I have tried to keep this as simple as I can. I have omitted many details, oversimplified things, and ignored some good coding practices (like checking the HRESULT that most COM methods return). The goal of this article is to show you that ADO (and COM in general) is nothing to fear, not to show you everything ADO can do. I have not even scratched the surface of what ADO can do for you. It is fast, easy to use, and much more powerful than DAO. Take a look at the article here at CodeGuru about how easy it is to use ADO to access stored procedures.

There are two good books out there that will get you started. One of the books you can read entirely for *free* (that's *free*) at www.mcp.com. The other you have to buy. (I would buy both books unless you have a computer in your bathroom and another next to your bed.) The books are *ADO 2.0* by WROC press. This book, like so many others, has very *few* C++ examples. But it is a great reference for all the methods and properties. After you get used to using ADO, porting the examples to C++ is relatively simple. The second book is *Learn Database Programming with Visual C++ in 21 days*. The information in it is great. Also you can read the *entire book* online at www.mcp.com. Both are worth the price. The first half of the "in 21 Days" book deals directly with ADO and how to use it (good stuff). The last half gets into database design and such (okay material).

Comments

To programmatically create a new database file, use the following code:

```
SQLConfigDataSource(NULL, ODBC_ADD_DSN, "Microsoft Access Driver
(*.mdb)\0", "CREATE_DB=D:\\temp\\MyDB\0DSN=MYDB\0Description=MYDB
Data Source\0FileType=Access\0DataDirectory=D:\\temp\0");
```

—Theresa Stites

For anyone developing a Win32 console application using ADO, make the following code changes:

Add

```
CoInitialize(NULL);
```

before the call to

```
MyCon.CreateInstance(__uuidof(Connection));
```

—Ovais Khan

ADO Is AOK—Part II (or How I Spent My Summer Vacation)

This article was contributed by Bob Place.

A little over a year ago, I wrote about the Generic Recordset. This was a simple class that wrapped CDaoRecordset and made it a lot simpler to use dynamic binding. Then along came ADO, which used dynamic binding, and it was goodbye Generic Recordset and DAO. To help others see how easy ADO really is and because of the lack of documentation about ADO and VC, I wrote "ADO Is AOK (a Simple ADO Tutorial)." Now I want to take that to the next level. This article will show you how to make ADO even simpler for all your future application development. But most of all, it will also show you a little more detail on how to use ADO (be it in your Active Template Library [ATL] COM object or just in an application). The example I will be using will show you how to use ADO in an ATL COM object. We use this all the time at the office to build business layer objects that handle all of the data I/O and rules. This allows not only a specific application to use these rules and the data, but also other related applications to do the same without the need for them to have an intimate knowledge of the application of the data. Anyway, here is what I will try to touch on in this article:

1. Creating an ATL project
2. Adding ADO to an ATL project (or any application)
3. Adding methods and properties to an interface
4. BSTR (_bstr_t), VARIANT(_variant_t), and SAFEARRAY
5. Creating global instances of the Connection, the Command, and the Recordset
6. Using the Connection to open/close a connection, to create a Recordset from SQL, and to be the active connection with a Command object
7. Using the Command object to run stored procedures with and without parameters
8. Turning a recordset into a delimited string and passing it back to the client application
9. Creating wrappers for business logic that access ADO through the ADO methods
10. Showing both Visual C++ and Visual Basic code to access all of the methods and properties we add to the COM object

As you can tell, this is a very long article. I could not cover everything as well as I would have liked to, so I will point you to other references if you want greater detail. I hope the time it took me to get a handle on this will help you get a handle on it. Once you get the basics down, neither ADO nor ATL is that intimidating.

Creating the Generic ADO COM Object Using ATL

The first thing we will need to do is create a new ATL COM object. We will let the wizards do this for us. We made our GenericAdo an EXE with the stub DLL; the choice is yours if you want it to be compiled as an EXE or a DLL. Creating it as an EXE will help stop it from crashing your application because it is not running in the same process. If you are a programming god and your code never crashes, then by all means make it a DLL. If you are a human like me, then I would suggest making it an EXE. But again, the choice is yours. If you have never created an ATL COM object, you will be pleasantly surprised at how simple it is:

1. Open a new project ATL COM AppWizard, naming it MyADO (or whatever you want to name it). Press OK.
2. Choose the server type, either EXE or DLL. We are not going to use MFC or choose anything else on this page, so just click Finish.

There. You have created a COM object (albeit a totally useless one). Now we have to add an interface to it:

1. Go to the Insert menu and select New ATL Object.
2. Double-click on the Simple Object icon. This will pop up a new dialog.
3. Enter the short name of ADO. This will populate all the other edit boxes.
4. Click on the Attributes tab, look at it, nod your head knowingly, but don't touch anything.
5. Click OK.

Is this simple or what? At this point I could go into topics about customer interfaces and cover what every option on the Attributes tab means, but that is way beyond the scope of this article. This article is meant to get you up and running in the shortest amount of time.

Okay, you have now created the MyADO COM object with the CADO class (also called coclasses), and the IADO interface. Here is a simple explanation of what we have so far. The CADO class is the C++ class that you can use to control what will happen. It is just like any other class that you have ever created. Nothing new there. The IADO interface is nothing more than the things that your COM client (the application that will use this COM server) can see. When you create a MyADO object, you will be able to use anything added to the interface. This will become a little clearer as we continue. It is important only to remember that an interface has two important pieces. They are a *property*, which looks to the COM client like a variable (though it really is not a variable) and a *method*, which is like a function. To use properties and methods from clients, you can use the following sample code:

Property:

VB:

```
MyADOObject.SomeProperty = 10
```

VC:

```
MyADOObject->put_SomeProperty(10);
```

Method:

VB:

```
Counter = MyADOObject.GetInt("SELECT COUNT(*) FROM some_table")
```

VC:

```
MyADOObject->GetInt("SELECT COUNT(*) FROM some_table",&Counter)
```

One important difference in accessing both ADO and COM methods in VB and VC is that there are no defaults when accessing with VC. For example, if the method takes five parameters, you must supply five parameters. In VB you can skip the ones you do not use. In my COM objects, I always have a global variable declared like this:

```
VARIANT m_vNull;
```

Then initialized in the constructor like this:

```
m_vNull.vt=VT_NULL;
m_vNull.scode = DISP_E_PARAMNOTFOUND;
```

This variable can be used whenever you want to use the default value of a parameter. You can use this as a parameter whenever you want to use a default parameter of a method.

So now we have a very simple COM object with one interface. We now need to add the ability to use ADO. This is done by editing the stdfx.h file for the application. You will need to add the same code to import ADO as you do in any application. I have the location of the ADO files in the "include" files (Tools, Options, Directories tab), so all we need to do is add this line:

```
#import "msado15.dll" no_namespace rename("EOF","adoEOF")
```

If you do not have the directory listed, you will have to add the entire path to the ADO files. If you read "ADO Is AOK (a Simple ADO Tutorial)," you will remember that we use no_namespace so that we do not have to use namespaces, and we have to rename EOF because of a nasty naming problem.

Now we are ready to move ahead. The first thing we will be doing is creating a global instance of _ConnectionPtr, _CommandPtr, and _RecordsetPtr. While we will be constantly creating new instances of the _RecordsetPtr, we will need at least one to do some fancy stuff later. Now let's add these as follows:

1. Right-click on CGAdo.
2. Choose Add Member Variable.
3. The data type is _ConnectionPtr, named m_Connection.
4. Do the same for data type _CommandPtr, named m_Command, and _RecordsetPtr, named m_Recordset.

Because our sample will only connect to one database at a time, we can use a global Connection and a global Command. Remember that the Connection object is what is used to connect to the database, and the Command is used to access the stored procedures. Usually, one of these per COM session will be enough. There is nothing saying that you cannot add additional ones if you like, but we have found that simpler is better and having one has never failed us yet.

Now that we have our global Connection and Command, we will need to initiate them in the constructor. Add the following code to the CADO constructor:

```
m_Connection.Createinstance(__uuidof(Connection));
m_Command.Createinstance(__uuidof(Command));
m_Recordset.CreateInstance(__uuidof(Recordset));
```

Now we must also add the code needed to eliminate these in the destructor, so add the following code:

```
try
{
    if(m_Connection->State == adOpen)
    {
        // the connection is still open so we need to close it
        m_Connection->Close();
    }
    if(m_Recordset->State == adOpen)
    {
        // the connection is still open so we need to close it
        m_Recordset->Close();
    }
    m_Connection = NULL;
    m_Command = NULL;
    m_Recordset = NULL;
}
catch(_com_error &e){} // error handling here
catch(...){}// all other exceptions here
```

Notice that we are checking to make sure that the connection and the recordset are not open before we set them to NULL. That is all there is to adding ADO to the COM server and adding a global connection, command, and recordset variable.

Now we have to decide what we want to have the ADO COM object do. But first, let's take a look at SAFEARRAYS, VARIANTS, and BSTRS. You will be using these over and over, so we will have to have an understanding of how they work. (You also might want to take a look at the STD string and strstream templates, which are a great alternative to the CString class you cannot use.) Because we like to keep things simple and our COM server may be used by any client regardless of the language it was written in, we like to keep the marshaling simple, and we never (never say never) use anything but standard data types. So using these three data types makes our lives simple.

The BSTR (and the Wrapper _bstr_t)

This is a variable type that holds a string. In a nut shell, it is a string that is preceded by a number that tells you how long the string is. To use BSTRs is rather simple, but you have to make sure that you allocate and de-allocate the memory for them. There are several ways to do this. The most common is using ::SysAllocString to allocate the memory and ::SysFreeString to free it. I, on the other hand, like to use the _bstr_t wrapper. Using this allows you to completely ignore any of the allocating or de-allocating because it is all done for you. Let's use _bstr_t:

```
#include <comdef.h> // this is where the _bstr_t is
_bstr_t BstrHolder("this is a BSTR");
```

To get the char* from a _bstr_t, you simply cast it:

```
char *holder = (char*)BstrHolder;
```

We use this to pass the information to and from the COM object. Once you have it in the CGAdo class or in your client, you can convert it to whatever you like: char*, CString, whatever. We will only be using it to pass information (string information) to and from the COM server (and to and from ADO in our COM server). If you search for _bstr_t in VC Help, you will get the lowdown on what you can and cannot do with this.

This may be a good time to consider memory allocation and the BSTR. The BSTR is created with the same variation of ::SysAllocString. But who should create and who should delete the memory? Well, the rules are actually rather simple:

1. If a parameter is [in], the client must allocate and free the memory. The COM object cannot change it.

2. If the parameter is [out], the client must allocate it; the COM object can re-allocate it, but the client must free it.

3. If a variable is created internally in the COM object, the COM object must free it.

The VARIANT (and the Wrapper _variant_t)

This is a huge union of different data types. You have several different ints: bool, char char* IDispatch, date, and others. The _variant_t gives you a simple way of extracting the data from the VARIANT. This simple way is to cast the _variant_t variable into the data type you want. VARIANTs are used throughout VB and scripting languages. Once you get used to them, they are also rather useful in C++. We will use the VARIANT to pass information to and from the COM object when we are not using the simple data types or when we want a return that could be one of several different things (for example, a string or an error code number). The calling program can check the vt property of the VARIANT to see what data type it is and take the appropriate action. We will use this ability in our Recordset calls. But first let's take a look at creating a VARIANT using the _variant_t wrapper:

```
#include <comdef.h> // this is where the _bstr_t is
_bstr_t BstrHolder("this is a Bstr");
_variant_t Holder(BStrHolder)
```

or

```
_variant_t Holder;
Holder = BstrHolder;
// then to extract the information
char * cHolder = (char*)_bstr_t(Holder);
```

Basically, all we have done here is created a _bstr_t, made it into a _variant_t, and then converted it back using casts. Not a really functional example, but it demonstrated the point that the VARIANT holds different types of data and can easily (using _variant_t) extract that data, too. As mentioned before, this union ability is going to come in handy when we start passing different types back and forth to the COM objects.

The SAFEARRAY (Sorry, No Wrapper Here)

This is a way for us to easily pass arrays to and from a COM object. (Of course, *easy* is a relative term.) I personally think they stink, but they are what we are stuck with. This is how you use them. There are several parts to what everyone calls a SAFEAR-RAY. In actuality we are making a VARIANT of the type VT_ARRAY.

The SAFEARRAYBOUND is how you set the bounds of your array. You have to set the upper and lower bounds. First we create a SAFEARRAYBOUND showing how many dimensions it will have. You could look at each of the dimensions as a field in a record. So let's create a two-dimensional SAFEARRAY:

```
SAFEARRAYBOUND MyBound[2];
```

Now, for each of the dimensions, you have to tell it how big it is and whether we are starting the count at 0 or 1:

```
// First how many elements do we have?
MyBound[0].cElements = 10);
MyBound[1].cElements = 10;
// Are we starting our counting at 1 or 0?
MyBound[0].lLbound = 0;
MyBound[1].lLBound = 0;
```

So now we have set up an array with 2 columns and 10 rows. You could, in theory, make a safe array a duplicate of a recordset if you wanted. The next thing we have to do is initialize a VARIANT. This VARIANT can either be passed to us from the client application or created right here. Remember, we are only using the VARIANT as a safe array. You can also use a SAFEARRAY variable, but since we are passing it back to our client, we will use a VARIANT. We initialize it like this:

```
VariantInit(pVariant);
```

Now we have to tell the array what kind of data it will be holding. The SAFEARRAY can only hold one data type at a time. We are going to use an array of variants because by using the variant we actually have an array where each column can be a different data type. (See the article "Using a Multidimensional SAFEARRAY to Pass Data Across from COM Objects" written by Aravind Corera to get a little more in-depth with this idea.)

```
pVariant->vt = VT_VARIANT ¦ VT_ARRAY;
```

The next thing we do is create the safe array in the VARIANT. The parameters to the SafeArrayCreate function are the type of data it will hold, the dimensions, and the name of the bound that you just created:

```
pVariant->parray = SafeArrayCreate(VT_VARIANT,2,MyBound);
```

or

```
SAFEARRAY pArray = SafeArrayCreate(VT_VARIANT,2,MyBound);
➥// if you were using SAFEARRAY rather than a VARIANT
```

Okay, let's recap here: First we created a SAFEARRAYBOUND variable and set the bounds. Then a variable called pVariant was sent to us as a parameter (that's how we got it). We used VariantInit() to initialize pVariant, and then we set the vt member to VT_VARIANT | VT_ARRAY. Last, we created the SAFEARRAY as the variable in the VARIANT (pVariant). This was done using SafeArrayCreate(). We basically told the function to create a SAFEARRAY for us that will hold VARIANTs. (Remember, we are holding VARIANTs because we may have different data types and a VARIANT can hold many different data types.) The size of the array is 2×10, which is 2 columns and 10 rows.

Now we have to fill the array with something. You can do this any way you like: Manually put it in; do it through a loop of some sort; the choice is yours. I am just going to fill them manually for this sample, as I think it demonstrates exactly what is happening better. I create a VARIANT to use and then fill it with some data (in this case a BSTR, which is created with the SysAllocateString() function and an integer):

```
VARIANT Column1(SysAllocString("COW"));
VARIANT Column2(100);
```

Now we have to add this VARIANT to the array using the SafeArrayPutElement() function. The first parameter is a SAFEARRAY (now called pVariant->parray). The second parameter is an array of ints that matches the dimensions of the array we just created (int MyPosition[2]). The numbers in the two columns represent the position in your array, [0,0], [1,0], or whatever. The last parameter is the VARIANT you just made:

```
int MyPosition[2];
MyPosition[0] = 0;
MyPosition[1] = 0;
SafeArrayPutElement(pVariant->parray,MyPosition,&Column1);
MyPosition[0] = 1;
MyPosition[1] = 0;
Dimension[0] = 0;
SafeArrayPutElement(pVariant->parray,lDimension,&Column2);
```

Note the second element we put in was a number, so both of our columns contain different data types. Well, that is about it for SAFEARRAYs. They are convenient for passing structured data back to the client application, especially when sending information from COM to a VB application.

So let's move on now. Remember, the most important things to know about a SAFEARRAY are

- SAFEARRAYBOUND sets the bounds (upper and lower limits) of the SAFEARRAY.
- SAFEARRAY and VT_ARRAY are basically the same thing.
- You create a SAFEARRAY with the SafeArrayCreate() function. It takes three parameters: the data type, the dimensions, and the SAFEARRAYBOUND.
- You access items in the safe array with a dimension integer, which is an array of ints with the same dimensions as the SAFEARRAY.
- You use SafeArrayGetElement and SafeArrayPutElement to get and put the information into a SAFEARRAY item.

Now, Let's Move On to the Component

What Methods Do We Need?

Well, the answer to this question is up to you. We have a ton of them covering just about everything you can think of (or at least everything we could think of). In this article I will cover several different types so that you have an idea of what we will be doing. You can expand your personal version to include everything you think you need. First let's take a look at the opening and closing of the connection. We all have to do that.

Opening a Connection

In our ADO model, we have the rule that every ADO COM object knows what database it is supposed to talk to. So, by default, you need to send no parameters to the ADOOpenConnection method. We create the method by right-clicking on IADO and then choosing New Method. Out parameters are entered as

```
[in] BSTR ConnectionString, [in] BSTR UserId, [in] BSTR Password,
➥[out,retval] int *Result
```

The [in] means that this parameter is being sent from the client application, the out means that we are sending it back to the client, and retval means that this will appear as the returned value of the method to clients written in VB (and similar languages).

The client application sends us the connection string, the user ID, and the password, and the COM object will send back the result. Now let's look at the method and what we need to do to make it work:

```
STDMETHODIMP CADO:ADOOpenConnection(BSTR ConnectionString,
➡BSTR UserId, BSTR Password, int *Result)
{
    _bstr_t TempConnectionString(ConnectionString);
    if(TempConnectionString.length() <1)
    {
        // There is no connection string  This would normally be set
➡up to connect to the ADO main database
        // It will change with each ADO COM Object
        std::string Holder = "MY_DSN";
        // Now open the connection only if it is not already open
        try
        {
            if(m_Connection->State != adStateOpen)
            {
                HRESULT hr = m_Connection->Open
➡(_bstr_t(Holder.c_str()),_bstr_t("Admin"),_bstr_t("ORAIDERS"),-1);
                if(hr != S_OK)
                {
                    Result = 0;
                    return S_FALSE;
                }
            }
        }
        catch(_com_error &e){} // error handling here
        catch(...){}// all other exceptions here
        return S_OK;
    }
    else
    {
        try
        {
            m_Connection->Open(ConnectionString,UserId,Password,adAsyncConnect);
        }
        catch(_com_error &e){} // error handling here
        catch(...){}// all other exceptions here
        return S_OK;
    }
}
```

Let's look at what is happening here. First we put that nasty BSTR into a _bstr_t so that we can work with it a little easier. Then we check to see if there is anything in it. If not, we are using the default. If there is something in it, we will try to use what the user sent us. The next thing we do is simply use the ADO Open method, passing it with the default or what the user sent. Notice we are using the STD string template here for our strings. The error-checking we are doing should also be noted: *basically none*. You should send appropriate messages back to the client when there is an error. For no other reason than my laziness, I have only included the simplest catching of errors in this article. To call this method you do this:

VB:

```
Result = MyADOObject.ADOOpenConnection "","",""
```

VC:

```
MyADOObject->ADOOpenConnection("","","",&Result);
```

After this method is called, your COM object now has a connection to the database. So let's close it. Again we will add a method to the IADO interface by right-clicking on it, and then choosing New Method. This time there are no parameters, so we can just press OK. Let's look at the code:

```
STDMETHODIMP CADO::ADOCloseConnection()
{
    try
    {
        if(m_Connection->State == adStateOpen)
            m_Connection->Close();
    }
    catch(_com_error &e){} // error handling here
    catch(...){}// all other exceptions here
    return S_OK;
}
```

Again, we simply wrapped the ADO.Close() method with our wrapper. So now we can open and close a database connection.

Let's get it to do something. In our ADO COM object, we decided we would return information three different ways. The first would be to return the Recordset, the second would be to return a delimited string, and the third would be to return a specific piece of information (one value). We also decided that we needed to be able to run both a SQL query and a stored procedure. So with this in mind, we came up with these generic methods:

- **ADOExecuteReturnDelimited)(/*[in]*/ BSTR SQL, /*[in]*/ BSTR Delimiter, /*[out,retval]*/VARIANT *Result);** This function will run the Connection.Execute method and return a string delimited by whatever the user wants it delimited by (including nothing).
- **ADOExecute)(/*[in]*/ BSTR SQL, /*[out,retval]*/ _Recordset **Result);** This function will run the Connection.Execute method and return a _RecordsetPtr.

- **ADOExecuteSPReturnDelimited)(/*[in]*/ BSTR SPName, /*[in]*/ VARIANT ParameterArray, /*[in]*/BSTR Delimiter, /*[out,retval]*/ VARIANT *Result);**　This will run a stored procedure, passing it an array of parameters and returning a delimited string containing the result.
- **ADOExecuteSP)(/*[in]*/ BSTR SPName, /*[in]*/ VARIANT ParameterArray, /*[out,retval]*/ _Recordset **Result);**　This will run any stored procedure and return a _RecordsetPtr.
- **ADOGetVariant)(/*[in]*/ BSTR SQL, /*[out,retval]*/ VARIANT *Result);**　This will return one value of any type. By default this will be the first column in the first recordset of whatever SQL statement you send.

To create any of these, you do that right-click thing on the interface again and choose New Method. Then enter the parameters as listed above. But wait a second.... When you try to compile this, you will get an error stating that there is no such thing as a _Recordset. To fix this you will need to add several things to your application. First is a file called helper.h. This contains the following (exactly like this):

```
struct _Recordset;
#if !defined(__cplusplus) || defined(CINTERFACE)
typedef struct _Recordset _Recordset;
#endif
```

You will also need to create a helper.idl file that contains the following (exactly like this):

```
import "msado15.idl";
```

And in your ADO.h file you need to add

```
#include "helper.h"
```

And in your application.idl file you need to add

```
import "helper.idl";
```

The above allows you to pass a recordset back to the client application. There is a KB article on this. Also take a look at the article "Creating a Disconnected Recordset in C++ for VB" by Jeff Lundgren here at CodeGuru. It has the KB references too.

Once you have added this to your application, you are ready to compile and to pass recordsets back to the client application. Let's look at these methods:

```
STDMETHODIMP CADO::ADOExecute(BSTR SQL, _Recordset **Result)
{
    VARIANT RecordsEffected;
    RecordsEffected.vt = VT_INT;
    try
    {
```

```
            if(m_Recordset == NULL)
                m_Recordset.CreateInstance(__uuidof(Recordset));
            if(m_Recordset->State == adStateOpen)
                m_Recordset->Close();
            m_Recordset = m_Connection->Execute
➥(_bstr_t(SQL),&RecordsEffected,adCmdText);
            *Result = m_Recordset.Detach();
        }
        catch(_com_error &e){} // error handling here
        catch(...){}// all other exceptions here
    }
```

Okay, the first thing we do is make sure that our m_Recordset is valid and closed:

```
if(m_Recordset == NULL)
    m_Recordset.CreateInstance(__uuidof(Recordset));
if(m_Recordset->State == adStateOpen)
    m_Recordset->Close();
```

After that, we use the m_Connection Execute method, sending it the SQL string and the other parameters needed:

```
m_Recordset = m_Connection->Execute(_bstr_t(SQL),&RecordsEffected,adCmdText);
```

We then detach the global recordset from the Result (which is also a recordset):

```
*Result = m_Recordset.Detach();
```

You would use the following method:

VB:

```
Dim MySet as Object
Object = MyADOObject.ADOExecute("SELECT * FROM some_table")
```

VC:

```
_RecordsetPtr MySet;
MyADOObject->ADOExecute(_bstr_t("SELECT * FROM some_table),&MySet);
```

The method is pretty straightforward. All we are doing here is wrapping the Connection.Execute method and returning the result. This may be a good time to ask: Since this is actually so much more work then simply creating a connection and a recordset in the client, why go through all this trouble? To answer that, let's remember what we are actually building here. We are building a way for an application that has no knowledge of how our data is set up to be able to access that data via different methods in our COM object. The methods we are currently building (the ADO wrappers) will be used internally in the COM object to simplify writing these application-specific methods. I have included the ADO wrapper methods so that the client developer can access them; you may want to hide them from the client developer. The choice is yours. The bottom line is when we want to use the Execute function on our connection.

From this point on, we do not have to worry about anything but the SQL statement. A little less typing, and when you see some of the application-specific methods we will be using, the need for the ADO wrappers will be even more obvious.

Now let's look at the return delimited method:

```
STDMETHODIMP CADO::ADOExecuteReturnDelimited(BSTR SQL, BSTR Delimiter,
➥VARIANT *Result)
{
    VARIANT RecordsEffected;
    RecordsEffected.vt = VT_INT;
    *Result = _variant_t("");
    try
    {
        _RecordsetPtr PopSet;
        PopSet.CreateInstance(__uuidof(Recordset));
        PopSet->CursorLocation = adUseClient;
        if(m_Connection->State != adStateOpen)
        {
            *Result = _variant_t("VISP_COM_ERROR_CONNECTION_NOT_OPEN");
            return S_FALSE;
        }
        ADOExecute((char*)_bstr_t(SQL),&PopSet);
        if(!PopSet->adoEOF)
        {
            BSTR bstrResult = NULL;
            _bstr_t btColDelim(L",");
            _bstr_t btRowDelim(L"\r\n");
            _bstr_t btNullExp(L"");
            PopSet->raw_GetString(adClipString,-
➥1,btColDelim,btRowDelim,btNullExp,&bstrResult);
            *Result = _variant_t(bstrResult);
        }
        else
            *Result = _variant_t("");
    }
    catch(_com_error &e){} // error handling here
    catch(...){}// all other exceptions here
    return S_OK;
}
```

Okay, you can see here that we are using a local instance of a _RecordsetPtr.

```
_RecordsetPtr PopSet;
PopSet.CreateInstance(__uuidof(Recordset));
PopSet->CursorLocation = adUseClient;
```

We can do this because when we leave this method, we do not care about the record-set anymore; we already have the information we want in the BSTR we receive from the raw_GetString method. It is *important* to note here that there is a known bug in the GetString method that will sometimes throw an unhandled exception. You should not use the GetString method, but you can use the raw_GetString method. In this method we use *our* ADOExecute rather than the Connection.Execute method. There is no reason for this other than it takes less typing.

```
ADOExecute((char*)_bstr_t(SQL),&PopSet);
```

When we get our recordset back, we check to make sure there are records there, and then we use the raw_GetString method to convert the recordset into a delimited string.

```
if(!PopSet->adoEOF)
{
    BSTR bstrResult = NULL;
    _bstr_t btColDelim(L",");
    _bstr_t btRowDelim(L"\r\n");
    _bstr_t btNullExp(L"");
    PopSet->raw_GetString(adClipString,-1,btColDelim,btRowDelim,
➡btNullExp,&bstrResult);
    *Result = _variant_t(bstrResult);
}
else
    *Result = _variant_t("");
```

Now you can get some rather large recordsets into these strings. I have not played with it enough to see if there is a max size recordset you can return. If someone wants to do that, I would be interested in hearing what they find out. After we get the string, we send it back to the client application. A typical call to this method would be:

VB:

```
ResultString = MyADOObject.ADOExecuteReturnDelimited
➡("SELECT * FROM some_table",",")
```

VC:

```
BSTR ResultString;
MyADOObject->ADOExecuteReturnDelimited(_bstr_t("SELECT * FROM
➡some_table"),_bstr_t(","),&Result);
```

Okay, at this point we have created an ATL COM object, added ADO support to it, and added four methods (all of which simply wrap existing ADO methods). Now let's take a look at what we can do to make this more application specific. Let's say in your company several applications need a customer name and the current balance. In your application database they are kept in two tables, cust_info and cust_credit. The fields of importance are cust_info.cust_id, cust_info.cust_name, and lastly cust_credit.cust_balance. For another application to access this data, it needs to know the names of the tables, the names of the fields, and the fact that they are linked with cust_id.

Now, if we take this "intimate knowledge" about the database and application and put it into a method, we can give the client application the information and still hide it from the database. Let's create this new method:

```
STDMETHODIMP CADO::sGetCustomerNameAndBalance(BSTR CustKey, VARIANT *Result)
{
    // std stream used to create the SQL statement
    std::strstream SQL;
    // Put the BSTR into something we can deal with
    _bstr_t Holder(CustKey);
    SQL.str("");
    SQL<<"SELECT a.cust_name, b.cust_balance FROM cust_info as a, cust_credit
➡as b WHERE a.cust_id = '"<<(char*)Holder
➡<<"' AND a.cust_key = b.cust_key";
    ADOExecuteReturnDelimited(_bstr_t(SQL.str().c_str()),_bstr_t(","),Result);
    return S_OK;
}
```

Whoa, was that easy or what? Let's look at what we did here. First we created a strstream. This is an STD template that allows us to have a formatted string:

```
std::strstream SQL;
```

The next thing we did was convert the BSTR the client sent to us into a _bstr_t. I do this all the time because I think it is much easier to use _bstr_t than BSTR. There are other methods you can use, too. (CComBstr, I think, is one of them.) The choice is yours. I like _bstr_t.

Anyway, we know what the SQL statement needs to be to extract this information, the client should not need to know this. So we create our SQL statement using the strstream variable:

```
SQL.str("");// this resets it to nothing
SQL<<"SELECT a.cust_name, b.cust_balance FROM cust_info as a, cust_credit as
➡b WHERE a.cust_id = '"<<(char*)_bstr_t(CustKey)
➡<<"' AND a.cust_key = b.cust_key";
```

Then the last thing we do is call the ADOExecuteReturnDelimited() method we created a few minutes ago to run the query and return a delimited string:

```
ADOExecuteReturnDelimited(_bstr_t(SQL.str().c_str()),_bstr_t(","),Result);
```

So now we have a method in our COM object that will return important information to the client application, but will hide from the client anything it doesn't need to know about our database. Of course the client application had to know that we had the COM object, that there was a method that got the information they needed, and that this method required them to send the customer ID. But that information should be given out with your ADO COM object to the client developers. So let's see what this takes from VB and from VC:

VB:

```
MyResult = MyADOObject.sGetCustomerNameAndBalance(SomeCustID)
```

VC:

```
VARIANT MyResult;
MyADOObject.->sGetCustomerNameAndBalance(SomeCustID,MyResult);
```

Now this example was rather simple, but I think you can see the power that an ADO COM object could have. The client application did not (necessarily) need to know the connection information, the table names, how to use a recordset, how to extract the information from the recordset, or anything about SQL to get the information. It needed one call to a method in our COM object, knowing that it needed to send a customer ID and that it would get back a comma-delimited string containing the customer name and the balance.

What we have done with most of our application-specific functions (the ones dealing with our application and our database) is to create two methods that are identical. One will return a delimited string (the method name is prefixed with an *s*); the other will return a recordset. Let's look at the sister to this function that will return a recordset rather than a delimited string:

```
STDMETHODIMP CADO::sGetCustomerNameAndBalance
➥(BSTR CustKey, _Recordset **Result)
{
    // std stream used to create the SQL statement
    std::strstream SQL;
    // Put the BSTR into something we can deal with
    _bstr_t Holder(CustKey);
    SQL.str("");
    SQL<<"SELECT a.cust_name, b.cust_balance FROM cust_info as a,
➥cust_credit as b WHERE a.cust_id = '"<<(char*)
➥Holder<<"' AND a.cust_key = b.cust_key";
    ADOExecute(_bstr_t(SQL.str().c_str()),_bstr_t(","),Result);
    return S_OK;
}
```

The only difference is that we use our ADOExecute method rather than the delimiter method, and our retval parameter is a _Recordset rather than a VARIANT. To call this from our client would look something like this:

VB:

```
dim MySet as object
MySet = MyADOObject.GetCustomerNameAndBalance(CustID)
```

VC:

```
_RecorsetPtr MySet;
MyADOObject->GetCustomerNameAndBalance(CustID,&MySet);
```

Okay, now we have a way to run SQL statements from the client application, but what about running a stored procedure? To do this we have to create two methods. One will run a stored procedure and return a delimited string; the other will return a recordset. Let's look at the recordset method first:

```
STDMETHODIMP CADO::ADOExecuteSP(BSTR SPName, VARIANT ParameterString,
➥_Recordset **Result)
{
    VARIANT RecordsEffected;
    RecordsEffected.vt = VT_INT;
    if(m_Recordset == NULL)
        m_Recordset.CreateInstance(__uuidof(Recordset));
    if(m_Recordset->State == adStateOpen)
        m_Recordset->Close();
    try
    {
        // Now set up the command object
        m_Command->ActiveConnection = m_Connection;
        // enter the SP name
        m_Command->CommandText = _bstr_t(SPName);
        // Now execute it
        m_Recordset = m_Command-
➥>Execute(&RecordsEffected,&ParameterString,adCmdStoredProc);
        *Result = m_Recordset.Detach();
    }
    catch(_com_error &e){} // error handling here
    catch(...){}// all other exceptions here
    return S_OK;
}
```

Okay, let's see what we did here. The beginning of this method looks like our SQL method. We made sure our global recordset was valid, but not open.

```
if(m_Recordset == NULL)
    m_Recordset.CreateInstance(__uuidof(Recordset));
if(m_Recordset->State == adStateOpen)
    m_Recordset->Close();
```

After this we set up our command variable by setting the ActiveConnection and entering the name of the stored procedure we wanted to use.

```
// Now set up the command object
m_Command->ActiveConnection = m_Connection;
// enter the SP name
m_Command->CommandText = _bstr_t(SPName);
```

Last, we have to run the Command.Execute method sending the parameters, and then populate the Result we are sending back.

```
m_Recordset = m_Command->Execute(&RecordsEffected,&ParameterString,
➥adCmdStoredProc);
*Result = m_Recordset.Detach();
```

Let's take a look at this parameter list. The parameter we need to send is an array of
VARIANTs (hmmm…SAFEARRAY). In VB it is really easy to do this:

VB:

```
dim MySet as Object
MySet = MyADOObject.ADOExecuteSP("some_stored_procedure",
➥Array("param_1",2,"param_3))
```

VC:

```
SAFEARRAYBOUND MyBound[1];
MyBound[0].cElements = 2);
MyBound[0].lLbound = 0;
VARIANT ParamHolder;
VariantInit(ParamHolder);
ParamHolder->vt = VT_VARIANT ¦ VT_ARRAY;
pVariant->parray = SafeArrayCreate(VT_VARIANT,2,MyBound);

VARIANT Param1(SysAllocString("123ABC"));
VARIANT Param2(100);

int MyPosition;
MyPosition = 0;
SafeArrayPutElement(pVariant->parray,MyPosition,&Param1);
SafeArrayPutElement(pVariant->parray,lDimension,&Param2);

_RecordsetPtr MySet;
MyADOObject->ADOExecuteSP(_bstr_t("some_stored_procedure"),ParamHolder,&MySet);
```

Quite a bit more work from VC, but not too bad. The majority of what you have to
do here is setting up the SAFEARRAY. This is what I do not like about the
SAFEARRAY. It is just way too much work to do something relatively simple. Once
you have the SAFEARRAY, though, the call to run the stored procedure is just as
simple in VC as it is in VB. Of course we have to have a sister method to this that will
return a delimited string. It looks like this:

```
STDMETHODIMP CADO::ADOExecuteSPReturnDelimited(BSTR SPName,
➥VARIANT ParameterArray, BSTR Delimiter, VARIANT *Result)
{
    VARIANT RecordsEffected;
    RecordsEffected.vt = VT_INT;
    *Result = _variant_t("");
    try
    {
        _RecordsetPtr PopSet;
        PopSet.CreateInstance(__uuidof(Recordset));
        PopSet->CursorLocation = adUseClient;
        if(m_Connection->State != adStateOpen)
        {
            *Result = _variant_t("VISP_COM_ERROR_CONNECTION_NOT_OPEN");
            return S_FALSE;
        }
```

```
                // Now set up the command object
                m_Command->ActiveConnection = m_Connection;
                // enter the SP name
                m_Command->CommandText = _bstr_t(SPName);
                // Now execute it

                PopSet = m_Command->Execute(&RecordsEffected,
➥&ParameterArray,adCmdStoredProc);
                if(!PopSet->adoEOF)
                {
                    BSTR bstrResult = NULL;
                    _bstr_t btColDelim(Delimiter);
                    _bstr_t btRowDelim(L"\r\n");
                    _bstr_t btNullExp(L"");
                    PopSet->raw_GetString(adClipString,-
➥1,btColDelim,btRowDelim,btNullExp,&bstrResult);
                    *Result = _variant_t(bstrResult);
                }
                else
                    *Result = _variant_t("");
        }
        catch(_com_error &e){} // error handling here
        catch(...){}// all other exceptions here

        return S_OK;
}
```

Again, you can see the similarity between the SQL execute methods and the stored procedure methods. To save a ton of typing, I am not going to walk through the code on this method. After looking at the code, I am sure that you can see what we are doing based on what I have already explained. Here is how you would call this from your clients:

VB:

```
MyResult = MyADOObject.ADOExecuteSPReturnDelimited("some_stored_procedure",
➥Array("param_1",2,"param_3"), ",")
```

VC:

```
SAFEARRAYBOUND MyBound[1];
MyBound[0].cElements = 2);
MyBound[0].lLbound = 0;
VARIANT ParamHolder;
VariantInit(ParamHolder);
ParamHolder->vt = VT_VARIANT | VT_ARRAY;
pVariant->parray = SafeArrayCreate(VT_VARIANT,2,MyBound);

VARIANT Param1(SysAllocString("123ABC");
VARIANT Param2(100);
```

```
int MyPosition;
MyPosition = 0;
SafeArrayPutElement(pVariant->parray,MyPosition,&Param1);
SafeArrayPutElement(pVariant->parray,lDimension,&Param2);
VARIANT MyResult;;
MyADOObject->ADOExecuteSPReturnDelimited(_bstr_t("some_stored_procedure"),
➥ParamHolder,_bstr_t(","),&MyResult);
```

Okay, now let's take the last step. Let's make an ADO-specific method that will return both a recordset and a delimited string based on a stored procedure. You will see since we have created our ADO stored procedure wrappers, creating an ADO-specific function will be easy. We are going to create an ADO-specific method that will run a stored procedure that takes one parameter. The client application only sees a method that asks for a Rep key. It expects to get a recordset containing all information about that employee. In our database we have created a stored procedure called GetEmployeeInfo. It takes one parameter, that is the employee ID.

```
STDMETHODIMP CADO::GetEmployeeName(BSTR RepKey, _Recordset **Result)
{
    SAFEARRAYBOUND MyBound[0];
    MyBound[0].cElements = 1);
    VARIANT ParamHolder;
    VariantInit(ParamHolder);
    ParamHolder->vt = VT_VARIANT | VT_ARRAY;
    pVariant->parray = SafeArrayCreate(VT_VARIANT,1,MyBound);
    VARIANT Param1(RepKey);
    int MyPosition;
    MyPosition = 0;
    SafeArrayPutElement(pVariant->parray,MyPosition,&Param1);
    ADOExecuteSP(_bstr_t("GetEmployeeInfo"),ParamHolder,Result);
}
```

Okay, what we have done here is we created a SAFEARRAY of VARIANTs, added one item (the BSTR sent to us from the client), and used the ADOExecuteSP method we just created. Let's see the client code needed to make this work:

VB:

```
dim MySet as Object
MySet = MyADOObject.GetEmployeeInfo("123ABC")
```

VC:

```
_RecordsetPtr MySet;
MyADOObject->GetEmployeeInfo(_bstr_t("123ABC"),&MySet);
```

The client application has it really easy. It does not need to know the name of the stored procedure, the parameters it takes, how to use the Command object, and in the case of the VC client, how to use SAFE arrays. Quite a bit of time saved. You can wrap all of the stored procedures you want with methods like these. The client application needs to know nothing. Of course we can also return a delimited string if we want to with a similar method:

```
STDMETHODIMP CADO::sGetEmployeeName(BSTR RepKey, VARIANT *Result)
{
    SAFEARRAYBOUND MyBound[0];
    MyBound[0].cElements = 1);
    VARIANT ParamHolder;
    VariantInit(ParamHolder);
    ParamHolder->vt = VT_VARIANT ¦ VT_ARRAY;
    pVariant->parray = SafeArrayCreate(VT_VARIANT,1,MyBound);
    VARIANT Param1(RepKey);
    int MyPosition;
    MyPosition = 0;
    SafeArrayPutElement(pVariant->parray,MyPosition,&Param1);
    ADOExecuteSPReturnDelimited(_bstr_t("GetEmployeeInfo"),
➡ParamHolder,_bstr_t(","),Result);
}
```

And the call from the clients:

VB:

```
MyResult = MyADOObject.GetEmployeeInfo("123ABC")
```

VC:

```
VARIANT MyResult;
MyADOObject->GetEmployeeInfo(_bstr_t("123ABC"),&MyResult);
```

Okay, let's look at what we now know:

1. Making an ATL COM object is really simple. Basically follow the wizards and you are done.

2. We can add an interface through the wizard and add both properties and methods to the interface by following some simple steps.

3. We can add ADO to our ATL project just as simply as we can add it to any application.

4. We know how to pass VARIANTs, BSTRs, and SAFEARRAYs to methods we create.

5. We know the difference in calling our methods from VB and VC.

6. We know how to use the SAFEARRAY, _bstr_t, and _variant_t.

7. We know how to wrap the ADOExecute method to return either a recordset or a delimited string based on a query.

8. We know how to access stored procedures through the command interface and return either a recordset or a delimited string.

9. We know how to use methods to hide the database from the client, eliminating the need for them to understand anything about the database.

FROM THE FORUM

Question (bayram):

I am trying to retrieve binary data from a database using ADO. How can I do this?

Answer (Tamer Omari):

One method is by using stream interface as shown:

```
pRecSet .... // perform a query

_StreamPtr pStm(__uuidof(Stream));
_variant_t varOptional(DISP_E_PARAMNOTFOUND,VT_ERROR);
pStm->Type =adTypeBinary;

hr = pStm->raw_Open(varOptional, adModeUnknown,
    adOpenStreamUnspecified,NULL,NULL);
hr = pStm->Write(pRecSet->GetCollect(L"Field"));

pRecSet->Close(); // you can close the recordset now
```

At this point your data can be accessed through the stream interface.

Now for a Cool Trick

Now I will show you one more really cool trick. We use our ADO COM object all the time when developing ASP Web pages. Also on our Web pages, we use tables all the time. Now I will show you how to make a table based on any query or any stored procedure! Check this out:

```
STDMETHODIMP CADO::ADOMakeWebTable(BSTR SQL, VARIANT *Result)
{
    VARIANT RecordsEffected;
    RecordsEffected.vt = VT_INT;
    BSTR bstrResult = NULL;
    std::strstream Holder;
    try
    {
        _RecordsetPtr PopSet;
        PopSet.CreateInstance(__uuidof(Recordset));
        PopSet->CursorLocation = adUseClient;
        if(m_Connection->State != adStateOpen)
        {
            *Result = _variant_t("VISP_COM_ERROR_CONNECTION_NOT_OPEN");
            return S_FALSE;
        }
        PopSet = m_Connection->Execute((char*)_bstr_t(SQL),
➥&RecordsEffected,adCmdText);
        if(!PopSet->adoEOF)
        {
            _bstr_t btColDelim(L"</TD><TD>");
            _bstr_t btRowDelim(L"</TD></TR><TR><TD>");
```

```
        _bstr_t btNullExp(L"");
        PopSet->raw_GetString(adClipString,-
➡1,btColDelim,btRowDelim,btNullExp,&bstrResult);
        Holder.str("");
        Holder<<"<TABLE BORDER="<<m_Border<<" BGCOLOR="<<(char*)
➡m_BGColor<<" STYLE='color="<<(char*)m_FGColor<<"'><TR>
➡<TD>"<<(char*)_bstr_t(bstrResult)<<"</TD></TR></TABLE>";
        *Result = _variant_t(_bstr_t(Holder.str().c_str()));
    }
    else
        *Result = _variant_t("");
}
catch(_com_error &e){} // error handling here
catch(...){}// all other exceptions here

return S_OK;
}
```

Okay, what this method does is it allows the ASP to create a table based on any query. The call from ASP is like this:

ASP:

```
Response.write MyADOObject.ADOMakeWebTable("SELECT * FROM some_table")
```

By adding that one line of code, you have made a table on your Web page based on the SQL. There is nothing else for you to do. We use this all the time!

As a matter of fact, we have a method that will allow us to change the parameters of the Web table:

```
STDMETHODIMP CADO::ADOSetWebTableInfo(int Border, BSTR FGColor, BSTR BGColor)
{
    // This is where we set up the variables for the WEB tables
    if(Border <0 || Border > 5)
        m_Border = 0;
    else
        m_Border = Border;
    m_FGColor = FGColor;
    m_BGColor = BGColor;
    return S_OK;
}
```

This method allows me to change the border size and foreground and background colors of the Web table. You can easily add more options to this if you like. Because you are using the Response.write method, any styles that you are using will be carried over to the Web table. I cannot tell you how much time this little method can (and will) save us!

Here is the version for creating a Web table from a stored procedure:

```
STDMETHODIMP CADO::ADOMakeSPWebTable(BSTR SPName, VARIANT ParamArray,
➥VARIANT *Result)
{
    VARIANT RecordsEffected;
    RecordsEffected.vt = VT_INT;
    BSTR bstrResult = NULL;
    std::strstream Holder;
    *Result = _variant_t("");
    try
    {
        _RecordsetPtr PopSet;
        PopSet.CreateInstance(__uuidof(Recordset));
        PopSet->CursorLocation = adUseClient;
        if(m_Connection->State != adStateOpen)
        {
            *Result = _variant_t("VISP_COM_ERROR_CONNECTION_NOT_OPEN");
            return S_FALSE;
        }
        // Now set up the command object
        m_Command->ActiveConnection = m_Connection;
        // enter the SP name
        m_Command->CommandText = _bstr_t(SPName);
        // Now execute it

        PopSet = m_Command->Execute(&RecordsEffected,&ParamArray,
➥adCmdStoredProc);
        if(!PopSet->adoEOF)
        {
            _bstr_t btColDelim(L"</TD><TD>");
            _bstr_t btRowDelim(L"</TD></TR><TR><TD>");
            _bstr_t btNullExp(L"");
            PopSet->raw_GetString(adClipString,-
➥1,btColDelim,btRowDelim,btNullExp,&bstrResult);
            Holder.str("");
            Holder<<"<TABLE BORDER="<<m_Border<<" BGCOLOR="<<(char*)m_BGColor
➥<<" STYLE='color="<<(char*)m_FGColor<<"'><TR><TD>"
➥<<(char*)_bstr_t(bstrResult)<<"</TD></TR></TABLE>";
            *Result = _variant_t(_bstr_t(Holder.str().c_str()));
        }
        else
            *Result = _variant_t("");
    }
    catch(_com_error &e){} // error handling here
    catch(...){}// all other exceptions here

    return S_OK;
}
```

And of course, you can wrap these with application-specific methods like this:

```
STDMETHODIMP CADO::GetEmployeeTable(VARIANT *Result)
{
    ADOMakeSPWebTable(_bstr_t("EmployeeList"),m_vNull,Result);
    return S_OK;
}
```

Now you have given the client application the ability to make a table on a Web page with one call like this:

ASP:

```
Response.Write MyADOObject.GetEmployeeTable()
```

Conclusion

If you have made it this far, I hope something in this article has helped you. I have tried to cover the basics for you and hope that you will find ADO a little easier after reading this article. I wish there were some more books on ADO. Heck, who knows? Maybe I will get off my butt and write one. But until that time, have fun with ADO and ATL. Once you start to get an understanding of how they work, you will find that they really are not that bad. Good luck with your programming!

Creating Database Objects Using ADOX

This article was contributed by J. Smits.

Environment: VC6 SP5

This code creates an MDB with three tables in it using ADOX.

General

ADOX stands for *extended ADO*. It extends ADO in that you can create tables, databases, columns, and so on without the use of Create Table–like SQL statements.

Steps

1. Use AppWizard to create an MFC application. Make it dialog based.

2. In AppWizard, be sure to leave Include ActiveX Controls checked.

   (This is apparently needed to communicate with ADOX, which is also true for ADO.)

3. Paste this statement into your StdAfx.h file:

```
#import "C:\Program Files\Common Files\System\ado\msadox.dll"
    no_namespace rename("EOF", "EndOfFile")
```

(Check whether the path is valid for your system.)

(Check other sites at CodeGuru if you want to omit the full path.)

4. Make sure you have the following lines in your InitInstance function:

```
BOOL CADOXApp::InitInstance()
{
  AfxEnableControlContainer();

  if (!AfxOleInit())
  {
    return FALSE;
  }
}
```

In your CPP file:

This code supposes the existence of

- A dialog called CADOXDlg
- A button called Createmdb
- Four edit boxes where the user will add the MDB filename and the name of the three tables

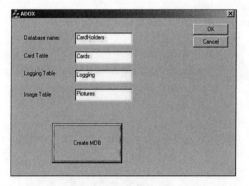

Figure 31.1

```
void CADOXDlg::OnCreatemdb()
{
  //Create MDB file with 3 tables, using ADOX! Leuk, leuk, leuk.

  char cDBName[80], cCardsTable[80],
       cLoggingTable[80], cImageTable[80];
```

```
//Read contents of Editboxes into their variables:
UpdateData(TRUE);

strcpy(cDBName,m_sMDBName);
strcpy(cCardsTable,m_sTable1);
strcpy(cLoggingTable,m_sTable2);
strcpy(cImageTable,m_sTable3,79);

// Define ADOX object pointers to Catalog (Database),
//   Table and Column objects.
_CatalogPtr m_pCatalog  = NULL;
_TablePtr m_pTable  = NULL;
_ColumnPtr m_pColumn  = NULL;

//Create object instances:
m_pCatalog.CreateInstance(__uuidof (Catalog));
m_pTable.CreateInstance(__uuidof (Table));

//Create Database
m_pCatalog->Create((const char *)(CString(
        "Provider=Microsoft.Jet.OLEDB.4.0;Data Source=F:\\") +
        cDBName + ".mdb"));

//Create First table
m_pTable->PutName(cCardsTable);

m_pTable->Columns->Append("EmpID",adInteger,0); //Third argument is
                                                //sort of optional.
                                                //Enter '0' if not
                                                //specified.
m_pTable->Columns->Append("FirstName",adVarWChar,30);
m_pTable->Columns->Append("LastName",adVarWChar,30);
m_pTable->Columns->Append("Address",adVarWChar,24);
m_pTable->Columns->Append("City",adVarWChar,24);
m_pCatalog->Tables->Append(_variant_t((IDispatch *)m_pTable));
m_pTable  = NULL;        //Reset pointer so as to use again

//Create Second table
m_pTable.CreateInstance(__uuidof (Table));
m_pTable->PutName(cLoggingTable);

m_pTable->Columns->Append("ID",adInteger,0);
m_pTable->Columns->Append("FirstName",adVarWChar,30);
m_pTable->Columns->Append("LastName",adVarWChar,30);
m_pTable->Columns->Append("Address",adVarWChar,24);
m_pTable->Columns->Append("City",adVarWChar,24);
m_pTable->Columns->Append("ChangedBy",adVarWChar,24);
m_pCatalog->Tables->Append(_variant_t((IDispatch *)m_pTable));
m_pTable  = NULL;

//Create Third table
m_pTable.CreateInstance(__uuidof (Table));
m_pTable->PutName(cImageTable);
```

```
    m_pTable->Columns->Append("ID",adInteger,0);
    m_pTable->Columns->Append("Length",adInteger,0);
    m_pTable->Columns->Append("Picture",adLongVarBinary,0);
    m_pTable->Columns->Append("Type",adInteger,0);
    m_pCatalog->Tables->Append(_variant_t((IDispatch *)m_pTable));
    m_pTable  = NULL;
}
```

Comments

To define a field within a table as being the primary key, use the following code sample:

```
pTable->Columns->Append("ID",adInteger, 0);
pTable->Keys->Append("PK", adKeyPrimary, "ID", "", "");
```

—Boris

It is possible that there could be problems with the connection string for Microsoft Access databases with different versions. You may need to change the following string to the value of 4 for the database engine if you are using Access 2000, for example. The sample shown uses 3.5, which is appropriate for Access 97.

```
m_pCatalog->Create((const char *) (CString("Provider=Microsoft.
➥Jet.OLEDB.3.5;Data Source=F:\\") + cDBName + ".mdb"));
```

—J. Smits

32

ODBC

In this chapter

Open Database Connectivity, or ODBC, is a C programming interface to access a variety of database management systems. Active Data Objects, or ADOs, were developed to provide a single easy-to-use approach to using a wide variety of data sources, programming tools, and platforms.

The benefit of using ODBC is its open nature in dealing with a large number of diverse data sources from many independent vendors.

- "Interactive SQL Tool (Using MFC)" describes a query tool that can be used to query ODBC data sources, author SQL scripts, and queries.

Interactive SQL Tool (Using MFC)

This article was contributed by George Poulose.

Environment: Visual C++ 5 (and above)

Interactive SQL is a query tool that allows you to query ODBC data sources, author SQL scripts, and queries and to return query results to a grid or text, retrieve ODBC driver information, execute multiple SQL scripts or stored procedures simultaneously, retrieve multiple query result sets (depends on the data source), and so on.

Acknowledgments

Thanks to Ronald Pihlgren of Microsoft Corporation for his ODBCInfo MFC database sample.

FROM THE FORUM

Question (hongcheng):

I am using ODBC to open a database. I would like to query the connection to determine the driver name, DSN, and login name. How can I do this?

Answer (ALM):

You can use SQLGetInfo to query the connection string as follows:

```
CString strInfo;
SWORD nResult;

AFX_SQL_SYNC(::SQLGetInfo(m_db.m_hdbc, SQL_DBMS_NAME,
    strInfo.GetBuffer(MAX_TNAME_LEN), MAX_TNAME_LEN, &nResult));
strInfo.ReleaseBuffer();
```

Use SQL_DATA_SOURCE_NAME and SQL_USER_NAME in place of the SQL_DBMS_NAME shown to query the DSN and login name.

FROM THE FORUM

Question (AnOnYmOuS):

How can I get a list of all the ODBC DSNs on the local machine?

Answer (PeterK):

This will retrieve all DSNs stored on the local machine:

```
HENV hEnv;
UCHAR tmpDSN[256];
SWORD tmpDSNLen = 255;
SWORD ResultLen;
UCHAR tmpDriver[256];
SWORD tmpDriverLen = 255;
SWORD ResultDescLen;
RETCODE ReturnCode = SQL_SUCCESS;

ReturnCode = ::SQLAllocEnv(&hEnv);
if (SQL_SUCCESS == ReturnCode)
{
    ReturnCode = ::SQLDataSources(hEnv, SQL_FETCH_FIRST, tmpDSN, tmpDSNLen,
        &ResultLen, tmpDriver, tmpDriverLen, &ResultDescLen);

    while (SQL_SUCCESS == ReturnCode)
    {
        //
        // Store tmpDSN to your list or array here.
        //

        ReturnCode = ::SQLDataSources(hEnv, SQL_FETCH_NEXT, tmpDSN,
            tmpDSNLen, &ResultLen, tmpDriver, tmpDriverLen,
            &ResultDescLen);
    }
}

::SQLFreeEnv(hEnv);
```

33

Stored Procedures

In this chapter

Stored procedures are scripted functions that are stored within the database and called as needed by client applications.

This type of stored procedure has potentially huge performance gains for certain types of client/server-based applications.

- "Executing Stored Procedures Using ADO" describes the use of stored procedures using ADO.

Executing Stored Procedures Using ADO

This article was contributed by Chakrapani Ramachandran.

chakrapani@rocketmail.com

2323 West Dunlap Avenue, #174

Phoenix, AZ 85021

ActiveX Data Objects (ADOs) enable you to write a client application to access and manipulate data in a database server through a provider.

ADO's primary benefits are ease of use, high speed, low memory overhead, and a small disk footprint.

This sample project is for ADODB, an implementation of ADO optimized for use with Microsoft OLE DB providers, including the Microsoft ODBC provider for OLE DB.

Using this we can execute stored procedures, pass arguments, and retrieve value. To use this sample, you will have to create the two stored procedures mentioned next.

For using this project, you need MFC 5.0 *or* above plus ADO in your machine.

```
{
    CString strTmp;

    CString m_sdatasource; // Data source name
    CString m_sUserID;     // User Id
    CString m_sPassword;   // Password
```

```
    // GET the above values from the user
    //Without creating Datasource we can use database by the following code
    /* strTmp.Format( "driver={sql server};"
                      "server=%s;"
                      "Database=%s;""UID=%s;""PWD=%s;",
                      m_server,m_sdatabase,m_sUserID,m_sPassword );*/

    strTmp.Format( "dsn=%s;""UID=%s;""PWD=%s;",m_sdatasource,m_sUserID,
➡m_sPassword );
    _bstr_t          bstrSQLServerConnect;
    _bstr_t bstrProc =( L"sp_StartByteImport" );;  //Stored procedure name
    _variant_t Final;
    bstrSQLServerConnect = (LPCTSTR) strTmp;
    m_status="Empty File";
    _ConnectionPtr  Conn1; // connection object pointer
    _CommandPtr     Cmd1;  // command object pointer
    _RecordsetPtr   Rs1; // recordset object pointer
    bool            bvalid = false;
    try
    {
        Conn1.CreateInstance( __uuidof( Connection ) ); // Instantiating
➡connection object
        Conn1->ConnectionString = bstrSQLServerConnect; // giving the
➡sqlconnection
        Conn1->Open( bstrEmpty, bstrEmpty, bstrEmpty ); // open the
➡connection object
        Cmd1.CreateInstance( __uuidof( Command ) ); // creating command
➡object
        Cmd1->ActiveConnection = Conn1;             // giving the connection
➡handle
        Cmd1->CommandText       = _bstr_t( bstrProc ); // passing the stored
➡procedure
        Cmd1->CommandType       = adCmdStoredProc;     // type
        Cmd1->Parameters->Refresh();                   // passing string value
➡as argument to stored procedure
        Cmd1->Parameters->Item[ _variant_t( (long) 1 ) ]->Value =
➡ _variant_t( (LPCTSTR)m_sfilename );
        Rs1 = Cmd1->Execute( &vtEmpty, &vtEmpty2, adCmdUnknown ); //
➡executing the stored procedure and storing the recordset value
        bvalid = true;
        Final = Rs1->Fields->GetItem( _variant_t( 0L ) )->Value; // getting
➡the first column value of the result row
        strTmp.Format( "%s", CrackStrVariant( Final) ); // to see the value
        // put your code to see all column values
    }
    catch( CException *e ) // trapping all error messages
    {
        TCHAR    szCause[255];
      e->GetErrorMessage(szCause, 255);
        m_status=szCause;
    }
    catch( _com_error &e )
    {
```

```
                m_status=e.ErrorMessage( );
        }
        catch(...)
        {
                m_status="Error while executing the Import";

        }
            //we need to create the stored procedures below before running the
➥application
                //CREATE PROCEDURE sp_AddAccountingInfo @nfinal int, @pcDate datetime,
                //@pcURL varchar (250), @pcTop varchar (250),
                //@pcQueryString varchar (250), @pcBytes int, @pcRequests int AS
                /*
                        Do your operation here
                */
                //CREATE PROCEDURE sp_AddAccountingInfo
                //@nfinal int,
                //@pcDate datetime,
                //@pcURL varchar (250),
                //@pcTop varchar (250),
                //@pcQueryString varchar (250),
                //@pcBytes int,
                //@pcRequests int
                //AS
                /*
                        Put your code here
                */
        }
```

Comments

To provide this functionality when using a Microsoft Access database, you may need to change the sample code as follows:

```
_Recordset* CADORecordsetFromQuery::OpenQueryWithKey(LPCTSTR lpszQueryName,
➥long lKey)
{
    // Create a command object
    _CommandPtr pCommand = _CommandPtr("ADODB.Command");
    pCommand->PutActiveConnection(m_qConnection.GetInterfacePtr());
    pCommand->PutCommandText(lpszQueryName);

    // Now query the database
    _variant_t vtRecordsAffected(0L);
    COleVariant varParams(lKey);
    m_pRecordset = pCommand->Execute(&vtRecordsAffected, &varParams,
➥adCmdUnknown);

    return m_pRecordset;
}
```

—Paul Wolfensberger

FROM THE FORUM

Question (VGirish):

How can I get a list of the available stored procedures in a database?

Answer (avm):

There are a couple of ways to do this. Using SQLProcedures, use the following code:

```
RETCODE rc;
HENV henv;
HDBC hdbc;
HSTMT hstmt;
rc=SQLAllocEnv(&henv);
rc=SQLAllocConnect(henv,&hdbc);
rc=SQLSetConnectOption( hdbc,SQL_LOGIN_TIMEOUT,5 );

rc=SQLConnect(hdbc,(unsigned char *)"dstest",SQL_NTS,(unsigned char *)
➥"user1",SQL_NTS,(unsigned char*)"user123",SQL_NTS);
rc=SQLAllocStmt(hdbc,&hstmt);
short a,b,c;

rc= SQLProcedures(hstmt,NULL,a,NULL,b,NULL,c);
char dbname[21];
char owner[21];
char name[50];

rc=SQLBindCol(hstmt,1,SQL_C_CHAR,dbname,21,(long *)&a);
rc=SQLBindCol(hstmt,2,SQL_C_CHAR,owner,21,(long *)&a);
rc=SQLBindCol(hstmt,3,SQL_C_CHAR,name,50,(long *)&a);

while ((rc = SQLFetch(hstmt)) != SQL_NO_DATA_FOUND)
{

    AfxMessageBox(name );
    //name is the stored procedure name

}

rc=SQLFreeStmt(hstmt,NULL);
rc=SQLDisconnect(hdbc);
rc=SQLFreeConnect(hdbc);
rc=SQLFreeEnv(henv);
```

Alternatively, you can run the following query on either SQL Server or Oracle to retrieve a list of all stored procedures:

```
SELECT name FROM sysobjects WHERE type = 'p'
```

FROM THE FORUM

Question (olstar):

How can I return a value from a stored procedure into a variable in my application?

Answer (Alex Fedotov):

1. Construct a SQL statement that uses the ODBC CALL escape sequence. The statement uses parameter markers for each input, input/output, and output parameter, and for the procedure return value (if any):

   ```
   {? = CALL procname (?,?)}
   ```

2. Call SQLBindParameter for each input, input/output, and output parameter, and for the procedure return value (if any).

3. Execute the statement with SQLExecDirect.

The following code demonstrates these steps:

```
SQLRETURN rcd;
DWORD ProcRet = 0, OParm = 0;
long cbProcRet = 0, cbOParm = 0;

// Bind the return code
rcd = SQLBindParameter(hstmt, 1, SQL_PARAM_OUTPUT,
SQL_C_SLONG, SQL_INTEGER, 0, 0, &ProcRet, 0, &cbProcRet);

// Bind the output parameter
rcd = SQLBindParameter(hstmt, 2, SQL_PARAM_OUTPUT,
SQL_C_SLONG, SQL_INTEGER, 0, 0, &OParm, 0, &cbOParm);

// First ? marks the return code,
// second ? marks the output parameter
rcd = SQLExecDirect(hstmt, "{? = call odbcproc(?)}", SQL_NTS);
```

34

XML

In this chapter

Extensible Markup Language, or XML, is similar to HTML in its use of tags, and is a standard for encoding data.

XML is emerging as an accepted standard for transferring data between applications on a local and network level. Because of its rich hierarchical design and unlimited set of tags, XML is being used in progressively more applications, including across the Internet.

- "Creating XML Files from C++ Programs" provides a mechanism used to generate XML files from within an application.
- "Using the Microsoft XML Parser to Create XML Documents" describes generating XML documents using the Microsoft MXXMLWriter.

Creating XML Files from C++ Programs

This article was contributed by Petko Popov.

Environment: Win32, MSVC 6.0, STL

Sometimes it is necessary to create XML files from a program in C++. It is possible to use the very powerful set of IXMLDOMxxx interfaces, but this may add unnecessary requirements and overhead to the program. On the other hand, to create XML files from code is not a trivial task in the general case. Even when simple XML files are created, a set of wrapping classes can still be helpful.

The front-end class CXmlNode exposes a number of constructors to handle the output of different types of variables—strings, wide-character strings, numeric values, boolean variables. All constructors take as parameters a reference to an open output stream object and the XML element name. Most of the functionality is provided by the base class, CXmlNodeBase. When the method StartNode is called, the begin tag of the element is created in the output file. The destructor of the class automatically inserts the end tag if StartNode has been called.

To attach attributes to an element, it is necessary to construct a CXmlAttributeSet object and call AssignAttributeSet *before* StartNode is called. This will ensure that all attributes are properly put in the begin tag of the element.

Often XML elements are created in fixed order. A set of macros makes this task extremely easy. To create an element with child elements, use the macro bracket pair START_NODE ... CLOSE_NODE and create all child elements between these macros. The macro DO_NODE creates an element and immediately puts its end tag. The macros with suffix _A take an additional reference to a CXmlAttributeSet object for the attributes of the node.

When more complex processing is required, CXmlNode objects can be manipulated directly or through a smart pointer wrapper, as shown in the sample:

```
ofstream          ofs("test.xml");
CXmlAttributeSet  as("a1","v1");

as.AddAttribute("a2","v2");

UTL_PutXmlHeader(ofs);

START_NODE(ofs, "DemoDocument", CXmlNode::EMPTY_DATA);

  START_NODE_A(ofs, "e1", "t1", as);
    DO_NODE(ofs, "e11","t11")
    DO_NODE(ofs, "e12","t12")
    START_NODE(ofs, "e12","t12")
      DO_NODE_A(ofs, "e121","t121", CXmlAttributeSet("wee","jee"))
      DO_NODE(ofs, "answer", 42)
      DO_NODE(ofs, "NO_PI",3.1514)
      START_NODE(ofs, "fact","5  3")
        DO_NODE(ofs, "is ok", true)
      CLOSE_NODE
    CLOSE_NODE
  CLOSE_NODE

  as.AddAttribute("a3","v3");

  DO_NODE_A(ofs, "e2", CXmlNode::EMPTY_DATA, as);

  CXmlNode     * n3 = new CXmlNode(ofs,"e3",CXmlNode::EMPTY_DATA);
  SmartPtr<CXmlNode>      spXml(NULL);

  n3->StartNode();

  spXml = new CXmlNode(ofs,"e31", "t31");
  spXml->StartNode();
  spXml = NULL;

  spXml = new CXmlNode(ofs,"e32", "&reg;");
  spXml->StartNode();
  spXml = NULL;

  delete n3;

CLOSE_NODE
```

The sample does not catch the exceptions that the CXmlNode class can throw. A professional program would handle these exceptions in an appropriate way.

Using the Microsoft XML Parser to Create XML Documents

This article was contributed by Essam Ahmed.

Environment: VC 6, Windows 2000, MS XML Parser 3.0

XML provides a powerful and flexible means of expressing and communicating information between different (or unlike) systems. XML is a text-based format that's similar to HTML in many ways. For example, XML documents contain elements that consist of start tags (such as <font>) and end tags (such as </font>). Unlike HTML, however, you can use any XML tags you like—how many tags you use and what names you give them are left to you, the document's designer.

Basics of the MXXMLWriter Component

Part of the challenge of creating an XML document is making sure that the XML conforms to some basic formatting rules—like ensuring that elements don't overlap. Although it is easy to ensure that a new XML document conforms to the basic formatting rules the XML specification outlines, it is easier—and safer—to use a third-party component to manage the output. The component that I'll describe to you in this article is MXXMLWriter, part of Microsoft's version three XML parser.

When you think of a parser, you generally think of something that consumes a stream of data on its input and generates a series of tokens at its output. The Microsoft XML Parser generally works like a regular parser; it takes an XML document on its input and generates either an XML Document Object Model (DOM)—an in-memory, object-based representation of an XML Document—or a series of Simple API for XML (SAX) events. In either case, the input is an XML document.

MXXMLWriter is a part of Microsoft's XML parser and is useful for programmatically creating XML documents. The advantages of using the MXXMLWriter over creating an XML document yourself (by hard coding XML tags in your code) include

- The MXXMLWriter produces an XML document that conforms to the W3C XML 1.0 Namespace recommendation—no need to be concerned with formatting the output since the parser does the work for you.

- You can hook up the output of the MXXMLWriter to a SAX content handler (a stream-based XML consumer) for quick and low-memory overhead processing.

- The interface-based programming model makes your code easier to read and maintain. You can send the output to a string or a COM object that supports the IStream interface (such as the ASP Response object).

Basics of Processing XML Documents

Before you can use the MXXMLWriter component to create new XML documents, you need to know some information about processing existing XML documents since the MXXMLWriter component expects applications that use it to act as SAX event providers.

There are two ways to process an existing XML document: Use the DOM or use the SAX. Both approaches have their own advantages and roles in various applications—the DOM is great at querying XML documents as if they are tables in a database, whereas SAX is great at quickly processing very large XML documents and basically putting you in complete control of the parsing process.

Using the DOM to Process XML

When you load an XML document into a DOM, the XML parser reads through the entire document and creates a hierarchy of objects that represent the document in memory. Figure 34.1 shows a fragment of a simple XML document and how the DOM represents it in memory.

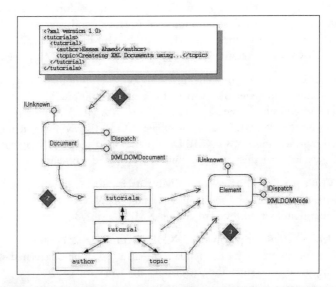

Figure 34.1   How the DOM represents an XML document.

Figure 34.1 illustrates that an instance of a Document represents an XML document (number 1 in Figure 34.1) that contains nodes (number 2 in Figure 34.1), which are instances of DOM Node objects (number 3 in Figure 34.1).

The DOM makes the XML document ready for you to use once it has read all of it into memory. You can work with the elements in a DOM by iterating over its contents using loops, querying for specific nodes using XPath expressions, or by randomly accessing parts of the DOM tree. The key point is that your application is in control over the document—your application essentially pulls information from an in-memory representation of the document.

Using SAX to Process XML

The SAX programming model is different from the programming model that the DOM offers. SAX puts your application much closer to the XML parser by allowing your application to intercept events that the XML parser raises as it processes an XML document. This is a push-programming model since events are pushed to your application, as shown in Figure 34.2; your application no longer acts as a point of control as it does when you use the DOM.

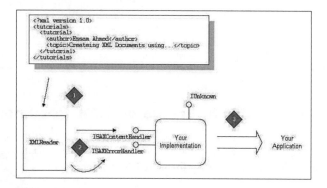

Figure 34.2 Using SAX to process an XML document.

Figure 34.2 illustrates that an XML Reader (number 1 in Figure 34.2) is responsible for reading the XML document. The XML Reader invokes a component that you provide and calls methods on its interfaces as it reads the XML document (number 2 in Figure 34.2); your application (number 3 in Figure 34.2) consumes the output your component provides.

A component that exposes the ISAXXMLReader represents the XML Reader in Figure 34.2. To process an XML document using SAX, you register a component that exposes, among other interfaces, the ISAXContentHandler interface. As the XML Reader encounters elements in a document, it calls ISAXContentHandler methods like startDocument, startElement, and characters that provide information about the element that the XML Reader picks up. Figure 34.3 illustrates a sequence of events (method calls on a component that expose the ISAXContentHandler interface) that the XML Reader raises as it processes the sample XML file (shown in Figures 34.1 and 34.2).

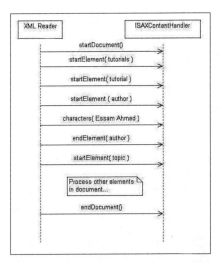

Figure 34.3 Sequence of events while processing an XML document.

Using MXXMLWriter to Create an XML Document

The MXXMLWriter component acts as a SAX consumer, meaning that applications that use the MXXMLWriter act as SAX providers. The MXXMLWriter consumes the SAX events and writes out a correctly formatted XML document.

The sample code that accompanies this article is a console application that reads a comma-separated file and produces an XML document. The XML document that the sample creates is shown on the screen, and you can capture its output to a text file to store it on disk. The sample uses the STL (Standard Template Library) to manage reading the input file and pick up its contents. Listing 34.1 shows the code that instantiates the MXXMLWriter and establishes pointers to interfaces like ISAXContentHandler.

Listing 34.1   Instantiating MXXMLWriter

```
// MSXML2::IMXWriterPtr is a smart pointer that's declared as a result
// of #importing msxml3.dll in StdAfx.h
MSXML2::IMXWriterPtr pXMLWriter;
pXMLWriter.CreateInstance(__uuidof(MSXML2::MXXMLWriter));

// ISAXContentHandler is an interface that's exposed by MXXMLWriter...
MSXML2::ISAXContentHandlerPtr pContentHandler;
pContentHandler=pXMLWriter;  //calls QI for ISAXContentHandler on pXMLWriter

// ...so is ISAXErrorHandler...
MSXML2::ISAXErrorHandlerPtr pErrorHandler;
pErrorHandler=pXMLWriter; //calls QI for ISAXErrorHandler on pXMLWriter
```

Listing 34.1 Continued

```
// ... and so is ISAXDTDHandler...
MSXML2::ISAXDTDHandlerPtr pDTDHandler;
pDTDHandler=pXMLWriter; //calls QI for ISAXDTDHandler on pXMLWriter

//sets output to go to a string
pXMLWriter->put_output(CComVariant(L""));
```

The code in the listing uses smart pointers that the compiler creates as a result of using the #import statement in stdafx.h. The listing also shows that, other than MXXMLWriter, all pointers refer to interfaces that MXXMLWriter exposes—refer to the comments in the code for details.

Once the MXXMLWriter is ready, the sample reads through the text file and raises SAX events for the MXXMLWriter to process, as shown in Listing 34.2.

Listing 34.2 Raising Events for the MXXMLWriter

```
std::getline(fileIn,lineFromFile);
while(fileIn.good())
{
    npos=lineFromFile.find_first_of(",",nlast);
    // make sure that there's a comma on the current line;
    //find_first_of returns std::wstring::npos if not found
    if(npos!=std::wstring::npos){
      wElementName=A2W(lineFromFile.substr(nlast,npos-nlast).c_str());

      // startElement...
      pContentHandler->startElement(L"",0,L"",0,
        const_cast<wchar_t*>(wElementName.c_str()),
        wElementName.length(),NULL);
      nlast= ++npos;

      // get the rest of the current line (element value)
      wElementValue=A2W(lineFromFile.substr(nlast).c_str());
      // characters...
      pContentHandler->characters(
        const_cast<wchar_t*>(wElementValue.c_str()),
        wElementValue.length());

        // endElement...
        pContentHandler->endElement(L"",0,L"",0,
          const_cast<WCHAR_T*>(wElementName.c_str()),
          wElementName.length());
    }
    std::getline(fileIn,lineFromFile);
    nlast=0;
}
```

The code in the listing resides in a loop that's controlled by the state of the input file. The code reads the input file line by line using the std::getline(...) method and stores the line in the lineFromFile variable, a std::string type. The MXXMLWriter expects its inputs as Unicode strings; however, the sample uses ANSI strings throughout to make parsing the document easier. As a result, the code converts the ANSI strings it picks up from the input file into Unicode strings just before it passes them on to the MXXMLWriter.

The input file is a text file that's formatted as an element and has an element value pair per line; the sample produces an XML document made up of the elements and values enclosed in a RootElement element (see Listing 34.3).

Listing 34.3   Sample Text File

```
author, Essam Ahmed
topic, Using the Microsoft XML Parser...

author, Essam Ahmed
topic, Using the Microsoft XML Parser...

<?xml version="1.0" encoding="UTF-16" standalone="no"?>
<RootElement>
  <author>Essam Ahmed</author>
  <topic>Using the Microsoft XML Parser...</topic>
</ RootElement>
```

The sample code prints its output on the screen; however, if you want to capture its output to a file, use the redirection character (>) to direct the output to a file.

Conclusion

This article introduced the MXXMLWriter, a component of the Microsoft XML 3.0 parser, to create XML documents. Using MXXMLWriter has several advantages over do-it-yourself implementations including on-going assurance that the XML documents your applications produce are conformant with current standards and without having to update your code as the standards change. (You need to ensure that the XML parser is up to date, but that is often just a matter of downloading and installing a newer version.)

The code that accompanies this article includes the sample featured in this article, a sample text file, and the resulting XML file. Open the project's file to review or change the code.

Essam Ahmed is the author of *JScript .NET Programming* (http://www.designs2solutions. com/jsnetprg), which includes an XML primer and information on using XML with ADO.NET and Web services.

FROM THE FORUM

Question (PeterShave):

How can I retrieve an XML stream and parse it?

Answer (Filbert Fox):

The following code converts an ADO recordset to XML, and XML to an ADO record-set. Just change the table, database, and file names to suit your needs:

```cpp
// ADO_XML.cpp : Defines the entry point for the console application.
//
#include "stdafx.h"

// 1. ADO Recordset <-> external xml file
// 2. ADO Recordset <-> ADO IStream Object
// 3. ADO Recordset <-> DOM Document

#import "C:\Program files\Common Files\System\Ado\msado15.dll"
➥rename_namespace("MSXML")  rename("EOF", "ADOEOF")

#import "c:\winnt\system32\msxml.dll"
using namespace MSXML;

#include <stdio.h>
#include <io.h>
#include <TCHAR.h>

void dump_error(_com_error &e) ; //exception handling

void main()
{
    HRESULT hr;
    CoInitialize(NULL);

    try
    {
        //open the connection, get the recordset ready
        _ConnectionPtr pConn;
        _RecordsetPtr pRs;

        hr = pConn.CreateInstance(__uuidof(Connection));
        hr = pRs.CreateInstance(__uuidof(Recordset));

        pConn->CursorLocation = adUseClient;

        _bstr_t strConn("Provider=Microsoft.Jet.OLEDB.4.0;Data
            Source=D:\\DPL.MDB");
        pConn->Open( strConn, _T(""), _T(""), adConnectUnspecified );

        _bstr_t strRs("SELECT * FROM [jobs]");
        pRs->Open( strRs, pConn.GetInterfacePtr(), adOpenForwardOnly,
            adLockReadOnly, adCmdText);
```

```
//preparation to save RS as xml file,
struct _finddata_t xml_file;
long hFile;
if( (hFile = _findfirst("d:\\dpl.xml", &xml_file )) != -1L)
{
    DeleteFile("d:\\dpl.xml"); //if the file exists, delete it
}

// 1. Persist it to an external xml file by calling Save with file
//    name and adPersistXML
hr = pRs->Save("d:\\dpl.xml", adPersistXML);

// 2. Persist it to ADO IStream Object
_StreamPtr    pStream ; //declare one first
pStream.CreateInstance( __uuidof(Stream) ); //create it after
hr = pRs->Save( pStream.GetInterfacePtr(), adPersistXML );
    //old trick, call Save

// 3. Persist it to DOM Document
IXMLDOMDocumentPtr pXMLDOMDoc;
pXMLDOMDoc.CreateInstance( __uuidof(DOMDocument) );
hr = pRs->Save( pXMLDOMDoc.GetInterfacePtr(), adPersistXML );
// if you want to check out the content call
// printf(pXMLDOMDoc->Getxml());

//Recycle the Recordset object
hr = pRs->Close();

// 4. load the recordset back from the file by calling Open
// with MSPersist provider and adCmdFile.
// the Recordset will be a ReadOnly, Forward only
/*    hr = pRs->Open("authors.xml", "Provider=MSPersist;",
      adOpenForwardOnly, adLockReadOnly,adCmdFile);
      hr = pRs->Close();

// 5.  Load from IStream object, call Open, first param
//     is pStream.GetInterfacePtr()

// Set the steam object position to the beginning of the stream:
pStream->Position = 0;

// call Open,  passing in vtMissing for connection string,
// see Q245485 for details
hr = pRs->Open(pStream.GetInterfacePtr(), vtMissing,
    adOpenForwardOnly, adLockReadOnly, adCmdFile);

hr = pRs->Close();

// 6 .Load from DOM Document, call Open, first param is
//    pXMLDOMDoc.GetInterfacePtr() and pass in
//    vtMissing for connection string, see Q245485
```

```
            hr = pRs->Open(pXMLDOMDoc.GetInterfacePtr(), vtMissing,
                adOpenForwardOnly, adLockReadOnly, adCmdFile);

            hr = pRs->Close();
*/
            //Don't forget to clean up the stream object
            hr = pStream->Close();

        }
        catch(_com_error &e)
        {
            dump_error(e);
        }
    }

    void dump_error(_com_error &e)
    {
        _bstr_t bstrSource(e.Source());
        _bstr_t bstrDescription(e.Description());

        // Print Com errors.
        printf("Error\n");
        printf("\tCode = %08lx\n", e.Error());
        printf("\tCode meaning = %s", e.ErrorMessage());
        printf("\tSource = %s\n", (LPCSTR) bstrSource);
        printf("\tDescription = %s\n", (LPCSTR) bstrDescription);

    }
```

VII

Internet and Networking

35

Socket Programming

In this chapter

Socket-based programming is based on the original Berkeley Software Distribution specification, and it is used to communicate over networks between many types of operating systems.

Socket-based communication is the primary means of network communication over local networks and the Internet.

- "Chat Room Comes Back with a New Face" describes a complete chat room application based upon the CSocket class.

Chat Room Comes Back with a New Face

This article was contributed by Yi Hai.

Environment: VC6, Win2K, WinXP

Preface

This is not an update of my previous article. Although this is also a chat room program, it was written in a totally different way from its predecessor. After my previous article was published, many people wrote to me with comments, which are highly appreciated. And many people wanted a Csocket-version chat room example too. So this article is an answer to their request. Since I am a physics student and have been busy playing with the detector simulation instead of Visual C++, I'd not even studied the CSocket mechanism until Matthew Millman's excellent article came to the front page of CodeGuru (http://www.codeguru.com/network/netmsg-fxx.html).

Inspired by the elegant implementation of his NetMsg program, I decided to rewrite my chat room with CSocket too.

Another reason for me to do this piece of work was a realistic one: I'm on my way to graduation, and I want to begin my career as a programmer. And I hope my code will interest any potential employers. Please see the following statement for details.

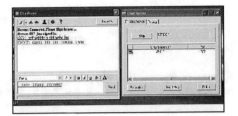

Figure 35.1

Basis

Before I dive into the details of my code, I'd like to share some ideas about the programming with you guys, which I believe you'll benefit from as I have.

Java, C++, Basic—no matter what language you prefer to use, some principles are always to be held dear:

- Think. Dr. Stroustrup said in his *The C++ Programming Language,* "Always think more before coding." Always think the problem over and over—knowing what you are going to solve and the possible solution.

- Keep the data process code and the GUI code separate always; the GUI module is supposed to collect the data from some place (end user, I suppose?) and do the data presentation. Your program should always have one or more *information centers* to hold these data (through variables) and manipulate them (through the methods or functions) and, at the right time, inform the GUI to update the presentation through the interface. Take MFC SDI/MDI or dialog_base programs as examples. For simple cases, the main dialog and the document class are an okay place for the information center. For larger projects, you might use the self-sufficient logic units as the building blocks, which have their own data manager classes, and have looser relations with each other.

Advantages of Using CSocket

Now it's time to talk code. My previous program used the socket class from David Kruglinski's *Programming Visual C++.* One of the disadvantages of that class was that it's extremely hard for the developer to send and receive data types other than character streams.

But CSocket uses the wonderful concepts of CSocketFile and CArchive. If you have used CFile and CArchive before, you might realize how convenient it is to deal with different data. Its counterpart, CSocketFile, together with CArchive, can do the same thing for the network data streaming.

After some simple initialization work to link CSocket, CSocketFile, and CArchive objects, we can focus our attention on the collecting and processing of all kinds of data. I did have some problems dealing with the pointer, which is also a member for streaming in my program. Later, I converted it into a DWORD so that it went to Archive happily. Then you can wrap them into a package and send it to the CArchive object; MFC will take care of the rest—sending the package to the other computers with the predefined data order. So the whole programming process became nothing more than the collecting, assembling, distributing, and parsing of the data. See the following diagrams.

Another advantage of CSocket is its virtual function override mechanism. Once the virtual functions of Csocket, like OnReceive and OnAccept, have been overridden by the developer, we have set a network alert guard. (For example, when there is an incident message, OnReceive will alert and forward it to your corresponding handler.) Similarly, once a request of connection comes, OnAccept sends an alert to the handler too.

Diagrams and Explanations

Client

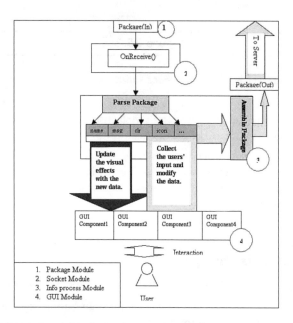

Figure 35.2

I believe the diagram speaks for itself. Still, I have to point out that the actual code would not strictly follow the building blocks shown in Figure 35.2, as the design programming is always an interactive activity that requires continuous modification.

Server

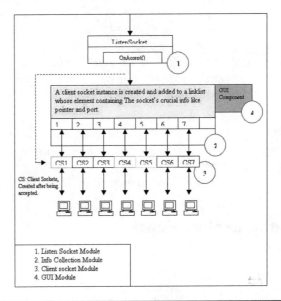

Figure 35.3

The design of the server is a little different from the client:

- Two CSocket-derived classes are used. One is listening to the ports; once a request for connection is coming, a new clientsocket is created and its info is added to a linklist maintained by the main dialog (in my case, CChatServer).

- I removed the burden of sending/receiving messages from the main dialog (CChatServer) to the client socket class. The main dialog is responsible for the forwarding and coordination of the messages between clients—in other words, a manipulation of the linklist.

How to Test This Program

Since only source file is provided, you need Visual C++ for compilation.

- Open the chat-server project, run it, click the Start button, and the IP of the current machine appears on the right.

- Open the chat–client project, click the Connection button, change the IP address to the one shown on the server side, and then click the OK button. Next, click the Sign In button and begin to chat.

- Functionality of the buttons in Figure 35.4 are (from left to right): Connection, Sign In, Sign Out, My Icon (N/A), On Leave (N/A), and About.

Figure 35.4

I used Visual C++ 6.0, Windows XP/2K to do the test.

Features

- Rich text editing.
- Persistence (Your customized setting will be remembered and recalled next time.)

Known Bugs

I did find some bugs when I operated the server a lot (stop, start, stop, start) while the clients were still linking. For example, if the client logs off during the period when the server stops services, the other clients of course couldn't get their log-off info. Since in the normal circumstance, the server is not supposed to be bothered after it's started, I did not bother to fix that part.

I tested on a single machine (Windows XP installed) and also tested in the LAN of my lab (Windows 2K installed). I was careful to avert the possible error. So I believe you guys will find many more bugs—don't hesitate to let me know. Of course, if you can solve them on your own, that'd be better.

Suggestions for Updates

There is a lot of room for updates:

- The icon button is a fake—no response to the users' input. It needs to be improved.
- The contact list box on the right is a fake—no icons, just names, and it can't do anything. It needs to be improved for personal talk.
- The persistence is machine dependent instead of account dependent, which means different users get the same setting if they run this program on the same machine. It's not a mistake, but the account–dependent setting is more professional. Suggestion: Use GetProfileIni/WriteProfileIni to do the persistence.
- Private conversations. People need to single out a certain person for a private talk. Like MSN message, Matthem Millman did that with multithread. But automation tech might be an alternative.
- File transfer.
- Pop3 mail reminder.

I'll do these updates in the coming days—maybe after graduation.

Acknowledgments

I finished this project (maybe not yet) within two weeks by myself, in my spare time at night. However, without the genius idea and code on CodeGuru, I wouldn't have made it. So many thanks should go to the people contributing their effort to this great Web site. Also, direct help from the following guys is highly appreciated:

- Matthem Millman for his NetMsg and the clear presentation of the usage of CSocket

- Kirk W. Stowell for his cool CFlatcombobox control

- Daniel G. Hyams for his great expansion dialog code, which goes into my code perfectly

- Bogdan Matasaru for his powerful Property Sheet Wizard, which helped me to construct my server in a professional way

Also, many thanks go to the people who emailed me, commented on my previous article, and answered my questions on the discussion board. I sincerely request continuing support for this one too.

Statement

As I mentioned at first, I am now looking for a proper job as a programmer. I like to use C/C++ and Java as my programming languages. My preferred IDE is Visual C++ Studio and Forte from SUN. My computer skills include, but are not limited to, my programming abilities. Web authoring and script writing are also my interests. I use Linux and IRIX from SGI for doing my work, as well. I also sometimes consult on campus. I like to talk with people on all topics. At last, my loyalty and diligence is of no doubt because this kind of work is something I'm really fond of.

Work area includes any state within the United States. Any offer or suggestion is quite welcome. Please contact me through

yihai@grant.phys.subr.edu or swayhand@hotmail.com

I'll send you my resume and I'll be ready to answer your questions.

Thank you all, and enjoy coding!

FROM THE FORUM

Question (Anarchi):

Many programs are able to check online and determine whether any newer versions of the software are available. How could I implement something like this?

Answer (Brandon Parker):

Using a CSocket object with MFC, you can connect to the server and read a text file containing the current version. If this is greater than the version of your installed application, there is an update available. You can retrieve the text from the file as follows:

```
AfxSocketInit();
CSocket* sock = new CSocket;
sock->Create();

sock->Connect("theserver.com",80);
CString send;
send+= "GET /update/version.txt HTTP/1.1\r\n";
send+= "User-Agent: Mozilla/5.05 (Win95;I)\r\n";
send+= "Host: theserver.com:80\r\n";
send+= /* End Of Header */ "\r\n";
sock->Send(send,send.GetLength());

char buf[1024];
::ZeroMemory(buf,sizeof(buf));
sock->Receive(buf,sizeof(buf));

CString version = buf;
// version contains the version information here
```

FROM THE FORUM

Question (roaceves):

How can I connect to a site and retrieve time information from it?

Answer (Brandon Parker):

Using a CSocket connection, you can use the following:

```
void CMyClass::DoConnection()
{
    // Create String to send
    CString send = "GET http://132.16.4.101/index.html HTTP/1.1\r\n";
    send+= "User-Agent: Mozilla/5.05 (Win95;I)\r\n";
    send+= "Connection: close\r\n";
    send+= "Host: 132.16.4.101\r\n";
    send+= /* End Of Header */ "\r\n";
```

```
// Initialize Sockets
AfxSocketInit();

// Create buffer to receive data
char rcvbuf [200];

// Create new Socket
CSocket* pSocket = new CSocket;
pSocket->Create();

// Connect to Server
pSocket->Connect("132.163.4.101",14);

// Clear Memory in buffer
::ZeroMemory(rcvbuf,sizeof(rcvbuf));

// Send Data to Server
pSocket->Send(send,send.GetLength());

// Receive dada from server
pSocket->Receive(rcvbuf,sizeof(rcvbuf));

// Display Time;
AfxMessageBox(rcvbuf);

// Delete Socket
delete pSocket;
}
```

36

Named Pipes

In this chapter

A *named pipe* is a method of communication between a server and one or more clients. These clients can be on the same machine or some remote machine.

Named pipes can be configured as having either one-way or duplex communication, and each instance using the pipe can have its own buffers and handles.

- "Named Pipe Wrapper for Win32 Platforms" provides an interesting way of using anonymous pipes based on the Win32 API routines with the same functionality as named pipes, thereby making this functionality available to Windows 95, 98, and ME operating systems, which typically do not support named pipes.
- "Connection Pipe Classes" describes simple methods of implementing robust named pipes using MFC.

Named Pipe Wrapper for Win32 Platforms

This article was contributed by Clemens Fischer.

Environment: VC6/MFC, Win9X/WinME/NT40/W2k

Background

Using pipes is not too complicated on Windows NT platforms, but on Windows 9X, it's not that easy because named pipes are not supported.

FROM THE FORUM

Question (Grit):

What is the maximum length I can use for a named pipe?

Answer (fblaha):

The name can be up to 256 characters long and is not case sensitive.

The Wrapper

cPipe is a C++ wrapper class encapsulating named pipes, providing a simple interface to create named pipes and to perform read/write operations. In addition, an application–defined callback function, which is called by the framework if data is available, can be specified on creation. (The server side of the sample demonstrates the usage of the callback function.)

cPipe contains the public methods shown in Table 36.1, fully documented within the source.

Table 36.1   cPipe Public Methods

Method	Description
Create	Creates and registers the necessary pipe(s).
Close	Closes the pipe(s).
ReadPipe	Performs read operation on the pipe.
WritePipe	Performs write operation on the pipe.
GetLastError	Returns the latest cPipe error code.

The Sample

The sample provides two tiny applications to demonstrate IPC. For the server side, run core.exe, and for the client side, run client.exe. For demonstration, the server side just mirrors the data sent by the client application. I tested the sample applications on the following platforms: Windows 98, NT 4.0, and W2k.

Figure 36.1 Server.

Figure 36.2 Client.

Comments

There are problems when using the sample code in a Microsoft Terminal Server environment with multiple clients. To correct this, make the following changes to the sample code:

```
BOOL cPipe::RegisterPipe ( void )
{
    ...

    // Create registry key

    // insert the desktop HWND before the m_PipeName
    CString strDesktopWnd;
    strDesktopWnd.Format("%lu", GetDesktopWindow());

//    m_SubKey = "SOFTWARE\\" + m_GUID + "\\" + m_PipeName;
    m_SubKey = "SOFTWARE\\" + m_GUID + "\\" + strDesktopWnd + "\\"
➥+ m_PipeName;

    ...
```

```
    }

    BOOL cPipe::RetrievePipe ( void )
    {

        ...

        // Open registry key

        // insert the desktop HWND bevore the m_PipeName
        CString strDesktopWnd;
        strDesktopWnd.Format("%lu", GetDesktopWindow());

//      m_SubKey = "SOFTWARE\\" + m_GUID + "\\" + m_PipeName;
        m_SubKey = "SOFTWARE\\" + m_GUID + "\\" + strDesktopWnd + "\\"
➥+ m_PipeName;

        ...

    }
```
—Walter

Connection Pipe Classes

This article was contributed by Ion Tichy (iont@hotmail.com).

http://www.iont.20m.com

Environment: VC6, Windows NT4, Windows 2000

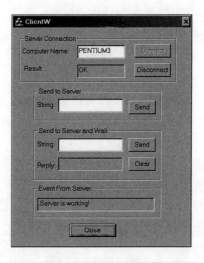

Figure 36.3

Figure 36.4

Purpose

Simple and fast communication between all types of MFC applications on single or multiple computers in Windows NT.

Main Features

- Data transmission from clients to server and their processing and results return, if needed.
- Data transmission from server to clients, informing them about any event.
- Different schemes of buffer allocations.
- Automatic Server loading.
- Automatic Server termination without clients, if needed.
- Utilities for registration, automatic loading, tracing, and wizard.

Introduction

Several years ago, I wrote classes by using Mailslots for communication between clients and servers. According to the project requirements, these classes had to work in Windows 95. In spite of numerous problems and limitations of Mailslots, these classes work properly in Windows 95 and Windows NT.

The aforementioned problems are the following:

- Eight-byte limitation for Mailslot names in Windows 95
- Numerous data transmissions across Mailslots between computers if they have several identical installed communication protocols

Microsoft considers this as "by design." In other words, it is not an error, but I don't agree.

In these classes, the server has the receiving thread and clients send data with the identifier of Client (computer name and client name) to this thread. It increases summary data that clients transmit across Mailslots, and it is the disadvantage of this method.

I took a course of COMs and ATL. After that, it was evident that there were many undocumented things in that technology. ATL is a convenient tool, but I have discovered several limitations (for example, it is impossible to make ATL-Server from the existing MFC application).

DCOM implementation needs great efforts too. For example, I wrote my first program with DCOM in almost two weeks and had to ask Microsoft for numerous consultations. That's why, in spite of my wish to use COM/DCOM in my new project, I had to give up this idea.

The new project that I have begun to work at had high requirements for the speed of data processing. This factor had to be taken into account in the design of the new communication tool. Fortunately, unlike COM, there were no requirements to the design of the universal tool and this made the development easier.

For the new project, I have chosen the protocol Named Pipes, working only in Windows NT. In literature, this protocol is defined as the following:

> An inter-process communication mechanism that allows one process to communicate with another local or remote process.

I have tried to implement the ideas that I used in my first project with Mailslots as well as the ideas of COM. In the next section, you'll learn the client-server architecture based on the Named Pipes protocol.

Client-Server Architecture

Following are the two types of connections between client and server:

- Client and server are on a single computer.
- Client and server are on multiple computers.

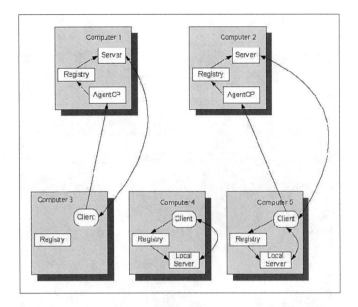

Figure 36.5

When the server is loaded, the client tries to get into connection with the server.

If the server is not loaded and the client and server are on a single computer, the client gets information about the server from the Registry of this computer (see Computer 4 in Figure 36.5).

If the server is not loaded and the client and server are on multiple computers, the client gets information about the server from the Registry of the remote server computer across the utility AgentCP (see Computers 1 and 2 in Figure 36.5). This program searches the server information in the Registry of the server computer and loads it.

As seen from Figure 36.5, for successful functioning of the aforementioned process, it is necessary

- To write information about the server in the Registry of the server computer.
- To run the utility AgentCP on the remote computer previously.

Thus, the server automatic loading is carried out. The process server may be terminated automatically if clients are not connected.

Here you may see the WizardCP application:

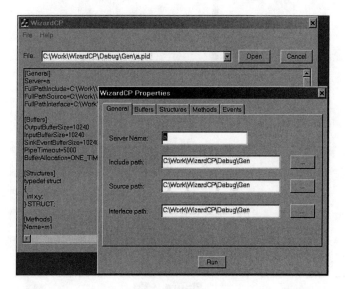

Figure 36.6

FROM THE FORUM

Question (rafias):

I am having problems trying to connect to a named pipe in a service on another machine within my domain. I keep getting access-denied errors when trying to connect.

Answer (Alex Fedotov):

You should specify the UNC path of the server when trying to connect, such as "\\server-name\\pipe\\pipe-name" and you should also modify the Local System account that is running the pipe on the server to give it network credentials to be authenticated by other computers. Configure the service to run under a specific domain account.

37

Network Information

In this chapter

Networking is at times a complex deployment environment, where from machine to machine, network configuration and settings can vary. In these situations, it can be useful to have some software functionality available to determine at runtime the current status of the network connectivity.

In this chapter, you will find some very useful and practical examples of how to gather this information.

- "Get the Hostname and IP Address of a Local Computer" provides a simple solution to

one of the more fundamental issues when attempting to determine network information.

- "Function to Verify if Connected to the Internet" shows how you can determine whether the computer has an active connection to the Internet.

- "PC Clock Synchronizing Using HTTP" describes a useful way of interacting with the Internet to determine the time and synchronize to that time.

Get the Hostname and IP Address of a Local Computer

This article was contributed by Jeff Lundgren.

This code will get the host name and IP for the computer on which the code is run. This works in Visual C++ 5 SP1/2 and on NT4 and 95.

Requirements:

- #include <winsock2.h>
- Link with Wsock32.lib

That's it.

```
{
    WORD wVersionRequested;
    WSADATA wsaData;
    char name[255];
    CString ip;
    PHOSTENT hostinfo;
    wVersionRequested = MAKEWORD( 2, 0 );

    if ( WSAStartup( wVersionRequested, &wsaData ) == 0 )
    {

        if( gethostname ( name, sizeof(name)) == 0)
        {
            if((hostinfo = gethostbyname(name)) != NULL)
            {
                ip = inet_ntoa (*(struct in_addr *)
➥*hostinfo->h_addr_list);
            }
        }

        WSACleanup( );
    }
}
```

Comments

There may be problems in using the sample code when using different versions of the Winsock network driver. For example, some versions of Windows 95 only use WinSock version 1.1. To use the two different versions, you can make the following changes to the sample code:

When using WinSock version 1.1:

- #include "WinSock.h"
- Use wVersionRequested = MAKEWORD (1, 1);
- Link with Wsock32.lib

When using WinSock version 2:

- #include "WinSock2.h"
- Use wVersionRequested = MAKEWORD (2, 0);
- Link with WS2_32.lib

—Nitin

FROM THE FORUM

Question (gvirdi):

How can I get a list of user accounts on a Windows NT network?

Answer (ZogMan):

Here's a code snippet that will fill a list box with usernames obtained from the primary domain controller. This only works on NT:

```
DWORD dwNextIndex = 0;
DWORD dwREC = 0;
PNET_DISPLAY_USER pBuffer = NULL, p = NULL;
NET_API_STATUS NetStat = NERR_Success;
CString szUserString;
LPTSTR lpPDC = NULL;

//
// Get all user accounts from the PDC.
//

NetStat = NetGetDCName(NULL, NULL, (LPBYTE*)&lpPDC);

// Test the returned buffer for validity
ASSERT(AfxIsValidAddress(lpPDC, 1, false));

do
{
    NetStat = NetQueryDisplayInformation(/* Server = */ lpPDC, /* Level= */1,
    /* Index = */ dwNextIndex, /* EntriesRequested = */ 50, /*
    PrefferredMaximumLength = */ 1024,
    /* ReturnedEntryCount */ &dwREC, /* SortedBuffer */ (void**)&pBuffer);

    // Test the returned buffer for validity
    ASSERT(AfxIsValidAddress(pBuffer, 1, false));

    if (NetStat == NERR_Success ¦¦ NetStat == ERROR_MORE_DATA)
    {
        // This will be the index pointer
        p = pBuffer;

        // Cycle through all returned entries and
        // place them in the list box.
        for (; dwREC > 0; dwREC--)
        {
            szUserString.Format(_T("%s\t%s\t%s"), p->usri1_name, p-
                >usri1_full_name, p->usri1_comment);
```

```
            m_ctlUsers.AddString(szUserString);
            dwNextIndex = p->usri1_next_index;
            p++;
        }

        // Free the buffer so we can use it again.
        NetApiBufferFree(pBuffer);
    }

// Keep going until we've seen them all.
} while (NetStat == ERROR_MORE_DATA);

// And free the PDC name buffer
NetApiBufferFree(lpPDC);
```

Function to Verify if Connected to the Internet

This article was contributed by Dmitri Utenkov.

Acknowledgments

As many of you are aware, there is already an article on CodeGuru, "BOOL IsInternetConnected()" (http://codeguru.developer.com/internet/isinternetconnected. shtml) by Ran (ranidf@iname.com), that contains a function that checks for Internet connectivity. However, while Ran's version of this function is very good, in my experience I found that it wasn't the best for my applications. One of the problems that I ran into was that the application loses focus while the function attempts to check for the Internet connection. To that extent, I present to you this alternative.

In addition, I'd like to add that this function is based on the comments made on this site by Jarek Gibek (jmg2001@hotmail.com) as well as the article "Get Hostname and IP Address of Local Computer(2)" (http://codeguru.developer.com/internet/local_ hostname2.shtml) by Jaroslav Pisk (jerryiii@sprynet.com).

How It Works

The way this function works is that it attempts to define which are the IP addresses that can automatically be excluded from consideration. Then it defines which IP addresses would signify that the computer is connected to the Internet. Here's a sampling of some of the IP addresses and what they mean to the function that should help to illustrate my point.

- **127.0.0.1** – localhost;
- Private Address area(RFC 1597)
  - **10.*.*.*** – Class A;
  - **172.16–31.*.*** – Class B;
  - **192.168.*.***– Class C;
- **169.254.*.*** Microsoft AutoNet address area (See http://lancanyon.com/autonet.htm for details.)

Please note that I do not exclude other specific IP addresses such as **0.0.0.0** or **255.2555.255.255** because the local host can't have either of these IP addresses.

The Function

While the function is stated (and commented) here, you can also download it from the disc.

```
#include "winsock2.h"

BOOL IsInternetConnection()
{
 char szHostName[128];

 BOOL bPrivateAdr = false; // Private Address area
 BOOL bClassA = false;     // Class A definition
 BOOL bClassB = false;     // Class B definition
 BOOL bClassC = false;     // Class C definition
 BOOL bAutoNet = false;    // AutoNet definition
 CString str;

 if (gethostname(szHostName, 128) == 0 )
 {
 // Get host adresses
 struct hostent * pHost;
 int i;
 UINT ipb;
 pHost = gethostbyname(szHostName);

 for (i = 0;
      pHost!= NULL && pHost->h_addr_list[i]!= NULL;
      i++ )
 {
  int j;
  str="";
```

```
   bClassA = bClassB = bClassC = false;
   for( j = 0; j < pHost->h_length; j++ )
   {
    CString addr;

    if( j > 0 )    str += ".";
    ipb = (unsigned int)((unsigned char*)pHost->h_addr_list[i])[j];

    // Define the IP range for exclusion
    if(j==0)
    {
     if(bClassA = (ipb == 10)) break; // Class A defined
     bClassB = (ipb == 172);
     bClassC = (ipb == 192);
     bAutoNet = (ipb == 169);
    }
    else if (j==1)
    {
     // Class B defined
     if(bClassB = (bClassB && ipb >= 16 && ipb <= 31)) break;

     // Class C defined
     if(bClassC = (bClassC && ipb == 168)) break;

     //AutoNet pasibility defined
     if(bAutoNet = (bAutoNet && ipb == 254)) break;
    }

    addr.Format("%u", ipb );
    str += addr;
   }
   // If any address of Private Address
   // area has been found bPrivateAdr = true
   bPrivateAdr = bPrivateAdr || bClassA || bClassB || bClassC;

   // If any address of Internet Address area
   // has been found returns TRUE
   if (!bClassA
   && !bClassB
   && !bClassC
   && !bAutoNet
   && str != "127.0.0.1"
   && !str.IsEmpty())
    return TRUE;
  }
 }

if (bPrivateAdr)
{
 // The system has IP address from Private Address
 // area,only. Internet from the computer can be accessable
 // via Proxy. If user turn on proxy connection flag, the
```

```
  // function believe Internet accessable.
  return bProxyConnection;
 }

 return false;
}
```

PC Clock Synchronizing Using HTTP

This article was contributed by Alex Rest (info@brigsoft.com).

Environment: VC6, VC7, Windows 9x/NT/2000/XP with IE4 or higher

Introduction

The standard way to synchronize a PC's clock through the Internet is by using a special Network Time Protocol (NTP). It was mainly developed at Delaware University in the United States. Three versions of NTP were defined: the first in 1988, the second in 1989, and the third in 1992. The current version is the third, which is compatible with the previous ones. To make using NTP on personal computers easier, in 1995 the Simplified NTP (SNTP) was defined. Unfortunately, standard Windows software for versions Win95/98/ME/NT/W2KPro does not support synchronizing a PC clock through the Internet.

When I decided to create a synchronization program, I chose Hypertext Transfer Protocol (HTTP) instead of SNTP. I like it because it is more universal. All WWW pages that you watch are brought to your PC's screen with this protocol. I created the program and called it "For Atomic Synchronization."

There are a lot of government and scientific sites that show atomic time. There is a small delay in the site opening and receiving information. I explored my program "For Atomic Synchronization" for several months. The net delay seldom exceeds 2 seconds. I took half of the delay and corrected the time according to it. As a result, I cannot find a difference between my PC clock's time and the time that I watch on a TV screen or hear on an FM receiver.

As a time source, I use the Time Service Department of the U.S. Naval Observatory's site. It is the official source of time for the Department of Defense and the standard of time for the United States. I have tested some others. They all work well but this one has a very simple format. The WWW page size is only 603 symbols (including the HTML tags). Try this URL, http://tycho.usno.navy.mil/cgi-bin/timer.pl, and you will see the same information that my program gets.

The "For Atomic Synchronization" program is big enough that it deserves description. To demonstrate the main principles of synchronization, I created a small project that is described next.

Reading WWW Sites by Using the Windows API

Modern Windows versions with Internet Explorer 4.0 or later have very nice Internet API functions. You need not work with such low terms as TCP/IP, sockets, ports, DNS, HTTP, and so forth. In this example, I use API functions instead of the same MFC classes because they are more universal and you can easily translate this code to VB or another programming language.

All API functions work as chains. The first function opens a Windows resource and returns its number, called a *handle*. Next, the function must use this handle. It could return another handle, return code, or something else. You must close the handle when you no longer need it.

Look at the function CBSAtomicEduDlg::OnSyncro (see the following code). It works with the Internet as user:

- The function InternetOpen opens the Internet connection. If you are offline now, it opens a Dialup connection window.
- The function InternetOpenUrl retrieves the site that you are looking for.
- The function InternetReadFile reads the site into the text buffer.

That is all! You have the text of the site! Do with it what you want!

And do not forget to check for errors and close handles (with the function InternetCloseHandle). By using this program, you can explore any information on the Internet!

Do not forget to include the Wininet.h file in the project!

Universal and Local Time

My watch shows 2:00 a.m. when it is midnight in London. The sun is rolling around the Earth, so there is different time in different places. (Note: I have heard about Copernicus and Jordano Bruno.) To define what time we use in the place where we are, we use a special time zone. Time zones are not strips on a globe. They were created not only according to geographical longitude, but also according to states (countries) delimiters too. If you want to use the Internet to synchronize your PC, you must have the right time zone information in your operating system. You set it when you installed your OS; you can change it any time later.

If you know Universal time (GMT) and your time zone, you can easily calculate your local time. Look at the function LocalZoneTime (see the following code). It calculates Universal time to local time using time zone information. I got the Universal time from a Web site. I received all the information about time zones that I needed by calling the Win API function GetTimeZoneInformation. Look at Microsoft's Help to understand how to use this information. The information includes the daylight saving time (DST) correction.

Links

http://www.brigsoft.com/bsatomic/—This all-around synchronization site includes a link to this article, project download links, "For Atomic Synchronization" program download link, and description.

http://tycho.usno.navy.mil/cgi-bin/timer.pl—This is the official source of time for the Department of Defense and the United States standard of time.

Source VC++ Code

This is a part of a dialog-based MFC project, which makes time synchronization.

```cpp
// LocalZoneTime function -- calculate Local time using Universal time.
// Time zone information is gotten from Windows using the
// GetTimeZoneInformation API function (see MSDN for more information).
// The function supports DST time.
// Created by Alex.

void LocalZoneTime(const SYSTEMTIME tmUniversal,
SYSTEMTIME& tmLocal)
{

    TIME_ZONE_INFORMATION TZI;
    DWORD retCode = GetTimeZoneInformation(TZI);

    int iStandardMonth = TZI.StandardDate.wMonth;
    int iDaylightMonth = TZI.DaylightDate.wMonth;

    long nZoneCorrection = TZI.Bias;

    if( retCode == TIME_ZONE_ID_STANDARD){
        nZoneCorrection = nZoneCorrection +
TZI.StandardBias;
    }
    else if( retCode == TIME_ZONE_ID_DAYLIGHT){
        nZoneCorrection = nZoneCorrection +
TZI.DaylightBias;
    }
    else{
        ASSERT(0);
    }

    nZoneCorrection = -nZoneCorrection;
    int nTotalMinutes = tmUniversal.wHour * 60 +
        tmUniversal.wMinute + nZoneCorrection;
    if(nTotalMinutes < 0){
        nTotalMinutes+=24*60;
    }
    if(nTotalMinutes>24*60){
        nTotalMinutes-=24*60;
    }
```

```
    tmLocal.wHour = nTotalMinutes /60;
    tmLocal.wMinute = nTotalMinutes - tmLocal.wHour*60;
    tmLocal.wSecond = tmUniversal.wSecond;


}


// OnSyncro is called after ID_SYNCRO dialog button is pressed.
// It opens an Internet connection, receives Universal Time,
// calculates Local Time, and set it in Windows.
// Created by Alex.

void CBSAtomicEduDlg::OnSyncro()
{

    // Open Internet connection.
    HINTERNET hInternet = ::InternetOpen("BSAtomicEdu",
    INTERNET_OPEN_TYPE_PRECONFIG , NULL, NULL, 0);
    if(!hInternet){
        AfxMessageBox( "Internet open error! Test your system and
        try again.", MB_OK | MB_ICONERROR );
        return;
    }
    // Open Naval Observatory site.
    unsigned long Context = 777;
    HINTERNET hHttp = ::InternetOpenUrl(hInternet,
    "http://tycho.usno.navy.mil/cgi-bin/timer.pl",
    NULL, -1L, INTERNET_FLAG_RELOAD, Context);
    if(!hHttp){
        AfxMessageBox("URL open
        error!", MB_OK | MB_ICONERROR );

        if(hInternet){
            InternetCloseHandle(hInternet);
        }
        return;

    }
    // Read the time from the site.
    CString buff(' ',1024);
    unsigned long NumberOfBytesRead = 0;
    BOOL bRet = ::InternetReadFile(hHttp, (void
    *)((LPCTSTR)buff), 1024L, & NumberOfBytesRead);
    // Close Internet connection.
    if(hHttp){
        InternetCloseHandle(hHttp);
    }
    if(hInternet){
        InternetCloseHandle(hInternet);
    }
    // Is received information correct?
    if(!bRet){
        AfxMessageBox( "URL reading error! Test
```

```
internet connection and try again.", MB_OK ¦
MB_ICONERROR );
    return;
}
if(NumberOfBytesRead != 603){
    AfxMessageBox( "Unrecognized communication
error!", MB_OK ¦ MB_ICONERROR );
return;
}


// Parse Universal time from string buffer to
// SYSTEMTIME struct.
SYSTEMTIME tmUniversal, tmLocal, dtOldTime;
ZeroMemory(&tmUniversal,sizeof(tmUniversal));
GetLocalTime(&tmLocal);
dtOldTime = tmLocal;
tmUniversal.wHour = atoi((LPCTSTR)buff.Mid(111,2));
tmUniversal.wMinute = atoi((LPCTSTR)buff.Mid(114,2));
tmUniversal.wSecond = atoi((LPCTSTR)buff.Mid(117,2));
// Calculate Local Time using received Universal Time.
LocalZoneTime(tmUniversal, tmLocal);
// Make Windows time correction.
SetLocalTime(&tmLocal);
// Show report dialog box.
CString sReport;
sReport.Format( "Successful synchronization!\n Time
before: %02d:%02d:%02d.\n Time after:
%02d:%02d:%02d.\n",
dtOldTime.wHour, dtOldTime.wMinute, dtOldTime.wSecond,
tmLocal.wHour, tmLocal.wMinute, tmLocal.wSecond);
AfxMessageBox( sReport, MB_OK ¦
MB_ICONINFORMATION );
return;
}
```

FROM THE FORUM

Question (nkarthik):

How can I determine whether DHCP is enabled on my Windows 98 machine?

Answer (Matthias Kring):

You could use GetAdaptersInfo(), which returns a structure IP_ADAPTER_INFO containing a value DhcpEnabled.

To get information about the network adaptors in your system, use the GetInterfaceInfo() call.

VIII

COM-based Technologies

38

COM

In this chapter

Component Object Model, or COM, is Microsoft's specification for developing distributed transaction-based applications.

A lot of the Windows operating system is based around this component-based technology, and it is being adopted for a whole range of new products.

- "DllUnregisterServer for MFC-based COM DLLs" describes how to programmatically unregister a COM component from an MFC application.

- "Passing Binary Data in COM" details a way to handle SAFEARRAY objects being passed between objects in a manageable way.

- "Undocumented AFX Function: AfxGetClassIDFromString" describes a very useful undocumented function that can be used to get a class ID based on a specified string.

- "COM Delegation Using the COM Channel Hook Mechanism" enables the use of delegation in COM components that normally do not support delegation.

DllUnregisterServer for MFC-based COM DLLs

This article was contributed by Alexei Evdokimov.

MFC usually saves you a lot of time when implementing COM components. For example, MFC-based COM DLL projects generated with AppWizard automatically provide you with the implementation of the DllRegisterServer function. However, there is no DllUnregisterServer in the AppWizard-generated DLL. This, generally, is not acceptable because every COM DLL should support self-registration as well as self-unregistration.

MFC-based implementation of DllRegisterServer() calls COleObjectFactory:: UpdateRegistryAll(). This method has an undocumented parameter, (BOOL bRegister = TRUE), so we can expect that calling COleObjectFactory:: UpdateRegistry(FALSE) will unregister COM DLL for us. This is, unfortunately, not the case. Looking at the source code quickly tells us that COleObjectFactory:: UpdateRegistryAll(BOOL bRegister) calls COleObjectFactory::UpdateRegistry (BOOL bRegister) passing the same value of BOOL parameter, but the implementation of COleObjectFactory::UpdateRegistry(BOOL bRegister) calls UpdateRegistry(LPCTSTR lpszProgID) that registers DLL only if bRegister is TRUE; otherwise it just does nothing!

Therefore, it is still necessary to write our own DllUnregisterServer(). The following code is a ready and easy-to-use implementation of DllUnregisterServer() for MFC-based COM DLLs. To use it

- Create a file DllUnregisterServer_MFC_Impl.inl.

- Copy/paste the code below into this file.

- Add the following line at the end of the main DLL .cpp file (dll_name.cpp):

  ```
  #include "DllUnregisterServer_MFC_Impl.inl"
  ```

- Add the following line to the EXPORTS section of the DLL .def file (dll_name.def):

  ```
  DllUnregisterServer PRIVATE
  ```

That's it! Now you can use "regsvr32 /u dll_name.dll" for DLL unregistration!

This code was tested with VC++ 5.0, VC++ 5.0 SP3, VC++ 6.0 (yeah, 6.0 still doesn't provide DllUnregisterServer for free) in ANSI builds. There should be no problems with Unicode as well.

```
//****************************************************************************
// Date : 11.15.98
// Header : DllUnregisterServer_MFC_Impl.inl
//
// Desc.:    DllUnregisterServer() helper for the inproc servers that were
//        registered via MFC's COleObjectFactory::UpdateRegistryAll()
//
// Usage:
//          Add '#include "DllUnregisterServer_MFC_Impl.inl"' to the end of
//        the main dll file (i.e. dll_name.cpp).
//
//          Add 'DllUnregisterServer    PRIVATE' to EXPORTS section of the
//        dll_name.def.
//
```

```
// Caution:
//          Code below uses undocumented, internal MFC data structures
//       and functions. Therefore, probably, it will be necessary to modify
//       it, according to the changes in the future versions of MFC.
//          Code below is based on the COleObjectFactory::UpdateRegistryAll(),
//       in src\olefact.cpp. (src\olereg.cpp - is actual implementation of
//       all registry work).
//*****************************************************************************
#include "stdafx.h"

// workaround MFC bug - no #ifndef/#endif for afximpl.h header
#if !defined(CRIT_OBJECTFACTORYLIST)
#include <..\src\afximpl.h>
#endif          //!CRIT_OBJECTFACTORYLIST
//*****************************************************************************
static HRESULT UnregisterCOMObject(REFCLSID p_clsid)
{
    LPOLESTR t_wzProgID(NULL);

    // get ProgID from CLSID and unregister...
    HRESULT t_hr = ::ProgIDFromCLSID(p_clsid, &t_wzProgID);
    if(FAILED(t_hr))
        return t_hr;

    // convert OLESTR to LPTSTR
    CString t_strProgID(t_wzProgID);
    LPCTSTR t_szProgID = t_strProgID.operator LPCTSTR();

    // free memory
    ::CoTaskMemFree(t_wzProgID);

    // unregister...
    if(AfxOleUnregisterServerClass(p_clsid,
                       t_szProgID,
                       t_szProgID,
                       t_szProgID,
                       OAT_DISPATCH_OBJECT))
        return S_OK;
    else
        return E_FAIL;
}
//*****************************************************************************
// by exporting DllUnregisterServer, you can use regsvr.exe
STDAPI DllUnregisterServer(void)
{
    AFX_MANAGE_STATE(AfxGetStaticModuleState());


    AFX_MODULE_STATE* pModuleState = AfxGetModuleState();
```

```
    AfxLockGlobals(CRIT_OBJECTFACTORYLIST);
    for(COleObjectFactory* pFactory = pModuleState->m_factoryList;
        pFactory != NULL;
        pFactory = pFactory->m_pNextFactory)
    {
        HRESULT t_hr = UnregisterCOMObject(pFactory->GetClassID());
        if(FAILED(t_hr))
        {
            AfxUnlockGlobals(CRIT_OBJECTFACTORYLIST);
            return t_hr;
        }
    }
    AfxUnlockGlobals(CRIT_OBJECTFACTORYLIST);

#ifdef _AFXDLL
    AfxLockGlobals(CRIT_DYNLINKLIST);
    // register extension DLL factories
    for(CDynLinkLibrary* pDLL = pModuleState->m_libraryList;
        pDLL != NULL;
        pDLL = pDLL->m_pNextDLL)
    {
        for(pFactory = pDLL->m_factoryList;
            pFactory != NULL;
            pFactory = pFactory->m_pNextFactory)
        {
            HRESULT t_hr = UnregisterCOMObject(pFactory->GetClassID());
            if(FAILED(t_hr))
            {
                AfxUnlockGlobals(CRIT_DYNLINKLIST);
                return t_hr;
            }
        }
    }
    AfxUnlockGlobals(CRIT_DYNLINKLIST);
#endif

    return S_OK;
}
//**************************************************************************
// end of DllUnregisterServer_MFC_Impl.inl
```

Passing Binary Data in COM

This article was contributed by Roy.

There are two ways we can pass binary data in COM: SAFEARRAY and a pointer.
By using a buffer pointer, we can get the best performance.

Here is the method declared in the server IDL:

```
HRESULT Transfer([in] long cbSize,
                 [in, size_is(cbSize)] unsigned char cBuffer[])
```

Here is the client code:

```
ITargetObj * pITargeObj ;
HRESULT hRC = ::CoCreateInstance(CLSID_TargetObj,
                                 NULL,
                                 CLSCTX_SERVER,
                                 IID_ITargetObj,
                                 (void **)&pITargetObj ) ;
if FAILED( hRC )
{
 AfxMessageBox( "Failed to make target object!" ) ;
 return FALSE ;
}

BYTE * pBuffer = (BYTE *)::CoTaskMemAlloc( 15 ) ;
CopyMemory( pBuffer, "HELLO WORLD!!!!", 15 ) ;
pITargetObj->Transfer( 15, pBuffer ) ;
::CoTaskMemFree( pBuffer ) ;
pITargetObj ->Release() ;
```

But it only works for an INPROC Server with an object supporting a custom interface. If the object is supporting a dual and dispatch interface, only the first character is transferred from client to server, because the size_is attribute is stripped out (it's not supported by Automation), and the type library is used to marshal the interface. Obviously, this will not do. By the way, one good way to pass an array that does work for dual and dispatch interfaces is to use a SAFEARRAY.

FROM THE FORUM

Question (asinro):

When I call the release on my ADO recordset, I get an exception error. Why is this?

Answer (lsajanyan):

Your recordset is based on _RecordsetPtr, a smart pointer. Smart pointers call the release for you automatically, so you should not bother to call it.

Using CBufferVariant

Well, it seems we have to use the SAFEARRAY. It's easy for a VB program, but I want the same for a VC program. I've created a class named CBufferVariant. Here are the cool things:

Here is the method declared in the server IDL:

```
HRESULT Transfer([in] VARIANT vData)
```

Here is the server code:

```
STDMETHODIMP CTargeObj::Transfer(VARIANT Data)
{
 CBufferVariant bvData=Data;
 if(bvData.GetLength()==0)
  return S_OK;
 send(m_nSocketFD,bvData,bvData.GetLength(),0);
 return S_OK;
}
```

Here is the client code:

```
#include "BufferVariant.h"

ITargetObj * pITargeObj ;
HRESULT hRC = ::CoCreateInstance(CLSID_TargetObj,
                                 NULL,
                                 CLSCTX_SERVER,
                                 IID_ITargetObj,
                                 (void **)&pITargetObj ) ;
if FAILED( hRC )
{
 AfxMessageBox( "Failed to make target object!" ) ;
 return FALSE ;
}

CBufferVariant bvData;

SomeStruct stData;
bvData.AssignData(&stData,sizeof(SomeStruct));
pITargetObj->Transfer( bvData );

bvData="Hello World!";
bvData+="\n";
pITargetObj->Transfer( bvData );

char buffer[2048];
File1.Read(buffer,2048);
bvData.AssignData(buffer,2048);
File2.Read(buffer,1024);
bvData.AppendData(buffer,1024);
pITargetObj->Transfer( bvData );

pITargetObj->Transfer( CBufferVariant("This is a ANSI string.") ) ;

pITargetObj->Release();
```

Comments

There may be an error in the result returned by the GetLength routine. This can be corrected by removing the –1 as follows:

```
long nLength;
SafeArrayGetUBound(m_varData.parray, 1, &nLength);
//return nLength-1;
return nLength; // CAII change it on 2001.8.16
```

—alwayscy

Undocumented AFX Function: AfxGetClassIDFromString

This article was contributed by G. De Leeuw.

Overview

Not a big deal until you need it—I was perusing through the AFX space when I came across this gem. This little function, AfxGetClassIDFromString, is an undocumented AFX function that does exactly as its name suggests. It enables you to compare a classid to a progid for things such as determining whether a given component has been installed. If the COM component does not exist, the function simply returns NULL.

Example

Here's an example of using it to determine the version of Microsoft Word for Windows that is currently installed on your system.

```
CAbsWordMngt::CAbsWordMngt()
{
 CString        strVersion;
 CLSID          clsid;

 CoInitialize(NULL);

 m_Version = 9;
 if ( AfxGetClassIDFromString("Word.Application.9", &clsid) )
 {
  m_Version = 8;
  if ( AfxGetClassIDFromString("Word.Application.8", &clsid) )
  {
   m_Version = 0;
   AfxMessageBox("WinWord version 8 or 9 not installed ...");
   return;
  }
 }
}
```

COM Delegation Using the COM Channel Hook Mechanism

This article was contributed by Paul Barvinko.

Environment: Windows NT, COM

In one of my projects, I needed a delegation feature for a COM mechanism. The server, running under high-privileged account, needed to issue COM calls on behalf of low-privileged clients to another COM server. After searching in MSDN, I have found that the current situation is pretty simple: COM does not support delegation. Although named pipes in the Windows NT environment support it for single-machine operation, COM does not. To overcome this situation, I created my own user-impersonation mechanism based on the usage of the COM channel hook interface.

The idea behind the usage of the COM channel hook mechanism is described in a very good and comprehensive way in the January 1998 issue of *MSJ*. In short, an application could register a COM callback interface that will be called by a COM engine when it sends or receives a call. So the application can add whatever information it needs in the transparent for the interface user way. The callback interface IChannelHook consists of the following functions:

```
void ClientGetSize(REFGUID uExtent,
                   REFIID riid,
                   ULONG *pDataSize);

void ClientFillBuffer(REFGUID uExtent,
                      REFIID riid,
                      ULONG *pDataSize,
                      void *pDataBuffer);

void ClientNotify(REFGUID uExtent,
                  REFIID riid,
                  ULONG cbDataSize,
                  void *pDataBuffer,
                  DWORD lDataRep,
                  HRESULT hrFault);

void ServerNotify(REFGUID uExtent,
                  REFIID riid,
                  ULONG cbDataSize,
                  void *pDataBuffer,
                  DWORD lDataRep);

void ServerGetSize(REFGUID uExtent,
                   REFIID riid,
                   HRESULT hrFault,
                   ULONG *pDataSize);
```

```
void ServerFillBuffer(REFGUID uExtent,
                      REFIID riid,
                      ULONG *pDataSize,
                      void *pDataBuffer,
                      HRESULT hrFault);
```

When a COM client issues a call to the server, first ClientGetSize is called on the client's side to determine the size of additional data, and then ClientFillBuffer is called to fill the buffer with actual data. When the COM call arrives at the server, the server side gets notified about the arrived data through the ServerNotify function. The functions ServerGetSize and ServerFillBuffer are called on the way back on the server's side and, finally, ClientNotify is called when the call returns on the client's side.

To make delegation possible, I attached the following information to the COM hook buffer:

- Process ID of the process that issued a call
- Network name of the computer that issued a call
- User token of the thread that issued a call (if it exists) or process-wide user token (if it does not)

When the data arrives on the server's side, the code first checks whether the client and server reside on the same machine, using the transferred machine's name because the user token that we have transferred as well makes sense only on the same machine. If the machine is the same, the server tries to open a process that issues a call and duplicate token, for the machine to be valid for the server's process. Then it uses the duplicated token to call the ImpersonateLoggedOnUser function to do the actual user impersonation.

All information about incoming calls is kept in the thread local storage (TLS) on a per-thread basis. To avoid losing information in case of recursive COM calls, the information about incoming calls is kept as a stack and every new call pushes its new context on the stack and removes it on the way back to the server.

The COM channel hook will be installed automatically as long as DLL is loaded into the memory of the process. This could be done either by an explicit call to the LoadLibrary function or implicitly by a CoCreateInstance call, creating an IClientInfo interface.

For the proper functionality of the discussed user-impersonation method, the channel hook must be installed both in the client and server processes. For my project, I managed to do it automatically for the client and for the server by initializing an interface to the IClientInfo from the Proxy-Stub DLL that is automatically generated by the MSVC Wizard. To do so, you need to create a new "c" file that looks like this:

```
#include <WINDOWS.H>
#include "..\COMchannelinfo\dcom_channel_info.h"
#include "..\dcomchannelinfo\dcom_channel_info_i.c"
```

```
//previous DLLMain function
BOOL WINAPI DllMain(HINSTANCE hinstDLL,
                    DWORD fdwReason,
                    LPVOID lpvReserved);

BOOL WINAPI newDllMain(HINSTANCE hinstDLL,
                       DWORD fdwReason,
                       LPVOID lpvReserved)
{
HRESULT hr;
static IClientInfo* client_info_iface;
switch (fdwReason)
{
    case DLL_PROCESS_ATTACH:
    {
    client_info_iface = NULL;
    hr = CoCreateInstance(&CLSID_ClientInfo,
                          NULL,
                          CLSCTX_INPROC_SERVER,
                          &IID_IClientInfo,
                          (void**)&client_info_iface);
        if (FAILED(hr))
        {
            return FALSE;
        };
    }; break;
    case DLL_PROCESS_DETACH:
    {
    __try
    {
        if (client_info_iface != NULL)
        {
        client_info_iface->lpVtbl->Release(client_info_iface);
        };
    } __except (1)
    {
        //we do not care if something has happened on shutdown
    };
    }; break;
};
return DllMain(hinstDLL, fdwReason, lpvReserved);
}
```

And then patch a generated make file for your proxy-stub DLL (usually it has the name of the project plus "ps.mk" at the end) and make the following changes to it:

```
rcserverps.dll: dlldata.obj rcserver_p.obj rcserver_i.obj
➥rcserverps_dllmain.obj
(this is a new object file)
    link /dll /out:rcserverps.dll /def:rcserverps.def /entry:newDllMain
(this is new DLL entry point) dlldata.obj rcserver_p.obj \
```

```
    rcserver_i.obj rcserverps_dllmain.obj (this
is a new object file) \
    kernel32.lib rpcndr.lib rpcns4.lib rpcrt4.lib oleaut32.lib uuid.lib
➥ole32.lib
(additional standard library)
```

The effect of this operation is the following: As soon as you make a first call to your COM interface, proxy-stub DLL will be loaded automatically by the COM engine and in its DLLMain it loads and installs our COM channel hook that transfers required information about the called user automatically! You have an advanced impersonation routine for free! :)

Interface Usage

You need to register the DLL with the call to regsvr32.exe dcom_channel_info.dll.

Sources, Demos, Updates, and Legal Stuff

- The latest sources and updates for the application can be found at http://www.geocities.com/pbarvinko.
- The interface itself is used in the Remote Control application (in its server part), which could be used as an example on usage of this impersonation method. It also can be found at http://www.geocities.com/pbarvinko.
- You can drop an email to the author at pbarvinko@yahoo.com.

Acknowledgments

Big thanks to Don Box (dbox@develop.com) for pointing out an elegant solution to my problem.

FROM THE FORUM

Question (cescobar):

I am trying to implement connection points to trap events that are raised by a custom COM class. How could I develop the sink class and the container or client class?

Answer (IndikaNiva):

Here is code to sink into an event loop. This code is for MS Word. By simply changing the UID and other minor modifications, you should be able to get events in your application.

Add the following to your header file:

```
COleDispatchDriver m_app;
IConnectionPoint *m_pConnectionPoint;
DWORD m_adviseCookie;

CWordAppEventSink::CWordAppEventSink(LPDISPATCH WordDispatch)
{
    EnableAutomation();
    DISPID dispID;
    unsigned short *ucPtr;
    BYTE *parmStr;
    ucPtr = L"visible";
    //_WordApplication WordApp = (_WordApplication) pWordApp;
    m_app.AttachDispatch(WordDispatch);
    m_app.m_lpDispatch->GetIDsOfNames(IID_NULL, &ucPtr, 1,
        LOCALE_USER_DEFAULT, &dispID );
    parmStr = (BYTE *)( VTS_VARIANT );
    m_app.InvokeHelper(dispID, DISPATCH_METHOD ¦ DISPATCH_PROPERTYPUT,
        VT_EMPTY, NULL, parmStr, &COleVariant((short)TRUE) );

    static const GUID IID_IWord8AppEvents =
    {0x000209f7,0x000,0x0000,{0xc0,0x00,0x0,0x00,0x00, 0x00, 0x00, 0x46 } };

    HRESULT hr;

    // Get server's IConnectionPointContainer interface.
    IConnectionPointContainer *pConnPtContainer;
    hr = m_app.m_lpDispatch->QueryInterface(IID_IConnectionPointContainer,
➥(void **)&pConnPtContainer );
    ASSERT(!FAILED(hr));

    // Find connection point for events we're interested in.
    hr = pConnPtContainer->FindConnectionPoint(IID_IWord8AppEvents,
        &m_pConnectionPoint );
    ASSERT(!FAILED(hr));

    // Get the IUnknown interface of our event implementation.
    LPUNKNOWN pUnk = GetInterface(&IID_IUnknown);
    ASSERT(pUnk);

    // Setup advisory connection!
    hr = m_pConnectionPoint->Advise(pUnk, &m_adviseCookie);
    ASSERT(!FAILED(hr));

    // Release IConnectionPointContainer interface.
    pConnPtContainer->Release();
}
```

39

DCOM

COM Security Primer, Part I

This article was contributed by Jeff Prosise.

Next to threading and apartments, security is the part of COM that seems to cause developers the most pain. Nearly everyone's first experience with DCOM is to attempt to launch a remote COM server, only to be met with an E_ACCEESSDENIED error. E_ACCESSDENIED may be the most hated HRESULT in all of COM because it tells you that the security subsystem prevented you from doing what you wanted to do, but it doesn't tell you why you were prevented from doing it.

I get regular email messages from developers who have written COM applications that work on one machine but fail miserably when they're deployed to work across machines. In almost every case, the problem is security. Security isn't a big deal when COM clients and COM servers reside on the same machine, but it's a huge deal when activation requests and method calls start flying between machines. COM can't simply allow someone to walk up to a machine, log in, and begin launching remote server processes on other machines; to do so would constitute a hole in security. If you want a COM client to launch a COM server on another machine, you must configure the security subsystem to allow it. And that's not all. There's also access control, remote server process identity, and authentication to think about. If you get a distributed COM application to work without factoring all these aspects of the COM security model into your design, you got lucky. And even though your application runs fine right now, something as simple as a user logging out from a remote server might cause it to fail.

The story of COM security is a story that needs to be told. In this article, the first in a two-part series, I'll discuss two important aspects of the COM security model: activation security and access security. Two articles can't hope to convey everything there is to know about COM security, but they can help you build the fundamental understanding necessary to have the security subsystem work for you instead of against you.

Activation Security

Let's say Bob walks up to a machine running Windows NT or Windows 2000, logs in, and runs an application that attempts to create a COM object on another machine on the network. By default, that attempt will fail. If Bob is to launch remote server processes on other machines, Bob—and anyone else who wishes to launch a server process remotely—must be granted permission to do so. COM refers to such permissions as launch permissions.

Launch permissions can be applied at two levels. First, the COM server that's to be launched remotely can be assigned launch permissions that apply only to it. Such launch permissions are called server-specific launch permissions. Second, the machine on which the remote COM server is installed can have default launch permissions defined. Server-specific launch permissions, if present, take precedence over default launch permissions. When a remote activation request arrives at its doorstep, COM first checks to see if server-specific launch permissions have been defined for the COM server targeted by the request. If the answer is yes, COM uses those launch permissions to determine whether to succeed or fail the activation attempt. If it finds no server-specific launch permissions, COM then falls back to the machine's default launch permissions.

Both types of launch permissions are recorded by writing access control lists (ACLs) to the registry of the machine on which the COM server is installed. An ACL is a standard NT security construct used to identify users and groups of users. Each entry in a launch ACL specifically grants or denies launch permission to a user or group of users. Server-specific launch permissions are applied by adding a value named LaunchPermission to the registry's HKCR\AppID\{...} key and assigning to that value a binary ACL. (HKCR stands for HKEY_CLASSES_ROOT; {...}is the COM server's AppID.) Default launch permissions are applied by adding a DefaultLaunchPermission value to the registry's HKLM\Software\Microsoft\Ole key and assigning it an ACL. (HKLM is short for HKEY_LOCAL_MACHINE.) Because it's no fun to encode ACLs by hand, launch permissions are normally added to the registry by running DCOMCNFG, a configuration tool that comes with COM.

The upshot of all this is that if Bob runs a COM client on machine A that launches a COM server on machine B, Bob must be granted launch permission on machine B. That permission can come from a LaunchPermission entry or a DefaultLaunchPermission entry, but it must come from one of the two. Bob must also be authenticatable on machine B. If Bob logged in using a domain account and both machine A and machine B belong to that domain, then Bob can be authenticated on both machines. However, if Bob logged onto machine A using a local account, then machine B must have an identical local account (same username and password), or else the activation request will fail.

Note that you can effectively disable activation security by granting launch permission to Everyone. Granting launch permission to Everyone is the only way to allow anonymous (unauthenticated) users to launch remote COM servers.

As an aside, I often receive email from developers asking whether it's possible for a COM client to launch a remote COM server using an alternate identity. For example, suppose Alice has permission to launch a particular COM server, but Bob doesn't. Can Bob launch a remote COM server as if he were Alice? The answer is yes—if Bob knows Alice's username and password. The trick is to initialize a COAUTHIDENTITY structure with Alice's credentials, put the address of the COAUTHIDENTITY structure in a COAUTHINFO structure, put the address of the COAUTHINFO structure in a COSERVERINFO structure, and pass the address of the COSERVERINFO structure to a COM activation function such as CoCreateInstanceEx or CoGetClassObject. If you do this, be sure to specify an impersonation level equal to or higher than RPC_C_IMP_LEVEL_IMPERSONATE in the COAUTHINFO structure's dwImpersonationLevel field. Otherwise, the activation request will fail.

Power COM Programming Tip

Ever been frustrated by CoCreateInstance or CoCreateInstanceEx calls that take a minute or more to succeed? The delay is probably due to the fact that an unauthenticatable caller is attempting to launch a remote server process, which is perfectly legal if you've granted launch permission to Everyone. The problem is that the local COM Service Control Manager (SCM) tries first to establish an authenticated connection to its counterpart on the remote machine, and only falls back to an unauthenticated connection after its earlier attempts fail—hence the delay.

The solution is to pass CoCreateInstanceEx a COSERVERINFO structure containing the address of a COAUTHINFO structure whose dwAuthnLevel field is set to RPC_C_AUTHN_LEVEL_NONE. This tells the local SCM to go directly to an unauthenticated connection and bypasses the time-consuming attempt to create an authenticated connection to a remote SCM.

Access Security

Activation security allows a system administrator—or anyone who has permission to edit the registry—to control who can launch remote server processes. Access security governs who can call into remote server processes once they're launched. Generally speaking, the same users and groups of users that enjoy launch permission should be granted access permission, too. There are exceptions, however. Occasionally it's useful to allow someone to call into a running server (or client) process but not grant them permission to launch the process to begin with.

Like launch permissions, access permissions can be applied to individual COM servers and to entire machines. ACLs used for server-specific access permissions are stored in the registry at HKCR\AppID\{...}\AccessPermission, where once more {...} is the COM server's AppID. Default access permissions, which define who can make method calls to a remote server process that isn't accompanied by server-specific access permissions, are stored at HKLM\Software\Microsoft\Ole\DefaultAccessPermission. The values assigned to AccessPermission and DefaultAccessPermission are serialized ACLs whose entries explicitly grant or deny access to individual users and groups. As with launch permissions, access permissions recorded in the registry are typically put there with DCOMCNFG.

That's one way to apply access permissions: Write them to the registry. But there's another way. CoInitializeSecurity is a COM API function that a process can use to create its own programmatic security blanket. It can only be called successfully once per process, so if you call it, you must call it early in the process's lifetime (before COM beats you to the punch). The first parameter to CoInitializeSecurity defines the process's access permissions. It can be set to any of the following values:

- NULL
- A pointer to a GUID that corresponds to a registered AppId
- A pointer to an IAccessControl interface
- A pointer to a security descriptor containing an ACL

Which type of value the first parameter holds is indicated by a flag passed in CoInitializeSecurity's eighth parameter (dwCapabilities). Setting the first parameter to NULL prevents access checks from being performed, effectively turning access control off for this process. Passing a pointer to an AppID causes COM to set access permissions according to the AccessPermission ACL found in the registry under that AppID. Passing a pointer to a security descriptor assigns access permissions using the ACL in the descriptor. Finally, passing a pointer to an IAccessControl interface permits a COM server to take control of access checking and to succeed or fail individual calls as they arrive based on the caller's identity—in effect, to implement its own security policy. By implementing IAccessControl, a COM server could, for example, accept calls from users whose usernames begin with A through K and reject all others.

Many programmers believe that setting access permissions with CoInitializeSecurity is superior to relying on ACLs in the registry. Why? Because CoInitializeSecurity ensures that your carefully applied access permissions can't be destroyed by someone with the freedom to edit the registry. It's unfortunate that launch permissions can't be applied with CoInitializeSecurity, too, but they can't because a process has to be launched before it can call CoInitializeSecurity, and once it's launched, it's too late for any API function to prevent the launch from occurring.

Whether you choose to apply access permissions declaratively (with DCOMCNFG) or programmatically (with CoInitializeSecurity), there's one detail you mustn't forget. Be sure to give the SYSTEM account—the built-in account under which most NT services run—access permission to your COM servers if you want clients to be able to activate them remotely. During one critical phase of the remote activation process, a part of COM that runs in an NT service must call into the freshly launched server process. If you've denied the SYSTEM account access permission, the call will fail and the client's activation request will fail, too. Due to a bug in Windows NT 4.0, the HRESULT returned to the client might be E_OUTOFMEMORY instead of E_ACCESSDENIED.

What it all means is that if you want Bob to be able to launch a remote server process, and then make method calls into that process, you should grant Bob access permission as well as launch permission. Failure to do both will result in the infamous E_ACCESSDENIED errors that COM programmers have come to know all too well.

Power COM Programming Tip

One of the errors that newbies often experience when they first begin tinkering with DCOM occurs when they fail to give a remote server process permission to perform callbacks to a client. Suppose a client on machine A launches a COM server on machine B and receives an interface pointer in return. Then that client passes an interface pointer of its own to the server so that the server can perform callbacks.

What's wrong with this picture? Nothing, except for the fact that callbacks will only be permitted if the server process is granted access permission to the client process. If the server process is assigned the identity Mister Server, then Mister Server must be granted access permission to the client process. One way to grant that access permission is to have the client process call CoInitializeSecurity. Another way is to include Mister Server (or Everyone) in the client machine's DefaultAccessPermission ACL.

What makes this error especially difficult to diagnose is that if connection points are involved, the failure typically doesn't occur when the server attempts its first callback; it occurs when the client passes its interface pointer to the server using IConnectionPoint::Advise. Most implementations of Advise, including ATL's, call QueryInterface on the client. But if the server process lacks access permissions in the client process, QueryInterface will fail. When Advise sees QueryInterface fail, Advise will fail, too.

The moral: If you're using connection points to facilitate callbacks from remote servers and IConnectionPoint::Advise returns E_ACCESSDENIED or E_OUTOFMEMORY, check the access permissions on the client. Chances are the security principal whose identity the server process has been assigned does not have permission to call into the client process.

Next Month...Identity and Authentication

Learning about activation security and access security is a good first step on the road to understanding COM security. But there's more—much more, as a matter of fact. In my next column , I'll talk about two more aspects of the COM security model: remote server process identity and authentication. If you found this month's discussion interesting, I think you'll find next month's to be even more so. Stay tuned....

COM Security Primer, Part II

This article was contributed by Jeff Prosise.

In my previous column, I began a two-part discussion on COM security by introducing launch permissions and access permissions. COM uses launch permissions to decide whether to allow or disallow remote activation requests, and it uses access permissions to determine who's allowed to make method calls to remote server processes. Failure to take launch and access permissions into account frequently leads to the E_ACCESSDENIED errors that COM developers so despise.

In Part II, I'll continue last month's discussion by explaining two more fundamental tenets of COM security—namely, remote server process identity and authentication.

Identity

When a person logs onto a machine running Windows NT or Windows 2000, that person is authenticated against a database of valid usernames and passwords. If the logon is approved, a new logon session is created and an access token is issued that identifies the person who performed the logon and the groups that he or she belongs to. Processes subsequently started by that user are tagged with the access token. Before NT or 2000 permits a process to access a system resource such as a file, it uses the access token and information encoded in the resource's security descriptor, if present, to determine whether or not to allow the access to occur. The operating system fails attempts to access the resource if the process performing the access lacks the necessary permissions. For example, if Bob is forbidden to read a certain file, then any process tagged with Bob's access token will utterly fail in its efforts to read that file.

Clearly, the fact that every running process is tagged with an access token is an essential element of operating system security. But when a remote server process is launched by a COM client, a fundamental question arises: Whose identity should the server process be assigned? On the surface, it might seem to make sense to assign the process the identity of the launching user—in other words, that of the client process that lodged the activation request. And while that is indeed one of the options available to you, it turns out to be the worst option for most distributed applications. I'll explain why momentarily.

When you configure a COM server to allow remote activation, one of the key choices you make is what identity to assign the server process when it's launched at the behest of a remote client. In the general case—that is, assuming the COM server is a regular EXE and not an NT service—your options are threefold:

- Interactive user
- Launching user
- A specific user ("this user")

If you choose interactive user, you're commanding COM to assign the server process the identity of the person logged in at the server console—the "interactive user"— when a launch occurs. If Alice is logged in when an activation request arrives from another machine, then the server process is assigned Alice's identity. It's as if the process had been launched by Alice herself, and it doesn't matter who lodged the remote activation request as long as that person has launch permission. Interactive user is a good choice for testing and debugging a distributed application because 1) it's the only option that lets you start the server process in a debugger, and 2) it's the only option that permits a remote server process to display message boxes and other GUI application elements on the screen. The drawback to interactive user is that the process can't be launched if there's no one logged in on the server—that is, if there is no interactive user. Therefore, interactive user is a poor choice for server identity unless you can ensure that someone is logged in on the server, and that the logged-on user has sufficient security permissions to do whatever it is the COM server is designed to do.

The second option is launching user. This option is sometimes referred to in COM literature as the *as activator* option. It also happens to be the default, which is unfortunate because launching user has crippled more than its fair share of distributed applications. Launching user simply tells COM to assign the server process the identity of the remote client process that did the launching. If Bob runs a COM client on machine A and that client launches a server process on machine B, then the server process is assigned Bob's identity. The good news is that this enables the process to launch even if no interactive user is logged in. The bad news is that every new security principal (Bob, Alice, and so on) who launches a server process this way will cause a unique instance of the server process to be launched, and in a unique winstation, no less. Among other things, this makes it impossible for two different clients to use CoCreateInstance[Ex] to connect to a singleton object in a remote server process unless both clients are logged in under the same account. Unless you truly do want COM to satisfy activation requests with different server processes, stay away from launching user.

The proper way to deploy most remote COM servers is to set up a special user account for each server to run under and to designate that account with the "this user" option. If a COM server is configured to run as Mister Object, and if Mister Object is a valid account on the server, then when launched, the remote server process is assigned the identity of Mister Object. It matters not who's logged in on the server (or if anyone is logged in at all) or who launched the process—all that matters is that Mister Object is a valid account on the machine that hosts the COM server. By assigning the remote server process a fixed and known identity, you can control the process's rights and privileges by exercising normal administrative control over the account. That's a win for everyone involved.

Remote server process identity is normally assigned by running DCOMCNFG on the server (see Figure 39.1). Choosing interactive user writes a RunAs entry to the server's registry-based AppID and assigns that entry the string Interactive User, as shown in Figure 39.2. If you choose this user instead, the account name is written to the RunAs entry in place of Interactive User. If you choose launching user in DCOMCNFG, no RunAs entry is created because launching user is the default. In other words, the absence of a RunAs entry means the server has been assigned the identity of the launching user. In most cases, that's bad.

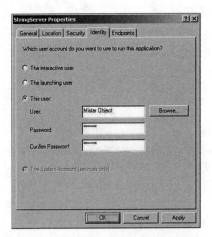

Figure 39.1   Using DCOMCNFG to assign an identity to a COM server.

Figure 39.2 RunAs entry added to the registry by DCOMCNFG.

Assigning an identity to a remote server process is easy with DCOMCNFG. But what if you want to write an installation program to do it for you? You can use the Reg functions in the Win32 API to write a new RunAs entry to the registry, but that's only half the job. You also have to tell COM what the account's password is. For security reasons, the password isn't stored in the registry; it's stored in a private location managed by the Local Security Authority, or LSA. Registering the password that goes with a RunAs account is accomplished with the LsaStorePrivateData API function. For sample code demonstrating how, see the DCOMPERM sample in the Windows 2000 Platform SDK. Pay particular attention to the function named SetRunAsPassword because it's that function that registers a password with the LSA.

Another issue to be aware of when writing custom installation programs for DCOM servers has to do with logon rights. An account used to provide an identity for a remote COM server—that is, an account referenced by a RunAs entry in the registry—must have the right to log on as a batch job. DCOMCNFG enables this right automatically when you use its "this user" option, but if you write a setup program that registers a RunAs account, you must enable this right programmatically. The same DCOMPERM sample that demonstrates how to register a RunAs password also shows how to enable an account's "logon as a batch job" right. See the DCOMPERM function named SetAccountRights for details.

Power COM Programming Tip

Not too long ago, a gentleman at a large computer company called me requesting help diagnosing a problem he was experiencing with a DCOM application. His app called for multiple clients, all running on different machines, to use CoCreateInstanceEx to connect to a singleton object on another machine. In testing, QA personnel found that the clients were able to connect just fine in one test scenario, but using a slightly different test script, each call to CoCreateInstanceEx caused a new server process to be launched, effectively negating the object's singleton behavior. Paradoxically, the code was identical in both cases. My friend's question to me: What could possibly cause this to happen?

The problem, as it turned out, was simple. Because the remote COM server had not been assigned an identity, it was defaulting to launching user. In the test scenario that worked, all test personnel were logged in under the same account—a special account established just for QA employees. In the scenario that didn't work, the testers were logged in using their normal domain user accounts. Get the picture? If 10 users log in as Bob and attempt to launch a remote server process configured to run as the launching user, then the system will happily allow them to connect to one server process. But if Bob logs in as Bob and Alice logs in as Alice and each calls CoCreateInstance[Ex], COM will launch two server processes—even if the object they're attempting to connect to is a singleton.

The moral of this story? Beware the launching user—especially if you want multiple clients out on the network to be able to "launch" into the same server process.

Authentication

Authentication is the answer to the question "How sure do I want to be that my callers are who they say they are? And how secure should my data be when COM method calls pass over the wire?" COM answers these questions by assigning an authentication level to all calls that travel between machines. You decide what the authentication level should be. Your choices, in order of ascending security, are listed in Table 39.1.

Table 39.1   Authentication Level Options

Authentication Level	Meaning
None	Do not authenticate callers.
Connect	Authenticate callers on their first call into the server process.
Call	Authenticate callers on every call into the server process.
Packet	Authenticate callers on every packet of every method call.
Packet Integrity	All of the above, plus verify that calls haven't been altered en route.
Packet Privacy	All of the above, plus encrypt all data passed over the wire.

You choose an authentication level based on the level of security you desire. Authentication=None means you're not concerned about security and want to allow anonymous access to your server. (If you go this route, remember to grant launch and access permissions to Everyone; otherwise, no one will be able to use your COM server.) Authentication=Packet is a good middle ground if you want to prevent *spoofing*—callers gaining access to your server by posing as someone else. If you intend to transmit sensitive information such as credit card numbers and passwords in your method calls, then you might opt for Packet Privacy, which fully encrypts every bit of every packet comprising a COM method call. Packet Privacy provides the highest degree of security, but it's bad for performance. Don't use it unless you really need it.

Before you choose an authentication level, be aware that a server can't authenticate callers if the callers' credentials aren't valid on the server's machine. For example, if you specify that Bob has access permission to your COM server and pick an authentication level equal to, say, Connect, then Bob will only be able to call into the server process if the username and password that Bob logged in with are valid on the server, too. The easiest way to achieve this is to have both machines be members of the same domain. If Bob is a valid account in the domain, and if the client that Bob's logged in to and the server he's making calls to belong to that domain, then you can use any authentication level you desire. But if for any reason Bob can't be authenticated on the server—if, for example, the two PCs belong to different domains that don't enjoy a trust relationship, or if one or both of them don't belong to a domain—then the only good way to authenticate calls from Bob is to set up identical Bob accounts (same username, same password) on both machines. That's a pain from an administrative standpoint, but it can be done.

So how do you set the authentication level? One way to do it is to use DCOMCNFG. You can pick a default authentication level for processes on the host machine from the Default Authentication Level list on DCOMCNFG's Default Properties tab (Figure 39.3). Doing so writes the authentication level to the registry at HKEY_LOCAL_MACHINE\Software\Microsoft\Ole\LegacyAuthenticationLevel. In Windows 2000 and in NT 4.0 Service Pack 4 and higher, you can assign authentication levels to individual COM servers (Figure 39.4). Server-specific authentication levels, if used, override machine-wide default authentication levels, and are written to the registry under the COM server's AppID.

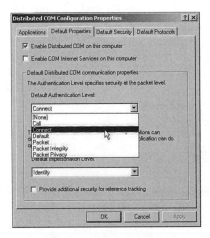

Figure 39.3   Setting a machine's default authentication level.

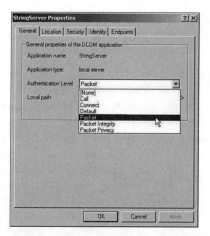

Figure 39.4   Setting an individual COM server's authentication level.

The second way to set the authentication level is to call CoInitializeSecurity. Passing an authentication value to CoInitializeSecurity sets the authentication level for the calling process and overrides authentication levels applied with DCOMCNFG. If desired, the authentication level can even be specified on a per-interface pointer basis using COM's IClientSecurity interface. That, however, is a topic for another day.

One point to be aware of concerning authentication levels is that you should set them at both ends of the wire—that is, on both the client and server PCs. When a client acquires an interface pointer from a remote COM server, COM examines the authentication levels in the two processes and encodes the higher of the two in the channel object that pairs the interface proxy and stub. The practical effect of this is that setting the authentication level to, say, Connect on the server doesn't necessarily mean that calls will be transmitted with an authentication level equal to Connect. If the client process has a higher authentication level—say, Packet—then calls will be performed with a Packet level of authentication. If you really want the server's authentication level to drive the authentication level of incoming calls, set the client's authentication level to None. Then, and only then, can you rest assured that the server's authentication level will be the one that's used.

FROM THE FORUM

Question (jeffro125):

I am attempting to operate a simple DCOM program over the local network and receiving the ERROR_NO 0x800706D3 message "Authentication Service is Unknown". This application works on the local Windows 98 machine but on no other, even after correct registration and enabling remote connections. What could be the problem?

Answer (Borgward):

This appears to be an authentication problem, possibly to do with Windows 98. You can use either DCOMCNFG to enable launching permissions or the following code to set the authentication level to zero, the default authentication level for proxies meaning that no authentication is used in the process:

```
CoInitializeSecurity(0, -1, 0, 0, RPC_C_AUTHN_LEVEL_NONE,
RPC_C_IMP_LEVEL_IMPERSONATE, 0, EOAC_ACCESS_CONTROL, 0)
```

Putting It All Together

Needless to say, there's much more that could be said about COM security. But hopefully these basics are enough to get you started and to help you overcome the security-related problems that bedevil many COM developers. Now, for example, if you encounter E_ACCESSDENIED errors attempting remote activations, you'll know to check the launch permissions on the server. If those are set correctly, then the next place you'd look is at the remote server process identity. If the server is configured to run as the interactive user but there is no interactive user, then bingo!—you've found the problem. To take this example a step further, suppose launch permissions are set to allow Bob to launch, that it's Bob who's attempting the launch, that Bob is a valid account on the server, that the server is set to run as launching user, and still you get E_ACCESSDENIED errors. The likely culprit? Check that the authentication level isn't equal to None. A server process can only be launched under the identity of the launching user if COM knows who the launching user is. But with authentication disabled, COM can't identify the launching user.

If you'd like to learn more about COM security, I highly recommend that you read Keith Brown's book *Programming Windows Security*. Chapter 9 especially contains valuable information that every COM developer should know, and by itself can justify the book's cost.

Instantiating _com_ptr_t Objects Remotely

This article was contributed by Keith Rule.

I was going along, cheerfully using COM with Microsoft's smart pointers, when I discovered a glaring omission in the underlying _com_ptr_t code. It turns out that there is no way to use CreateInstance() to instantiate an object remotely. And there is no equivalent member function to CreateInstanceEx().

After a bit of digging around, I ended up writing this (partially tested) macro that I believe allows remote or local instantiation of Microsoft's smart COM pointers.

Normally, you create COM instances using Microsoft's smart pointers as follows:

```
m_pMyCOMObj.CreateIntance(CLSID_MyCOMObj);
```

When using this macro, replace the previous code with the following:

```
HRESULT hr = CreateInstanceEx<IIMyCOMObjPtr>(m_pMyCOMObj, CLSID_MyCOMObj,
➥_T("RemoteHostname"));
```

This should allow you to connect to your remote host simply by specifying the host-name or IP address in the third argument. Don't forget to check the return value for success.

The code follows:

```
// This template is used to invoke either local or remote instances of
// C++ builtin smart COM objects.
template <typename ObjPtr>
HRESULT CreateInstanceEx(ObjPtr& output, const CLSID& rclsid,
    const CString& hostname = _T(""), IUnknown* pOuter = NULL, DWORD
➥dwClsContext = CLSCTX_ALL)
{
    USES_CONVERSION;
    HRESULT hr;

    if (!hostname.IsEmpty()) {
        // Create Distributed Object

        // Declare some locals
        IUnknown*       pIUnknown;
        COSERVERINFO*   pServerInfo = NULL;
        MULTI_QI        rgmqResults;
        COSERVERINFO    ServerInfo;

        // Zero structures
        memset(&rgmqResults, 0, sizeof(rgmqResults));
        memset(&ServerInfo, 0, sizeof(ServerInfo));

        // Initialize data items
        dwClsContext = CLSCTX_REMOTE_SERVER;
        ServerInfo.pwszName = T2W(hostname);
        pServerInfo = &ServerInfo;
        rgmqResults.pIID = &IID_IUnknown;

        // Create the IUnknown object for the remote object object
        hr = CoCreateInstanceEx(rclsid, pOuter, dwClsContext, pServerInfo, 1,
➥&rgmqResults);

        // If successful, then get the internal interface we really wanted.
        if (SUCCEEDED(hr)) {
            pIUnknown = rgmqResults.pItf;
            if (SUCCEEDED(hr)) {
```

```
            hr = pIUnknown->QueryInterface(ObjPtr::GetIID(),
➥reinterpret_cast<void**>(&output));
            }
            pIUnknown->Release(); // IUnknown has served its purpose. Nuke it.
        }
    } else {
        // It's not remote so use the simpler call.
        hr = CoCreateInstance(rclsid, pOuter, dwClsContext, ObjPtr::GetIID(),
reinterpret_cast<void**>(&output));
    }

    return hr;
}
```

Caveats

Don't forget to include _WIN32_DCOM in the preprocessor definitions of your project, or you will get a syntax error telling you that CoCreateInstanceEx() is not defined. You also need to make sure that OleInit() has been called prior to using the CreateInstanceEx() macro.

FROM THE FORUM

Question (dodo):

I am getting the following errors when trying to use CoCreateInstanceEx:

```
error C2039: 'CoCreateInstanceEx' : is not a member of '`global namespace''
error C2065: 'CoCreateInstanceEx' : undeclared identifier
```

Why is this?

Answer (dodo):

I found the answer myself. The _WIN32_DCOM preprocessor definition must be defined either in the project settings or in stdafx.h before CoCreateInstanceEx can be used.

RNSO—A Remote Notifiers, Subjects, and Observers Server Over DCOM

This article was contributed by Pierre Mellinand.

What Is RNSO?

RNSO is a server where the well-known Observer Design Pattern is implemented with Distributed COM. The Observer Design Pattern helps you to build applications where data changes need to be communicated to another of your applications. The pieces of data are called *subjects*, and parts of applications interested in the changes are *observers*. Subjects send *notifications* of changes to observers through a server (called the *manager*). Only the manager knows about the observers who want to be notified. It maintains the connections, which are called *subscriptions*.

Generally, observers indicate that they want to be notified by a method:

```
Observer1.Subscribe( pSubject ) ;
Observer2.Subscribe( pSubject ) ;
```

Subjects prevent changes by another method:

```
Subject.Notify( ..something ) ;
```

Here, the two observers Observer1 and Observer2 will be notified.

This design pattern is very useful for GUI applications (MDI), but this can be used in several other cases. As an example, if you build a DLL to access hardware equipment and you'd like to use it on a remote machine, you'll be able to with RNSO.

RNSO allows you to build client-server applications over DCOM without knowing about DCOM or the Observer Design Pattern. It is also independent of applications. The server can serve several applications at the same time, even if they have no relationships with each other.

How Does RNSO Work?

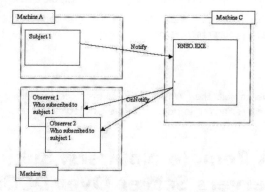

Figure 39.5

Subject1 communicates about changes. The server (RNSO.EXE), which is automatically launched by the OS, notifies the observers who subscribed to the subject.

Observers have a sink interface used by the server to notify them. This is also a component with a mailbox. The mailbox is read by a thread of the component, so the server is not blocked by clients.

Data that a subject can notify is binary, so you can transmit all you want.

Binaries of RNSO

I made several binaries for RNSO:

- **RNSO.exe.** The server.
- **RNSOSupport.DLL.** The DLL used both by the server and the clients.
- **RNSOClient.DLL.** The DLL used to build the observer's clients (you also need RNSOSupport.DLL). You don't need it if you just build a Subject.

The binaries are built with Visual C++ 6.0.

The Sample Application

The sample application shows you

- How to make a CDialog as an observer and a subject.
- How to use classes and ready-to-use components.

Figure 39.6 shows two instances of the application.

1. On the left, we declared the name of the object for the dialog: Subject1.
2. On the right, we declared the dialog as an observer to Subject1.
3. On the left, the subject notified a change My Message.
4. On the right, the subscriber received the notification.

You can start several apps and subscribe to Subject1. All of them will be notified. When a subject is going down, subscribers receive a notification.

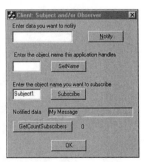

Figure 39.6

In my sample, I derived my CDialog from CDialog and from RnsoNotificationRout. This class has two virtual methods. Overload them to handle notifications:

```
class AFX_EXT_CLASS     RnsoNotificationRout
{
    public:
    RnsoNotificationRout();
    virtual    ~RnsoNotificationRout();
    virtual void OnNotifyNOTIFY(ObserverNotification*    pNotification);
    virtual void OnNotifyNOTIFY_SUBJECTBROKEN(DWORD dwSubjectID);
};
```

You aren't obliged to have a dialog or a window to build an observer or a subject. You can also make your class just an observer or just a subject.

This is very simple.

Why Use This Framework?

You don't have to maintain subscriptions yourself with lists, arrays, and so on. You also can build interprocess/intermachine apps.

40

ActiveX

In this chapter

ActiveX controls are based upon COM technology and are designed to be reusable components that can quickly add specialized functionality to many desktop and Web-based applications.

- "ActiveX Control Tutorial" provides a detailed description of ActiveX controls and their creation.

- "ActiveX Shell Registration" shows an easy way to add ActiveX registration and unregistration capabilities to your Windows shell.

- "Menu in ActiveX Controls" describes how to add menu support to ATL- and MFC-based ActiveX controls.

ActiveX Control Tutorial

This article was contributed by Kapil Chaturvedi.

Figure 40.1

Introduction

This article is for those enthusiastic VC++ developers who want to build their own ActiveX controls but don't know where to start. This article will help you to build your first ActiveX control. This article will show you the step-by-step methods to build a control that draws different waveforms (Sin/Cos). I assume that you are familiar with VC++ and know some basics of ActiveX controls.

Creating an ActiveX Control

Simply follow these steps in order to create an ActiveX control.

1. Using the AppWizard to Create an ActiveX Control Project

1. Select New from the File menu.
2. Click the Projects tab and select the type of project as MFC ActiveX Control Wizard from the list.
3. Name the new project Plot and then click the OK button.
4. Take all the default values of the next dialog (titled MFC ActiveX Control Wizard - Step 1 of 2) and click the Next button.
5. From the next dialog (titled MFC ActiveX Control Wizard - Step 2 of 2), locate the combo box with the prompt "Which window class, if any, should this control subclass?" Drop down the list and select the entry STATIC from that list. We're using a static control in this example since we'll just be displaying data (and not accepting input).
6. Click the Advanced button and check the Flicker Free Activation checkbox.
7. Now click the Finish button. At this point, the AppWizard will generate the following three classes on your behalf:

   - CPlotApp—The ActiveX "application" class is derived from COleControlModule. The COleControlModule class is the base class from which you derive an OLE control module object. This class provides member functions for your control module's initialization (InitInstance) and cleanup code (ExitInstance).
   - CPlotCtrl—The second class is derived from COleControl and will provide most of the functionality to your control. This is the class where you will write the majority of your code.
   - CPlotPropPage—The third class is CPlotPropPage (derived from COlePropertyPage). This class is used to manage the property page dialog of your control. In addition to this class, a dialog resource is also created that will serve as the property page for the control.

2. Adding "Stock" Properties

The term *stock property* means that it's one of a set of common properties that MFC code stores and initializes for you. The MFC code also performs appropriate action when the value of a stock property is changed. The Class Wizard provides code for changing nine such properties. Since these properties are built-in, they are obviously the easiest to deal with in terms of the work required by the developer. As you'll see shortly, you literally don't add a single line of code to add a stock property to your control!

The Class Wizard provides code for the following stock properties:

- Appearance
- BackColor
- ForeColor
- BorderStyle
- Font
- Caption
- Enable
- Text
- hWnd

From these, we will work with the Appearance, BackColor, ForeColor, and BorderStyle properties.

We'll start by adding the BackColor stock property.

1. From the Class Wizard, click the Automation tab.
2. Ensure that the CPlotCtrl class is selected in the Class Name combobox. Now, click the Add Property button to display the Add Property dialog.
3. Once the Add Property dialog does appear, select the BackColor property from the External Name combo box. (It is called the "external name" because this is how users of the control will refer to it.)
4. Verify that the Stock radio button is selected in the Implementation groupbox.
5. Click the OK button to finish the generation of the stock property. At this point, the Class Wizard will store the value of the BackColor property and initialize it to the background color of the container window. The Class Wizard will also add the following line to your control's ODL file:

```
[id(DISPID_BACKCOLOR), bindable, requestedit] OLE_COLOR BackColor;
```

Finally, Class Wizard will also add the code to invalidate the control whenever the value of the BackColor property changes, thereby forcing the OnDraw function to redraw the control. The only thing you have to do is to use the color contained in the property to paint the background color of the control.

6. At this point, add the following two lines of code to the end of the CPlotCtrl::OnDraw member function:

```
CBrush bkBrush(TranslateColor(GetBackColor()));
pdc->FillRect(rcBounds,&bkBrush);
```

7. Now, let's add a Color property page to the program. This page will allow users of the control to change the BackColor of our newly added property at design time. To do this, simply open the PlotCtrl.cpp file and locate the // Property pages comment.

Once you've done that, you should see the following:

```
BEGIN_PROPPAGEIDS(CPlotCtrl, 1)
  PROPPAGEID(CPlotPropPage::guid)
END_PROPPAGEIDS(CPlotCtrl)
```

The first line tells the compiler how many pages exist. Notice that it's set to 1. Change this value to 2 as we're going to add a new page.

Now insert the following line just before the END_PROPPAGEIDS line. (The CLSID_CColorPropPage is defined automatically since this is a property page CLSID for a stock property.)

```
PROPPAGEID(CLSID_CColorPropPage)
```

Once you've finished, your new property page ID map should look like the following:

```
BEGIN_PROPPAGEIDS(CPlotCtrl, 2)
  PROPPAGEID(CPlotPropPage::guid)
  PROPPAGEID(CLSID_CColorPropPage)
END_PROPPAGEIDS(CPlotCtrl)
```

Once you make the above changes, the stock property page is automatically linked to the BackColor property.

8. Now that you've seen how to add the BackColor stock property to an ActiveX control, follow these same steps in order to add the Appearance, ForeColor, and BorderStyle properties. *Note that you do not need to add a property page for the other properties.*

9. After adding these stock properties, build your control and test it using ActiveX Test Container (which is usually found under the Tools menu). As you can see in Figure 40.2, the Class Wizard has added the appropriate controls for changing the stock properties.

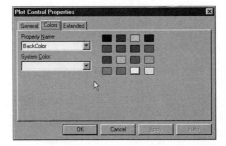

Figure 40.2

FROM THE FORUM

Question (manjula123):

How can I call my ActiveX control from an Active Server Page?

Answer (claudiu_t):

You can use an ActiveX component on an ASP using the following HTML code:

```
<OBJECT id="MyControl" CLSASSID="clsid:XXX-XX..." width="100"
height="100"></OBJECT>
```

In client-side JavaScript code, you can call methods and access properties of this control using the specified ID:

```
<script language="JavaScript">
function myFunc() {
document.all("MyControl").someMethod();
document.all("MyControl").aProperty = "hello";
}
</script>
```

3. Adding Custom Properties

Custom properties are properties you devise yourself for your control. For the plot control I have added only four custom properties, including "Grid On/Off" and "X-Log." The grid properties will control the visibility of the control grid. The "X-log" property will be used to plot the horizontal axis in the logarithmic scale. Let's start with the grid properties.

1. From the Class Wizard, click the Automation tab.

2. Ensure that the CPlotCtrl class is selected in the Class Name combobox. Now, Click the Add Property button to display the Add Property dialog.

3. Once the Add Property dialog is displayed, enter ShowGrid into the External Name combo box.

4. Select BOOL as the properties type.

5. Verify that the Member Variable radio button is selected in the Implementation group box.

6. Click the OK button to have the Class Wizard create a boolean custom property named ShowGrid. Also note that the internal member variable name (the name used in the control's code) is m_showGrid. Now, whenever the container changes the value of this property, the MFC code will reflect that value in the m_showGrid member variable and will call the CPlotCtrl::OnShowGridChanged notification function.

7. Because ShowGrid is a custom property, we have to write our own initialization and implementation code. Add the following code (marked in bold) in order to initialize the m_showGrid member variable.

```
void CPlotCtrl::DoPropExchange(CPropExchange* pPX)
{
ExchangeVersion(pPX, MAKELONG(_wVerMinor, _wVerMajor));
COleControl::DoPropExchange(pPX);

PX_Bool(pPX,_T("ShowGrid"),m_showGrid,FALSE);
}
```

Locate the CPlotCtrl::OnShowGridChanged member function that the Class Wizard added to your code when you created the ShowGrid property. (It should be at the end of the PlotCtl.cpp file.) Insert the following line (marked in bold) to that function. (This call simply invalidates the control when the ShowGrid property value is changed.)

```
void CPlotCtrl::OnShowGridChanged()
{
InvalidateControl();
SetModifiedFlag();
}
```

8. Since ShowGrid is a custom property, we have to do a little more work to have it included on the property page. To do this, open the Resource View tab and open the Property page dialog (IDD_PROPPAGE_PLOT).

9. Using the dialog editor, add a check box with the ID IDC_CHECK1 and text value of "Show Grid."

10. Run the Class Wizard, and select the Member Variables tab.

11. Add a member variable for the control ID IDC_CHECK1 called m_bShowGrid of type BOOL. Make sure that you set the Optional property name to ShowGrid. When you're finished, the dialog should look like Figure 40.3.

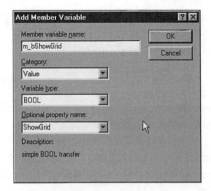

Figure 40.3

12. Now, add the custom property "X-Log" where the following values are shown in Figure 40.4.

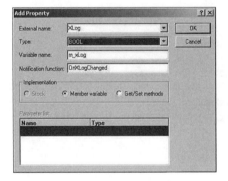

Figure 40.4

13. Add the following line of code to the CPlotCtrl::DoPropExchange member function:

```
PX_Bool(pPX,_T("ShowGrid"),m_xLog,FALSE);
```

14. Just as you did with the ShowGrid property, add a checkbox to the control's property page for the X-Log property and then add a member variable for it as well.

15. Insert the following code (marked in bold) in the CPlotCtrl::OnXLogChanged member function:

```
void CPlotCtrl::OnXLogChanged()
{
  InvalidateControl();
    SetModifiedFlag();
}
```

16. To implement these properties, add the following members to the control:

```
private:
CRect wndRect,m_DrawRect;
CDC* m_pDC;

//Function to Intialize DC and mapping mode
void PrepareForPlotting(CRect rect);
void DrawGrid();
```

17. Modify the CPlotCtrl::OnDraw member function as follows. (Note: You will need to include the math.h file due to the use of the sin function.)

```
//Function to plot Grid
void CPlotCtrl::OnDraw(CDC* pdc,
                       const CRect& rcBounds,
                       const CRect& rcInvalid)
{
DoSuperclassPaint(pdc, rcBounds);

m_pDC = pdc;
m_DrawRect = rcBounds;
wndRect = rcBounds;

PrepareForPlotting(&rcBounds);

CBrush hbrBackground(TranslateColor(GetBackColor()));
pdc->FillRect (m_DrawRect,&hbrBackground);

if(m_showGrid)
 DrawGrid();

float y;
m_pDC->SelectObject(CPen(PS_SOLID,1,GetForeColor()));
m_pDC->MoveTo(m_DrawRect.right/2,
m_DrawRect.bottom/2);
for (int i=0;i<2000;i=i++)
{
 y = 512*sin(2*3.1415926535*i/1000)+512;
 m_pDC->MoveTo(i , y);
 m_pDC->LineTo(i+1 ,
 512*sin(2*3.1415926535*(i+1)/1000)+512);
}
}
```

18. Add the following code for the DrawGrid function that you declared.

```
void CPlotCtrl::DrawGrid()
{
 CPen Pen (PS_SOLID¦PS_INSIDEFRAME,1,TranslateColor(GetForeColor()));
 CPen* oldPen = m_pDC->SelectObject (&Pen);

 switch(m_xLog)
 {
  case FALSE:
   int i;

   for (i = m_DrawRect.left;
        i <= m_DrawRect.right ;
        i = i+(( m_DrawRect.right - m_DrawRect.left )/10))
   {
    m_pDC->MoveTo (i, m_DrawRect.top );
    m_pDC->LineTo (i, m_DrawRect.bottom );
   }

   for (i = m_DrawRect.top;
        i <= m_DrawRect.bottom;
        i = i+ (( m_DrawRect.bottom - m_DrawRect.top )/8))
   {
    m_pDC->MoveTo (m_DrawRect.left,i );
    m_pDC->LineTo (m_DrawRect.right,i);
   }
  break;

  case TRUE:
   int x,X;

   for(int j=1;j<= 10;j++)
   {
    x= (int)(log10(j)*285.7143);
    m_pDC->MoveTo (x,m_DrawRect.top);
    m_pDC->LineTo (x,m_DrawRect.bottom );
   }

   X= x;

   m_pDC->SelectObject(&Pen);
   m_pDC->MoveTo (x,m_DrawRect.top);
   m_pDC->LineTo (x,m_DrawRect.bottom );
   m_pDC->SelectObject (&Pen);
   m_pDC->TextOut (x,m_DrawRect.bottom-5,"10.0K");
```

```
for( j=1;j<= 10;j++)
{
 x= X+(int)(log10(j)*285.7143);
 m_pDC->MoveTo (x,m_DrawRect.top);
 m_pDC->LineTo (x,m_DrawRect.bottom );
}

X= x;

m_pDC->SelectObject(&Pen);
m_pDC->MoveTo (x,m_DrawRect.top);
m_pDC->LineTo (x,m_DrawRect.bottom );
m_pDC->SelectObject (&Pen);
m_pDC->TextOut (x,m_DrawRect.bottom-5,"100.0K");

for( j=1;j<= 10;j++)
{
 x= X+(int)(log10(j)*285.7143);
 m_pDC->MoveTo (x,m_DrawRect.top);
 m_pDC->LineTo (x,m_DrawRect.bottom );
}

X= x;

m_pDC->SelectObject(&Pen);
m_pDC->MoveTo (x,m_DrawRect.top);
m_pDC->LineTo (x,m_DrawRect.bottom );
m_pDC->SelectObject (&Pen);
m_pDC->TextOut (x,m_DrawRect.bottom-5,"1.0M");

for( j=1;j<= 10;j++)
{
 x= X+(int)(log10(j)*285.7143);
 m_pDC->MoveTo (x,m_DrawRect.top);
 m_pDC->LineTo (x,m_DrawRect.bottom );
}

X= x;

m_pDC->SelectObject(&Pen);
m_pDC->MoveTo (x,m_DrawRect.top);
m_pDC->LineTo (x,m_DrawRect.bottom );
m_pDC->SelectObject (&Pen);
m_pDC->TextOut (x,m_DrawRect.bottom-5,"10.0M");
```

```
for( j=1;j<= 10;j++)
{
 x= X+(int)(log10(j)*285.7143);
 m_pDC->MoveTo (x,m_DrawRect.top);
 m_pDC->LineTo (x,m_DrawRect.bottom );
}

X= x;

m_pDC->SelectObject(&Pen);
m_pDC->MoveTo (x,m_DrawRect.top);
m_pDC->LineTo (x,m_DrawRect.bottom );
m_pDC->SelectObject (&Pen);
m_pDC->TextOut (x,m_DrawRect.bottom-5,"10.0M");

for( j=1;j<= 10;j++)
{
 x= X+(int)(log10(j)*285.7143);
 m_pDC->MoveTo (x,m_DrawRect.top);
 m_pDC->LineTo (x,m_DrawRect.bottom );
}

X= x;

m_pDC->SelectObject(&Pen);
m_pDC->MoveTo (x,m_DrawRect.top);
m_pDC->LineTo (x,m_DrawRect.bottom );
m_pDC->SelectObject (&Pen);
m_pDC->TextOut (x,m_DrawRect.bottom-5,"10.0M");

for( j=1;j<= 10;j++)
{
 x= X+(int)(log10(j)*285.7143);
 m_pDC->MoveTo (x,m_DrawRect.top);
 m_pDC->LineTo (x,m_DrawRect.bottom );
}

break;
}
}
```

19. Add the following code for the PrepareForPlotting function that you declared.

```
void CPlotCtrl::PrepareForPlotting(CRect rect)
{
 m_pDC->SetMapMode(MM_HIMETRIC);
 m_pDC->SetMapMode(MM_ANISOTROPIC);
 m_pDC->SetWindowExt (2000,1024);
 m_pDC->SetViewportExt (rect.right , rect.bottom );
 m_pDC->DPtoLP(&m_DrawRect);

 return;
}
```

At this point, you have completed your control and should be able to build and test it using the ActiveX Test Container. Figure 40.5 shows an example of the control being tested.

Figure 40.5

About the Author

Kapil is a software engineer at Scientific Mes-Technik. He has been working with Visual C++ for the past three years, developing ActiveX controls. Presently he is looking for a job offer from a U.S. company.

Comments

There may be a problem registering controls that are using long filenames with the sample code. To correct this, make the following changes to the code:

"%l" should be replaced with "%L" to enable long filename support.

—Stefan Migowsky

ActiveX Shell Registration

This article was contributed by Emmanuel KARTMANN.

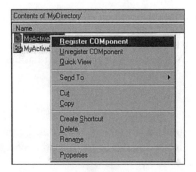

Figure 40.6

Environment: Windows NT4 SP4, Windows 95/98

For those among us who develop ActiveX/COM objects, here's a little trick to help you with registering/unregistering your components easily. With a simple modification to the registry, you will have additional register/unregister menu options (accessible with the right-mouse button) integrated in your Windows shell, as shown in Figure 40.6.

You can also register a component by double-clicking on it!

Note that if you're paranoid with .reg files (like me ;-)), you can manually create the register/unregister menu for your components (see the section "Manual Installation" below).

I also shipped in the kit a new version of regsvr32.exe (called regsvr33) that prints a clear-text error message if registration fails (instead of an error code).

Automatic Installation

To install the additional menu options in your shell

1. Open Windows Explorer.
2. Browse to the directory where the .reg files are located:
   DLL_Register_Unregister.reg
   OCX_Register_Unregister.reg
3. Double-click on the file DLL_Register_Unregister.reg.

4. A dialog box pops up, saying

    "Information in DLL_Register_Unregister.reg has been successfully entered into the registry."

5. Click on the OK button.

6. Double-click on the file OCX_Register_Unregister.reg.

7. A dialog box pops-up, saying

    "Information in OCX_Register_Unregister.reg has been successfully entered into the registry."

8. Click on the OK button.

The program regsvr32.exe must be in your PATH. Put the program (if you don't already have it, it's in the .zip file for this article) in your system directory ("C:\winnt\system32" on Windows NT).

Manual Installation

To install the additional menu options in your shell

1. Start Windows Explorer.

2. Select the menu option View/Options....

3. Click on the tab File Types.

4. Click on the button New Type....

5. Type the description of type: **ActiveX COMponent**

6. Type the Content Type (MIME): **application/ocx**

7. Type the Default Extension for Content Type: **.OCX**

8. Click on the checkbox Enable Quick View.

9. Click on the button New... (below Action).

10. Type the Action name: **Register**

11. Type the application used to perform action: **regsvr32.exe "%1"**

    CAUTION: Do not forget the double-quotes before and after **%1**.

12. Click on the OK button.

13. Select the action Register, and click on the button Set Default.

14. Click on the button New... (below Action).

15. Type the Action name: **Unregister**

16. Type the application used to perform action: **regsvr32.exe /u "%1"**

    CAUTION: Do not forget the double-quotes before and after **%1**.

17. Click on OK.

18. Click on the button Change Icon....

19. Pick up a cool icon in shell32.dll, like in Figure 40.7.

Figure 40.7

20. Click on OK.

Note that there is a difference with automatic registration: You can't add the menu option for DLLs. (There's no associated file type in Windows Explorer.) Only automatic registration can do that.

Usage

Registering a COMponent

1. Start Windows Explorer.

2. Browse to the directory containing your component.

3. Double-click on your component.

    or

    Select the OCX or DLL file, click on the right mouse button, and select the option Register COMponent.

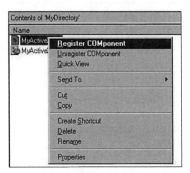

Figure 40.8

4. A dialog box pops-up, saying that registration is successful, as in Figure 40.9.

Figure 40.9

Unregistering a COMponent

1. Start Windows Explorer.

2. Browse to the directory containing your component.

3. Select the OCX or DLL file, click on the right mouse button, and select the option Unregister COMponent.

Figure 40.10

4. A dialog box pops-up, saying that unregistration is successful.

Comments

There may be a problem registering controls that are using long filenames with the sample code. To correct this, make the following change to the code:

"%l" should be replaced with "%L" to enable long filename support.

—Stefan Migowsky

Menu in ActiveX Controls

This article was contributed by Robert Nagy.

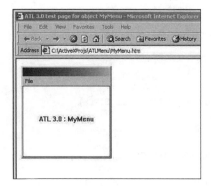

Figure 40.11

Environment: VC6, Windows 2000

It took me some time to figure out how to enable a menu in an ATL/MFC ActiveX control, and I think the result is simple but instructive. You simply have to change the style of the window of the AX control. ActiveX is the third generation of COM (Basic COM and Automation are the first and second), and it added support to the following weeknesses of its predeccessors: lack of a user interface, standardized storage, custom events, and optimization for the Internet. Basic COM and Automation servers could display and use dialog boxes, but not through the COM system. Being an elementary thing in a user interface, the menu is very important.

ATL

Let's create a simple ATL AX Control:

Start Visual C++, select the File/New/ATL COM AppWizard, specify a location, and let the project name be ATLMenu. Click OK, then Finish, and then OK. Now you will insert a Full Control through the menu items Insert/New ATL Object. Select Controls and Full Control, and click Next. In the Short Name box, enter MyMenu, then click on the Miscellaneous tab, click Windowed Only, and then click OK. Now select Insert/Resource/Menu from the VC's menu and click New. Type File then MsgBox in the menu items and ID_MSGBOX as the identifier for the MsgBox menu item. Choose the Class View tab of the Workspace window, right-click on CMyMenu, and select Add Windows Message Handler. Expand the tree if necessary. Select

WM_CREATE, and then click on Add Handler and OK. Now select the FileView tab of the Workspace window and expand the tree until MyMenu.h. Double-click on it, locate the OnCreate function, and type the following:

```
LRESULT OnCreate( UINT uMsg,
                  WPARAM wParam,
                  LPARAM lParam,
                  BOOL& bHandled)
{
  long lStyle;
  HMENU hMenu;

  lStyle = ::GetWindowLong(m_hWnd, GWL_STYLE);

  lStyle &= WS_DISABLED;
  lStyle |= WS_CAPTION;
  //lStyle |= WS_OVERLAPPEDWINDOW;

  ::SetWindowLong(m_hWnd, GWL_STYLE, lStyle);

  hMenu = ::LoadMenu( _Module.GetModuleInstance(),
                      MAKEINTRESOURCE(IDR_MENU1));
  ::SetMenu(m_hWnd, hMenu);

  return 0;
}
```

Now you will add the code to handle the message sent by the menu item. Locate the BEGIN_MSG_MAP macro and alter it like this (COMMAND_ID_HANDLER):

```
BEGIN_MSG_MAP(CMyMenu)
  CHAIN_MSG_MAP(CComControl<CMyMenu>)
  DEFAULT_REFLECTION_HANDLER()
  MESSAGE_HANDLER(WM_CREATE, OnCreate)
  COMMAND_ID_HANDLER(ID_MSGBOX, OnMsgBox)
END_MSG_MAP()
```

Now add the handler function too, and you are ready to compile:

```
LRESULT OnMsgBox( WORD wNotifyCode,
                  WORD wID,
                  HWND hWndCtl,
                  BOOL& bHandled)
{
  ::MessageBox( m_hWnd,
                "Hello World!",
                "From Menu",
                MB_OK);
  return 0;
}
```

Select Build/Set Active Configuration, set it to Release MinDependency, and click OK. Now Build your AX Control by selecting Build/Build ATLMenu.dll. The wizard automatically generates a MyMenu.html file in your project's folder. Double-click on it and test your work.

It's interesting that you can drag your AX Control by its caption and move it. You can prevent dragging by overriding WM_NCLBUTTONDOWN:

```
LRESULT OnNcLButtonDown( UINT uMsg,
                         WPARAM wParam,
                         LPARAM lParam,
                         BOOL& bHandled)
{
  // TODO : Add Code for message handler.
  // Call DefWindowProc if necessary.
  if (HTCAPTION == (INT)wParam)
  {
    ::SetActiveWindow(m_hWnd);
    return 1;
  }
  ::DefWindowProc(m_hWnd, uMsg, wParam, lParam);
  return 0;
}
```

You can manipulate your Control by using the interfaces derived from IOleWindow. Add IOleInPlaceObject::SetObjectRects to your Control's class. This will be called by the Container as a response to a call to IOleInPlaceSite::OnPosRectChange by your Control or when the user makes changes to the Container's window. When necessary, call OnPosRectChange, which is implemented by the Container from your Control (m_spInPlaceSite->OnPosRectChange(&rc), where m_spInPlaceSite is a pointer to the Container's IOleInplaceSite interface).

```
STDMETHODIMP SetObjectRects( LPCRECT prcPos,
                             LPCRECT prcClip)
{
  //Call ::SetWindowPos Win32 API function
  return NOERROR;
}
```

MFC

It's almost the same as in ATL, but it's much easier because of the powerful Class Wizard:

Select File/New/MFC ActiveX Control Wizard, and just click next and OK everywhere. Insert the menu resource and add menu items. Use Class Wizard to add WM_CREATE and the menu item handler code to the project. Add the code needed to the OnCreate function. (See the ATL way in the previous section, but change from HMENU to CMenu, and so on, or use the Win32 API functions just like in the case of ATL above.) Finally, add AfxMessageBox("Hello World!") to your menu item handler code. Build and register your AX Control (Tools/Register Control menu). The wizard won't generate an .html file this time, so you have to write it or create an MFC AppWizard (exe) container project and test it there.

It's interesting that if you test your MFC control in IE, the window acts like a child of the Control (you can drag it only in the Control's client area), but it has a menu. It's strange because as far as I know, a child window can't have a menu. But if you test it in a dialog-based MFC container, it works fine.

You should override the WM_NCLBUTTONDOWN message like this in case of MFC:

```
void CMFCMenuCtrl::OnNcLButtonDown( UINT nHitTest,
                                    CPoint point)
{
  if (HTCAPTION == nHitTest)
     return;
  COleControl::OnNcLButtonDown(nHitTest, point);
}
```

The pointer to an IOleInPlaceSite interface is m_pInPlaceSite in the case of MFC.

FROM THE FORUM

Question (Cloud Lee):

I have written an ActiveX control using C++, but some of my users wish to use it with Delphi 6 and Visual Basic. The control is currently using CString to output some data that is unknown to Delphi and VB. What should I use to return string data to the calling application?

Answer (Markus W.):

You can use a variant to return string data to either a VB or Delphi application:

```
void CMyControl::GetText(VARIANT FAR* vText)
{
    CString strTmp = "some text";
    vText->vt = VT_BSTR;
    vText->bstrVal = strTmp.AllocSysString();
}
```

Then to call this from VB, use:

```
Dim strText as string
Dim vText as Variant
MyControl1.GetText vText
strText = vText
```

41

ATL and WTL

In this chapter

Microsoft introduced the Active Template Library, or ATL, as a small library to provide support for the most common COM tasks, such as implementing the standard COM interfaces and component registration.

The Windows Template Library, or WTL, was developed by Microsoft as an extension to ATL, allowing the creation of controls, dialogs, GDI objects, and other UI components.

- "An ATL Project to View Type Library Information" describes a very useful and informative

utility built using ATL to allow viewing of all kinds of type libraries.

- "ATL Tear-Off Interfaces" shows how to use tear-off interfaces that are only created when explicitly requested, thus saving resources.

- "Using DDX and DDV with WTL" examines the use of Dynamic Data Exchange and Dynamic Data Validation with WTL that can save a great deal of development time.

An ATL Project to View Type Library Information

This article was contributed by Mihai Filimon.

Lib2Usr ATL Component

Here is an ATL project for viewing all "classes" from a dll, tlb, or ocx, which are in fact library files. A user can read some information, like functions (methods and properties) from a file, but only if that file has a resource "TYPELIB"\1 in the resource component. I use the LoadTypeLib file to provide a pointer to a ITypeLib interface. From the ITypeLib interface you can find all that the library knows (functions, variables, names, and so on).

Classes and interfaces used in the project:

- *ILib2Me (CLib2Me)*—This interface provides two functions: Load and Class. The Load function loads the file as TypeLibrary. If the function is successful, you can call the Class function to provide one-by-one all the interfaces, enums, coclasses, and so on defined in the library. The function will return a pointer to an ILClass interface.

- *ILClass (CLClass)*—This interface provides information about one "class." I define "class" to be one of the following: enum, record, module, interface, dispatch, coclass, alias, union, or max. The user can find the name (get_Name), kind (get_Kind), count of functions, function (get_Function), count of variables, or variable (get_Variable) of this "class." The get_Function(int nIndex) function returns a pointer (ILFucntion★) to the function nIndex from the class. The get_Variable(int nIndex) function returns a pointer (ILVariable★) to the variable nIndex from the class. In both cases, the functions will return NULL if nIndex is not found in the range (0..GetCount...() - 1).

- *ILFunction(CLFunction)*—This interface provides information about one function. The user can find the name (get_Name), kind (get_Kind - virtual,pure-virtual,nonvirtual,static,dispatch), invoke kind (get_InvokeKind--function(1), get(2), put(4),putref(8)), documentation (get_Documentation), ID (get_ID), parameters, and return type. If you want one of the function's parameters, you have to call the get_Parameter function. You have to pass the index of the parameter, and this parameter will return the pointer to one parameter interface (ILParameter★).

- *ILVariable(CLVariable)*—This interface provides information such as the name, type, and kind (persistence, static, const, or dispatch) of one variable.

- *ILParameter(CLParameter)*—This interface will return information such as the name (get_Name) and type (get_Type) of one parameter.

DEMO Program and Source (Updated)

Now one can even watch interfaces of a particular object. Demo application in VC++ included.

The DEMO VB program looks like Figure 41.1.

Figure 41.1

A new DEMO program has been added in VC++, as shown in Figure 41.2.

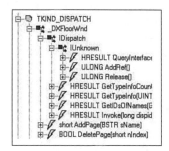

Figure 41.2

The demo VB project requires the XPropertiesWnd ActiveX control. This can be obtained from the CodeGuru article "A Set of Two ActiveX Controls."

FROM THE FORUM

Question (Arrigoni):

I am building an ATL COM DLL and exporting it to be used by a Visual Basic client. I can see the interfaces from VB, but how can I have some enums exported too?

Answer (Abdul Kareem):

You can define enums as shown below to work with Visual C++ and VB clients:

```
// This file will be processed by the MIDL tool to
// produce the type library (XXXX.tlb) and marshalling code.

import "oaidl.idl";
import "ocidl.idl";

typedef enum eEnum{
EnumVal1 = 1,
EnumVal2 = 2,
}eEnum;

[
object,
uuid(173FF9FF-FB99-11D4-8484-006008119967),
dual,
helpstring("IYourIn Interface"),
pointer_default(unique)
]
interface IYourIn : IDispatch
{
//Your interface methods..............
};
```

ATL Tear-Off Interfaces

This article was contributed by Andrew Whitechapel.

If an interface of an object is not used often, it might be more efficient to delay the creation of the interface until it is actually requested, especially if the initialization of the object is expensive. The interface will be created only when a client needs it, and it will be released after the client is finished using the interface. In other words, the code for the interface will be instantiated only when the client explicitly requests the interface by calling QueryInterface. Such an interface is known as a *tear-off interface*.

A tear-off interface maintains its own reference counting, through the CComTearOffObjectBase ATL class. Note that this is not entirely consistent with the usual COM model where the object maintains an object-wide reference count. In implementing the tear-off interface, you actually need to implement it in a separate C++ class and instantiate this class separately from the main object class. Also, therefore, the tear-off interface doesn't feature the multiple inheritance of the main implementation class.

If a tear-off interface takes a long time to get created, it could be inefficient to release it each time the reference count becomes zero. If a tear-off interface is likely to be called more than once, you can create it as a cached tear-off interface. The interface pointer of such an interface is cached and returned the next time a client asks for the interface.

In the following example, we will create two types of tear-off interfaces: a regular tear-off and a cached tear-off.

1. Create a new ATL COM AppWizard project. Call it Ripper. Everything default. Insert a new ATL Object. Use the short name OuterObject. Everything default. Add a property to the IOuterObject interface, called Name, with the parameter list shown below—make it a "get" only property. This is an arbitrary property—we'll use it for testing by outputting simple strings:

   ```
   [out, retval] BSTR *pVal
   ```

2. Implement the get_Name method to create and allocate a string:

   ```
   *pVal = ::SysAllocString(L"IOuterObject");
   return S_OK;
   ```

3. Now for the regular tear-off. We need to declare a separate class, but for convenience we'll put it in the OuterObject header file. At the top, declare a new class to manage the reference counting for the first tear-off interface. This class will support a dual interface and have a normal COM map. However, it must derive from CComTearOffObjectBase and not CComObjectRootEx:

   ```
   class CTearOff1:
    public IDispatchImpl<ITEAROFF1, &LIBID_RIPPERLib &__uuidof(ITearOff1),,
    public CComTearOffObjectBase
   {
   public:
   CTearOff1(){}
   ~CTearOff1(){}

   BEGIN_COM_MAP(CTearOff1)
     COM_INTERFACE_ENTRY(ITearOff1)
   END_COM_MAP()
   };
   ```

   Note: For this to compile, you'll have to forward-declare the COuterObject class just before the CTearOff1 class.

4. Add the corresponding entries to the IDL file, as shown below (and don't forget to list the tear-off interface in the coclass):

```
[
object,
uuid(9B8A71F7-DB54-11CF-9462-00AA00BBAD7F),
dual,
helpstring("ITearOff1 Interface"),
pointer_default(unique)
]
interface ITearOff1 : IDispatch
{
};
```

5. Next, add a Name get property to this tear-off interface, with exactly the same signature and implementation as the Name property in the outer interface (but creating a different string):

```
*pVal = ::SysAllocString(L"ITearOff1");
```

6. Update the outer object's COM map with the special ATL macro shown below. Then build the server.

```
COM_INTERFACE_ENTRY_TEAR_OFF(IID_ITearOff1, CTearOff1)
```

Just step aside for a minute, and note the definition of this macro:

```
#define COM_INTERFACE_ENTRY_TEAR_OFF(iid, x)\
{&iid,\
 (DWORD)&_CComCreatorData<\
  CComInternalCreator< CComTearOffObject< x > >\
 >::data,\
 _Creator},
```

As you can see, when QueryInterface is called, this entry in the COM map will call CComObjectBase::_Creator, passing _CComCreatorData<CCOMINTERNAL-CREATOR<CCOMTEAROFFOBJECT>>::data as a parameter. This data is an _ATL_CREATORDATA, which is a struct that has only one member, an _ATL_CREATORFUNC*, which is just a typedefed function pointer, and data that will be initialized to CreateInstance. The definitions are in atlcom.h and atlbase.h:

```
typedef HRESULT (WINAPI _ATL_CREATORFUNC)(void* pv,
REFIID riid, LPVOID* ppv);

struct _ATL_CREATORDATA
{
 _ATL_CREATORFUNC* pFunc;
};
```

```
template <class Creator>
class _CComCreatorData
{
public:
 static _ATL_CREATORDATA data;
};

template <class Creator>
_ATL_CREATORDATA _CComCreatorData<Creator>::data =
{Creator::CreateInstance};

struct _ATL_CACHEDATA
{
 DWORD dwOffsetVar;
 _ATL_CREATORFUNC* pFunc;
};

// ...

static HRESULT WINAPI _Creator(void* pv, REFIID iid,
void** ppvObject, DWORD dw)
{
 _ATL_CREATORDATA* pcd = (_ATL_CREATORDATA*)dw;
 return pcd->pFunc(pv, iid, ppvObject);
}
```

So, QueryInterface calls _Creator, which calls CreateInstance, which calls new to instantiate a new CComTearOffObject:

```
template <class T1>
class CComInternalCreator
{
public:
 static HRESULT WINAPI CreateInstance(void* pv,
                                      REFIID riid,
                                      LPVOID* ppv)
 {
  ATLASSERT(*ppv == NULL);
  HRESULT hRes = E_OUTOFMEMORY;
  T1* p = NULL;
  ATLTRY(p = new T1(pv))
  if (p != NULL)
  {
   p->SetVoid(pv);
   p->InternalFinalConstructAddRef();
   hRes = p->FinalConstruct();
   p->InternalFinalConstructRelease();
   if (hRes == S_OK)
```

```
      hRes = p->_InternalQueryInterface(
      riid, ppv);
      if (hRes != S_OK)
      delete p;
     }
     return hRes;
    }
};
```

Bearing in mind ATL's upside-down inheritance, you won't be surprised to see that the object that actually gets instantiated at the bottom of the hierarchy is a CComTearOffObject instead of the more usual CComObject. Also, instead of the usual CComObjectRootEx, the base for this is CComTearOffObjectBase as shown below (although, of course, CComTearOffObjectBase itself is derived from CComObjectRootEx). From this you'll see that the tear-off interface object caches a pointer to its owner object. In your code, you might use this pointer to call into the members of the owning object for your own purposes.

```
template <class Owner, class ThreadModel = CComObjectThreadModel>
class CComTearOffObjectBase : public CComObjectRootEx<ThreadModel>
{
public:
 typedef Owner _OwnerClass;
 CComObject<Owner>* m_pOwner;
 CComTearOffObjectBase() {m_pOwner = NULL;}
};
```

The CComTearOffObject class uses this pointer to forward requests for the IUnknown methods (after having taken care of its own reference count):

```
template <class Base>
class CComTearOffObject : public Base
{
public:
 CComTearOffObject(void* pv)
 {
  ATLASSERT(m_pOwner == NULL);
  m_pOwner = reinterpret_cast< CComObject <
  Base::_OwnerClass > *>(pv);
  m_pOwner->AddRef();
 }

 // Set refcount to 1 to protect destruction
 ~CComTearOffObject()
 {
  m_dwRef = 1L;
  FinalRelease();
```

```
  m_pOwner->Release();
 }

 STDMETHOD_(ULONG, AddRef)() {return InternalAddRef();}
 STDMETHOD_(ULONG, Release)()
 {
  ULONG l = InternalRelease();
  if (l == 0)
  delete this;
  return l;
 }

 STDMETHOD(QueryInterface)(REFIID iid, void ** ppvObject)
 {
  return m_pOwner->QueryInterface(iid, ppvObject);
 }
};
```

7. Now write a client: a console project, called TestRipper. Above main, import the Ripper type library (with no namespace, and named guids). Inside main, use CoInitialize/CoUninitialize as normal, and set up a try...catch block. In the try block, declare and initialize an IOuterObject smart pointer object. Use this smart pointer to call the GetName wrapper function, and print out the results, for example:

```
IOuterObjectPtr pOuter(CLSID_OuterObject);
BSTR b1 = pOuter->GetName();
_tprintf(_T("%S\n"), b1);
SysFreeString(b1);
```

8. Build and test. Then, write additional client code to test the tear-off, that is

```
ITearOff1Ptr pT1 = pOuter;
b1 = pT1->GetName();
_tprintf(_T("%S\n"), b1);
SysFreeString(b1);
```

9. Finally, write a second tear-off—a cached tear-off called CTearOff2. Set this up in exactly the same way as the first tear-off—you can copy and paste the IDL code and the C++ code, replacing TearOff1 with TearOff2. Implement the Name get property as before, but with an appropriate different string. The first difference for a cached tear-off is in the outer object's COM map. You need this macro instead of the regular one:

```
COM_INTERFACE_ENTRY_CACHED_TEAR_OFF(IID_ITearOff2,
                                    CTearOff2,
                                    m_pUnkTearOff2.p)
```

Where m_pUnkTearOff2 is a public data member in the outer object class of the CComPtr ATL interface pointer wrapper class, that is

```
CComPtr<IUnknown> m_pUnkTearOff2;
```

10. The cached tear-off macro uses the CComCachedTearOffObject ATL class, and this makes use of the GetControllingUnknown function, so you also need to add this macro to the outer object class:

```
DECLARE_GET_CONTROLLING_UNKNOWN()
```

Again, take a moment to reflect on the ATL macros for cached tear-offs:

```
#define COM_INTERFACE_ENTRY_CACHED_TEAR_OFF(iid, \
                                            x, \
                                            punk)\
{&iid,\
(DWORD)&_CComCacheData<\
CComCreator< CComCachedTearOffObject< x > >,\
(DWORD)offsetof(_ComMapClass, punk)\
>::data,\
_Cache},
```

An important part of this macro is the CComCacheData, which is defined as follows:

```
struct _ATL_CACHEDATA
{
DWORD dwOffsetVar;
_ATL_CREATORFUNC* pFunc;
};

template <class Creator, DWORD dwVar>
class _CComCacheData
{
public:
 static _ATL_CACHEDATA data;
};

template <class Creator, DWORD dwVar>
_ATL_CACHEDATA _CComCacheData<Creator, dwVar>::data =
{dwVar, Creator::CreateInstance};
```

So, this makes the data an _ATL_CACHEDATA, which contains two members— a creator function pointer and also an offset. This offset is from the base of the owner class to the member data that will be used to cache the pointer to the tear-off. The _Cache function uses the offset to work out the address of the pointer and to check to see if it needs to create a new tear-off object:

```
static HRESULT WINAPI CComObjectRootBase::_Cache(
void* pv, REFIID iid, void** ppvObject, DWORD dw)
{
 HRESULT hRes = E_NOINTERFACE;
 _ATL_CACHEDATA* pcd = (_ATL_CACHEDATA*)dw;
 IUnknown** pp = (IUnknown**)((DWORD)pv + pcd->dwOffsetVar);

 if (*pp == NULL)
  hRes = pcd->pFunc(pv, IID_IUnknown, (void**)pp);

 if (*pp != NULL)
  hRes = (*pp)->QueryInterface(iid, ppvObject);

 return hRes;
}
```

11. Build the revised server. Then enhance the client to use the second (cached) tear-off, as shown:

```
ITearOff2Ptr pT2 = pOuter;
b1 = pT2->GetName();
_tprintf(_T("%S\n"), b1);
SysFreeString(b1);
```

12. Build and test. The client, as you would expect, is blissfully unaware of the devilish machinations going on behind the scenes.

Okay, so now you know how to set up regular and cached tear-offs with the ATL. But what about the pros and cons?

- **PRO #1:** The more interfaces you implement with one class, the bigger the C++ class object, since it will have a vtbl pointer for each interface. Using tear-offs reduces this vptr bloat. If clients use an interface only rarely, this overhead is unwarranted.

- **CON #1:** Since the tear-off is implemented in a separate class with its own reference counting, we trade the 4-byte vptr reduction against 4 bytes for the vptr in the separate C++ object, plus 4 bytes for the separate reference count, plus 4 bytes for a back-pointer to the main object class.

- **JUDGEMENT #1:** If you only use the tear-off pattern for rarely used interfaces (and can back up the surmise with profiling data), the pros outweigh the cons.

- **CON #2:** If the object is being used across an apartment boundary, the stub will cache the object-wide reference count with no accommodation for the tear-off, so any benefit is lost.

- **CON #2a:** If you are doing anything in the construction or destruction of the tear-off object that you assume is transient because the tear-off is transient (like, say, holding resources, file handles, database connections) and you're going across apartments, you lose the transience.

- **CON #3:** In a regular tear-off, the tear-off is created when QueryInterface is called on the main object. This means that your tear-off should be stateless, since multiple QI calls will result in multiple tear-off instances, each with their own state.

- **PRO #2:** One valid reason for using a cached tear-off is exactly the opposite: to maintain state information, since once created the tear-off is thereafter cached and multiple instances do not occur.

As you can see, there are more cons than pros listed here. The ATL does supply some very convenient macros for implementing regular and cached tear-offs, but the strategy is essentially an implementation trick for performance optimization. The bottom line is that tear-offs will sometimes be only marginally useful and therefore, you need to base your decision on the specifics of the system involved. Hopefully, what you've learned today will make that decision-making process a bit easier.

FROM THE FORUM

Question (sugi):

How can I go about creating a method in an ATL-based component that returns an array of strings?

Answer (Alex Fedotov):

The method should be declared in the .idl file as

```
HRESULT GetArrayofStrs([out, retval] SAFEARRAY(BSTR) * pArray);
```

The implementation might look like

```
HRESULT CMyObject::GetArrayofStrs(SAFEARRAY ** pArray)
{
SAFEARRAYBOUND sab;
sab.lLbound = 0;
sab.cElements = 3; // number of strings

SAFEARRAY * psa = SafeArrayCreate(VT_BSTR, 1, &sab);
if (psa == NULL)
return E_OUTOFMEMORY;

LONG lIndex;
CComBSTR bstr;
HRESULT hRes;

lIndex = 0;
bstr = L"String 1";
```

```
hRes = SafeArrayPutElement(psa, &lIndex, (BSTR)bstr);
if (FAILED(hRes))
{
SafeArrayDestroy(psa);
return hRes;
}

lIndex = 1;
bstr = L"String 2";
hRes = SafeArrayPutElement(psa, &lIndex, (BSTR)bstr);
if (FAILED(hRes))
{
SafeArrayDestroy(psa);
return hRes;
}

lIndex = 2;
bstr = L"String 3";
hRes = SafeArrayPutElement(psa, &lIndex, (BSTR)bstr);
if (FAILED(hRes))
{
SafeArrayDestroy(psa);
return hRes;
}

*pArray = psa;
return S_OK;
}
```

Using DDX and DDV with WTL

This article was contributed by Less P. Wright II.

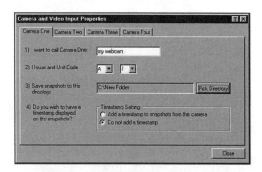

Figure 41.3

Environment: VC6 SP4, Win2K, Win98/ME

Introduction

One of the more tedious parts of UI coding is simply doing the grunt work of passing member data into various dialogs for user interaction, and then pulling it back out and ensuring the data is valid before recommitting it to the core part of your program. MFC realized this and has long had the concept of DDX (dynamic data exchange) and DDV (dynamic data validation). However, those of us who are focused on download size stick to ATL- and SDK-style coding, meaning lots of rote code has to be done to enable the user to modify various properties and settings in our UI dialogs. With WTL, however, we now have the opportunity to gain a lot of the ease of MFC coding without the bulk. This article will show you how to make use of WTL's DDX/DDV implementation, show two custom extensions I added to WTL's implementation to extend its reach, and provide code taken from a real-life example using WTL's property sheet implementation (CPropertyPageImpl).

What Is DDX/DDV Exactly?

As alluded to earlier, the purpose of DDX is to provide a framework for handling the passing (both loading and retrieving) of data between your application and the UI it presents to the user via dialogs, property sheets, and so on. The goal of DDV is to enable automatic verification of any changes the user made to ensure they have entered valid data, where valid is defined by your application. The benefit of using DDX is efficient, easy-to-read-and-maintain mappings between your application's variables and their presentation/modification in your various dialogs. Additionally, you will see a significant reduction in the amount of time you spend coding the basic infrastructure needed to support interactive UI.

With the overview out of the way, let's get into coding to start explaining the details involved in utilizing DDX in your app. WTL provides DDX/DDV handling via the header atlddx.h, which contains macros for creating a DDX map (same concept as ATL's message map), and the templatized class CWinDataExchange.

Thus, the first step to make use of DDX/DDV is

```
#include <ATLddx.h>
```

into your StdAfx.h or other primary header file. The one caveat here is that if you are using WTL's Cstring, you must include AtlMisc.h before AtlDDx.h.

Thus, I always simply add the following to my StdAfx.h:

```
#include <atlmisc.h> //CString support
#include <atlddx.h>
```

in StdAfx.h, right beneath atlwin.h and forget about it. Because the sample code in this article will also use property sheets to demonstrate DDX, we have to add the include for atldlgs.h, giving us a final StdAfx.h that has this segment of code in it:

```
#include <atlbase.h>
#include <atlapp.h>

extern CAppModule _Module;

#include <atlwin.h>

#include <atlmisc.h>
#include <atlddx.h>
#include <atldlgs.h>
```

The next step is to ensure the dialog class you are using inherits from CWinDataExchange to get support for DDX like so:

```
class CCameraBase : public CPropertyPageImpl<CCameraBase>,
                    public CWinDataExchange<CCameraBase>
```

After that, we can now get to the heart of it, which is actually connecting your application's variables to their respective UI components. This is done via the DDX message map, of which a simplistic example is listed here:

```
BEGIN_DDX_MAP(<your dialog class>)
DDX_TEXT(<dlg resource id>,<string variable>)
DDX_TEXT_LEN(<dlg resource id2>,
             <string variable2>,
             <max text length>)
END_DDX_MAP()
```

Within the message map is where you direct WTL's DDX class as to how to hook up your variables to your dialog's UI elements. There are a number of macros that can be used for various data types, but let's briefly look at the two preceding entries. The first one, DDX_TEXT, simply states that the value in <string variable> should be assigned to <dlg resource id> on load—typically a string variable mapping to an edit box.

On the close of the dialog, the mapping is done in reverse—the current contents of <dlg resource id> are pulled out and placed back into <string variable>. Very nice and tidy. The second macro shown above, DDX_TEXT_LEN, has similar functionality to DDX_TEXT in that it joins the <dlg resource id2> to <string variable2>, but you can see there is a third parameter, <max text length>. Specify a value here, and if the user's text entry exceeds it, the DDV error handler will kick in. You can override the default handler, or you can use the default handler, which will beep and set the focus back to the offending control to prompt the user to correct it. (You implement your own handler by overriding the function void OnDataValidateError(UINT id, BOOL bSave,_XData& data), which is demonstrated in the sample app.)

There are a number of macros for the message map, usually with a variation of one for pure linkage (ala DDX_TEXT) and one for linkage and validation (ala DDX_TEXT_LEN).

With that, the final step is to actually tell WTL when to fire the actual data exchange. This is done by calling DoDataExchange(BOOL fParam) with FALSE to load the dialog with your data values, and TRUE to retrieve the data from your dialog. Where to do this is up to you, but OnInitDialog (handler for WM_INITDIALOG) is a good spot for the DoDataExchange(FALSE), or load call. For pulling back the modified data, you could put the DoDataExchange(TRUE) call (retrieve) in OnOK for a dialog, and for property pages, you probably want to handle it in OnKillActivate().

DDX in Action

With an understanding of the fundamentals involved in utilizing DDX/DDV, let's move on to the sample application, where we can see DDX in action, as well as examine some limitations I found and how to work around them.

The sample application is based on a subset of code from a commercial application that handles the viewing/monitoring of multiple wireless cameras. The relevant part of this app is that it has to allow the user to specify individual settings for up to 16 cameras and do so in a clean UI. The solution I chose was to use WTL's property page implementation to allow a nice tabbed dialog for each camera, and then use DDX/DDV to simplify the transfer back and forth of the individual settings. The sample app simply lets you play with four settings, so that you can see in the debugger how the settings are transferred and validated. I'll give an overview here of some of the more interesting parts, and after that, just tracing the code in the debugger should cement your understanding of DDX/DDV.

Because the camera settings were going to be globally used throughout the app, I made a global struct as follows (from stdafx.h):

```
struct _cameraprops
{
 CString ssFriendlyName;
 UINT iHouseCode;
 UINT iUnitCode;
 CString ssSaveDir;
 BOOL fIsInSnapshotCycle;
 BOOL fAddTimestamp;
};

extern _cameraprops g_cameraProps[4];
```

and allocated storage in the main cpp file (propsheetddx.cpp):

```
#include "maindlg.h"

CAppModule _Module;

_cameraprops g_cameraProps[4];
```

With our central storage structure setup, the next step was to create the header for handling the property sheet and create the base class for the property page handler.

```
class CCameraBase : public CPropertyPageImpl<CameraBas>,
                    public CWinDataExchange<CameraBas>
```

I then created a single dialog in VC, which looked like Figure 41.4.

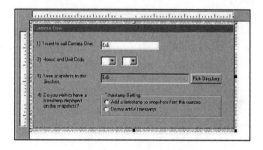

Figure 41.4

Next, I added the DDX message map to specify the linkage between the UI and the global struct g_cameraprops:

```
BEGIN_DDX_MAP(CCameraBase)
DDX_TEXT_LEN(IDC_edit_CameraTitle,
             g_cameraProps[m_iIdentity].ssFriendlyName,
             35)
DDX_COMBO_INDEX(IDC_cmbo_HouseCode,
                g_cameraProps[m_iIdentity].iHouseCode)
DDX_COMBO_INDEX(IDC_cmbo_UnitCode,
                g_cameraProps[m_iIdentity].iUnitCode)
DDX_TEXT(IDC_edit_FileDirectory,
         g_cameraProps[m_iIdentity].ssSaveDir)
DDX_BOOL_RADIO(IDC_radio_AddTimeStamp,
               g_cameraProps[m_iIdentity].fAddTimestamp,
               IDC_radio_NoTimeStamp)
END_DDX_MAP()

enum { IDD = IDD_PROP_PAGE1 };
```

And of course we had to invoke the DoDataExchange for load:

```
LRESULT OnInitDialog(...)
{
...
InitComboBoxes(hwndComboHouse, hwndComboUnit, m_iIdentity);
CenterWindow();

DoDataExchange(FALSE);
...
}
```

And for validating and pulling the modified data back:

```
BOOL OnKillActive()
{
 DoDataExchange(TRUE);
 return true;
}
```

Since we have to scale up to 16 cameras (4 in the sample though), I modified the constructor of the CCameraBase class to take an integer to identify what camera it was handling:

```
CCameraBase(int _index)
{
 m_iIdentity = _index;
 ...
}
```

With that done, we now have a basic layout for a property page, a framework for transferring the data and pulling it back after the user has modified it, and an index to allow us to reuse the same class for all cameras. Now, to actually implement this 4x in our UI, we turn to our derived CPropertySheetImpl class, CCameraProperties. There isn't too much to it, as shown:

```
class CCameraProperties : public CPropertySheetImpl<CameraProperties>
{
public:
 CCameraBase m_page1;
 CCameraBase m_page2;
 CCameraBase m_page3;
 CCameraBase m_page4;

 CCameraProperties():m_page1(1),m_page2(2),m_page3(3),m_page4(4)
 {
  m_psh.dwFlags |= PSH_NOAPPLYNOW;

AddPage(m_page1);
AddPage(m_page2);
AddPage(m_page3);
AddPage(m_page4);
SetActivePage(0);

SetTitle(_T("Camera and Video Input Properties"));
}
```

Note the use of the member initialization list above to show where we actually id each of the class instances with their respective camera. After that, call AddPage to hook up the classes into the tabbed layout, and specify your first page via SetActivePage. There is a small message map omitted above, but beyond that, you now have the handler for the full property sheet.

Extending DDX in WTL

Of course, things didn't all just fall into place—there were two immediate problems I hit that required adding new extensions to <ATLDDX.H> to get the DDX framework to do some additional handling. The first item was regarding the combo boxes— the generic DDX implementation would be to specify DDX_INT and pass in the combo box id to handle the mapping of the camera's unit code and house code to their respective combo box. However, the gotcha is that DDX_INT calls Get/SetDlgItemInt underneath, which merely places or retrieves the textual representation of an integer. For the cameras, which use X10 wireless protocol, both the unit code and house code represented an index into an array of values, not the values themselves. Example: House code A is represented by 0, B is 1, and so on. Under the default DDX implementation, if I passed in its intrinsic value 0, I would get a combo box showing 0, which is not what I wanted.

Since I think its very common to have combo boxes representing indexes into arrays or enums rather than trying to represent the literal textual value, I added a new macro and macro handler called DDX_COMBO_INDEX. This will handle the passing and retrieval of an index value, rather than the literal textual translation. The sample has the modified code, but it ended up like this:

```
#define DDX_COMBO_INDEX(nID, var) \
 if(nCtlID == (UINT)-1 ¦¦ nCtlID == nID) \
 { \
  if(!DDX_Combo_Index(nID, var, TRUE, bSaveAndValidate)) \
    return FALSE; \
 }
```

Followed by

```
template <class Type>
BOOL DDX_Combo_Index(UINT nID,
                     Type& nVal,
                     BOOL bSigned,
                     BOOL bSave,
                     BOOL bValidate = FALSE,
                     Type nMin = 0,
                     Type nMax = 0)
{
 T* pT = static_cast<>(this);
 BOOL bSuccess = TRUE;
```

```
if(bSave)
{
 nVal = ::SendMessage((HWND) (Type)pT->GetDlgItem(nID),
                      CB_GETCURSEL,
                      (WPARAM) 0,
                      (LPARAM) 0);
 bSuccess = (nVal == CB_ERR ? false : true);
}
else
{
 ATLASSERT(!bValidate || nVal >= nMin && nVal <= nMax);
 int iRet =     ::SendMessage((HWND) (Type)pT->GetDlgItem(nID),
                              CB_SETCURSEL,
                              (WPARAM) nVal,
                              (LPARAM) 0);

 bSuccess = (iRet == CB_ERR ? false : true);
}

if(!bSuccess)
{
 pT->OnDataExchangeError(nID, bSave);
}
else if(bSave && bValidate)     // validation
{
 ATLASSERT(nMin != nMax);
 if(nVal < nMin || nVal > nMax)
 {
  _XData data;
  data.nDataType = ddxDataInt;
  data.intData.nVal = (long)nVal;
  data.intData.nMin = (long)nMin;
  data.intData.nMax = (long)nMax;
  pT->OnDataValidateError(nID, bSave, data);
  bSuccess = FALSE;
 }
}
return bSuccess;
}
```

With this, I could successfully handle indexes within my combo box UI.

The other gotcha was that the UI I wanted to use was to have two radio buttons, representing a true/false choice for the user (see the option #4, "do you wish to have timestamps added"). Initially, I thought DDX_RADIO was what I wanted, but that didn't do it, and neither did DDX_CHECK (it didn't handle the toggling of the UI to create an exclusive selection between the two radio buttons). Thus, I added another extension, DDX_BOOL_RADIO, which took two resource ids as follows:

```
DDX_BOOL_RADIO(<primary radio buttonID>,
               <OOL variable>,
               <secondary radio buttonID>)
```

This extension ensures that in the load, only one of the two buttons is selected, based on the state of the bool variable. If true, the primary ID radio is checked, the secondary radio button is initialized to unchecked, and the reverse happens if the initial load value is false. Obviously, you could simply use one radio button to represent the true/false state, but I wanted to make it really clear to the user what they were selecting by explicitly calling it out with two buttons and associated text. You can also find the code for DDX_BOOL_BUTTON in the modified <ATLDDX.H> file.

With that, the basic code framework for the sample application is complete—we now have a UI that can elegantly handle the transfer back and forth of data between UI and internal variables via WTL's DDX/DDV, allow the user to understand what they are selecting via a tabbed property dialog, and, finally, we have a codebase that can scale any number of cameras with minimal change to the code.

Hopefully, a quick run of the sample app under the debugger will clear up any remaining questions, and you will now be able to take advantage of WTL's DDX/DDV framework to ensure you no longer have to keep writing reams of rote GetDlgItem/SetDlgItem-style code for your future UI.

If you have recommendations for improving this article or write your own extensions to atlddx.h, I would appreciate hearing about them. You can email me at less_wright@hotmail.com.

Default Data Handlers

Here's the list of default DDX/DDV handlers:

```
DDX_TEXT(nID, var)
DDX_TEXT_LEN(nID, var, len)

DDX_INT(nID, var)
DDX_INT_RANGE(nID, var, min, max)

DDX_UINT(nID, var)
DDX_UINT_RANGE(nID, var, min, max)

DDX_FLOAT(nID, var)
DDX_FLOAT_RANGE(nID, var, min, max)

// NOTE: you must define _ATL_USE_DDX_FLOAT to
//       exchange float values.

DDX_CONTROL(nID, obj)
DDX_CHECK(nID, var)
DDX_RADIO(nID, var)
```

42

Apartments and Threading

In this chapter

COM features concurrency boundaries to protect COM servers from COM clients with incompatible threading characteristics. These boundaries are called *apartments*. These apartments, along with the threading models associated with them, cause the most problems to COM programmers.

In this chapter you will find an explanation of the correct use of these apartments and also the threading models using them.

- "Understanding COM Apartments, Part I" describes

what apartments are and how to avoid some of the problems associated with them.

- "Understanding COM Apartments, Part II" continues the description of apartments, giving practical examples and useful rules to follow.

- "Getting a Feel for COM Threading Models" explains the types of COM threading models available, showing some practical examples of their use.

Understanding COM Apartments, Part I

This article was contributed by Jeff Prosise.

Let me begin my inaugural column for CodeGuru by stating that I'm on a crusade—a crusade to stamp out bugs related to COM concurrency. COM features a concurrency mechanism that's capable of intercepting and serializing concurrent method calls to objects that were designed to process only one method call at a time. That mechanism centers around the notion of abstract boundaries called apartments. When I troubleshoot COM systems that don't work, probably 40% of the bugs that I find result from a lack of understanding of apartments. This deficiency of knowledge shouldn't be surprising because apartments are at once one of the most complex areas of COM and also the least well documented. Microsoft's intentions were good, but when they introduced apartments to COM in Windows NT 3.51, they laid a mine field for unwary developers. Play by the rules and you can avoid stepping on mines. But it's hard to obey the rules when you don't know what the rules are.

This article is the first in a two-part series that describes what apartments are, why they exist, and how to avoid the problems that they introduce. In Part I, I'll describe COM's apartment-based concurrency mechanism. In Part II, I'll provide a set of rules that you can follow to avoid some of the nastiest and most insidious bugs that afflict COM programmers.

Apartment Basics

An *apartment* is a concurrency boundary; it's an imaginary box drawn around objects and client threads that separates COM clients and COM objects that have incompatible threading characteristics. The primary reason that apartments exist is to enable COM to serialize method calls to objects that aren't thread-safe. If you don't tell COM that an object is thread-safe, COM won't allow more than one call at a time to reach the object. Tell COM that the object is thread-safe, however, and it will happily allow the object to field concurrent method calls on multiple threads.

Every thread that uses COM and every object that those threads create is assigned to an apartment. Apartments never span process boundaries, so if an object and its client reside in two different processes, they reside in different apartments, too. When a client creates an in-proc object, COM must decide whether to place the object in its creator's apartment or in another apartment in the client process. If COM assigns the object and the thread that created it to the same apartment, the client has direct, unimpeded access to the object. But if COM places the object in another apartment, calls to the object from the thread that created it are marshaled.

Figure 42.1 depicts the relationship between threads and objects that share an apartment and threads and objects that are assigned to different apartments. Calls from thread 1 travel directly to the object that it created. Calls from thread 2 go through a proxy and a stub. COM creates the proxy/stub pair when it marshals the interface pointer to thread 2's apartment. As a rule, an interface pointer must be marshaled when it's passed across apartment boundaries. This means that when custom interfaces are involved, the same proxy/stub DLL (or type library if you prefer typelib marshaling) you use to provide marshaling support for cross-process and cross-machine method calls is needed even for in-proc objects if those objects will be communicating with clients in other apartments.

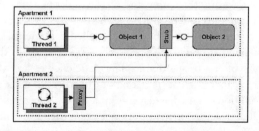

Figure 42.1   Calls to objects in other apartments are marshaled even if the object and its caller belong to the same process.

Windows NT 4.0 supports two different types of apartments; Windows 2000 supports three. The three types of apartments are

- Single-threaded apartments, or STAs (Windows NT 4.0 and Windows 2000)
- Multithreaded apartments, or MTAs (Windows NT 4.0 and Windows 2000)
- Neutral-threaded apartments, or NTAs (Windows 2000 only)

Single-threaded apartments are limited to one thread each but can host an unlimited number of objects. Additionally, COM places no limit on the number of STAs in a given process. The very first STA created in a process is referred to as the process's main STA. What's important about STAs is that every call destined for an object in an STA is transferred to the STA's thread before being delivered. Since all of the object's calls execute on the same thread, it's impossible for an STA-based object to execute more than one call at a time. COM uses STAs to serialize incoming calls to non–thread-safe objects. If you don't explicitly tell COM that an object is thread-safe, it will place instances of that object in an STA so that the object won't suffer concurrent thread accesses.

One of the more interesting aspects of an STA's operation is how COM transfers calls destined for an STA-based object to the STA's thread. When it creates an STA, COM creates a hidden window to go with it. The window is accompanied by a window procedure that knows how to handle private messages representing method calls. When a method call destined for an STA comes out of COM's RPC channel, COM posts a message representing that call to the STA's window. When the thread in the STA retrieves the message, it dispatches it to the hidden window, and the window's window procedure delivers the call to the stub. The stub, in turn, executes the call to the object. Because a thread retrieves, dispatches, and processes just one message at a time, putting an object in an STA enacts a crude (but effective) call serialization mechanism. As shown in Figure 42.2, if *n* method calls are placed to an STA-based object at exactly the same time, the calls are queued and delivered to the object one at a time.

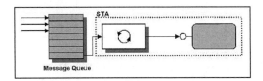

Figure 42.2   Calls entering an STA are converted into messages and posted to a message queue. Messages are retrieved from the message queue and converted back into method calls one at a time by the thread running in the STA.

Something equally important happens when a call leaves an STA. COM can't simply allow the thread to block inside the RPC channel because a callback would induce deadlock. (Imagine what would happen if an STA thread called an object in another apartment and that object, in turn, called an object in the calling thread's apartment. If the thread were blocked, the call would never return because the one and only thread that can process the callback is waiting in the RPC channel for the original call to return.) Therefore, when a call leaves an STA, COM blocks the calling thread in such a way that the thread can be awakened to process callbacks. To enable such callbacks to occur, COM tracks the causality of each and every method call. This enables it to recognize when an STA thread that's waiting in the RPC channel for a call to return should be released to process another incoming call. By default, a call that arrives at the entrance to an STA blocks if the STA's thread is currently waiting for an outbound call to return and the inbound and outbound calls are not part of the same causality chain. You can change this default behavior by writing a message filter, but that's a topic for another day.

Multithreaded apartments are different animals altogether. COM limits each process to one MTA, but it places no limit on the number of threads or objects in an MTA. If you look inside a process, you might find several STAs containing one thread each, but you'll never see more than one MTA. However, that one MTA, if it exists, can host any number of threads.

How do MTAs differ from STAs? Besides the fact that each process is limited to one MTA and that a given MTA can host any number of threads, an MTA has no hidden window and no message queue. Calls inbound to an object in an MTA are transferred to threads randomly selected from an RPC thread pool and are not serialized (see Figure 42.3). This means that objects placed in an MTA better be thread-safe because in the absence of an external synchronization mechanism guaranteeing that an MTA-based object will only receive one call at a time, that object is likely to see calls execute concurrently on different RPC threads.

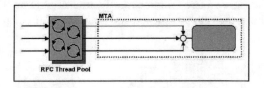

Figure 42.3   Calls entering an MTA are transferred to RPC threads but are not serialized.

When a call leaves an MTA, COM does nothing special. The calling thread is simply allowed to block inside the RPC channel, and if a callback occurs, no deadlock will occur because the callback will be transferred to another RPC thread.

Windows 2000 introduced a third apartment type: the neutral-threaded apartment, or NTA. COM limits processes to a maximum of one NTA each. Threads are never assigned to the NTA; the NTA hosts objects only. What's important about the NTA is the fact that calls to NTA-based objects do not incur thread switches as they enter the NTA. In other words, when a call emanates from an STA or MTA to an NTA in the same process, the calling thread temporarily leaves the apartment it's in and executes code directly in the NTA. Contrast this to STA- and MTA-based objects, which always incur thread switches when called from other apartments. This thread switching accounts for the bulk of the overhead incurred when a call is marshaled between apartments. Eliminating these thread switches improves performance. Therefore, you can think of the NTA as an optimization that allows interapartment method calls to execute more efficiently. In addition, Windows 2000 supports an external synchronization mechanism based on activities that lets you specify separately whether calls to NTA-based objects should be serialized. Activity-based call serialization is more efficient than message-based serialization and can be enacted (or not enacted) on an object-by-object basis.

How Threads Are Assigned Apartments

One of the cardinal rules of COM programming is that every thread that uses COM in any way must first initialize COM by calling either CoInitialize or CoInitializeEx. When a thread calls either of these functions, it is placed in an apartment. What type of apartment it's placed in depends on which function the thread called and how it called it. If a thread calls CoInitialize, COM creates a new STA and places the thread inside it:

```
CoInitialize (NULL); // STA
```

If the thread calls CoInitializeEx and passes in the parameter COINIT_APARTMENTTHREADED, it, too, is placed in an STA:

```
CoInitializeEx (NULL, COINIT_APARTMENTTHREADED); // STA
```

Calling CoInitializeEx with a COINIT_MULTITHREADED parameter places the thread inside the process's one and only MTA:

```
CoInitializeEx (NULL, COINIT_MULTITHREADED); // MTA
```

To a very large extent, a process's apartment configuration is driven by how the threads in that process call CoInitialize[Ex]. There are instances in which COM will create a new apartment outside of a call to CoInitialize[Ex], but for now we won't muddy the water by considering such circumstances.

For the sake of example, suppose that a new process is begun and that a thread in that process (thread 1) calls CoInitialize:

```
CoInitialize (NULL); // Thread 1
```

Furthermore, suppose that thread 1 starts threads 2, 3, 4, and 5, and that these threads initialize COM with the following statements:

```
CoInitializeEx (NULL, COINIT_APARTMENTTHREADED); // Thread 2
CoInitializeEx (NULL, COINIT_MULTITHREADED);     // Thread 3
CoInitializeEx (NULL, COINIT_MULTITHREADED);     // Thread 4
CoInitialize (NULL);                             // Thread 5
```

Figure 42.4 shows the resulting apartment configuration. Threads 1, 2, and 5 are assigned to STAs because of how they called CoInitialize and CoInitializeEx. They're placed in separate STAs because STAs are limited to one thread each. Threads 3 and 4, on the other hand, go in the process's MTA. Remember, COM never creates more than one MTA in a given process, but it's willing to place any number of threads in that MTA.

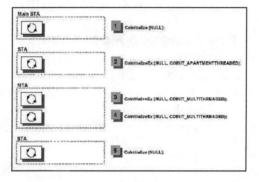

Figure 42.4   A process with five threads distributed among three STAs and one MTA.

If you're a nuts and bolts person, you might be curious to know more about the physical nature of an apartment—that is, how COM represents apartments internally. Whenever it creates a new apartment, COM allocates an apartment object on the heap and initializes it with important information such as the apartment ID and apartment type. When it assigns a thread to an apartment, COM records the address of the corresponding apartment object in thread-local storage (TLS). Thus, if COM is executing on a thread and it wants to know which, if any, apartment the thread belongs to, all it has to do is reach into thread-local storage and look for the address of an apartment object.

How In-Proc Objects Are Assigned Apartments

Now that we know how threads are assigned to apartments, we should consider the other half of the equation—that is, how objects are assigned apartments. The algorithm that COM uses to decide which apartment to create an object in differs depending on whether the object is an in-proc object or out-of-proc object. The in-proc case tends to be the most interesting because only in-proc objects can be created in their creator's apartment. We'll discuss the in-proc case first and then double back to discuss apartment considerations for out-of-proc objects.

COM determines which apartment an in-proc object will be created in by reading the object's ThreadingModel value from the registry. ThreadingModel is a named value assigned to the InprocServer32 key that identifies the object's DLL. The following registry entries, shown here in REGEDIT format, identify an object whose CLSID is 99999999-0000-0000-0000-111111111111, whose DLL is MyServer.dll, and whose ThreadingModel is Apartment:

```
[HKEY_CLASSES_ROOT\CLSID\{99999999-0000-0000-0000-111111111111}]
@="My Object"
[HKEY_CLASSES_ROOT\CLSID\{99999999-0000-0000-0000-111111111111}
\InprocServer32]
@="C:\\COM Servers\\MyServer.dll"
"ThreadingModel"="Apartment"
```

Apartment is one of four threading models supported by Windows NT 4.0, and one of five supported by Windows 2000. The five threading models—and the operating systems in which they're supported—are shown in Table 42.1.

Table 42.1 ThreadingModel Operating System Support

Threading Model	Apartment Type	NT 4.0	Windows 2000
None	Main STA	X	X
Apartment	Any STA	X	X
Free	MTA	X	X
Both	STA or MTA	X	X
Neutral	NTA		X

The column labeled Apartment Type indicates how COM treats an object with the designated ThreadingModel value. For example, COM restricts an object that has no ThreadingModel value ("ThreadingModel=None") to the process's main STA. ThreadingModel=Apartment allows the object to be created in any STA (not just the main STA), while ThreadingModel=Free restricts the object to the MTA, and ThreadingModel=Neutral restricts it to the NTA. Only ThreadingModel=Both offers COM any real choice in the matter by giving it permission to create an object in either an STA or an MTA.

COM tries its best to place in-proc objects in the same apartments as the threads that create them. For example, if an STA thread creates an object marked ThreadingModel=Apartment, COM will create the object in the creating thread's STA. If an MTA thread creates a ThreadingModel=Free object, COM will place the object in the MTA alongside the creating thread. Sometimes, however, COM can't put an object in its creator's apartment. If an STA thread, for example, creates an object marked ThreadingModel=Free, the object will be created in the process's MTA and the creating thread will access the object through a proxy and stub. Similarly, if an MTA thread creates a ThreadingModel=None or ThreadingModel=Apartment object, calls from that thread will be marshaled from the MTA to the object's STA. Table 42.2 documents what happens when a thread in either an STA or an MTA creates an object marked with any valid ThreadingModel value (or no ThreadingModel value).

Table 42.2   ThreadingModel Value Results

	None	Apartment	Free	Both	Neutral
STA	Main STA	Creator's STA	MTA	Creator's STA	NTA
MTA	Main STA	STA	MTA	MTA	NTA

Why does ThreadingModel=None restrict an object to a process's main STA? Because only then can COM ensure that multiple instances of an object that knows nothing about thread safety can execute safely. Suppose that two ThreadingModel=None objects are created from the same DLL. If the objects access any global variables in that DLL (and they almost certainly will), COM must execute all calls to both objects on the same thread, or else the objects might attempt to read or write the same global variable at once. Restricting object instances to the main STA is COM's way of getting the objects on the same thread.

Although it might not be obvious at first, the threading model that you choose has important implications for the code that you write. For example, an object marked ThreadingModel=Free or ThreadingModel=Both should be completely thread-safe since calls to MTA-based objects aren't serialized. Even a ThreadingModel=Apartment object should be partially thread-safe because ThreadingModel=Apartment doesn't prevent multiple objects created from the same DLL from colliding over shared data. We'll explore this subject in my next column.

How Out-of-Proc Objects Are Assigned Apartments

Out-of-process objects don't have ThreadingModel values because COM uses a completely different algorithm to assign out-of-proc objects to apartments. To make a long story short, COM places an out-of-proc object in the same apartment as the thread in the server process that creates the object. Most out-of-proc (EXE) COM servers begin by calling either CoInitialize or CoInitializeEx to place their primary thread in an STA. They then create class objects for the object types that they're capable of creating and register them with CoRegisterClassObject. When an activation request reaches a server that's initialized this way, the request is processed in the process's STA. As a result, objects created in the server process are placed in the process's STA, too.

You can move out-of-proc objects to the MTA by placing the thread that registers the objects' class objects in the MTA. Incoming activation requests will then arrive on RPC threads that execute in the server process's MTA. Objects created in response to these activation requests will reside in the MTA as well.

The upshot is that in most cases involving EXE COM servers, the apartment that hosts the thread that calls CoRegisterClassObject is also the apartment that hosts the objects that the server creates. Exceptions do exist; EXE COM servers written with ATL's CComAutoThreadModule and CComClassFactoryAutoThread classes, which create multiple STAs in the server process and divide objects evenly among those STAs, are one example. These, however, account for a tiny fraction of the EXE COM servers that exist today and can very much be considered the exception rather than the rule.

Coming Up Next

So what does it all mean? Much of the detail presented in this article may seem too arcane to have any practical value. The reality, however, is that understanding COM apartments is absolutely essential if you want to avoid some of the most common—and potentially most dangerous—pitfalls that afflict COM programmers. You'll see what I mean in my next column.

Understanding COM Apartments, Part II

This article was contributed by Jeff Prosise.

In my previous column, I described the hows and whys of COM apartments. If you read it, you now know that when a thread calls COM's CoInitialize or CoInitializeEx function, that thread is placed in an apartment. And you know that when an object is created, it, too, is placed in an apartment, and that COM uses ThreadingModel values in the registry to determine what types of apartments to place in-proc objects in.

You also know that there are three types of apartments: single-threaded apartments, or STAs; multithreaded apartments, or MTAs; and neutral-threaded apartments, or NTAs. Windows 2000 supports all three apartment types; Windows NT 4.0 supports only two (STAs and MTAs). COM apartment types have the following distinguishing characteristics:

- STAs are limited to one thread each, but COM places no limit on the number of STAs per process. When a method call enters an STA, it is transferred to the STA's one and only thread. Consequently, an object in an STA will only receive and process one method call at a time, and every method call that it receives will arrive on the same thread. COM transfers an incoming call to an STA thread by posting a private message to the hidden window that serves that STA.

- MTAs are limited to one per process, but do not limit the number of threads that can run inside them. Method calls destined for an object in an MTA are transferred to arbitrary RPC threads as they enter the apartment. COM makes no attempt to serialize method calls bound for MTAs, so an MTA-based object can receive concurrent calls on concurrent threads. Because incoming calls are transferred to RPC threads, every call to an MTA-based object is likely to arrive on a different thread—even if every one of those calls comes from the same caller.

- NTAs were added to Windows 2000 as a performance optimization. Method calls entering STAs and MTAs incur thread switches that account for most of the overhead involved in interapartment method calls. Calls entering an NTA incur no thread switching. If an STA or MTA thread calls an NTA-based object in the same process, the thread temporarily leaves the apartment that it's in and executes code in the NTA.

Some of the information presented in last month's "Into the IUnknown" column must have seemed hopelessly abstract at the time. This month you'll see why understanding the arcana of apartments is important if you wish to avoid the pitfalls that afflict all too many COM programmers. It all boils down to understanding (and obeying) two sets of rules: one for COM clients, another for COM servers. Obey the rules and life with COM will be as joyous as that scene from *The Sound of Music* where Julie Andrews sings the movie's theme song while spinning like a top in an Alpine meadow. Break the rules, and you'll probably encounter insidious errors that are difficult to reproduce and even more difficult to diagnose. I get email about these errors all the time. It's time to do something about them.

Writing COM Clients That Work

Here are three rules for writing COM clients that work. Take them to heart and you'll avoid many of the crippling mistakes made by developers who write COM clients.

Rule 1: Client Threads Must Call CoInitialize[Ex]

Before a thread does anything that involves COM, it should call either CoInitialize or CoInitializeEx to initialize COM. If a client application has 20 threads and 10 of those threads use COM, then each of those 10 threads should call CoInitialize or CoInitializeEx. Inside these API functions, the calling thread is assigned to an apartment. If a thread isn't assigned to an apartment, COM is powerless to enforce the laws of COM concurrency for that thread. Don't forget, too, that a thread that calls CoInitialize or CoInitializeEx successfully needs to call CoUninitialize before it terminates. Otherwise, the resources allocated by CoInitialize[Ex] aren't freed until the process ends.

It sounds simple—remembering to call CoInitialize or CoInitializeEx before using COM—and it is simple. It's one function call. Yet you'd be amazed at how often this rule is broken. Most of the time the error manifests itself in the form of failed calls to CoCreateInstance and other COM API functions. But occasionally the problems don't show up until much later and have no obvious connection to the client's failure to initialize COM.

Ironically, one of the reasons that developers sometimes don't call CoInitialize[Ex] is that Microsoft tells them they don't have to. MSDN contains a document advising developers that COM clients can sometimes avoid calling these functions. The document goes on to say that access violations may result. I recently got a call from a developer whose client threads' calls to Release were locking up or generating access violations. The reason? Some of the threads were placing method calls without first calling CoInitialize or CoInitializeEx. When calls to Release blow up, you have problems. Fortunately, fixing the problem was a simple matter of adding a few calls to CoInitialize[Ex].

Remember: It's never harmful to call CoInitialize[Ex], and it should be considered mandatory for any and all threads that call COM API functions or utilitize COM objects in any way.

Rule 2: STA Threads Need Message Loops

Rule 2 isn't very obvious unless you understand the mechanics of single-threaded apartments. When a client places a call to an STA-based object, the call is transferred to the thread that lives in that STA. COM accomplishes the transfer by posting a message to the STA's hidden window. So what happens if the thread in that STA doesn't retrieve and dispatch messages? The call will disappear into the RPC channel and never return. It will languish in the STA's message queue forever.

When developers call me and ask why method calls aren't returning, the first thing I ask them is "Is the object that you're calling in an STA? And if so, does the thread that drives that STA have a message loop?" More often than not, the answer is "I don't know." If you don't know, you're playing with fire. When a thread calls CoInitialize, when it calls CoInitializeEx with a COINIT_APARTMENTTHREADED parameter, or when it calls MFC's AfxOleInit function, it's assigned to an STA. If objects are later created in that STA, those objects can't receive method calls from clients in other apartments if the STA's thread lacks a message pump. The message pump can be as simple as this:

```
MSG msg;
while (GetMessage (&msg, 0, 0, 0))
  DispatchMessage (&msg);
```

Be wary of placing a thread in an STA if it lacks these simple statements. One common scenario in which it happens is when an MFC application launches a worker thread (MFC worker threads are, by definition, threads that lack message pumps) and that thread calls AfxOleInit, which places it in an STA. You'll get away with it if the

STA doesn't end up hosting any objects, or if it does host objects but the objects don't have clients in other apartments. But if that STA ends up hosting objects that export interface pointers to other apartments, calls placed through those interface pointers will never return.

Rule 3: Never Pass Raw, Unmarshaled Interface Pointers Between Apartments

Suppose you're writing a COM client that has two threads. Both threads call CoInitialize to enter an STA, and one thread—thread A—uses CoCreateInstance to create a COM object. Thread A wants to share the interface pointer that it received from CoCreateInstance with thread B. So thread A sticks the interface pointer in a global variable and signals thread B that the pointer is ready. Thread B reads the interface pointer from the global variable and proceeds to place calls to the object through the interface pointer. What, if anything, is wrong with this picture?

The scenario that I just described is an accident waiting to happen. The problem is that thread A passed a raw, unmarshaled interface pointer to a thread in another apartment. Thread B should only communicate with the object through an interface pointer that has been marshaled to thread B's apartment. *Marshaling* in this context means giving COM the opportunity to create a new proxy in thread B's apartment so that thread B can safely call out. The consequences of passing raw interface pointers between apartments range from extremely timing-dependent (and difficult to reproduce) data corruption errors to outright lockups.

Thread A can safely share an interface pointer with thread B if it marshals the interface pointer. There are two basic ways a COM client can marshal an interface to another apartment:

- The COM API functions CoMarshalInterThreadInterfaceInStream and CoGetInterfaceAndReleaseStream. Thread A calls CoMarshalInterThreadInterfaceInStream to marshal the interface pointer; thread B calls CoGetInterfaceAndReleaseStream to unmarshal it. Inside CoGetInterfaceAndReleaseStream, COM creates a new proxy in the caller's apartment. If the interface pointer doesn't need to be marshaled (if, for example, the two threads share an apartment), CoGetInterfaceAndReleaseStream is smart enough not to create a proxy.

- The Global Interface Table (GIT), which debuted in Windows NT 4.0 Service Pack 3. The GIT is a per-process table that enables threads to safely share interface pointers. If thread A wants to share an interface pointer with other threads in the same process, it can use IGlobalInterfaceTable::RegisterInterfaceInGlobal to put the interface pointer in the GIT. Then, threads that want to use that interface pointer can call IGlobalInterfaceTable::GetInterfaceFromGlobal to retrieve it. The magic is that when a thread retrieves an interface pointer from the GIT, COM marshals the interface pointer to the retrieving thread's apartment.

Are there times when it's OK not to marshal an interface pointer that you intend to share with another thread? Yes. If the two threads share an apartment, which can only happen if the threads belong to the MTA, they can share raw, unmarshaled interface pointers. But if in doubt, marshal. It's never harmful to call CoMarshalInterThreadInterfaceInStream and CoGetInterfaceAndReleaseStream or use the GIT because COM won't marshal the pointer if it doesn't have to.

Writing COM Servers That Work

There's an equally binding set of rules that you should follow when you write COM servers. They're described in the following sections.

Rule 1: Protect Shared Data in ThreadingModel=Apartment Objects

One of the most common misconceptions about COM programming is that marking an object ThreadingModel=Apartment absolves the developer from having to think about thread safety. It doesn't. When you register an in-proc object ThreadingModel=Apartment, you're implicitly promising COM that instances of that object (and other objects created from that DLL) access shared data in a thread-safe manner. That means you use critical sections or other thread synchronization primitives to ensure that only one thread can touch the data at a time. Data shared between object instances typically comes in three forms:

- Global variables declared in a DLL
- Static member variables in C++ classes
- Static local variables

Why is thread synchronization so important for ThreadingModel=Apartment objects? Consider the case in which two objects—object A and object B—are created from the same DLL. Suppose that both objects read and write a global variable declared in that DLL. Because the objects are marked ThreadingModel=Apartment, they might be created in separate STAs and run, therefore, on two different threads. But the global variable that they access is shared because it's only instanced into the process one time. If calls go out to objects A and B at about the same time, and if object A writes to that variable at the same time thread B reads from it (or vice versa), the variable could be corrupted—unless you serialize the threads' actions. Fail to provide a synchronization mechanism and you'll get away with it most of the time. But eventually the two threads will probably collide over the shared data, and there's no telling what might happen as a result.

Is it ever safe to allow COM objects to access shared data without synchronizing those accesses? Yes, under the following circumstances:

- Objects that have no ThreadingModel value registered (which we refer to as ThreadingModel=None or ThreadingModel=Single) all run on the same thread in the same STA and therefore can't collide over shared data.

- If you're sure that the objects will run in the same STA even though they're marked ThreadingModel=Apartment (for example, if they're all created by the same STA thread).
- If you're sure that the objects won't process method calls concurrently.

Absent these circumstances, make sure any ThreadingModel=Apartment objects that you write access shared data in a thread-safe manner. Only then can you rest assured that you've fulfilled your end of the bargain.

Rule 2: Objects Marked ThreadingModel=Free or ThreadingModel=Both Should Be Wholly Thread-Safe

When you register an object ThreadingModel=Free or ThreadingModel=Both, the object either will be (Free) or could be (Both) placed in an MTA. Remember that COM does not serialize calls to MTA-based objects. Therefore, unless you know beyond the shadow of a doubt that these objects' clients will not place concurrent calls to them, the objects should be entirely thread-safe. That means your classes must synchronize access to their own nonstatic member variables in addition to synchronizing accesses to data shared by object instances. Writing thread-safe code isn't easy, but you must be prepared to do it if you plan to use the MTA.

Rule 3: Avoid Using TLS in Objects Marked ThreadingModel=Free or ThreadingModel=Both

Some Windows developers use thread-local storage (TLS) as a temporary data store. Imagine that you're implementing a COM method and you want to cache some information about the current call where you can retrieve it when the next call arrives. You might be tempted to use TLS. And in an STA, it would work. But if the object you're writing resides in an MTA, you should avoid TLS like the plague.

Why? Because calls that enter an MTA are transferred to RPC threads. Each call is liable to arrive on a different RPC thread, even if every one of those calls originated from the same thread and the same caller. Thread B can't access thread A's thread-local storage, so if call number 1 arrives on thread A and the object tucks data away in TLS, and if call number 2 arrives on thread B and the object attempts to retrieve the data it wrote to TLS in call number 1, the data won't be there. Plain and simple.

Beware using TLS to cache data between method calls in MTA-based objects. It'll only work if all the calls come from the same thread in the same MTA that the object resides in.

You're Kidding, Right?

Am I serious about all these rules? You bet. Roughly half of all bugs I find in COM-based applications stem from violations of the rules prescribed in this article. Even if you don't understand them, abide by them. The world will be a better place if you do.

FROM THE FORUM

Question (Tsatsek):

I have a COM server in which I need to create a worker thread to perform some functionality using an interface pointer from the calling thread. The threading model of the CoClass that implements the interfaces is Apartment and the threading model of the new thread is Single Thread. Is there a simple way I can perform the marshalling of the interface pointer?

Answer (Marius Cabas):

You can pass an IStream pointer to the CoGetInterfaceAndReleaseStream function as shown:

```
// STA1
IMyInterface* pMyInterface;
hr = CoCreateInstance(CLSID_MyCOMClass, NULL, CLSCTX_LOCAL_SERVER,
    IID_IMyInterface, (void**)&pMyInterface);

// Marshal interface pointer to stream.
IStream* pStream;
hr = CoMarshalInterThreadInterfaceInStream(IID_IMyInterface, pMyInterface,
➥&pStream);

// Spawn new thread; pass pStream to new thread.
DWORD threadId;
CreateThread(NULL, 0, (LPTHREAD_START_ROUTINE)ThreadRoutine, pStream, 0,
➥&threadId);

// Do other work...

pMyInterface->Release();
...

void __stdcall ThreadRoutine(IStream* pStream)
{
    // Create STA2.
    CoInitializeEx(NULL, COINIT_APARTMENTTHREADED);

    // Unmarshal interface pointer from stream.
    IMyInterface* pMyInterface;
    hr = CoGetInterfaceAndReleaseStream(pStream, IID_IMyInterface,
        (void**)&pMyInterface);

    // Do work with pMyInterface...

    pMyInterface->Release();

    CoUninitialize();
}
```

Getting a Feel for COM Threading Models

This article was contributed by Rama Krishna.

The purpose of this article is to explain the various COM threading models with the aid of a tutorial.

Before We Begin

For this tutorial the following are required:

- Visual C++ version 5.0 or 6.0 (preferred)
- OLE/COM Object Viewer
- Spy++ (Window Spying Utility that comes with VC)

Before we proceed further take a look at the tutorial projects. The tutorial consists of a main workspace, COMThreading. This has three projects as follow:

- **Server:** A COM DLL server application implemented in ATL. It has one object supporting a single nondual interface IServer. The interface IServer has a single method—SimpleMethod—which just displays a message box.
- **ServerPS:** A simple Win32 DLL project for building the proxy-stub DLL from the files generated from the MIDL compiler.
- **Client:** A simple console application that uses the Server Object. We will be dealing almost entirely with this project in this tutorial.

Unzip the Comthreading.zip file and open the workspace COMThreading.dsw in VC++. All three projects described previously must be visible in the workspace.

1. To start with, set Server as the active project and build it. This builds and registers Server.dll.

2. Once the Server project is built, it is time to open OLE/COM Object Viewer and see what we have got. From the Tools menu use VC or otherwise open the OLE/COM Object Viewer.

3. Next, in the View menu of OLE/COM Object Viewer, make sure that Expert Mode is checked. Under object classes expand All Objects. Scroll down until you see the ServerApp Class item in the tree view. It should look something like the screen shot shown in Figure 42.5. Note that it shows the interface IUnknown only and not IServer. This is because IServer is not a recognized interface in the Registry.

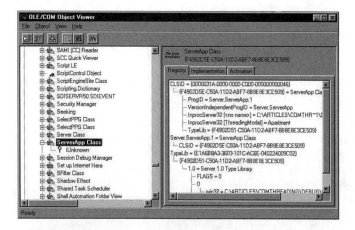

Figure 42.5

The First Client Application

4. Next it is the time to build the client application. In the client application I have used compiler COM support for simplicity. This enables us to create a ServeApp object and invoke its SimpleMethod conveniently using smart interface pointers.

This is the code for the client application:

```
#include <windows.h>
#pragma hdrstop

#import "Server.tlb" no_namespace
#include "MyComutl.h"

int main(int , char** )
{
    CComInit cominit(COINIT_APARTMENTTHREADED);

    IServerPtr spServer(__uuidof(ServerApp));

    spServer->SimpleMethod();

    return 0;

}
```

CComInit is a class whose constructor initializes COM by calling CoInitializeEx in the constructor and uninitializes COM by calling CoUninitialize in the destructor. Thus in the main function, the destructor of IServerPtr for spServer (which Releases spServer) is called before the destructor of CComInit for cominit. After cominit has been declared, an object of ServerApp and the interface pointer to IServer are obtained in the smart pointer spServer. Finally, the method SimpleMethod is invoked.

5. Now it's the time to run the client application. Place a breakpoint in the first line where an object of CComInit is being declared and do a Debug - Go (or press F5).

6. Leaving the execution at the breakpoint (don't step over), open Spy++ (from the Tools menu or in any other way). From the Spy Menu of Spy++, select processes. Under the tree of processes, expand Client. The screen would look something like Figure 42.6.

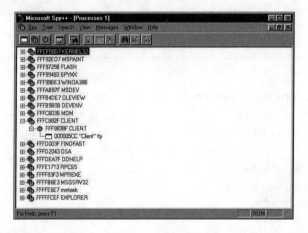

Figure 42.6

Note that Spy++ has recognized the Client process. The child item 0000005CC "Client" tty that is shown is the window handle, the title, and the window class name of the console window belonging to the process.

7. Now step over a line of code in the debugger. After stepping over switch back to Spy++ and refresh the view by pressing F5. Under the Client tree item, the child items look like they do in Figure 42.7.

Figure 42.7

Note that a new window (hidden) named OleMainThreadWndName of class OleMainThreadWndClass has been created in the process due to a call to CoInitializeEx(NULL, COINIT_APARTMENTTHREADED). In a process, whichever thread calls CoInitialize(NULL) or CoInitializeEx(NULL, COINIT_APARTMENTTHREADED) first is called the Main STA (Single-Threaded Apartment). (I will delve into terminology later.) Thus the window name OleMainThreadWndName is significant.

8. Just do a Debug - Go on the rest of the code. Dismiss the message box that is displayed by pressing the OK button.

The significant point that we observed going through all this ordeal was that the COM runtime (basically routines in OLE32.dll) creates a hidden window when COM is initialized using CoInitialize(Ex). The purpose of this window will become clear in the next steps.

Client Application 2: Entering the MultiThreaded World

In the COM world the component and the client may be created independently. Now suppose the client application uses multiple threads, but the poor component was built with the assumption that there would be only a single thread accessing the component at any time, and the data and routines were not protected because nobody took multiple threading into consideration. If the client tries to access the component using multiple threads, the component code is bound to fail or behave weirdly due to this. Luckily, COM helps to protect the code in such a case.

In a simple DLL-based server, the interface pointers can of course be passed to different threads, but if the DLL is not built to handle multiple threads, there will be failures, and in some cases it might even lead to hard-to-detect bugs because the code may fail randomly due to synchronization issues. How can a COM interface obtained from an object created in one thread (more precisely apartment, but for the present moment let us leave it as a thread and not go into terminology) be safely used by another thread in the same process? COM provides an answer—Marshal the interface from one thread to the other thread. Though marshaling used to be associated with RPC communications (and it still is), in the current context marshaling has something to do with ensuring thread safety. I am purposely being vague here as it will become clear as we see practically what happens.

What exactly does marshaling do and how does it ensure thread safety? We will see this next.

9. For marshaling to work we need to build and register the proxy stub dll. So build the ServerPS project. This automatically registers the proxy stub dll. To actually see that the proxy stub dll has been registered, switch back once again to the OLE/COM Object Viewer. Now it can be seen that the OLE/COM Object Viewer shows the IServer interface when the ServerApp Class item is expanded, as in Figure 42.8.

Figure 42.8

This does all the background preparation to be able to marshal interfaces from one thread to another.

10. Now we need to add some code in the client application to handle multiple threads. The entire code that we will be going to add is in the mycomutl.cpp and client1.cpp files. All that needs to be done is to cut and paste code from client1.cpp to client.cpp or remove client.cpp from the project and add client1.cpp—whichever way is convenient.

11. Each thread in the process that needs to call COM functions should Initialize COM using CoInitialize(Ex) and unintialize it before it terminates. To do this I have a simple helper function, BeginCOMThread (mycomutl.cpp), like this:

```
HANDLE BeginCOMThread(DWORD dwTM, THREADFN pfnStart)
{
    unsigned int dwId;

    COMThreadingHelper* pCT = new COMThreadingHelper;

    pCT->dwTM = dwTM;
    pCT->pfnStart = pfnStart;

    return (HANDLE) _beginthreadex(
                    NULL,           //Security
                    0,              //Stack Size
                    ThreadProc,     //Start Address
                    (void*)(pCT),   //Parameter
                    0,              //Creation Flag
                    &dwId           //Thread Id
                    );
}
```

Where COMThreadingHelper struct has been defined as

```
typedef void (*THREADFN)();

struct COMThreadingHelper
{
    DWORD dwTM; //Threading model
    THREADFN pfnStart;
};
```

This defintion is in an unnamed namespace in MyComutl.cpp. This is the C++ way of making functions and structs local to a file.

Finally, the function ThreadProc has been defined as

```
unsigned int _stdcall ThreadProc(LPVOID pParam)
{
    COMThreadingHelper* pCT = reinterpret_cast<COMThreadingHelper*>(pParam);

    //Initialize COM using the threading model passed in
    CComInit cominit(pCT->dwTM);

    //call the user function
    (pCT->pfnStart)();

    delete pCT;

    return 0;
}
```

A point worth mentioning is that the C runtime function _beginthreadex has been used instead of the Win32 function CreateThread. The main reason behind this is that C runtime maintains thread-specific global data like errno. By using _beginthreadex it is ensured that thread-specific data of C runtime is maintained. This would not be done if Win32 CreateThread had been used.

12. Now we are ready with a function that creates a thread with COM initialized. So let us now understand how to marshal the IServer interface pointer from one thread to another. This is done by one of the longest functions (by name) in the OLE32 API: CoMarshalInterThreadInterfaceInStream. Now the main function looks like this:

```
int main(int , char** )
{
    CComInit cominit(COINIT_APARTMENTTHREADED);

    IServerPtr spServer(__uuidof(ServerApp));

    spServer->SimpleMethod();

    //marsahl the spServer Interface pointer
    HRESULT hr = CoMarshalInterThreadInterfaceInStream(__uuidof(IServer),
➡//The IID of inteface to be marshaled
                                            spServer, //The interface
➡pointer
                                            &g_pStm   //IStream pointer
                                            );

    //Begin a thread in an STA
    HANDLE hThread = BeginCOMThread(COINIT_APARTMENTTHREADED, AThread);
```

```
//Wait for the thread to finish execution
//A thread handle is signaled is thread execution
//is complete
WaitForSingleObject(hThread, INFINITE);

//_endthreadex doesnot close handle unlike _endthread
//When th efunction called by _beginthreadex completes
//execution _endthreadex is called automatically
//Therefore we need to Close the handle of the thread
CloseHandle(hThread);

return 0;

}
```

A Global variable g_pStm of type IStream* has been defined. This is used by COM functions for marshaling. This stream pointer is effective only for a single marshaling.

Since the main application should not exit before the worker thread we have created, we have to use the WaitForSingleObject function.

The AThread function, which obtains the marshaled interface, looks like this:

```
void AThread()
{
    //This functions executes in a separate thread
    IServerPtr spServer;

    HRESULT hr = CoGetInterfaceAndReleaseStream(g_pStm,
                        __uuidof(IServer),
                        reinterpret_cast<LPVOID*>(&spServer));

    spServer->SimpleMethod();
}
```

13. Now place a breakpoint just at the beginning of the AThread function, and run the debugger. As soon as the execution stops at the AThread function, open the Spy++ application again and observe the client process again. This time it should look something like Figure 42.9.

Figure 42.9

This time Spy++ shows both the threads.

14. Step over to the next line and find that after a call to CoGetInterfaceAndReleaseStream, the value of the spServer pointer is valid. Step over to the next line. What happens? The application hangs. All that can be done is to select Stop Debugging from the Debug menu.

    If the call to spServer->SimpleMethod had been a direct call to a function in the dll, the application should not hang. But we have marshaled the interface to the other thread and we are accessing the marshaled interface in the other thread. A call to spServer->SimpleMethod no longer is direct but instead has to pass through the system code until it reaches the actual SimpleMethod function in Server.dll.

    Since the interface pointer which was obtained by the marshaling process actually belongs to an object created in another thread and the object cannot handle multiple threads, the SimpleMethod function in the object should be called from the same thread that created the object. This means that the thread FFF81C03 (it may be different on your machine) should somehow tell thread FFFD8147 that it needs to call the function SimpleMethod from it. The execution context has to be changed. How can this be done? This is not difficult given that a hidden window has been created by thread FFFD8147. All that thread FFF81C03 needs is to SendMessage to the hidden window. As the window messages are delivered in the respective threads, this method would change the execution context to thread FFFD8147. But we have not implemented any message loop in FFFD8147 and instead we are waiting for the other thread to complete execution. Thus there is a deadlock.

    Therefore, we need to implement a message loop in the main thread (FFFD8147); more precisely, we need to dispatch window messages to the respective window procedures. But we also need to wait for the execution of thread FFF81C03 to complete. Luckily, Win32 API provides the function MsgWaitForMultipleObjects, which returns when either a message is there in the message queue of the thread or the objects have been signalled. For details of this function, please consult the documentation.

15. Now, the main function needs to be modified to incorporate message dispatching. The WaitForSingleObject function now needs to be replaced with the following code (you can cut and paste it from Client2.cpp):

```
//Wait for the thread to finish execution
//A thread handle is signaled if thread execution
//is complete
for(;;)
{
    DWORD dwRet = MsgWaitForMultipleObjects(
                            1, //Count of objects
                            &hThread, //pointer to the array of objects
                            FALSE,    //Wait for all objects?
                            INFINITE, //Wait How Long?
                            QS_ALLINPUT //Wait for all messages
                            );
```

```
//This means that the object is signaled
if (dwRet != WAIT_OBJECT_0 + 1)
    break;


//Remove the messages from the queue
MSG msg;

while (PeekMessage(&msg, NULL, 0, 0, PM_REMOVE) > 0)
{
    //Not essential
    TranslateMessage(&msg);
    //Let the windowproc handle the message
    DispatchMessage(&msg);
}
    }
}
```

16. Placing the breakpoint at the AThread function, start the program again in the debugger. When the execution stops, open Spy++ and expand the client tree item again. It would look almost the same as in the previous case. Now place a breakpoint in CServerApp::SimpleMethod. This is in the Server project ServerApp.cpp file. Just allow the debugger to continue execution and the execution will stop at the SimpleMethod function. Now just see the call stack to get an idea of how the execution reached this point. The call stack would look something like Figure 42.10:

Figure 42.10

As is obvious from the call stack, the execution reached this function through routines in Kernel32.dll, rpcrt4.dll, and ole32.dll instead of being called directly from the client application. This is what is done by marshaling. For a method call to even an in-proc server, the execution has to go through system-level code. All this is being done to ensure thread safety to the component's methods.

17. Next, keeping the breakpoint at the same place in the AThread function, rerun the application again in the debugger. After the execution passes through CoGetInterfaceAndReleaseStream, open Spy++ again. This time it would appear something like Figure 42.11.

The difference is that now both the main thread and the thread running in the function AThread (FFFAFA97) have windows created in them. In the other thread there is a hidden window of the same class but a different title (OLEChannelWnd). It would be good to experiment with what messages are being sent to each of these windows. Spy++ again helps us; just right-click on each of the windows and select messages from the pop-up menu. Now any messges being sent to these windows will be shown by Spy++.

18. Let the application finish execution. Now revert back to Spy++, and you will find the message log. It appears something like in Figure 42.12.

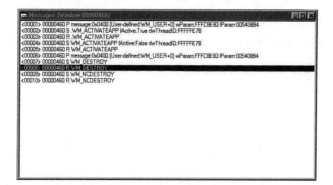

Note the two WM_USER messages. The wParam of the two messages can immediately be recognized as the handle of the other thread. So, it becomes clear that COM sends WM_USER messages to the hidden window associated with the thread where the object belongs, if the object's method is invoked from another thread through a marshaled interface. This is all done by the marshaling code residing mainly in rpcrt4.dll.

In this article I primarily focused on a single interface of a single object being accessed by different threads. There are many cases and concepts (especially that of an Apartment) that I plan to cover as separate articles in the same series, depending on the feedback. Please give your feedback on this tutorial.

FROM THE FORUM

Question (Jon Blanchard):

I'm writing a COM component with ATL. A single instance of the component should be accessible from more than one thread in the client application. Certain method calls should be limited to one thread at a given time. What would I need to do in both the client and server to achieve this?

Answer (AnOnYmOuS):

The following should work as you need:

Use the following macro to make sure that there is only one instance of your interface. You need this macro for each COM interface you want to implement:

```
DECLARE_CLASSFACTORY_SINGLETON(CYourClass)
```

If you want to make sure that there is only one instance of your object, then use a mutex and implement it somewhere in your constructor.

```
HANDLE hHandle = CreateMutex(NULL, FALSE, "Blah"); (Substitute Blah with your
➥own unique string)
...
ReleaseMutex(Hhandle); // Don't forget to release in the destructor!!
```

Your object should live in an MTA (Multi-threaded Apartment), and your threading model should be FREE.

```
HRESULT hRes = CoInitializeEx(NULL, COINIT_MULTITHREADED);
```

Make sure you have the following line in your main CPP file. This means that multiple clients can access this object:

```
hRes = _Module.RegisterClassObjects(CLSCTX_LOCAL_SERVER, REGCLS_MULTIPLEUSE);
```

Now for the client threads, you need to use either critical sections or mutexes when you make your calls.

Index

X-Z

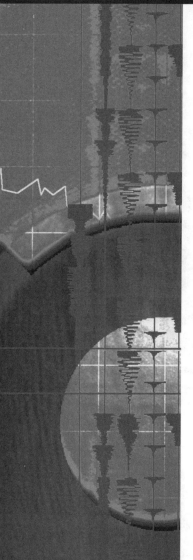